DATE DUE

DEMCO 38-296

THOMAS REID

AN INQUIRY
INTO THE
HUMAN MIND

ON THE PRINCIPLES OF
COMMON SENSE

The Edinburgh Edition of Thomas Reid

Series Editor: Knud Haakonssen

THOMAS REID

AN INQUIRY INTO THE HUMAN MIND

ON THE PRINCIPLES OF COMMON SENSE

A Critical Edition

EDITED BY

Derek R. Brookes

EDINBURGH UNIVERSITY PRESS

©Derek R. Brookes, 1997

Edinburgh University Press Ltd
22 George Square, Edinburgh

Typeset in 10½ on 13½ pt Times
by Bibliocraft Dundee, and
printed and bound in Great Britain

A CIP record for this book is available
from the British Library

ISBN 0 7486 0722 6

CONTENTS

PREFACE

Thomas Reid's *Inquiry into the Human Mind* has long been recognised as a classic philosophical text. Since its first public appearance in 1764 there have followed no fewer than forty editions, five of which were issued in the second half of the twentieth century. The proliferation of secondary literature further indicates that Reid's work is flourishing as never before. Yet, surprisingly, neither a complete nor critical representation of the *Inquiry* has been available to present-day readers.

Most university libraries will house *The Works of Thomas Reid*, edited by the Scottish philosopher Sir William Hamilton (1788–1856). Hamilton based his text on the last edition of the *Inquiry* published in Reid's lifetime, noting 'variations of importance'[1] with the first. However, the edition is severely marred, not only by Hamilton's obtrusive footnotes, but also by frequent textual inaccuracies. Hamilton plainly took it upon himself to 'correct' Reid's entire work in matters of typography, punctuation and spelling. Duggan's edition (1970) claims to be based on a text chosen for 'its authenticity',[2] and to have reproduced the *Inquiry* 'in its entirety'.[3] Yet the text is based on an 1813 American edition, and Reid's 'Dedication' is entirely absent. The edition by Lehrer and Beanblossom (1983) is an abridged reproduction of Hamilton's eighth edition, and omits large portions of the *Inquiry*. The recent photo-facsimile of the 1785 edition (1990), introduced by Wood and published by Thoemmes, is therefore the only current edition available that faithfully represents one of the original editions.

There remains, however, an urgent need for a critical edition of Reid's work.[4] Reid scholars, for instance, have been acutely aware of proceeding without the full textual evidence. There exist thousands of unpublished manuscript pages in Reid's hand, many of which relate directly to the composition of the *Inquiry*. Furthermore, no account has been taken of the successive alterations made to the four editions published in Reid's lifetime – alterations which require not only a meticulous record, but a principled editing of the final, definitive text. The present edition therefore aims to present a complete, critically edited text of the *Inquiry*, accompanied by a judicious selection of manuscript evidence relating to its composition.

1. *The Works of Thomas Reid . . .*, ed. W. Hamilton, 8th ed. (Edinburgh, J. Thin, 1895, reprint with introduction by H. M. Bracken, Hildesheim, Georg Olms Verlag, 1985): p. 94.
2. *An Inquiry into the Human Mind*, ed. T. Duggan (Chicago, University of Chicago Press, 1970): p. vii.
3. *ibid*, fly-leaf.
4. The literature is replete with invitations: 'There is, as yet, no standard edition of Reid's works worthy of the name.' R. D. Gallie, *Thomas Reid and 'The Way of Ideas'* (Dordrecht, Kluwer Academic Publishers, P.S.S. 45, 1989): p. 266; 'Reid's other works must be quoted from the old Hamilton edition, which is neither critical nor complete, and whose replacement by a new critical edition is a major desideratum.' B. Smith and K. Schuhmann, 'Elements of Speech Act Theory in the Work of Thomas Reid', *History of Philosophy Quarterly 7* (1990): p. 62, n.9.

ACKNOWLEDGEMENTS

The critical text for this edition was completed while I was a Visiting Fellow at the Thomas Reid Institute for Research in Cultural Studies and the Humanities in the University of Aberdeen in 1993. I am very grateful for the research grants provided by the Thomas Reid Institute and the Research School of Social Sciences at the Australian National University. I would like to acknowledge my indebtedness to Knud Haakonssen and M.A. Stewart for their personal support and academic guidance during the preparation of this edition. My thanks to Wendy Hare for computer-typing the text of the *Inquiry*; and to the staff of the University of Aberdeen Library Archives for their assistance during my study of the Reid manuscript collection. My family have been a constant source of love and encouragement. This work is dedicated to them.

Derek R. Brookes
Yale University
1996

ABBREVIATIONS

Libraries

AUL   Aberdeen University Library
NLS   National Library of Scotland

Works by Thomas Reid

HM   *An Inquiry into the Human Mind on the Principles of Common Sense* (present edition).

IP   *Essays on the Intellectual Powers of Man* (Edinburgh, Printed for J. Bell, Parliament Square, and G. G. J. & J. Robinson, London, 1785). Hamilton editions include the 1785 pagination.

Orations   *The Philosophical Orations of Thomas Reid delivered at Graduation Ceremonies in King's College Aberdeen*, 1753, 1756, 1759, 1762, ed. D. D. Todd, trans. S. M. L. Darcus, *Philosophical Research Archives* 3 (1977): pp. 916–990.

Manuscript References

Manuscripts referred to in the editor's *Introduction* are identified by the MS location (e.g. AUL) and the catalogue number (e.g. 2131/4/I/27) followed by the page or folio number (e.g. AUL MS 2131/4/I/27, 2r). See the *Editorial Principles* for further detail.

INTRODUCTION

1. The Philosophical Problem

Most of us take it that we know something of the external world. We believe that there are external objects, such as roses, trees and candles; and we even think we know a good deal about what they are like. The question is, do we have any good evidence to support these beliefs?

We might take it that our beliefs about the world are justified in view of our sense experience. Our sensations, we might think, appear to be a rich and articulate source of information about external objects. Our beliefs regarding the colour, size, shape and texture of a rose, for instance, are, in some way, 'grounded upon' our visual and tactile sensations. Indeed, we would ordinarily take our sensations to be some kind of *evidence* for our beliefs about the rose. If someone asked how it is that we knew that a certain rose was red, we would explain to them that we had experienced visual sensations in its presence, and these had seemed to us to be such as to indicate the colour of the rose.

Now this kind of answer might suggest that our sensations somehow represent the external world to the mind. Indeed, we might think that our sensations are a kind of mental image or picture of the rose, thus resembling it in certain respects. And if so, then it might be that our beliefs are justified by means of an inference from like effect to like cause. The problem is, when we reflect upon the nature of our sensations, we find that they are not in the least like a rose. The rose has a certain colour, size, shape and texture; whereas our sensations have nothing like these attributes.

One response might be that this is merely a crude stab at a very difficult problem; and that, given sufficient time and philosophical ingenuity, we should be able to come up with an adequate account of how the external world is represented to the mind. But suppose that we are so constituted that *the* solution is beyond our intellectual capacity; or, less extravagantly, suppose that no adequate solution is currently available. What ought to be our epistemic position in the meantime? Given that we do not, at present, appear to have sufficient reason to think that our mind represents the world in a reliable manner, should we not then adopt a sceptical stance? One problem with this approach, is that it would have most unpalatable implications. For example, it would entail that the achievements and discoveries of the empirical sciences are nothing but an 'enchanted illusion'. Again, it would be likely to lead to a deeply pessimistic and even contemptuous view of the human condition.

There is, however, a more serious reason why this kind of scepticism is untenable. The operation of mind by which we form beliefs is largely involuntary and irresistible, much like breathing or swallowing. Hence, it would not be psychologically possible to maintain a stance of disbelief, at least not for any extended period. It follows that any professed sceptic would only be diagnosed as either profoundly insincere or the victim of some cognitive dysfunction.

2. Historical Origins

This line of reasoning sets up the problem with which Thomas Reid's *Inquiry into the Human Mind on the Principles of Common Sense* is largely concerned. The question Reid took himself to be confronting was 'whether there was any such thing as truth within the reach of the human faculties'.[1] But he also perceived that the doubts about this epistemological question drew their strength, in part, from the enigma of how it is that 'a thing that is external, or a thing that is past, & has now no existence, or a thing which never had or never will have existence, can be represented to the mind'.[2]

The philosophical problem is ancient. But the naturalistic manner in which Reid addresses it in the *Inquiry* is strikingly contemporary. Many philosophers have accordingly reaped important and stimulating dividends from taking the text at face-value. But there is a world behind the text. The argument of the *Inquiry* did not spring into existence *ex nihilo*. Its roots lie in the cluster of ideas introduced in Reid's education at Aberdeen's Marischal College (1723–31). During his twenty year ministry in the Church of Scotland (1731–51) it was nurtured by a small philosophical club, fuelled by his close reading of philosophers such as Berkeley, Locke, and Butler, and ignited by his encounter with Hume's *Treatise*. It was then systematically developed and presented to students and peers during his regency at King's College, Aberdeen (1751–64);[3] and, in its final phase, prior to publication, was submitted to the private review of several prominent philosophers – including its primary target, David Hume.

There is, then, a fascinating story to be told about the historical origins of the *Inquiry*.[4] There are also good philosophical reasons for doing so.

For such an account may explain how and why Reid formed the central argument of his *Inquiry*.

3. Providential Naturalism and the Ideal System

The basic contours of Reid's mature thought were carved out in his early years at Marischal College. It was under the regency of George Turnbull (1723–26), that the adolescent Reid was immersed in a world-view that we may call Providential Naturalism.[5] This view consisted of four interconnected tenets: first, Newton's *regulæ philosophandi* were taken to provide the criteria for theoretical or explanatory success in both the natural sciences and the philosophy of mind;[6] second, the laws of nature could be given no further explanation than the providential purposes of God; third, determining the laws of nature would serve to establish a naturalistic means of discovering the end or purpose for which a thing had been created;[7] and fourth, the end or purpose of our cognitive processes was, among other things, to furnish us with true beliefs.

It was during this early phase that Reid also inherited an account of human cognition that had been promulgated, in various forms, by almost every major philosopher, namely, the theory of ideas or, using Reid's terminology, the 'ideal system'. The mind was, on this account, taken to obtain information about the world by means of images that were conveyed to it by the senses.

Reid was thus lulled into the apparent security of taking Providential Naturalism to be wedded happily to the ideal system.[8] The first told him that the mind could obtain epistemic access to itself and to the external world by means of cognitive processes designed for that purpose by God. The second explained just how this process was supposed to work. But the honeymoon was short-lived. In 1739 Hume published his *Treatise on Human Nature*, with the explicit intention of putting the two asunder.

4. Hume's Sceptical Argument

On the ideal system, any so-called truth about the world, was not, Hume argued, within the reach of our faculties. Our knowledge of the external world must be either direct or indirect. For it to be direct, external things must be immediately present to the mind. On the ideal system, the only things with which the mind could be in immediate contact were sensations or, in Hume's terminology, 'impressions'. It followed that no external object could be immediately present to the mind; consequently, our knowledge of the external world could not be direct. Could it then be indirect? Do our sensations constitute reason or evidence for an external world? Hume's answer was negative; and Reid was entirely in agreement.

First, by Newton's second rule of philosophising, like causes may be inferred from like effects. But the conception we have of external objects is such that they appear to be nothing like our sensations. Indeed, such is the disparity between the two that all our sensations might have been exactly as they are, 'though no body, nor quality of body, had ever existed'.[9] Hence we can make no causal inference from sensations to external objects.

Second, any enumerative induction would invariably suffer from a kind of circularity. Reid held the mind to be constituted by natural or innate faculties, individuated by their function in the cognitive economy. Consciousness, memory, perception, imagination, and reasoning, for instance, constitute individual faculties. In the case of sense perception, enumerative evidence may well confirm the reliability of that faculty; perception is, indeed, eminently successful in respect of predictability, consistency and the like. But these considerations will only support the faculty's trustworthiness from within; for the evidence upon which they are based can only be gathered by using perception itself. For instance, a person may gather the inductive evidence required for believing that something hard exists only if she already has good reason to believe that, normally, when she has the sensation of hardness, something hard exists – which clearly begs the epistemic question at hand.[10]

Third, suppose, following Descartes, we attempted to show that our faculties were trustworthy by producing an argument to the effect that there is a perfectly good Creator. The problem with this approach, as Reid pointed out, is that, to arrive at this conclusion, we must use the faculty of reasoning. But if we can rely upon the deliverances of at least one faculty without first showing it to be reliable, what prevents us from treating our other faculties likewise? It would be no more than rationalistic imperialism to give the faculty of reasoning this privileged status.[11] On the other hand, if we refuse to trust the deliverances of any faculty until such time as it can be shown to be reliable, we can hardly rely upon any reasoning that purports to demonstrate the existence of God.

5. The Evolution of Reid's Response to Hume

Reid was thus faced with a dilemma: either he must accept Hume's sceptical conclusion or deny the ideal system. Reid of course resisted the former; but not from an aversion to scepticism *per se*. Prior to Hume's *Treatise*, Reid had accepted Bishop Berkeley's system in its entirety,[12] along with what he took to be its denial of a material world. The difference, Reid held, was that Berkeley, in his concern to retain his religious and moral beliefs, reduced everything in nature to spirits and ideas; whereas Hume accepted only 'ideas and impressions'.[13] Reid's philosophical crisis, then, was stimulated primarily by his view that Hume's system threatened the very possibility of rational religion and morality.[14]

We might therefore expect to see Reid turning his immediate attention to the project of refuting the ideal system. But the evidence is not forthcoming. Reid's refusal to accept Hume's sceptical conclusion was, for almost two decades, supported entirely by an appeal to common sense; and not by any direct refutation of the ideal system. For example, in one of Reid's earliest dated manuscripts (1748), he argues for a common sense view of the self, against what he took to be Hume's theory of the self – apparently without having yet rejected the ideal system (see *Manuscripts* § 3.1). Again, in Reid's second Oration, delivered as late as 1756, the target is, among other things, Hume's scepticism; yet the ideal system is not once mentioned. Instead, Reid argues that to wage war on common sense, as Hume does, is indicative of either insincerity or insanity. Finally, in his discourse to the Aberdeen Philosophical Society, dated 14 June 1758, Reid argues that there are two 'General prejudices' against Hume's system of mind: the first being that Hume claimed to have given an 'entire system' of the mind; and second, that Hume's system 'waged war' on common sense. Reid does not suggest that he has located any intrinsic fallacy in Hume's system. On the contrary, he argues that, 'Such philosophy is justly ridiculous even to those who cannot show the fallacy of it'[15] (see *Manuscripts* § 2.1).

This is not to say that Reid continued to accept the ideal system. Rather, he seems, at some stage, to have taken Hume's sceptical argument as a *reductio* of the ideal system. His next strategy was to determine precisely where the system had gone wrong.[16] Thus, in July 1758, Reid delivered a paper to the Aberdeen Philosophical Society; a paper of which there are more draft versions than any other from this period. The paper was entitled: 'Are the objects of the human mind properly divided into impressions & ideas? & must every idea be a copy of a preceding impression?' (see *Manuscripts*, § 2.2). Its purpose was to present a detailed refutation of the ideal system. This paper, then, appears to mark the first breakthrough in Reid's second strategy. The most compelling evidence for this is found in Reid's third Oration, delivered in April 1759. The Oration, being a development of the arguments found in the July 1758 paper, opens with the remark: 'formerly I suspected, but now I know for certain', that the ideal system is merely an hypothesis rather than 'an accurate analysis of the operations of the intellect'.[17] This would appear to confirm the thesis that, prior to 1758, Reid believed that he had not directly refuted the ideal system.

The aftermath of this discovery was a burst of intellectual energy, in which Reid sought to develop his own account of human cognition; one that would fully accord with the four tenets of Providential Naturalism. The first substantial paper to emerge from this period is dated December 1, 1758. This is Reid's first substantive treatment of the operations of mind, in particular that of perception, and the natural principles of belief (see *Manuscripts*, § 3.2).

6. The Argument of the *Inquiry*

Reid's response to Hume was thus a three-stage process that stretched over four decades: first, his commitment to Providential Naturalism led him to take Hume's sceptical argument as a *reductio* of the ideal system; his primary task was then to expose the errors within the theory; once this had been accomplished, he was able to construct a new system of the mind. This evolutionary story effectively explains the structure of the *Inquiry*'s central argument:

> *the ideal system* . . . hath some original defect; that this scepticism is inlaid in it, and reared along with it; and, therefore, that we must lay it open to the foundation, and examine the materials, before we can expect to raise any solid and useful fabric of knowledge on this subject.[18]

There is an important anomaly in this account, however. Reid's second major paper, entitled 'The Analysis of the Sensations of smell & Taste', was delivered on 14 March 1759, again to the Aberdeen Philosophical

Society.[19] Of particular interest is a large section containing an examination of the ideal system. The composition of this section was not a trivial undertaking for Reid. There are at least two extant draft copies (see *Manuscripts*, § 2.2), and much of it makes its way into Reid's Orations III and IV (April 1759, 1762). The mystery, however, is that, while most of the 1759 paper made its way into the *Inquiry*, Reid dropped the entire section containing his criticisms of the ideal system. In its place, Reid tells us that the system will be examined further on in the text, and gives a *précis* of the key objections he intends to raise.[20] Yet this intention is never fulfilled. Instead, we find, at the end of the *Inquiry*, the confession: 'I have thought it proper to drop this part of my design'.[21]

How do we explain this change of mind? Why would Reid omit from the *Inquiry* the crucial second stage of his response to Hume? There are several possibilities. After reading an early draft of the *Inquiry*, Hume complained that Reid frequently digressed: 'For Instance, under the Article of Smelling, he gives you a Glimpse of all the Depths of his Philosophy'.[22] Reid defended himself by arguing that he would consider something a digression only if it did not tend 'either to give any new light to the Operations of the human Mind, or to correct any of the received opinions concerning it'.[23] Nevertheless, the 'Article' on smell is the very portion of the *Inquiry* from which Reid withdrew his section against the ideal system; and within that section itself, Reid describes his examination as a 'long digression'.[24] Perhaps Hume's complaint proved, in the end, to be compelling. Reid himself seems to suggest this as the reason for its removal: 'we shall not now examine . . . the doctrine of the ideal philosophy', he writes, so that 'we may not interrupt the thread of the present investigation'.[25]

There is, however, a more interesting explanation. Hume had also complained of Reid's having falsely charged him with providing no argument to support his principle that all our ideas are copied from impressions.[26] In fact, Hume writes, he had proffered two arguments:

> The first is desiring any one to make a particular Detail of all his Ideas, where he woud always find that every Idea had a correspondent & preceeding Impression. If no Exception can ever be found, the Principle must remain incontestible. The second is, that if you exclude any particular Impression, as Colours to the blind, Sound to the Deaf, you also exclude the Ideas.[27]

The section Reid removed from the *Inquiry* contained a battery of objections to the system of ideas. What he retained was a single *experimentum crucis*:

> If what we call Extension, Figure, Motion, Hardness or Softness, Roughness or Smoothness have any Resemblance to the Sensations that correspond to them, then I must Subscribe to Mr Humes Creed and cannot avoid it. But if there is no such resemblance then his System falls to pieces as well as all the other Systems I have named, and we are to seek for a new one.[28]

Hume's complaint may therefore explain this simplification in Reid's strategy. For, on Hume's own account, Reid needed only to show that some of his conceptions did not resemble any preceding impression.

The problem with this explanation is that there are passages in the *Inquiry* that suggest Reid took Hume's principle to be 'incontestible', and perhaps for good reason. In his comments on the draft of the *Inquiry*, Hume suggested that Reid's doctrine 'leads us back to innate Ideas'.[29] In his published work, Hume defined an innate idea as that which is 'original and copied from no precedent perception'.[30] He must therefore have taken Reid to be claiming that certain meaningful or existent ideas were not derived from our impressions.

Hume appears, in his comments, to concede that this return to innate ideas was no objection to Reid's doctrine: 'For nothing', he writes, 'ought ever to be supposd finally decided in Philosophy, so as not to admit of a new Scrutiny'.[31] But this response seems more sardonic than conciliatory, given Hume's published views. In the *Treatise*, for instance, we find the following argument: Any meaningful or existent idea is either innate or derived from our impressions. The doctrine of innate ideas 'has been already refuted, and is now almost universally rejected in the learned world'. Hence, any putative idea that cannot be shown to derive from our impressions is 'impossible and imaginary'.[32] If so, it must follow that Hume's principle is, after all, 'incontestible'. For suppose some putative idea were found not to be derived from any impression. Instead of showing that his principle was false, Hume would simply conclude that no such idea could exist or be meaningful.[33] As Reid colourfully puts it:

> there is a tribunal of inquisition erected by certain modern philosophers, before which every thing in nature must answer. The articles of inquisition are few indeed, but very dreadful in their consequences. They are only these: Is the prisoner an impression, or an idea? If an

idea, from what impression copied? Now, if it appears that the prisoner is neither an impression, nor an idea copied from some impression, immediately, without being allowed to offer any thing in arrest of judgment, he is sentenced to pass out of existence, and to be, in all time to come, an empty unmeaning sound, or the ghost of a departed entity.[34]

If Reid was aware of this, why does he accept Hume's *experimentum crucis*? Following Locke, Reid held that we are not capable of creating anything *ex nihilo*, we can only combine or disjoin: simple things are made complex, and complex, simple. Our simple conceptions cannot therefore be, ultimately, the product of our own reason, error or prejudice. They must instead be 'the work of nature, and the result of our constitution'.[35] Hence, if it is discovered that we have simple conceptions of the external world that cannot be explained by reference to sensations, then this would constitute a phenomenon of nature not to be denied, but to be explained. Hume's system, however, would not be able to explain such phenomena. Hence, to discover these conceptions, would be to show that Hume's system failed to satisfy Newton's rules of philosophising.

> That we have clear and distinct conceptions of extension, figure, motion, and other attributes of body, which are neither sensations, nor like any sensation, is a fact of which we may be as certain, as that we have sensations. . . . These facts are phænomena of human nature, from which we may justly argue against any hypothesis, however generally received. But to argue from a hypothesis against facts, is contrary to the rules of true philosophy.[36]

This, I suggest, accounts for Reid's removal of the section against the ideal system. It also serves to explain Reid's claim that it was his investigation into Hume's principle that led him 'gradually' into his 'present way of thinking with regard to the human Mind'.[37] For Reid was aware that it would not be enough to refute Hume's system. The problem of accounting for our perceptual knowledge remained. An alternative would therefore need to be formulated.

7. Reid's System of Mind

Reid's account of the human mind is driven by the four tenets of Providential Naturalism. Following Newton, he held that the phenomenon of two things being 'constantly and invariably connected in the course of Nature' could only be accounted for by showing this connection to be a necessary consequence of some known law of nature. If there were no such law, then the connection must be considered either a law of nature itself, or else a consequence of some law of nature yet to be discovered; and if the latter, it would be taken to have the same authority as a law of nature.[38] The account Reid presents in the *Inquiry* is an application of this method to certain operations of the mind. For example, he argues that it is a phenomenon of nature that certain sensations are invariably connected with the conception and belief of certain external objects; this connection is not a necessary consequence of any known law of nature; hence, it must be considered 'to be itself a Law of the human Mind, untill we find some more general Law of which it is the consequence'.[39]

Second, Reid held that the laws of nature themselves can be given no account other than that they are a consequence of the will of the Author of nature. Thus, the lawful operation of mind that connects our sensations with our conception of and belief in an external world can be accounted for only by reference to the intentional agency of its Creator.

> Who taught all the muscles that are concerned in sucking, in swallowing our food, in breathing, and in the several natural expulsions, to act their part in such regular order and exact measure? It was not custom surely. It was that same powerful and wise Being who made the fabric of the human body, and fixed the laws by which the mind operates upon every part of it, so that they may answer the purposes intended by them.[40]

Third, Reid held that it is in determining the laws by which the human mind operates, that we can discover their particular end or purpose. It would appear that our operations of mind are, among other things, designed to furnish us with true beliefs: 'our Senses are given us by nature not to deceive but to give us true information of things within their Reach'.[41] Hence truth, on this account, appears to be within the reach of the human faculties. Of course, we may be entirely wrong about this: our perceptual faculties may well be entirely deceptive. But if so, then, Reid states, 'we are deceived by Him that made us, and there is no remedy'. [42]

8. Providentialist Epistemology

Reid has often been read as moving, in Cartesian fashion, from premises asserting the existence and nature of God, to a conclusion about the reliability of our faculties of mind. This view contains a deep misunderstanding of Reid's epistemology. Our day-to-day faith in the reliability of

our faculties is, he held, shared by theist and non-theist. The reason for
this common ground is that the intellectual operations are, for the most
part, involuntary and irresistible. We cannot help but form a conception
of and belief in external objects upon having certain kinds of sensations.
Furthermore, whenever we choose to act, we give expression to our
belief that these deliverances are, for the most part, reliable. Reid's point,
however, is that the *rationality* of this belief is best sustained within the
context of Providential Naturalism. For on this account, there is no reason
to believe that scepticism about the external world is a live possibility.
Providential Naturalism is a philosophical system, a set of beliefs of which
no member either affirms or leads to the denial of the reliability of our
faculties – a feature, Reid argued, that could not be claimed of a system
such as David Hume's.[43]

One crucial member of this set is, of course, the belief in God. But
theism does not serve a Cartesian function in Reid's epistemology. Reid
held that any appeal to an argument for the existence of God would, in this
context, result in a glaring *petitio principii*: 'if our faculties be fallacious,
why may they not deceive us in this reasoning as well as in others?'[44] For
Reid, the process by which a person forms the belief in God is, like every
other belief, a natural phenomenon. As such, its epistemic status is taken
to arise from within the explanatory resources of his system.

Reid held it to be a law of nature that there is an immediate, non-
inferential connection between the perception of certain kinds of objects
or events and the belief that these are effects brought about by the design
and intelligence of an agent. One application of this law is the process
by which we form beliefs about human agency upon perceiving human
behaviour; another is 'design and wisdom in the works of Nature'.[45] Like
our belief in other minds, then, the non-inferential connection between the
belief in God and certain kinds of perceptual beliefs is a law of nature for
which there can be no further explanation than the providential purposes
of God. Our belief in other minds and the belief in God, Reid held, are
therefore in the same epistemic category:[46]

> if a Man has the same Rational Evidence for the Existence of a Deity
> as he has for the Existence of his Father his Brother or his Friend, this I
> apprehend, is sufficient to satisfy every man that has common Sense.[47]

A second crucial belief for Reid is that the 'Author of our nature' does
not intend to deceive us. But why should we believe this? Again, Reid's
answer is naturalistic. Our belief in the trustworthiness of our senses is

an immediate deliverance of a lawful operation of mind: in this case, analogous to the operation by which we form our belief in the trustworthiness of human persons. In infancy, a person tends to believe, by a kind of natural instinct, the guidance and testimony of her parents and teachers. With hindsight, she might reflect that they had, on the whole, been fair, honest and beneficent. Of course, this natural credulity meant that, at times, she was 'imposed upon by deceivers'. However, it seems clear to her that, had she refrained from believing her elders until she had evidence of their reliability, she would either have perished or arrived at adulthood 'little better than a changeling'. Thus she concludes that, subject to overriding evidence, it appears more reasonable than not to continue to place her confidence and trust in those of whose 'integrity and veracity' she has experience.[48] Likewise, Reid argues,

> I gave implicit belief to the informations of Nature by my senses, for a considerable part of my life, before I had learned so much logic as to be able to start a doubt concerning them. And now, when I reflect upon what is past, I do not find that I have been imposed upon by this belief. I find, that without it I must have perished by a thousand accidents. I find, that without it I should have been no wiser now than when I was born. I should not even have been able to acquire that logic which suggests these sceptical doubts with regard to my senses. Therefore, I consider this instinctive belief as one of the best gifts of Nature. I thank the Author of my being who bestowed it upon me, before the eyes of my reason were opened, and still bestows it upon me to be my guide, where reason leaves me in the dark. And now I yield to the direction of my senses, not from instinct only, but from confidence and trust in a faithful and beneficent Monitor, grounded upon the experience of his paternal care and goodness.[49]

NOTES

1. AUL MS 2131/2/III/1, 1.
2. AUL MS 3107/1/3, 67; cf. 2131/1/I/3, 7.
3. For an account of Reid's academic environs, see Paul B. Wood, *The Aberdeen Enlightenment: The Arts Curriculum in the Eighteenth Century* (Aberdeen, Aberdeen University Press, 1993).
4. For a discussion of the events leading up to the publication of the *Inquiry* and its immediate reception, see Paul B. Wood's Introduction in the Thoemmes reprint of the 1785 edition of the *Inquiry*.
5. This term was first used by David Fate Norton, 'From Moral Sense to Common Sense: An Essay on the Development of Scottish Common

Sense Philosophy, 1700–1765' (University of California, San Diego, Ph.D. Dissertation, Philosophy, 1966): Ch. VI.

6. See *Explanatory Notes*, 12/9.

7. Cf. 'Now it is only by strictly examining the structure and fabrick of the mind, the frame and connexion of all its powers and affections, and the manner of their operation that we can ascertain the end and purpose of our being. . . .' George Turnbull, *The Principles of Moral (and Christian) Philosophy: An Enquiry into the Wise and Good Government of the Moral World. . . .* Fascimile reprint of the 1740–41 London edition. Anglistica & Americana 167. (Olms, Hildesheim, 1976): Vol. I, p. v.

8. Some acknowledgement of this unquestioning phase is hinted at in Reid's cautionary tale about the enduring influence of education, even in one such as Isaac Newton: 'Is it not possible, that this great philosopher, as well as many of a lower form, having been led into this opinion at first by education, may have continued in it, because he never thought of calling it in question? I confess this was my own case for a considerable part of my life.' HM, p. 165/39–166/4.

9. HM, p. 57/33–4; cf. HM, p. 26/33–5.

10. IP, p. 307. Cf. William P. Alston, *The Reliability of Sense Perception* (Ithaca and London, Cornell University Press, 1993).

11. Cf. HM, p. 169/4–9; IP, p. 592.

12. IP, p. 162.

13. HM, p. 20/9. Several recent authors have argued that Reid misrepresented the views of those whom he criticised. D. Raynor, for example, argues that Reid, among others, misread Hume as a Berkeleyan immaterialist. 'Hume and Berkeley's Three Dialogues', in *Studies in the Philosophy of the Scottish Enlightenment*, ed. M. A. Stewart (Oxford, Clarendon Press, 1990): pp. 247–50. Again, J. W. Yolton argues that 'Reid found skepticism in the way of ideas because he thought (wrongly) that the only concept of ideas, or the dominant concept was [that of 'ideas as entities']. *Perceptual Acquaintance: From Descartes to Reid* (Minneapolis, University of Minnesota Press, 1984): p. 208.

14. HM, p. 5/7–12; cf. *Manuscripts* § 3.1.

15. AUL MS 3107/1/1, 18; cf. HM, p. 21/24–5.

16. Reid seems to suggest that Hume thought of his argument as serving the same objective: 'I conceive the sceptical writers to be a set of men, whose business it is, to pick holes in the fabric of knowledge wherever it is weak and faulty; and when these places are properly repaired, the whole building becomes more firm and solid than it was formerly.' HM, p. 4/20–3. Perhaps Hume agreed. In a letter to Reid, he writes: ' I shall only say, that if you have been able to clear up these abstruse & important Subjects, instead of being mortifyd, I shall be so vain as to pretend to a share of the Praise, and shall think, that my Errors, by having at least some Coherence, had led you to make a more strict Review of my Principles which were the common ones, and to perceive their futility.' AUL MS 2814/I/42, 1r–v. Reid replied: 'I agree with you therefore that if this System shall ever be demolished, you have a just claim to a great share of the Praise, both because you have made it a distinct and determinate mark to be aimed at, and have furnished proper artillery for the purpose.' NLS MS 23157, Letter 3, 1v. See *Manuscripts* § 1.3, 1.4.

17. *Orations*, p. 956.
18. HM, p. 23/20–5.
19. AUL MS 3107/1/3, 58–72.
20. HM, p. 28/24–32; see also HM, p. 91/28.
21. HM, p. 217/33–4.
22. AUL MS 2814/1/39, 2.
23. AUL MS 2/III/1, 7.
24. AUL MS 3107/1/3, 71; see *Manuscripts* § 2.2.
25. HM p. 28/22.
26. Reid seems to have retained the charge against Hume: 'It is a fundamental principle of the ideal system, That every object of thought must be an impression, or an idea, that is, a faint copy of some preceding impression. This is a principle so commonly received, that the author above mentioned, although his whole system is built upon it, never offers the least proof of it.' HM, p. 33/22–7.
27. AUL MS 2814/1/39, 1v; cf. David Hume, *A Treatise of Human Nature*, ed. L. A. Selby-Bigge and P. H. Nidditch, 2nd ed. (Oxford, Clarendon Press, 1978): pp. 4–5; David Hume, *Enquiries Concerning Human Understanding*, ed. L. A. Selby-Bigge and P. H. Nidditch, 3rd ed. (Oxford, Clarendon Press, 1975): pp. 19–20.
28. AUL MS 2/III/1, 4; HM, p. 70/16–27.
29. AUL MS 2814/1/39, 1v.
30. Hume, *Enquiries*, p. 22, n. 1.
31. AUL MS 2814/1/39, 1v.
32. Hume, *Treatise*, p. 158.
33. See Hume, *Enquiries*, p. 22.
34. HM, p. 98/14–22.
35. HM, p. 70/10.
36. HM, p. 76/3–13.
37. AUL MS 2/III/1, 3.
38. HM, pp. 132/19–133/8.
39. AUL MS 2/III/1, 4.
40. HM, p. 113/28–33.
41. AUL MS 8/II/22, 2–3.
42. HM, p. 72/15–6.
43. Cf. Alvin Plantinga, *Warrant and Proper Function* (Oxford, Oxford University Press, 1993): pp. 236–7.
44. IP, p. 592. In his Glasgow lectures, Reid presented a variety of arguments for the existence of God. These lectures survive in two student transcriptions: MS AUL 160, and The Mitchell Library, Glasgow MS A104929. For a transcription of the latter, see E. H. Duncan, *Thomas Reid's Lectures on Natural Theology* (1780) (Washington, DC., University Press of America, 1981).
45. IP, p. 629.
46. Cf. Alvin Plantinga, *God and Other Minds* (Ithaca and London, Cornell University Press, 1990).
47. AUL MS 8/II/20a, 8. Cf. IP, p. 632.
48. HM, pp. 170/31–171/4.
49. HM, p. 170/16–30.

CRITICAL TEXT

AN

INQUIRY

INTO THE

HUMAN MIND,

On the PRINCIPLES of

COMMON SENSE.

By THOMAS REID, D.D.
Professor of Moral Philosophy in the University of GLASGOW.

The inspiration of the Almighty giveth them understanding.

JOB.

The FOURTH EDITION Corrected.

LONDON:
Printed for T. CADELL in the Strand, London; and
J. BELL and W. CREECH, Edinburgh.

M,DCC,LXXXV.

TO

THE RIGHT HONOURABLE

JAMES Earl of FINDLATER

and SEAFIELD,

CHANCELLOR of the University of

OLD ABERDEEN.

My LORD,

THOUGH I apprehend that there are things new, and of some importance, in the following inquiry, it is not without timidity that I have consented to the publication of it. The subject has been canvassed by men of very great penetration and genius: for who does not acknowledge Des Cartes, Malebranche, Locke, Berkeley, and Hume, to be such? A view of the human understanding, so different from that which they have exhibited, will, no doubt, be condemned by many without examination, as proceeding from temerity and vanity.

But I hope the candid and discerning Few, who are capable of attending to the operations of their own minds, will weigh deliberately what is here advanced, before they pass sentence upon it. To such I appeal, as the only competent judges. If they disapprove, I am probably in the wrong, and shall be ready to change my opinion upon conviction. If they approve, the Many will at last yield to their authority, as they always do.

However contrary my notions are to those of the writers I have mentioned, their speculations have been of great use to me, and seem even to point out the road which I have taken; and your Lordship knows, that the merit of useful discoveries is sometimes not more justly due to those that have hit upon them, than to others who have ripened them, and brought them to the birth.

I acknowledge, my Lord, that I never thought of calling in question the principles commonly received with regard to the human understanding, until the *Treatise of human nature* was published, in the year 1739. The ingenious author of that treatise, upon the principles of Locke, who was no sceptic, hath built a system of scepticism, which leaves no ground to believe any one thing rather than its contrary. His reasoning appeared to me to be just: there was therefore a necessity to call in question the principles upon which it was founded, or to admit the conclusion.

5 But can any ingenuous mind admit this sceptical system without reluctance? I truly could not, my Lord: for I am persuaded, that absolute scepticism is not more destructive of the faith of a Christian, than of the science of a philosopher, and of the prudence of a man of common understanding. I am persuaded, that the unjust *live by faith* as well as the 10 *just*; that, if all belief could be laid aside, piety, patriotism, friendship, parental affection, and private virtue, would appear as ridiculous as knight-errantry; and that the pursuits of pleasure, of ambition, and of avarice, must be grounded upon belief, as well as those that are honourable and virtuous.

15 The day-labourer toils at his work, in the belief that he shall receive his wages at night; and if he had not this belief, he would not toil. We may venture to say, that even the author of this sceptical system, wrote it in the belief that it should be read and regarded. I hope he wrote it in the belief also, that it would be useful to mankind: and perhaps it may prove so at 20 last. For I conceive the sceptical writers to be a set of men, whose business it is, to pick holes in the fabric of knowledge wherever it is weak and faulty; and when these places are properly repaired, the whole building becomes more firm and solid than it was formerly.

For my own satisfaction, I entered into a serious examination of the 25 principles upon which this sceptical system is built; and was not a little surprised to find, that it leans with its whole weight upon a hypothesis, which is ancient indeed, and hath been very generally received by philosophers, but of which I could find no solid proof. The hypothesis I mean is, That nothing is perceived but what is in the mind which perceives 30 it: That we do not really perceive things that are external, but only certain images and pictures of them imprinted upon the mind, which are called *impressions* and *ideas*.

If this be true; supposing certain impressions and ideas to exist in my mind, I cannot, from their existence, infer the existence of any thing else; 35 my impressions and ideas are the only existences of which I can have any knowledge or conception; and they are such fleeting and transitory beings, that they can have no existence at all, any longer than I am conscious of them. So that, upon this hypothesis, the whole universe about me, bodies and spirits, sun, moon, stars, and earth, friends and relations, all things without exception, which I imagined to have a permanent existence, whether I thought of them or not, vanish at once;

And, like the baseless fabric of a vision,
Leave not a track behind.

I thought it unreasonable, my Lord, upon the authority of philosophers, to admit a hypothesis, which, in my opinion, overturns all philosophy, all religion and virtue, and all common sense: and finding that all the systems concerning the human understanding which I was acquainted with, were built upon this hypothesis, I resolved to inquire into this subject anew, without regard to any hypothesis.

What I now humbly present to your Lordship, is the fruit of this inquiry, so far only as it regards the five senses; in which I claim no other merit, than that of having given great attention to the operations of my own mind, and of having expressed, with all the perspicuity I was able, what I conceive every man, who gives the same attention, will feel and perceive. The productions of imagination, require a genius which soars above the common rank; but the treasures of knowledge are commonly buried deep, and may be reached by those drudges who can dig with labour and patience, though they have not wings to fly. The experiments that were to be made in this investigation suited me, as they required no other expence, but that of time and attention, which I could bestow. The leisure of an academical life, disengaged from the pursuits of interest and ambition; the duty of my profession, which obliged me to give prelections on these subjects to the youth; and an early inclination to speculations of this kind, have enabled me, as I flatter myself, to give a more minute attention to the subject of this inquiry, than has been given before.

My thoughts upon this subject were, a good many years ago, put together in another form, for the use of my pupils; and afterwards were submitted to the judgment of a private philosophical society, of which I have the honour to be a member. A great part of this inquiry was honoured even by your Lordship's perusal. And the encouragement which you, my Lord, and others, whose friendship is my boast, and whose judgment I reverence, were pleased to give me, counterbalanced my timidity and diffidence, and determined me to offer it to the public.

If it appears to your Lordship to justify the common sense and reason of mankind, against the sceptical subtilties which, in this age, have endeavoured to put them out of countenance; if it appears to throw any

new light upon one of the noblest parts of the divine workmanship; your
Lordship's respect for the arts and sciences, and your attention to every
thing which tends to the improvement of them, as well as to every thing
else that contributes to the felicity of your country, leave me no room

5   to doubt of your favourable acceptance of this essay, as the fruit of my
industry in a profession wherein I was accountable to your Lordship;
and as a testimony of the great esteem and respect wherewith I have the
honour to be,

10

My LORD,

Your LORDSHIP'S

most obliged, and

15   most devoted servant,

THO. REID.

CONTENTS.

CHAPTER I.
INTRODUCTION.

CHAP. II.
Of SMELLING.

CHAP. VII.
CONCLUSION.

AN

INQUIRY

INTO THE

HUMAN MIND.

CHAP. I.

INTRODUCTION.

SECT. I.

The importance of the subject, and the means of prosecuting it.

THE fabric of the human mind is curious and wonderful, as well as that of the human body. The faculties of the one are with no less wisdom adapted to their several ends, than the organs of the other. Nay, it is reasonable to think, that as the mind is a nobler work, and of a higher order than the body, even more of the wisdom and skill of the divine Architect hath been employed in its structure. It is therefore a subject highly worthy of inquiry on its own account, but still more worthy on account of the extensive influence which the knowledge of it hath over every other branch of science.

In the arts and sciences which have least connection with the mind, its faculties are the engines which we must employ; and the better we understand their nature and use, their defects and disorders, the more skilfully we shall apply them, and with the greater success. But in the noblest arts, the mind is also the subject upon which we operate. The painter, the poet, the actor, the orator, the moralist, and the statesman, attempt to operate upon the mind in different ways, and for different ends; and they succeed, according as they touch properly the strings of the human frame. Nor can their several arts ever stand on a solid foundation, or rise to the dignity of science, until they are built on the principles of the human constitution.

Wise men now agree, or ought to agree in this, that there is but one way to the knowledge of nature's works; the way of observation and experiment. By our constitution, we have a strong propensity to trace particular facts and observations to general rules, and to apply such general rules to account for other effects, or to direct us in the production of them. This procedure of the understanding is familiar to every human creature in the common affairs of life, and it is the only one by which any real discovery in philosophy can be made.

The man who first discovered that cold freezes water, and that heat turns it into vapour, proceeded on the same general principles, and in the same method, by which Newton discovered the law of gravitation and the properties of light. His *regulæ philosophandi* are maxims of common sense, and are practised every day in common life; and he who philosophizes by other rules, either concerning the material system, or concerning the mind, mistakes his aim.

Conjectures and theories are the creatures of men, and will always be found very unlike the creatures of God. If we would know the works of God, we must consult themselves with attention and humility, without daring to add any thing of ours to what they declare. A just interpretation of nature is the only sound and orthodox philosophy: whatever we add of our own, is apocryphal, and of no authority.

All our curious theories of the formation of the earth, of the generation of animals, of the origin of natural and moral evil, so far as they go beyond a just induction from facts, are vanity and folly, no less than the vortices of Des Cartes, or the Archæus of Paracelsus. Perhaps the philosophy of the mind hath been no less adulterated by theories, than that of the material system. The theory of ideas is indeed very ancient, and hath been very universally received; but as neither of these titles can give it authenticity, they ought not to screen it from a free and candid examination; especially in this age, when it hath produced a system of scepticism, that seems to triumph over all science, and even over the dictates of common sense.

All that we know of the body, is owing to anatomical dissection and observation, and it must be by an anatomy of the mind that we can discover its powers and principles.

SECT. II.

The impediments to our knowledge of the mind.

BUT it must be acknowledged, that this kind of anatomy is much more difficult than the other; and therefore it needs not seem strange, that mankind have made less progress in it. To attend accurately to the operations of our minds, and make them an object of thought, is no easy matter even to the contemplative, and to the bulk of mankind is next to impossible.

An anatomist who hath happy opportunities, may have access to examine with his own eyes, and with equal accuracy, bodies of all different ages, sexes, and conditions; so that what is defective, obscure, or preternatural in one, may be discerned clearly, and in its most perfect state in another. But the anatomist of the mind cannot have the same advantage. It is his own mind only that he can examine, with any degree of accuracy and distinctness. This is the only subject he can look into. He may, from outward signs, collect the operations of other minds; but these signs are for the most part ambiguous, and must be interpreted by what he perceives within himself.

So that if a philosopher could delineate to us, distinctly and methodically, all the operations of the thinking principle within him, which no man was ever able to do, this would be only the anatomy of one particular subject; which would be both deficient and erroneous, if applied to human nature in general. For a little reflection may satisfy us, that the difference of minds is greater than that of any other beings, which we consider as of the same species.

Of the various powers and faculties we possess, there are some which nature seems both to have planted and reared, so as to have left nothing to human industry. Such are the powers which we have in common with the brutes, and which are necessary to the preservation of the individual, or the continuance of the kind. There are other powers, of which nature hath only planted the seeds in our minds, but hath left the rearing of them to human culture. It is by the proper culture of these, that we are capable of all those improvements in intellectuals, in taste, and in morals, which exalt and dignify human nature; while, on the other hand, the neglect or perversion of them makes its degeneracy and corruption.

The two-legged animal that eats of nature's dainties, what his taste or appetite craves, and satisfies his thirst at the crystal fountain, who propagates his kind as occasion and lust prompt, repels injuries, and takes alternate labour and repose, is, like a tree in the forest, purely of nature's growth. But this same savage hath within him the seeds of the logician, the man of taste and breeding, the orator, the statesman, the man of virtue, and the saint; which seeds, though planted in his mind by nature, yet, through want of culture and exercise, must lie for ever buried, and be hardly perceivable by himself or by others.

The lowest degree of social life will bring to light some of those principles which lay hid in the savage state; and according to his training, and company, and manner of life, some of them, either by their native vigour, or by the force of culture, will thrive and grow up to great perfection, others will be strangely perverted from their natural form, and others checked, or perhaps quite eradicated.

This makes human nature so various and multiform in the individuals that partake of it, that, in point of morals, and intellectual endowments, it fills up all that gap which we conceive to be between brutes and devils below, and the celestial orders above; and such a prodigious diversity of minds must make it extremely difficult to discover the common principles of the species.

The language of philosophers, with regard to the original faculties of the mind, is so adapted to the prevailing system, that it cannot fit any other; like a coat that fits the man for whom it was made, and shows him to advantage, which yet will sit very aukward upon one of a different make, although perhaps as handsome and as well proportioned. It is hardly possible to make any innovation in our philosophy concerning the mind and its operations, without using new words and phrases, or giving a different meaning to those that are received; a liberty which, even when necessary, creates prejudice and misconstruction, and which must wait the sanction of time to authorise it. For innovations in language, like those in religion and government, are always suspected and disliked by the many, till use hath made them familiar, and prescription hath given them a title.

If the original perceptions and notions of the mind were to make their appearance single and unmixed, as we first received them from the hand of nature, one accustomed to reflection would have less difficulty in tracing them; but before we are capable of reflection, they are so mixed, compounded, and decompounded, by habits, associations, and abstractions, that it is hard to know what they were originally. The mind may in this respect be compared to an apothecary or a chemist, whose materials indeed are furnished by nature; but for the purposes of his art, he mixes, compounds, dissolves, evaporates, and sublimes them, till they put on a quite different appearance; so that it is very difficult to know what they were at first, and much more to bring them back to their original and natural form. And this work of the mind is not carried on by deliberate acts of mature reason, which we might recollect, but by means of instincts, habits, associations, and other principles, which operate before we come to the use of reason; so that it is extremely difficult for the mind to return upon its own footsteps, and trace back those operations which have employed it since it first began to think and to act.

Could we obtain a distinct and full history of all that hath passed in the mind of a child, from the beginning of life and sensation, till it grows up to the use of reason; how its infant faculties began to work, and how they brought forth and ripened all the various notions, opinions, and sentiments, which we find in ourselves when we come to be capable of reflection; this would be a treasure of natural history, which would probably give more light into the human faculties, than all the systems of philosophers about them since the beginning of the world. But it is in vain to wish for what nature has not put within the reach of our power. Reflection, the only instrument by which we can discern the powers of the mind, comes too late to observe the progress of nature, in raising them from their infancy to perfection.

It must therefore require great caution, and great application of mind, for a man that is grown up in all the prejudices of education, fashion, and philosophy, to unravel his notions and opinions, till he finds out the simple and original principles of his constitution, of which no account can be given but the will of our Maker. This may be truly called an *analysis* of the human faculties; and till this is performed, it is in vain we expect any just *system* of the mind; that is, an enumeration of the original powers and laws of our constitution, and an explication from them of the various phænomena of human nature.

Success in an inquiry of this kind, it is not in human power to command; but perhaps it is possible, by caution and humility, to avoid error and delusion. The labyrinth may be too intricate, and the thread too fine, to be traced through all its windings; but if we stop where we can trace it no farther, and secure the ground we have gained, there is no harm done; a quicker eye may in time trace it farther.

It is genius, and not the want of it, that adulterates philosophy, and fills it with error and false theory. A creative imagination disdains the mean offices of digging for a foundation, of removing rubbish, and carrying materials: leaving these servile employments to the drudges in science, it plans a design, and raises a fabric. Invention supplies materials where they are wanting, and fancy adds colouring, and every befitting ornament. The work pleases the eye, and wants nothing but solidity and a good foundation. It seems even to vie with the works of nature, till some succeeding architect blows it into rubbish, and builds as goodly a fabric of his own in its place. Happily for the present age, the castle-builders employ themselves more in romance than in philosophy. That is undoubtedly their province, and in those regions the offspring of fancy is legitimate, but in philosophy it is all spurious.

5

S E C T. III.

The present state of this part of philosophy.
Of Des Cartes, Malebranche, and Locke.

10

THAT our philosophy concerning the mind and its faculties, is but in a very low state, may be reasonably conjectured, even by those who never have narrowly examined it. Are there any principles with regard to the mind, settled with that perspicuity and evidence, which attends the principles of mechanics, astronomy, and optics? These are really sciences, built upon laws of nature which universally obtain. What is discovered in them, is no longer matter of dispute: future ages may add to it, but till the course of nature be changed, what is already established can never be overturned. But when we turn our attention inward, and consider the phænomena of human thoughts, opinions, and perceptions, and endeavour to trace them to the general laws and the first principles of our constitution, we are immediately involved in darkness and perplexity. And if common sense, or the principles of education, happen not to be stubborn, it is odds but we end in absolute scepticism.

Des Cartes finding nothing established in this part of philosophy, in order to lay the foundation of it deep, resolved not to believe his own existence till he should be able to give a good reason for it. He was, perhaps, the first that took up such a resolution: but if he could indeed have effected his purpose, and really become diffident of his existence, his case would have been deplorable, and without any remedy from reason or philosophy. A man that disbelieves his own existence, is surely as unfit to be reasoned with, as a man that believes he is made of glass. There may be disorders in the human frame that may produce such extravagancies, but they will never be cured by reasoning. Des Cartes indeed would make us believe, that he got out of this delirium by this logical argument, *Cogito, ergo sum*. But it is evident he was in his senses all the time, and never seriously doubted of his existence. For he takes it for granted in this argument, and proves nothing at all. I am thinking, says he, therefore I am: and is it not as good reasoning to say, I am sleeping, therefore I am?

15

20

25

30

35

or, I am doing nothing, therefore I am? If a body moves, it must exist, no doubt; but if it is at rest, it must exist likewise.

Perhaps Des Cartes meant not to assume his own existence in this enthymeme, but the existence of thought; and to infer from that the existence of a mind, or subject of thought. But why did he not prove the existence of his thought? Consciousness, it may be said, vouches that. But who is voucher for consciousness? Can any man prove that his consciousness may not deceive him? No man can: nor can we give a better reason for trusting to it, than that every man, while his mind is sound, is determined, by the constitution of his nature, to give implicit belief to it, and to laugh at, or pity the man who doubts its testimony. And is not every man, in his wits, as much determined to take his existence upon trust as his consciousness?

The other proposition assumed in this argument, That thought cannot be without a mind or subject, is liable to the same objection: not that it wants evidence; but that its evidence is no clearer, nor more immediate, than that of the proposition to be proved by it. And taking all these propositions together, – I think, – I am conscious, – Every thing that thinks, exists, – I exist, – would not every sober man form the same opinion of the man who seriously doubted any one of them? And if he was his friend, would he not hope for his cure from physic and good regimen, rather than from metaphysic and logic?

But supposing it proved, that my thought and my consciousness must have a subject, and consequently that I exist, how do I know that all that train and succession of thoughts which I remember, belong to one subject, and that the I of this moment, is the very individual I of yesterday, and of times past?

Des Cartes did not think proper to start this doubt: but Locke has done it; and, in order to resolve it, gravely determines, that personal identity consists in consciousness; that is, if you are conscious that you did such a thing a twelve-month ago, this consciousness makes you to be the very person that did it. Now, consciousness of what is past, can signify nothing else but the remembrance that I did it. So that Locke's principle must be, That identity consists in remembrance; and consequently a man must lose his personal identity with regard to every thing he forgets.

Nor are these the only instances whereby our philosophy concerning the mind appears to be very fruitful in creating doubts, but very unhappy in resolving them.

Des Cartes, Malebranche, and Locke, have all employed their genius

and skill, to prove the existence of a material world; and with very bad
success. Poor untaught mortals believe undoubtedly, that there is a sun,
moon, and stars; an earth, which we inhabit; country, friends, and relations, which we enjoy; land, houses, and moveables, which we possess.
But philosophers, pitying the credulity of the vulgar, resolve to have no
faith but what is founded upon reason. They apply to philosophy to furnish
them with reasons for the belief of those things which all mankind have
believed, without being able to give any reason for it. And surely one
would expect, that, in matters of such importance, the proof would not be
difficult: but it is the most difficult thing in the world. For these three great
men, with the best good will, have not been able, from all the treasures
of philosophy, to draw one argument, that is fit to convince a man that
can reason, of the existence of any one thing without him. Admired
Philosophy! daughter of light! parent of wisdom and knowledge! if thou
art she! surely thou hast not yet arisen upon the human mind, nor blessed
us with more of thy rays, than are sufficient to shed a darkness visible
upon the human faculties, and to disturb that repose and security which
happier mortals enjoy, who never approached thine altar, nor felt thine
influence! But if indeed thou hast not power to dispel those clouds and
phantoms which thou hast discovered or created, withdraw this penurious
and malignant ray; I despise Philosophy, and renounce its guidance: let
my soul dwell with Common Sense.

SECT. IV.

Apology for those philosophers.

BUT instead of despising the dawn of light, we ought rather to hope for
its increase: instead of blaming the philosophers I have mentioned, for
the defects and blemishes of their system, we ought rather to honour their
memories, as the first discoverers of a region in philosophy formerly
unknown; and however lame and imperfect the system may be, they have
opened the way to future discoveries, and are justly intitled to a great
share in the merit of them. They have removed an infinite deal of dust and
rubbish, collected in the ages of scholastic sophistry, which had obstructed
the way. They have put us in the right road, that of experience and accurate
reflection. They have taught us to avoid the snares of ambiguous and ill-
defined words, and have spoken and thought upon this subject with a
distinctness and perspicuity formerly unknown. They have made many

openings that may lead to the discovery of truths which they did not reach, or to the detection of errors in which they were involuntarily intangled.

It may be observed, that the defects and blemishes in the received philosophy concerning the mind, which have most exposed it to the contempt and ridicule of sensible men, have chiefly been owing to this: That the votaries of this Philosophy, from a natural prejudice in her favour, have endeavoured to extend her jurisdiction beyond its just limits, and to call to her bar the dictates of Common Sense. But these decline this jurisdiction; they disdain the trial of reasoning, and disown its authority; they neither claim its aid, nor dread its attacks.

In this unequal contest betwixt Common Sense and Philosophy, the latter will always come off both with dishonour and loss; nor can she ever thrive till this rivalship is dropt, these incroachments given up, and a cordial friendship restored: for, in reality, Common Sense holds nothing of Philosophy, nor needs her aid. But, on the other hand, Philosophy (if I may be permitted to change the metaphor) has no other root but the principles of Common Sense; it grows out of them, and draws its nourishment from them: severed from this root, its honours wither, its sap is dried up, it dies and rots.

The philosophers of the last age, whom I have mentioned, did not attend to the preserving this union and subordination so carefully as the honour and interest of philosophy required: but those of the present have waged open war with Common Sense, and hope to make a complete conquest of it by the subtilties of Philosophy; an attempt no less audacious and vain, than that of the giants to dethrone almighty Jove.

SECT. V.

Of Bishop Berkeley; the Treatise of human nature; and of scepticism.

THE present age, I apprehend, has not produced two more acute or more practised in this part of philosophy, than the Bishop of Cloyne, and the author of the *Treatise of human nature*. The first was no friend to scepticism, but had that warm concern for religious and moral principles which became his order: yet the result of his inquiry was, a serious conviction, that there is no such thing as a material world; nothing in nature but spirits and ideas; and that the belief of material substances, and of abstract ideas, are the chief causes of all our errors in philosophy, and of all infidelity and heresy in religion. His arguments are founded upon the principles which were formerly laid down by Des Cartes, Malebranche, and Locke, and which have been very generally received.

And the opinion of the ablest judges seems to be, that they neither have been, nor can be confuted; and that he hath proved by unanswerable arguments what no man in his senses can believe.

The second proceeds upon the same principles, but carries them to their full length; and as the Bishop undid the whole material world, this author, upon the same grounds, undoes the world of spirits, and leaves nothing in nature but ideas and impressions, without any subject on which they may be impressed.

It seems to be a peculiar strain of humour in this author, to set out in his introduction, by promising, with a grave face, no less than a complete system of the sciences, upon a foundation entirely new, to wit, that of human nature; when the intention of the whole work is to shew, that there is neither human nature nor science in the world. It may perhaps be unreasonable to complain of this conduct in an author, who neither believes his own existence, nor that of his reader; and therefore could not mean to disappoint him, or to laugh at his credulity. Yet I cannot imagine, that the author of the *Treatise of human nature* is so sceptical as to plead this apology. He believed, against his principles, that he should be read, and that he should retain his personal identity, till he reaped the honour and reputation justly due to his metaphysical *acumen*. Indeed he ingenuously acknowledges, that it was only in solitude and retirement that he could yield any assent to his own philosophy; society, like day-light, dispelled the darkness and fogs of scepticism, and made him yield to the dominion of Common Sense. Nor did I ever hear him charged with doing any thing, even in solitude, that argued such a degree of scepticism as his principles maintain. Surely if his friends apprehended this, they would have the charity never to leave him alone.

Pyrrho the Elean, the father of this philosophy, seems to have carried it to greater perfection than any of his successors: for if we may believe Antigonus the Carystian, quoted by Diogenes Laertius, his life corresponded to his doctrine. And therefore, if a cart run against him, or a dog attacked him, or if he came upon a precipice, he would not stir a foot to avoid the danger, giving no credit to his senses. But his attendants, who, happily for him, were not so great sceptics, took care to keep him out of harm's way; so that he lived till he was ninety years of age. Nor is it to be doubted, but this author's friends would have been equally careful to keep him from harm, if ever his principles had taken too strong a hold of him.

It is probable the *Treatise of human nature* was not written in company; yet it contains manifest indications, that the author every now and then relapsed into the faith of the vulgar, and could hardly, for half a dozen pages, keep up the sceptical character.

In like manner, the great Pyrrho himself forgot his principles on some occasions; and is said once to have been in such a passion with his cook, who probably had not roasted his dinner to his mind, that with the spit in his hand, and the meat upon it, he pursued him even into the market-place.

It is a bold philosophy that rejects, without ceremony, principles which irresistibly govern the belief and the conduct of all mankind in the common concerns of life; and to which the philosopher himself must yield, after he imagines he hath confuted them. Such principles are older, and of more authority, than Philosophy: she rests upon them as her basis, not they upon her. If she could overturn them, she must be buried in their ruins; but all the engines of philosophical subtilty are too weak for this purpose; and the attempt is no less ridiculous, than if a mechanic should contrive an *axis in peritrochio* to remove the earth out of its place; or if a mathematician should pretend to demonstrate, that things equal to the same thing are not equal to one another.

Zeno endeavoured to demonstrate the impossibility of motion; Hobbes, that there was no difference between right and wrong; and this author, that no credit is to be given to our senses, to our memory, or even to demonstration. Such philosophy is justly ridiculous, even to those who cannot detect the fallacy of it. It can have no other tendency, than to shew the acuteness of the sophist, at the expence of disgracing reason and human nature, and making mankind Yahoos.

SECT. VI.

Of the Treatise of human nature.

THERE are other prejudices against this system of human nature, which, even upon a general view, may make one diffident of it.

Des Cartes, Hobbes, and this author, have each of them given us a system of human nature; an undertaking too vast for any one man, how great soever his genius and abilities may be. There must surely be reason to apprehend, that many parts of human nature never came under their observation; and that others have been stretched and distorted, to fill up blanks, and complete the system. Christopher Columbus, or Sebastian Cabot, might almost as reasonably have undertaken to give us a complete map of America.

There is a certain character and style in Nature's works, which is never attained in the most perfect imitation of them. This seems to be wanting in the systems of human nature I have mentioned, and particularly in the last. One may see a puppet make variety of motions and gesticulations, which strike much at first view; but when it is accurately observed, and taken to pieces, our admiration ceases; we comprehend the whole art of the maker. How unlike is it to that which it represents! what a poor piece of work compared with the body of a man, whose structure the more we know, the more wonders we discover in it, and the more sensible we are of our ignorance! Is the mechanism of the mind so easily comprehended, when that of the body is so difficult? Yet, by this system, three laws of association, joined to a few original feelings, explain the whole mechanism of sense, imagination, memory, belief, and of all the actions and passions of the mind. Is this the man that Nature made? I suspect it is not so easy to look behind the scenes in Nature's work. This is a puppet surely, contrived by too bold an apprentice of Nature, to mimic her work. It shews tolerably by candle-light, but brought into clear day, and taken to pieces, it will appear to be a man made with mortar and a trowel. The more we know of other parts of nature, the more we like and approve them. The little I know of the planetary system; of the earth which we inhabit; of minerals, vegetables, and animals; of my own body, and of the laws which obtain in these parts of nature, opens to my mind grand and beautiful scenes, and contributes equally to my happiness and power. But when I look within, and consider the mind itself, which makes me capable of all these prospects and enjoyments; if it is indeed what the *Treatise of human nature* makes it, I find I have been only in an inchanted castle, imposed upon by spectres and apparitions. I blush inwardly to think how I have been deluded; I am ashamed of my frame, and can hardly forbear expostulating with my destiny: Is this thy pastime, O Nature, to put such tricks upon a silly creature, and then to take off the mask, and shew him how he hath been befooled? If this is the philosophy of human nature, my soul enter thou not into her secrets. It is surely the forbidden tree of knowledge; I no sooner taste of it, than I perceive myself naked, and stript of all things, yea even of my very self. I see myself, and the whole frame of nature, shrink into fleeting ideas, which, like Epicurus's atoms, dance about in emptiness.

SECT. VII.

The system of all these authors is the same, and leads to scepticism.

5   BUT what if these profound disquisitions into the first principles of human nature, do naturally and necessarily plunge a man into this abyss of scepticism? May we not reasonably judge so from what hath happened? Des Cartes no sooner began to dig in this mine, than scepticism was ready to break in upon him. He did what he could to shut it out. Malebranche

10   and Locke, who dug deeper, found the difficulty of keeping out this enemy still to increase; but they laboured honestly in the design. Then Berkeley, who carried on the work, despairing of securing all, bethought himself of an expedient: By giving up the material world, which he thought might be spared without loss, and even with advantage, he hoped by an impregnable

15   partition to secure the world of spirits. But, alas! the *Treatise of human nature* wantonly sapped the foundation of this partition, and drowned all in one universal deluge.

These facts, which are undeniable, do indeed give reason to apprehend, that Des Cartes's system of the human understanding, which I shall beg

20   leave to call *the ideal system*, and which, with some improvements made by later writers, is now generally received, hath some original defect; that this scepticism is inlaid in it, and reared along with it; and, therefore, that we must lay it open to the foundation, and examine the materials, before we can expect to raise any solid and useful fabric of knowledge on this

25   subject.

SECT. VIII.

We ought not to despair of a better.

30

BUT is this to be despaired of, because Des Cartes and his followers have failed? By no means. This pusillanimity would be injurious to ourselves, and injurious to truth. Useful discoveries are sometimes indeed the effect of superior genius, but more frequently they are the birth of time and of

35   accidents. A traveller of good judgment may mistake his way, and be unawares led into a wrong track; and while the road is fair before him, he may go on without suspicion, and be followed by others; but when it ends in a coal-pit, it requires no great judgment to know that he hath gone wrong, nor perhaps to find out what misled him.

In the mean time, the unprosperous state of this part of philosophy hath produced an effect, somewhat discouraging indeed to any attempt of this nature, but an effect which might be expected, and which time only and better success can remedy. Sensible men, who never will be sceptics
5   in matters of common life, are apt to treat with sovereign contempt every thing that hath been said, or is to be said, upon this subject. It is metaphysic, say they: Who minds it? Let scholastic sophisters intangle themselves in their own cobwebs; I am resolved to take my own existence, and the existence of other things, upon trust; and to believe that snow is
10   cold, and honey sweet, whatever they may say to the contrary. He must either be a fool, or want to make a fool of me, that would reason me out of my reason and senses.

I confess I know not what a sceptic can answer to this, nor by what good argument he can plead even for a hearing; for either his reasoning
15   is sophistry, and so deserves contempt; or there is no truth in the human faculties, and then why should we reason?

If therefore a man find himself intangled in these metaphysical toils, and can find no other way to escape, let him bravely cut the knot which he cannot loose, curse metaphysic, and dissuade every man from meddling
20   with it. For if I have been led into bogs and quagmires by following an *ignis fatuus*, what can I do better, than to warn others to beware of it? If Philosophy contradicts herself, befools her votaries, and deprives them of every object worthy to be pursued or enjoyed, let her be sent back to the infernal regions from which she must have had her original.

25   But is it absolutely certain that this fair lady is of the party? Is it not possible she may have been misrepresented? Have not men of genius in former ages often made their own dreams to pass for her oracles? Ought she then to be condemned without any farther hearing? This would be unreasonable. I have found her in all other matters an agreeable
30   companion, a faithful counsellor, a friend to Common Sense, and to the happiness of mankind. This justly intitles her to my correspondence and confidence, till I find infallible proofs of her infidelity.

CHAP. II.

Of SMELLING.

The order of proceeding. Of the medium and organ of smell.

IT is so difficult to unravel the operations of the human understanding, and to reduce them to their first principles, that we cannot expect to succeed in the attempt, but by beginning with the simplest, and proceeding by very cautious steps to the more complex. The five external senses may, for this reason, claim to be first considered in an analysis of the human faculties. And the same reason ought to determine us to make a choice even among the senses, and to give the precedence, not to the noblest, or most useful, but to the simplest, and that whose objects are least in danger of being mistaken for other things.

In this view, an analysis of our sensations may be carried on, perhaps with most ease and distinctness, by taking them in this order: Smelling, Tasting, Hearing, Touch, and, last of all, Seeing.

Natural philosophy informs us, that all animal and vegetable bodies, and probably all or most other bodies, while exposed to the air, are continually sending forth effluvia of vast subtilty, not only in their state of life and growth, but in the states of fermentation and putrefaction. These volatile particles do probably repel each other, and so scatter themselves in the air, until they meet with other bodies to which they have some chemical affinity, and with which they unite, and form new concretes. All the smell of plants, and of other bodies, is caused by these volatile parts, and is smelled wherever they are scattered in the air: and the acuteness of smell in some animals, shews us, that these effluvia spread far, and must be inconceivably subtile.

Whether, as some chemists conceive, every species of bodies hath a *spiritus rector*, a kind of soul, which causes the smell, and all the specific virtues of that body, and which, being extremely volatile, flies about in the air in quest of a proper receptacle, I do not inquire. This, like most other theories, is perhaps rather the product of imagination than of just induction. But that all bodies are smelled by means of effluvia which they emit, and which are drawn into the nostrils along with the air, there is no reason to doubt. So that there is manifest appearance of design in placing the organ of smell in the inside of that canal, through which the air is continually passing in inspiration and expiration.

Anatomy informs us, that the *membrana pituitaria*, and the olfactory nerves, which are distributed to the villous parts of this membrane, are the organs destined by the wisdom of nature to this sense; so that when a body emits no effluvia, or when they do not enter into the nose, or when the pituitary membrane or olfactory nerves are rendered unfit to perform their office, it cannot be smelled.

Yet, notwithstanding this, it is evident, that neither the organ of smell, nor the medium, nor any motions we can conceive excited in the membrane above mentioned, or in the nerve or animal spirits, do in the least resemble the sensation of smelling; nor could that sensation of itself ever have led us to think of nerves, animal spirits, or effluvia.

S E C T. II.

The sensation considered abstractly.

HAVING premised these things, with regard to the medium and organ of this sense, let us now attend carefully to what the mind is conscious of when we smell a rose or a lily; and since our language affords no other name for this sensation, we shall call it a *smell* or *odour*, carefully excluding from the meaning of those names every thing but the sensation itself, at least till we have examined it.

Suppose a person who never had this sense before, to receive it all at once, and to smell a rose; can he perceive any similitude or agreement between the smell and the rose? or indeed between it and any other object whatsoever? Certainly he cannot. He finds himself affected in a new way, he knows not why or from what cause. Like a man that feels some pain or pleasure formerly unknown to him, he is conscious that he is not the cause of it himself; but cannot, from the nature of the thing, determine whether it is caused by body or spirit, by something near, or by something at a distance. It has no similitude to any thing else, so as to admit of a comparison; and therefore he can conclude nothing from it, unless perhaps that there must be some unknown cause of it.

It is evidently ridiculous, to ascribe to it figure, colour, extension, or any other quality of bodies. He cannot give it a place, any more than he can give a place to melancholy or joy: nor can he conceive it to have any existence, but when it is smelled. So that it appears to be a simple and original affection or feeling of the mind, altogether inexplicable and unaccountable. It is indeed impossible that it can be in any body: it is a sensation, and a sensation can only be in a sentient thing.

5   The various odours have each their different degrees of strength or weakness. Most of them are agreeable or disagreeable; and frequently those that are agreeable when weak, are disagreeable when stronger. When we compare different smells together, we can perceive very few resemblances or contrarieties, or indeed relations of any kind between them. They are all so simple in themselves, and so different from each

10   other, that it is hardly possible to divide them into *genera* and *species*. Most of the names we give them are particular; as the smell of a *rose*, of a *jessamine*, and the like. Yet there are some general names; as *sweet, stinking, musty, putrid, cadaverous, aromatic*. Some of them seem to refresh and animate the mind, others to deaden and depress it.

15

S E C T. III.

Sensation and remembrance, natural principles of belief.

20   So far we have considered this sensation abstractly. Let us next compare it with other things to which it bears some relation. And first I shall compare this sensation with the remembrance, and the imagination of it.

I can think of the smell of a rose when I do not smell it; and it is possible that when I think of it, there is neither rose nor smell any where

25   existing. But when I smell it, I am necessarily determined to believe that the sensation really exists. This is common to all sensations, that as they cannot exist but in being perceived, so they cannot be perceived but they must exist. I could as easily doubt of my own existence, as of the existence of my sensations. Even those profound philosophers who have

30   endeavoured to disprove their own existence, have yet left their sensations to stand upon their own bottom, stript of a subject, rather than call in question the reality of their existence.

Here then a sensation, a smell for instance, may be presented to the mind three different ways: it may be smelled, it may be remembered, it

35   may be imagined or thought of. In the first case, it is necessarily accompanied with a belief of its present existence; in the second, it is necessarily accompanied with a belief of its past existence; and in the last, it is not accompanied with belief at all, but is what the logicians call *a simple apprehension*.

Why sensation should compel our belief of the present existence of the
thing, memory a belief of its past existence, and imagination no belief at
all, I believe no philosopher can give a shadow of reason, but that such
is the nature of these operations: They are all simple and original, and
therefore inexplicable acts of the mind.

Suppose that once, and only once, I smelled a tuberose in a certain
room where it grew in a pot, and gave a very grateful perfume. Next
day I relate what I saw and smelled. When I attend as carefully as I can
to what passes in my mind in this case, it appears evident, that the very
thing I saw yesterday, and the fragrance I smelled, are now the immediate
objects of my mind when I remember it. Further, I can imagine this pot
and flower transported to the room where I now sit, and yielding the same
perfume. Here likewise it appears, that the individual thing which I saw
and smelled, is the object of my imagination.

Philosophers indeed tell me, that the immediate object of my memory
and imagination in this case, is not the past sensation, but an idea of
it, an image, phantasm, or species of the odour I smelled: that this idea
now exists in my mind, or in my sensorium; and the mind contemplating
this present idea, finds it a representation of what is past, or of what
may exist; and accordingly calls it memory, or imagination. This is the
doctrine of the ideal philosophy; which we shall not now examine, that
we may not interrupt the thread of the present investigation. Upon the
strictest attention, memory appears to me to have things that are past, and
not present ideas, for its object. We shall afterwards examine this system
of ideas, and endeavour to make it appear, that no solid proof has ever
been advanced of the existence of ideas; that they are a mere fiction and
hypothesis, contrived to solve the phænomena of the human understanding; that they do not at all answer this end; and that this hypothesis of ideas
or images of things in the mind, or in the sensorium, is the parent of those
many paradoxes so shocking to common sense, and of that scepticism,
which disgrace our philosophy of the mind, and have brought upon it the
ridicule and contempt of sensible men.

In the mean time, I beg leave to think with the vulgar, that when
I remember the smell of the tuberose, that very sensation which I had
yesterday, and which has now no more any existence, is the immediate
object of my memory; and when I imagine it present, the sensation itself,
and not any idea of it, is the object of my imagination. But though the
object of my sensation, memory, and imagination, be in this case the
same, yet these acts or operations of the mind are as different, and as

easily distinguishable, as smell, taste, and sound. I am conscious of a difference in kind between sensation and memory, and between both and imagination. I find this also, that the sensation compels my belief of the present existence of the smell, and memory my belief of its past existence.

5 There is a smell, is the immediate testimony of sense; There was a smell, is the immediate testimony of memory. If you ask me, why I believe that the smell exists? I can give no other reason, nor shall ever be able to give any other, than that I smell it. If you ask, why I believe that it existed yesterday? I can give no other reason but that I remember it.

10 Sensation and memory therefore are simple, original, and perfectly distinct operations of the mind, and both of them are original principles of belief. Imagination is distinct from both, but is no principle of belief. Sensation implies the present existence of its object; memory its past existence; but imagination views its object naked, and without any belief
15 of its existence or non-existence, and is therefore what the schools call *simple apprehension.*

SECT. IV.

20 *Judgment and belief in some cases precede simple apprehension.*

But here again the ideal system comes in our way: it teaches us, that the first operation of the mind about its ideas, is simple apprehension; that is, the bare conception of a thing without any belief about it; and that after we
25 have got simple apprehensions, by comparing them together, we perceive agreements or disagreements between them; and that this perception of the agreement or disagreement of ideas, is all that we call belief, judgment, or knowledge. Now, this appears to me to be all fiction, without any foundation in nature: for it is acknowledged by all, that sensation must
30 go before memory and imagination; and hence it necessarily follows, that apprehension accompanied with belief and knowledge, must go before simple apprehension, at least in the matters we are now speaking of. So that here, instead of saying, that the belief or knowledge is got by putting together and comparing the simple apprehensions, we ought rather to say,
35 that the simple apprehension is performed by resolving and analysing a natural and original judgment. And it is with the operations of the mind, in this case, as with natural bodies, which are indeed compounded of simple principles or elements. Nature does not exhibit these elements separate, to be compounded by us; she exhibits them mixed and compounded in

concrete bodies, and it is only by art and chemical analysis that they can
be separated.

SECT. V.

Two theories of the nature of belief refuted.
Conclusions from what hath been said.

BUT what is this belief or knowledge which accompanies sensation and
memory? Every man knows what it is, but no man can define it. Does any
man pretend to define sensation, or to define consciousness? It is happy
indeed that no man does. And if no philosopher had endeavoured to define
and explain belief, some paradoxes in philosophy, more incredible than
ever were brought forth by the most abject superstition, or the most frantic
enthusiasm, had never seen the light. Of this kind surely is that modern
discovery of the ideal philosophy, that sensation, memory, belief, and
imagination, when they have the same object, are only different degrees
of strength and vivacity in the idea. Suppose the idea to be that of a future
state after death; one man believes it firmly; this means no more than
that he hath a strong and lively idea of it: Another neither believes nor
disbelieves; that is, he has a weak and faint idea. Suppose now a third
person believes firmly that there is no such thing; I am at a loss to know
whether his idea be faint or lively: If it is faint, then there may be a firm
belief where the idea is faint; if the idea is lively, then the belief of a future
state and the belief of no future state must be one and the same. The same
arguments that are used to prove that belief implies only a stronger idea of
the object than simple apprehension, might as well be used to prove that
love implies only a stronger idea of the object than indifference. And then
what shall we say of hatred, which must upon this hypothesis be a degree
of love, or a degree of indifference? If it should be said, that in love there
is something more than an idea, to wit, an affection of the mind; may it
not be said with equal reason, that in belief there is something more than
an idea, to wit, an assent or persuasion of the mind?

But perhaps it may be thought as ridiculous to argue against this strange
opinion, as to maintain it. Indeed, if a man should maintain, that a circle,
a square, and a triangle, differ only in magnitude, and not in figure, I
believe he would find nobody disposed either to believe him or to argue
against him; and yet I do not think it less shocking to common sense, to
maintain, that sensation, memory, and imagination, differ only in degree,

and not in kind. I know it is said, that in a delirium, or in dreaming, men are apt to mistake one for the other. But does it follow from this, that men who are neither dreaming, nor in a delirium, cannot distinguish them? But how does a man know, that he is not in a delirium? I cannot tell; neither can I tell how a man knows that he exists: but if any man seriously doubts whether he is in a delirium, I think it highly probable that he is, and that it is time to seek for a cure, which I am persuaded he will not find in the whole system of logic.

I mentioned before Locke's notion of belief or knowledge: he holds that it consists in a perception of the agreement or disagreement of ideas; and this he values himself upon as a very important discovery.

We shall have occasion afterwards to examine more particularly this grand principle of Locke's philosophy, and to shew that it is one of the main pillars of modern scepticism, although he had no intention to make that use of it. At present let us only consider how it agrees with the instances of belief now under consideration; and whether it gives any light to them. I believe that the sensation I have, exists; and that the sensation I remember, does not now exist, but did exist yesterday. Here, according to Locke's system, I compare the idea of a sensation with the ideas of past and present existence: at one time I perceive that this idea agrees with that of present existence, but disagrees with that of past existence; but at another time it agrees with the idea of past existence, and disagrees with that of present existence. Truly these ideas seem to be very capricious in their agreements and disagreements. Besides, I cannot for my heart conceive what is meant by either. I say a sensation exists, and I think I understand clearly what I mean. But you want to make the thing clearer, and for that end tell me, that there is an agreement between the idea of that sensation and the idea of existence. To speak freely, this conveys to me no light, but darkness; I can conceive no otherwise of it, than as an odd and obscure circumlocution. I conclude, then, that the belief which accompanies sensation and memory, is a simple act of the mind, which cannot be defined. It is in this respect like seeing and hearing, which can never be so defined as to be understood by those who have not these faculties; and to such as have them, no definition can make these operations more clear than they are already. In like manner, every man that has any belief, and he must be a curiosity that has none, knows perfectly what belief is, but can never define or explain it. I conclude also, that sensation, memory, and imagination, even where they have the same object, are operations of a quite different nature, and perfectly distinguishable by those who

are sound and sober. A man that is in danger of confounding them, is
indeed to be pitied; but whatever relief he may find from another art, he
can find none from logic or metaphysic. I conclude further, that it is no
less a part of the human constitution, to believe the present existence of
5   our sensations, and to believe the past existence of what we remember,
than it is to believe that twice two make four. The evidence of sense,
the evidence of memory, and the evidence of the necessary relations of
things, are all distinct and original kinds of evidence, equally grounded
on our constitution: none of them depends upon, or can be resolved into
10   another. To reason against any of these kinds of evidence, is absurd; nay,
to reason for them, is absurd. They are first principles; and such fall not
within the province of Reason, but of Common Sense.

SECT. VI.
15

Apology for metaphysical absurdities. Sensation without a sentient, a
consequence of the theory of ideas. Consequences of this strange opinion.

HAVING considered the relation which the sensation of smelling bears to the
20   remembrance and imagination of it, I proceed to consider, what relation
it bears to a mind, or sentient principle. It is certain, no man can conceive
or believe smelling to exist of itself, without a mind, or something that
has the power of smelling, of which it is called a sensation, an operation,
or feeling. Yet if any man should demand a proof, that sensation cannot
25   be without a mind, or sentient being, I confess that I can give none; and
that to pretend to prove it, seems to me almost as absurd as to deny it.
   This might have been said without any apology before the *Treatise of*
human nature appeared in the world. For till that time, no man, as far
as I know, ever thought either of calling in question that principle, or of
30   giving a reason for his belief of it. Whether thinking beings were of an
ethereal or igneous nature, whether material or immaterial, was variously
disputed; but that thinking is an operation of some kind of being or other,
was always taken for granted, as a principle that could not possibly admit
of doubt.
35   However, since the author above mentioned, who is undoubtedly one
of the most acute metaphysicians that this or any age hath produced, hath
treated it as a vulgar prejudice, and maintained, that the mind is only a
succession of ideas and impressions, without any subject; his opinion,
however contrary to the common apprehensions of mankind, deserves

respect. I beg therefore, once for all, that no offence may be taken at charging this or other metaphysical notions with absurdity, or with being contrary to the common sense of mankind. No disparagement is meant to the understandings of the authors or maintainers of such opinions. Indeed, they commonly proceed not from defect of understanding, but from an excess of refinement: the reasoning that leads to them, often gives new light to the subject, and shews real genius and deep penetration in the author; and the premises do more than atone for the conclusion.

If there are certain principles, as I think there are, which the constitution of our nature leads us to believe, and which we are under a necessity to take for granted in the common concerns of life, without being able to give a reason for them; these are what we call the principles of common sense; and what is manifestly contrary to them, is what we call absurd.

Indeed, if it is true, and to be received as a principle of philosophy, That sensation and thought may be without a thinking being; it must be acknowledged to be the most wonderful discovery that this or any other age hath produced. The received doctrine of ideas is the principle from which it is deduced, and of which indeed it seems to be a just and natural consequence. And it is probable, that it would not have been so late a discovery, but that it is so shocking and repugnant to the common apprehensions of mankind, that it required an uncommon degree of philosophical intrepidity to usher it into the world. It is a fundamental principle of the ideal system, That every object of thought must be an impression, or an idea, that is, a faint copy of some preceding impression. This is a principle so commonly received, that the author above mentioned, although his whole system is built upon it, never offers the least proof of it. It is upon this principle, as a fixed point, that he erects his metaphysical engines, to overturn heaven and earth, body and spirit. And indeed, in my apprehension, it is altogether sufficient for the purpose. For if impressions and ideas are the only objects of thought, then heaven and earth, and body and spirit, and every thing you please, must signify only impressions and ideas, or they must be words without any meaning. It seems, therefore, that this notion, however strange, is closely connected with the received doctrine of ideas, and we must either admit the conclusion, or call in question the premises.

Ideas seem to have something in their nature unfriendly to other existences. They were first introduced into philosophy, in the humble character of images or representatives of things; and in this character they seemed not only to be inoffensive, but to serve admirably well for explaining the operations of the human understanding. But since men began to reason clearly and distinctly about them, they have by degrees supplanted their constituents, and undermined the existence of every thing but themselves. First, they discarded all secondary qualities of bodies; and it was found out by their means, that fire is not hot, nor snow cold, nor honey sweet; and, in a word, that heat and cold, sound, colour, taste, and smell, are nothing but ideas or impressions. Bishop Berkeley advanced them a step higher, and found out, by just reasoning, from the same principles, that extension, solidity, space, figure, and body, are ideas, and that there is nothing in nature but ideas and spirits. But the triumph of ideas was completed by the *Treatise of human nature*, which discards spirits also, and leaves ideas and impressions as the sole existences in the universe. What if at last, having nothing else to contend with, they should fall foul of one another, and leave no existence in nature at all? This would surely bring philosophy into danger; for what should we have left to talk or to dispute about?

However, hitherto these philosophers acknowledge the existence of impressions and ideas; they acknowledge certain laws of attraction, or rules of precedence, according to which ideas and impressions range themselves in various forms, and succeed one another: but that they should belong to a mind, as its proper goods and chattels, this they have found to be a vulgar error. These ideas are as free and independent as the birds of the air, or as Epicurus's atoms when they pursued their journey in the vast inane. Shall we conceive them like the films of things in the Epicurean system?

> *Principio hoc dico, rerum simulacra vagari,*
> *Multa modis multis, in cunctas undique parteis*
> *Tenuia, quæ facile inter se junguntur in auris,*
> *Obvia cum veniunt.*   Lucr.

Or do they rather resemble Aristotle's intelligible species after they are shot forth from the object, and before they have yet struck upon the passive intellect? But why should we seek to compare them with any thing, since there is nothing in nature but themselves? They make the whole furniture of the universe; starting into existence, or out of it, without any cause; combining into parcels, which the vulgar call *minds*; and succeeding one another by fixed laws, without time, place, or author of those laws.

Yet, after all, these self-existent and independent ideas look pitifully naked and destitute, when left thus alone in the universe, and seem, upon

the whole, to be in a worse condition than they were before. Des Cartes, Malebranche, and Locke, as they made much use of ideas, treated them handsomely, and provided them in decent accommodation; lodging them either in the pineal gland, or in the pure intellect, or even in the divine
5 mind. They moreover clothed them with a commission, and made them representatives of things, which gave them some dignity and character. But the *Treatise of human nature*, though no less indebted to them, seems to have made but a bad return, by bestowing upon them this independent existence; since thereby they are turned out of house and home, and set
10 adrift in the world, without friend or connection, without a rag to cover their nakedness; and who knows but the whole system of ideas may perish by the indiscreet zeal of their friends to exalt them?

However this may be, it is certainly a most amazing discovery, that thought and ideas may be without any thinking being. A discovery big
15 with consequences which cannot easily be traced by those deluded mortals who think and reason in the common track. We were always apt to imagine, that thought supposed a thinker, and love a lover, and treason a traitor: but this, it seems, was all a mistake; and it is found out, that there may be treason without a traitor, and love without a lover, laws without
20 a legislator, and punishment without a sufferer, succession without time, and motion without any thing moved, or space in which it may move: or if, in these cases, ideas are the lover, the sufferer, the traitor, it were to be wished that the author of this discovery had farther condescended to acquaint us, whether ideas can converse together, and be under obligations
25 of duty or gratitude to each other; whether they can make promises and enter into leagues and covenants, and fulfil or break them, and be punished for the breach. If one set of ideas makes a covenant, another breaks it, and a third is punished for it, there is reason to think that justice is no natural virtue in this system.

30 It seemed very natural to think, that the *Treatise of human nature* required an author, and a very ingenious one too; but now we learn, that it is only a set of ideas which came together, and arranged themselves by certain associations and attractions.

After all, this curious system appears not to be fitted to the present state
35 of human nature. How far it may suit some choice spirits, who are refined from the dregs of common sense, I cannot say. It is acknowledged, I think, that even these can enter into this system only in their most speculative hours, when they soar so high in pursuit of those self-existent ideas, as to lose sight of all other things. But when they condescend to mingle

again with the human race, and to converse with a friend, a companion, or a fellow-citizen, the ideal system vanishes; common sense, like an irresistible torrent, carries them along; and, in spite of all their reasoning and philosophy, they believe their own existence, and the existence of
5   other things.

Indeed, it is happy they do so; for if they should carry their closet-belief into the world, the rest of mankind would consider them as diseased, and send them to an infirmary. Therefore, as Plato required certain previous qualifications of those who entered his school, I think it would be prudent
10   for the doctors of this ideal philosophy to do the same, and to refuse admittance to every man who is so weak, as to imagine that he ought to have the same belief in solitude and in company, or that his principles ought to have any influence upon his practice: for this philosophy is like a hobby-horse, which a man in bad health may ride in his closet,
15   without hurting his reputation; but if he should take him abroad with him to church, or to the exchange, or to the play-house, his heir would immediately call a jury, and seize his estate.

S E C T. VII.
20

The conception and belief of a sentient being or mind, is suggested by our constitution. The notion of relations not always got by comparing the related ideas.

25   LEAVING this philosophy therefore to those who have occasion for it, and can use it discreetly as a chamber-exercise, we may still inquire, how the rest of mankind, and even the adepts themselves, except in some solitary moments, have got so strong and irresistible a belief, that thought must have a subject, and be the act of some thinking being: how every man
30   believes himself to be something distinct from his ideas and impressions; something which continues the same identical self when all his ideas and impressions are changed. It is impossible to trace the origin of this opinion in history: for all languages have it interwoven in their original construction. All nations have always believed it. The constitution of all laws
35   and governments, as well as the common transactions of life, suppose it.

It is no less impossible for any man to recollect when he himself came by this notion: for, as far back as we can remember, we were already in possession of it, and as fully persuaded of our own existence, and the existence of other things, as that one and one make two. It seems, therefore, that this opinion preceded all reasoning, and experience, and instruction; and this is the more probable, because we could not get it by any of these means. It appears then to be an undeniable fact, that from thought or sensation, all mankind, constantly and invariably, from the first dawning of reflection, do infer a power or faculty of thinking, and a permanent being or mind to which that faculty belongs; and that we as invariably ascribe all the various kinds of sensation and thought we are conscious of, to one individual mind or self.

But by what rules of logic we make these inferences, it is impossible to show; nay, it is impossible to show how our sensations and thoughts can give us the very notion and conception either of a mind or of a faculty. The faculty of smelling is something very different from the actual sensation of smelling; for the faculty may remain when we have no sensation. And the mind is no less different from the faculty; for it continues the same individual being when that faculty is lost. Yet this sensation suggests to us both a faculty and a mind; and not only suggests the notion of them, but creates a belief of their existence; although it is impossible to discover, by reason, any tie or connection between one and the other.

What shall we say then? Either those inferences which we draw from our sensations, namely, the existence of a mind, and of powers or faculties belonging to it, are prejudices of philosophy or education, mere fictions of the mind, which a wise man should throw off as he does the belief of fairies; or they are judgments of nature, judgments not got by comparing ideas, and perceiving agreements and disagreements, but immediately inspired by our constitution.

If this last is the case, as I apprehend it is, it will be impossible to shake off those opinions, and we must yield to them at last, though we struggle hard to get rid of them. And if we could, by a determined obstinacy, shake off the principles of our nature, this is not to act the philosopher, but the fool or the madman. It is incumbent upon those who think that these are not natural principles, to show, in the first place, how we can otherwise get the notion of a mind and its faculties; and then to show, how we come to deceive ourselves into the opinion that sensation cannot be without a sentient being.

It is the received doctrine of philosophers, that our notions of relations can only be got by comparing the related ideas: but, in the present case, there seems to be an instance to the contrary. It is not by having first the notions of mind and sensation, and then comparing them together, that we perceive the one to have the relation of a subject or substratum, and the other that of an act or operation: on the contrary, one of the related things, to wit, sensation, suggests to us both the correlate and the relation.

I beg leave to make use of the word *suggestion*, because I know not one more proper, to express a power of the mind, which seems entirely to have escaped the notice of philosophers, and to which we owe many of our simple notions which are neither impressions nor ideas, as well as many original principles of belief. I shall endeavour to illustrate, by an example, what I understand by this word. We all know, that a certain kind of sound suggests immediately to the mind, a coach passing in the street; and not only produces the imagination, but the belief, that a coach is passing. Yet there is here no comparing of ideas, no perception of agreements or dis-agreements, to produce this belief; nor is there the least similitude between the sound we hear, and the coach we imagine and believe to be passing.

It is true that this suggestion is not natural and original; it is the result of experience and habit. But I think it appears, from what hath been said, that there are natural suggestions; particularly, that sensation suggests the notion of present existence, and the belief that what we perceive or feel, does now exist; that memory suggests the notion of past existence, and the belief that what we remember did exist in time past; and that our sen-sations and thoughts do also suggest the notion of a mind, and the belief of its existence, and of its relation to our thoughts. By a like natural principle it is, that a beginning of existence, or any change in nature, suggests to us the notion of a cause, and compels our belief of its existence. And in like manner, as shall be shewn when we come to the sense of touch, certain sensations of touch, by the constitution of our nature, suggest to us extension, solidity, and motion, which are nowise like to sensations, although they have been hitherto confounded with them.

SECT. VIII.

There is a quality or virtue in bodies, which we call their smell.
How this is connected in the imagination with the sensation.

WE have considered smell as signifying a sensation, feeling, or impression upon the mind; and in this sense, it can only be in a mind, or sentient being: but it is evident, that mankind give the name of *smell* much more frequently to something which they conceive to be external, and to be a quality of body: they understand something by it which does not at all infer a mind; and have not the least difficulty in conceiving the air

perfumed with aromatic odours in the deserts of Arabia, or in some uninhabited island, where the human foot never trod. Every sensible day-labourer hath as clear a notion of this, and as full a conviction of the possibility of it, as he hath of his own existence; and can no more doubt
5   of the one than of the other.

Suppose that such a man meets with a modern philosopher, and wants to be informed, what smell in plants is. The philosopher tells him, that there is no smell in plants, nor in any thing, but in the mind; that it is impossible there can be smell but in a mind; and that all this hath been demonstrated
10   by modern philosophy. The plain man will, no doubt, be apt to think him merry: but if he finds that he is serious, his next conclusion will be, that he is mad; or that philosophy, like magic, puts men into a new world, and gives them different faculties from common men. And thus philosophy and common sense are set at variance. But who is to blame for it? In my
15   opinion the philosopher is to blame. For if he means by smell, what the rest of mankind most commonly mean, he is certainly mad. But if he puts a different meaning upon the word, without observing it himself, or giving warning to others; he abuses language, and disgraces philosophy, without doing any service to truth: as if a man should exchange the meaning of
20   the words *daughter* and *cow*, and then endeavour to prove to his plain neighbour, that his cow is his daughter, and his daughter his cow.

I believe there is not much more wisdom in many of those paradoxes of the ideal philosophy, which to plain sensible men appear to be palpable absurdities, but with the adepts pass for profound discoveries. I resolve,
25   for my own part, always to pay a great regard to the dictates of common sense, and not to depart from them without absolute necessity: and therefore I am apt to think, that there is really something in the rose or lily, which is by the vulgar called *smell*, and which continues to exist when it is not smelled: and shall proceed to inquire what this is; how we come by
30   the notion of it; and what relation this quality or virtue of smell hath to the sensation, which we have been obliged to call by the same name, for want of another.

Let us therefore suppose, as before, a person beginning to exercise the sense of smelling: a little experience will discover to him, that the nose
35   is the organ of this sense, and that the air, or something in the air, is a medium of it. And finding, by farther experience, that when a rose is near, he has a certain sensation; when it is removed, the sensation is gone; he finds a connection in nature betwixt the rose and this sensation. The rose is considered as a cause, occasion, or antecedent, of the sensation; the

sensation as an effect or consequent of the presence of the rose: they are associated in the mind, and constantly found conjoined in the imagination.

But here it deserves our notice, that although the sensation may seem more closely related to the mind its subject, or to the nose its organ; yet neither of these connections operate so powerfully upon the imagination, as its connection with the rose its concomitant. The reason of this seems to be, that its connection with the mind is more general, and nowise distinguisheth it from other smells, or even from tastes, sounds, and other kinds of sensations. The relation it hath to the organ, is likewise general, and doth not distinguish it from other smells: but the connection it hath with the rose is special, and constant; by which means they become almost inseparable in the imagination, in like manner as thunder and lightning, freezing and cold.

SECT. IX.

That there is a principle in human nature, from which the notion of this, as well as all other natural virtues or causes, is derived.

IN order to illustrate further how we come to conceive a quality or virtue in the rose which we call *smell*, and what this smell is, it is proper to observe, that the mind begins very early to thirst after principles, which may direct it in the exertion of its powers. The smell of a rose is a certain affection or feeling of the mind; and as it is not constant, but comes and goes, we want to know when and where we may expect it, and are uneasy till we find something, which being present, brings this feeling along with it, and being removed, removes it. This, when found, we call the cause of it; not in a strict and philosophical sense, as if the feeling were really effected or produced by that cause, but in a popular sense: for the mind is satisfied, if there is a constant conjunction between them; and such causes are in reality nothing else but laws of nature. Having found the smell thus constantly conjoined with the rose, the mind is at rest, without inquiring whether this conjunction is owing to a real efficiency or not; that being a philosophical inquiry, which does not concern human life. But every discovery of such a constant conjunction is of real importance in life, and makes a strong impression upon the mind.

So ardently do we desire to find every thing that happens within our observation, thus connected with something else, as its cause or occasion, that we are apt to fancy connections upon the slightest grounds: and this weakness is most remarkable in the ignorant, who know least of the real connections established in nature. A man meets with an unlucky accident on a certain day of the year; and knowing no other cause of his misfortune, he is apt to conceive something unlucky in that day of the calendar; and if he finds the same connection hold a second time, is strongly confirmed in his superstition. I remember, many years ago, a white ox was brought into this country, of so enormous a size, that people came many miles to see him. There happened, some months after, an uncommon fatality among women in child-bearing. Two such uncommon events following one another, gave a suspicion of their connection, and occasioned a common opinion among the country-people, that the white ox was the cause of this fatality.

However silly and ridiculous this opinion was, it sprung from the same root in human nature, on which all natural philosophy grows; namely, an eager desire to find out connections in things, and a natural, original, and unaccountable propensity to believe, that the connections which we have observed in time past, will continue in time to come. Omens, portents, good and bad luck, palmistry, astrology, all the numerous arts of divination, and of interpreting dreams, false hypotheses and systems, and true principles in the philosophy of nature, are all built upon the same foundation in the human constitution; and are distinguished only according as we conclude rashly from too few instances, or cautiously from a sufficient induction.

As it is experience only that discovers these connections between natural causes and their effects; without inquiring further, we attribute to the cause some vague and indistinct notion of power or virtue to produce the effect. And in many cases, the purposes of life do not make it necessary to give distinct names to the cause and the effect. Whence it happens, that being closely connected in the imagination, although very unlike to each other, one name serves for both; and, in common discourse, is most frequently applied to that which, of the two, is most the object of our attention. This occasions an ambiguity in many words, which having the same causes in all languages, is common to all, and is apt to be overlooked even by philosophers. Some instances will serve both to illustrate and confirm what we have said.

Magnetism signifies both the tendency of the iron towards the magnet, and the power of the magnet to produce that tendency: and if it was asked, whether it is a quality of the iron or of the magnet? one would perhaps be puzzled at first; but a little attention would discover, that we conceive a power or virtue in the magnet as the cause, and a motion in the iron as the effect; and although these are things quite unlike, they are so united in the imagination, that we give the common name of *magnetism* to both. The same thing may be said of *gravitation*, which sometimes signifies the tendency of bodies towards the earth, sometimes the attractive power of the earth, which we conceive as the cause of that tendency. We may observe the same ambiguity in some of Sir Isaac Newton's definitions; and that even in words of his own making. In three of his definitions, he explains very distinctly what he understands by the *absolute* quantity, what by the *accelerative* quantity, and what by the *motive* quantity, of a centripetal force. In the first of these three definitions, centripetal force is put for the cause, which we conceive to be some power or virtue in the centre or central body: in the two last, the same word is put for the effect of this cause, in producing velocity, or in producing motion towards that centre.

Heat signifies a sensation, and *cold* a contrary one. But *heat* likewise signifies a quality or state of bodies, which hath no contrary, but different degrees. When a man feels the same water hot to one hand, and cold to the other, this gives him occasion to distinguish between the feeling, and the heat of the body; and although he knows that the sensations are contrary, he does not imagine that the body can have contrary qualities at the same time. And when he finds a different taste in the same body in sickness and in health, he is easily convinced, that the quality in the body called *taste* is the same as before, although the sensations he has from it are perhaps opposite.

The vulgar are commonly charged by philosophers, with the absurdity of imagining the smell in the rose to be something like to the sensation of smelling: but I think, unjustly; for they neither give the same epithets to both, nor do they reason in the same manner from them. What is smell in the rose? It is a quality or virtue of the rose, or of something proceeding from it, which we perceive by the sense of smelling; and this is all we know of the matter. But what is smelling? It is an act of the mind, but is never imagined to be a quality of the mind. Again, the sensation of smelling is conceived to infer necessarily a mind or sentient being; but smell in the rose infers no such thing. We say, This body smells sweet, that stinks; but we do not say, This mind smells sweet, and that stinks. Therefore smell in the rose, and the sensation which it causes, are not conceived, even by the vulgar, to be things of the same kind, altho' they have the same name.

From what hath been said, we may learn, that the smell of a rose signifies two things. *First*, A sensation, which can have no existence but when it is perceived, and can only be in a sentient being or mind. *Secondly*, It signifies some power, quality, or virtue, in the rose, or in effluvia proceeding from it, which hath a permanent existence, independent of the mind, and which, by the constitution of nature, produces the sensation in us. By the original constitution of our nature, we are both led to believe, that there is a permanent cause of the sensation, and prompted to seek after it; and experience determines us to place it in the rose. The names of all smells, tastes, sounds, as well as heat and cold, have a like ambiguity in all languages: but it deserves our attention, that these names are but rarely, in common language, used to signify the sensations; for the most part, they signify the external qualities which are indicated by the sensations. The cause of which phænomenon I take to be this. Our sensations have very different degrees of strength. Some of them are so quick and lively, as to give us a great deal either of pleasure or of uneasiness: When this is the case, we are compelled to attend to the sensation itself, and to make it an object of thought and discourse; we give it a name, which signifies nothing but the sensation; and in this case we readily acknowledge, that the thing meant by that name is in the mind only, and not in any thing external. Such are the various kinds of pain, sickness, and the sensations of hunger and other appetites. But where the sensation is not so interesting as to require to be made an object of thought, our constitution leads us to consider it as a sign of something external, which hath a constant conjunction with it; and having found what it indicates, we give a name to that: the sensation, having no proper name, falls in as an accessory to the thing signified by it, and is confounded under the same name. So that the name may indeed be applied to the sensation, but most properly and commonly is applied to the thing indicated by that sensation. The sensations of smell, taste, sound, and colour, are of infinitely more importance as signs or indications, than they are upon their own account; like the words of a language, wherein we do not attend to the sound, but to the sense.

SECT. X.

Whether in sensation the mind is active or passive?

THERE is one inquiry remains, Whether in smelling, and in other sensations, the mind is active or passive? This possibly may seem to be a question about words, or at least of very small importance; however, if it leads us to attend more accurately to the operations of our minds, than we are accustomed to do, it is upon that very account not altogether unprofitable. I think the opinion of modern philosophers is, that in sensation the mind is altogether passive. And this undoubtedly is so far true, that we cannot raise any sensation in our minds by willing it; and, on the other hand, it seems hardly possible to avoid having the sensation when the object is presented. Yet it seems likewise to be true, that in proportion as the attention is more or less turned to a sensation, or diverted from it, that sensation is more or less perceived and remembered. Every one knows, that very intense pain may be diverted by a surprise, or by any thing that entirely occupies the mind. When we are engaged in earnest conversation, the clock may strike by us without being heard; at least we remember not the next moment that we did hear it. The noise and tumult of a great trading city, is not heard by them who have lived in it all their days; but it stuns those strangers who have lived in the peaceful retirement of the country. Whether therefore there can be any sensation where the mind is purely passive, I will not say; but I think we are conscious of having given some attention to every sensation which we remember, though ever so recent.

No doubt, where the impulse is strong and uncommon, it is as difficult to withhold attention, as it is to forbear crying out in racking pain, or starting in a sudden fright: but how far both might be attained by strong resolution and practice, is not easy to determine. So that, although the Peripatetics had no good reason to suppose an active and a passive intellect, since attention may be well enough accounted an act of the will; yet I think they came nearer to the truth, in holding the mind to be in sensation partly passive and partly active, than the moderns, in affirming it to be purely passive. Sensation, imagination, memory, and judgment, have, by the vulgar, in all ages, been considered as acts of the mind. The manner in which they are expressed in all languages, shews this. When the mind is much employed in them, we say it is very active; whereas, if they were impressions only, as the ideal philosophy would lead us to conceive, we ought in such a case rather to say, that the mind is very passive: for I suppose no man would attribute great activity to the paper I write upon, because it receives variety of characters.

The relation which the sensation of smell bears to the memory and imagination of it, and to a mind or subject, is common to all our sensations, and indeed to all the operations of the mind: the relation it bears to the will, is common to it with all the powers of understanding: and the relation it bears to that quality or virtue of bodies which it indicates, is common to it with the sensations of taste, hearing, colour, heat, and cold: so that what hath been said of this sense, may easily be applied to several of our senses, and to other operations of the mind; and this, I hope, will apologize for our insisting so long upon it.

CHAP. III.

Of TASTING.

A GREAT part of what hath been said of the sense of smelling, is so easily applied to those of tasting and hearing, that we shall leave the application entirely to the reader's judgment, and save ourselves the trouble of a tedious repetition.

It is probable that every thing that affects the taste, is in some degree soluble in the *saliva*. It is not conceivable how any thing should enter readily, and of its own accord, as it were, into the pores of the tongue, palate, and *fauces*, unless it had some chemical affinity to that liquor with which these pores are always replete. It is therefore an admirable contrivance of nature, that the organs of taste should always be moist with a liquor which is so universal a menstruum, and which deserves to be examined more than it hath been hitherto, both in that capacity, and as a medical unguent. Nature teaches dogs, and other animals, to use it in this last way; and its subserviency both to taste and digestion, shews its efficacy in the former.

It is with manifest design and propriety, that the organ of this sense guards the entrance of the alimentary canal, as that of smell, the entrance of the canal for respiration. And from these organs being placed in such manner, that every thing that enters into the stomach must undergo the scrutiny of both senses, it is plain, that they were intended by nature to distinguish wholesome food from that which is noxious. The brutes have no other means of chusing their food; nor would mankind, in the savage state. And it is very probable, that the smell and taste, no way vitiated by luxury or bad habits, would rarely, if ever, lead us to a wrong choice of food among the productions of nature; although the artificial compositions of a refined and luxurious cookery, or of chemistry and pharmacy, may often impose upon both, and produce things agreeable to the taste and smell, which are noxious to health. And it is probable, that both smell and taste are vitiated, and rendered less fit to perform their natural offices, by the unnatural kind of life men commonly lead in society.

These senses are likewise of great use to distinguish bodies that cannot be distinguished by our other senses, and to discern the changes which the same body undergoes, which in many cases are sooner perceived by taste and smell than by any other means. How many things are there in the market, the eating-house, and the tavern, as well as in the apothecary

and chemist's shops, which are known to be what they are given out to be, and are perceived to be good or bad in their kind, only by taste or smell? And how far our judgment of things, by means of our senses, might be improved by accurate attention to the small differences of taste
5 and smell, and other sensible qualities, is not easy to determine. Sir Isaac Newton, by a noble effort of his great genius, attempted, from the colour of opaque bodies, to discover the magnitude of the minute pellucid parts, of which they are compounded: and who knows what new lights natural philosophy may yet receive from other secondary qualities duly
10 examined?

Some tastes and smells stimulate the nerves, and raise the spirits: but such an artificial elevation of the spirits is, by the laws of nature, followed by a depression, which can only be relieved by time, or by the repeated use of the like *stimulus*. By the use of such things we create an appetite
15 for them, which very much resembles, and hath all the force of a natural one. It is in this manner that men acquire an appetite for snuff, tobacco, strong liquors, laudanum, and the like.

Nature indeed seems studiously to have set bounds to the pleasures and pains we have by these two senses, and to have confined them within
20 very narrow limits, that we might not place any part of our happiness in them; there being hardly any smell or taste so disagreeable that use will not make it tolerable, and at last perhaps agreeable; nor any so agreeable as not to lose its relish by constant use. Neither is there any pleasure or pain of these senses which is not introduced, or followed, by some degree
25 of its contrary, which nearly balances it. So that we may here apply the beautiful allegory of the divine Socrates; That although pleasure and pain are contrary in their nature, and their faces look different ways, yet Jupiter hath tied them so together, that he that lays hold of the one, draws the other along with it.

30 As there is a great variety of smells, seemingly simple and uncompounded, not only altogether unlike, but some of them contrary to others; and as the same thing may be said of tastes; it would seem that one taste is not less different from another than it is from a smell: and therefore it may be a question, How all smells come to be considered as one *genus*,
35 and all tastes as another? What is the generical distinction? Is it only that the nose is the organ of the one, and the palate of the other? or, abstracting from the organ, is there not in the sensations themselves something common to smells, and something else common to tastes, whereby the one is distinguished from the other? It seems most probable that the latter is

the case; and that, under the appearance of the greatest simplicity, there is still in these sensations something of composition.

If one considers the matter abstractly, it would seem, that a number of sensations, or indeed of any other individual things, which are perfectly simple and uncompounded, are incapable of being reduced into *genera* and *species*; because individuals which belong to a species, must have something peculiar to each, by which they are distinguished, and something common to the whole species. And the same may be said of *species* which belong to one *genus*. And whether this does not imply some kind of composition, we shall leave to metaphysicians to determine.

The sensations both of smell and taste do undoubtedly admit of an immense variety of modifications, which no language can express. If a man was to examine five hundred different wines, he would hardly find two of them that had precisely the same taste: the same thing holds in cheese, and in many other things. Yet of five hundred different tastes in cheese or wine, we can hardly describe twenty, so as to give a distinct notion of them to one who had not tasted them.

Dr Nehemiah Grew, a most judicious and laborious naturalist, in a discourse read before the Royal Society, *anno* 1675, hath endeavoured to show, that there are at least sixteen different simple tastes, which he enumerates. How many compounded ones may be made out of all the various combinations of two, three, four, or more of these simple ones, they who are acquainted with the theory of combinations will easily perceive. All these have various degrees of intenseness and weakness. Many of them have other varieties: in some the taste is more quickly perceived upon the application of the sapid body, in others more slowly; in some the sensation is more permanent, in others more transient; in some it seems to undulate, or return after certain intervals, in others it is constant: the various parts of the organ, as the lips, the tip of the tongue, the root of the tongue, the *fauces*, the *uvula*, and the throat, are some of them chiefly affected by one sapid body, and others by another. All these, and other varieties of tastes, that accurate writer illustrates by a number of examples. Nor is it to be doubted, but smells, if examined with the same accuracy, would appear to have as great variety.

CHAP. IV.

Of HEARING.

SECT. I.

Variety of sounds. Their place and distance learned by custom,
without reasoning.

SOUNDS have probably no less variety of modifications, than either tastes or odours. For, first, sounds differ in tone. The ear is capable of perceiving four or five hundred variations of tone in sound, and probably as many different degrees of strength; by combining these, we have above twenty thousand simple sounds that differ either in tone or strength, supposing every tone to be perfect. But it is to be observed, that to make a perfect tone, a great many undulations of elastic air are required, which must all be of equal duration and extent, and follow one another with perfect regularity; and each undulation must be made up of the advance and recoil of innumerable particles of elastic air, whose motions are all uniform in direction, force, and time. Hence we may easily conceive a prodigious variety in the same tone, arising from irregularities of it, occasioned by the constitution, figure, situation, or manner of striking the sonorous body: from the constitution of the elastic medium, or its being disturbed by other motions; and from the constitution of the ear itself, upon which the impression is made.

A flute, a violin, a hautboy, and a French horn, may all sound the same tone, and be easily distinguishable. Nay, if twenty human voices sound the same note, and with equal strength, there will still be some difference. The same voice, while it retains its proper distinctions, may yet be varied many ways, by sickness or health, youth or age, leanness or fatness, good or bad humour. The same words spoken by foreigners and natives, nay, by persons of different provinces of the same nation, may be distinguished.

Such an immense variety of sensations of smell, taste, and sound, surely was not given us in vain. They are signs, by which we know and distinguish things without us; and it was fit that the variety of the signs should, in some degree, correspond with the variety of the things signified by them.

It seems to be by custom, that we learn to distinguish both the place of things, and their nature, by means of their sound. That such a noise is in the street, such another in the room above me; that this is a knock at my door, that a person walking up stairs, is probably learnt by experience. I remember, that once lying a-bed, and having been put into a fright, I heard my own heart beat; but I took it to be one knocking at the door, and arose and opened the door oftener than once, before I discovered that the sound was in my own breast. It is probable, that previous to all experience, we should as little know, whether a sound came from the right or left, from above or below, from a great or a small distance, as we should know whether it was the sound of a drum, or a bell, or a cart. Nature is frugal in her operations, and will not be at the expence of a particular instinct, to give us that knowledge which experience will soon produce, by means of a general principle of human nature.

For a little experience, by the constitution of human nature, ties together, not only in our imagination, but in our belief, those things which were in their nature unconnected. When I hear a certain sound, I conclude immediately, without reasoning, that a coach passes by. There are no premises from which this conclusion is inferred by any rules of logic. It is the effect of a principle of our nature, common to us with the brutes.

Although it is by hearing, that we are capable of the perceptions of harmony and melody, and of all the charms of music; yet it would seem, that these require a higher faculty, which we call *a musical ear.* This seems to be in very different degrees, in those who have the bare faculty of hearing equally perfect; and therefore ought not to be classed with the external senses, but in a higher order.

SECT. II.

Of natural language.

ONE of the noblest purposes of sound undoubtedly is language; without which mankind would hardly be able to attain any degree of improvement above the brutes. Language is commonly considered as purely an invention of men, who by nature are no less mute than the brutes, but having a superior degree of invention and reason, have been able to contrive artificial signs of their thoughts and purposes, and to establish them by common consent. But the origin of language deserves to be more carefully inquired into, not only as this inquiry may be of importance for the improvement of language, but as it is related to the present subject, and tends to lay open some of the first principles of human nature. I shall therefore offer some thoughts upon this subject.

By language I understand all those signs which mankind use in order to communicate to others their thoughts and intentions, their purposes and desires. And such signs may be conceived to be of two kinds: First, such as have no meaning, but what is affixed to them by compact or agreement among those who use them; these are artificial signs: Secondly, such as, previous to all compact or agreement, have a meaning which every man understands by the principles of his nature. Language, so far as it consists of artificial signs, may be called *artificial*; so far as it consists of natural signs, I call it *natural*.

Having premised these definitions, I think it is demonstrable, that if mankind had not a natural language, they could never have invented an artificial one by their reason and ingenuity. For all artificial language supposes some compact or agreement to affix a certain meaning to certain signs; therefore there must be compacts or agreements before the use of artificial signs; but there can be no compact or agreement without signs, nor without language; and therefore there must be a natural language before any artificial language can be invented: Which was to be demonstrated.

Had language in general been a human invention, as much as writing or printing, we should find whole nations as mute as the brutes. Indeed even the brutes have some natural signs by which they express their own thoughts, affections, and desires, and understand those of others. A chick, as soon as hatched, understands the different sounds whereby its dam calls it to food, or gives the alarm of danger. A dog or a horse understands, by nature, when the human voice caresses, and when it threatens him. But brutes, as far as we know, have no notion of contracts or covenants, or of moral obligation to perform them. If nature had given them these notions, she would probably have given them natural signs to express them. And where nature has denied these notions, it is as impossible to acquire them by art, as it is for a blind man to acquire the notion of colours. Some brutes are sensible of honour or disgrace; they have resentment and gratitude; but none of them, as far as we know, can make a promise, or plight their faith, having no such notions from their constitution. And if mankind had not these notions by nature, and natural signs to express them by, with all their wit and ingenuity they could never have invented language.

The elements of this natural language of mankind, or the signs that are naturally expressive of our thoughts, may, I think, be reduced to these three kinds; modulations of the voice, gestures, and features. By means of these, two savages who have no common artificial language, can converse together; can communicate their thoughts in some tolerable manner; can

5 ask and refuse, affirm and deny, threaten and supplicate; can traffic, enter into covenants, and plight their faith. This might be confirmed by historical facts of undoubted credit, if it were necessary.

Mankind having thus a common language by nature, though a scanty one, adapted only to the necessities of nature, there is no great ingenuity

10 required in improving it by the addition of artificial signs, to supply the deficiency of the natural. These artificial signs must multiply with the arts of life, and the improvements of knowledge. The articulations of the voice, seem to be, of all signs, the most proper for artificial language; and as mankind have universally used them for that purpose, we may reason-

15 ably judge that nature intended them for it. But nature probably does not intend that we should lay aside the use of the natural signs; it is enough that we supply their defects by artificial ones. A man that rides always in a chariot, by degrees loses the use of his legs; and one who uses artificial signs only, loses both the knowledge and use of the natural. Dumb people

20 retain much more of the natural language than others, because necessity obliges them to use it. And for the same reason, savages have much more of it than civilized nations. It is by natural signs chiefly that we give force and energy to language; and the less language has of them, it is the less expressive and persuasive. Thus, writing is less expressive than reading,

25 and reading less expressive than speaking without book; speaking without the proper and natural modulations, force, and variations of the voice, is a frigid and dead language, compared with that which is attended with them; it is still more expressive when we add the language of the eyes and features; and is then only in its perfect and natural state, and attended

30 with its proper energy, when to all these we superadd the force of action.

Where speech is natural, it will be an exercise, not of the voice and lungs only, but of all the muscles of the body; like that of dumb people and savages, whose language, as it has more of nature, is more expressive, and is more easily learned.

35 Is it not pity that the refinements of a civilized life, instead of supplying the defects of natural language, should root it out, and plant in its stead dull and lifeless articulations of unmeaning sounds, or the scrawling of insignificant characters? The perfection of language is commonly thought to be, to express human thoughts and sentiments distinctly by these dull

signs; but if this is the perfection of artificial language, it is surely the corruption of the natural.

Artificial signs signify, but they do not express; they speak to the understanding, as algebraical characters may do, but the passions, the affections, and the will, hear them not: these continue dormant and inactive, till we speak to them in the language of nature, to which they are all attention and obedience.

It were easy to show, that the fine arts of the musician, the painter, the actor, and the orator, so far as they are expressive; although the knowledge of them requires in us a delicate taste, a nice judgment, and much study and practice; yet they are nothing else but the language of nature, which we brought into the world with us, but have unlearned by disuse, and so find the greatest difficulty in recovering it.

Abolish the use of articulate sounds and writing among mankind for a century, and every man would be a painter, an actor, and an orator. We mean not to affirm that such an expedient is practicable; or, if it were, that the advantage would counterbalance the loss; but that, as men are led by nature and necessity to converse together, they will use every mean in their power to make themselves understood; and where they cannot do this by artificial signs, they will do it, as far as possible, by natural ones: and he that understands perfectly the use of natural signs, must be the best judge in all the expressive arts.

CHAP. V.

Of TOUCH.

SECT. I.

Of heat and cold.

THE senses which we have hitherto considered, are very simple and uniform, each of them exhibiting only one kind of sensation, and thereby indicating only one quality of bodies. By the ear we perceive sounds, and nothing else; by the palate, tastes; and by the nose, odours: These qualities are all likewise of one order, being all secondary qualities: Whereas by touch we perceive not one quality only, but many, and those of very different kinds. The chief of them are heat and cold, hardness and softness, roughness and smoothness, figure, solidity, motion, and extension. We shall consider these in order.

As to heat and cold, it will easily be allowed that they are secondary qualities, of the same order with smell, taste, and sound. And, therefore, what hath been already said of smell, is easily applicable to them; that is, that the words *heat* and *cold* have each of them two significations; they sometimes signify certain sensations of the mind, which can have no existence when they are not felt, nor can exist any where but in a mind or sentient being; but more frequently they signify a quality in bodies, which, by the laws of nature, occasions the sensations of heat and cold in us: A quality which, though connected by custom so closely with the sensation, that we cannot without difficulty separate them; yet hath not the least resemblance to it, and may continue to exist when there is no sensation at all.

The sensations of heat and cold are perfectly known; for they neither are, nor can be, any thing else than what we feel them to be; but the qualities in bodies which we call *heat* and *cold*, are unknown. They are only conceived by us, as unknown causes or occasions of the sensations to which we give the same names. But though common sense says nothing of the nature of these qualities, it plainly dictates the existence of them; and to deny that there can be heat and cold when they are not felt, is an absurdity too gross to merit confutation. For what could be more absurd, than to say, that the thermometer cannot rise or fall, unless some person be present, or that the coast of Guinea would be as cold as Nova Zembla, if it had no inhabitants?

It is the business of philosophers to investigate, by proper experiments and induction, what heat and cold are in bodies. And whether they make heat a particular element diffused through nature, and accumulated in the heated body, or whether they make it a certain vibration of the parts of the heated body; whether they determine that heat and cold are contrary qualities, as the sensations undoubtedly are contrary, or that heat only is a quality, and cold its privation: these questions are within the province of philosophy; for common sense says nothing on the one side or the other.

But whatever be the nature of that quality in bodies which we call *heat*, we certainly know this, that it cannot in the least resemble the sensation of heat. It is no less absurd to suppose a likeness between the sensation and the quality, than it would be to suppose, that the pain of the gout resembles a square or a triangle. The simplest man that hath common sense, does not imagine the sensation of heat, or any thing that resembles that sensation, to be in the fire. He only imagines, that there is something in the fire, which makes him and other sentient beings feel heat. Yet as the name of *heat*, in common language, more frequently and more properly signifies this unknown something in the fire, than the sensation occasioned by it, he justly laughs at the philosopher, who denies that there is any heat in the fire, and thinks that he speaks contrary to common sense.

SECT. II.

Of hardness and softness.

LET us next consider hardness and softness; by which words we always understand real properties or qualities of bodies, of which we have a distinct conception.

When the parts of a body adhere so firmly, that it cannot easily be made to change its figure, we call it *hard*; when its parts are easily displaced, we call it *soft*. This is the notion which all mankind have of hardness and softness: they are neither sensations, nor like any sensation; they were real qualities before they were perceived by touch, and continue to be so when they are not perceived: for if any man will affirm, that diamonds were not hard till they were handled, who would reason with him?

There is, no doubt, a sensation by which we perceive a body to be hard or soft. This sensation of hardness may easily be had, by pressing one's hand against the table, and attending to the feeling that ensues, setting aside, as much as possible, all thought of the table and its qualities, or of any external thing. But it is one thing to have the sensation, and another to attend to it, and make it a distinct object of reflection. The first is very easy; the last, in most cases, extremely difficult.

5   We are so accustomed to use the sensation as a sign, and to pass immediately to the hardness signified, that, as far as appears, it was never made an object of thought, either by the vulgar or by philosophers; nor has it a name in any language. There is no sensation more distinct, or more frequent; yet it is never attended to, but passes through the mind
10 instantaneously, and serves only to introduce that quality in bodies, which, by a law of our constitution, it suggests.

    There are indeed some cases, wherein it is no difficult matter to attend to the sensation occasioned by the hardness of a body; for instance, when it is so violent as to occasion considerable pain: then nature calls upon
15 us to attend to it, and then we acknowledge, that it is a mere sensation, and can only be in a sentient being. If a man runs his head with violence against a pillar, I appeal to him, whether the pain he feels resembles the hardness of the stone; or if he can conceive any thing like what he feels, to be in an inanimate piece of matter.

20   The attention of the mind is here entirely turned towards the painful feeling; and, to speak in the common language of mankind, he feels nothing in the stone, but feels a violent pain in his head. It is quite otherwise when he leans his head gently against the pillar; for then he will tell you that he feels nothing in his head, but feels hardness in the stone. Hath he
25 not a sensation in this case as well as in the other? Undoubtedly he hath: but it is a sensation which nature intended only as a sign of something in the stone; and, accordingly, he instantly fixes his attention upon the thing signified; and cannot, without great difficulty, attend so much to the sensation, as to be persuaded that there is any such thing, distinct from
30 the hardness it signifies.

    But however difficult it may be to attend to this fugitive sensation, to stop its rapid progress, and to disjoin it from the external quality of hardness, in whose shadow it is apt immediately to hide itself; this is what a philosopher by pains and practice must attain, otherwise it will
35 be impossible for him to reason justly upon this subject, or even to understand what is here advanced. For the last appeal, in subjects of this nature, must be to what a man feels and perceives in his own mind.

    It is indeed strange, that a sensation which we have every time we feel a body hard, and which, consequently, we can command as often, and

continue as long as we please, a sensation as distinct and determinate as
any other, should yet be so much unknown, as never to have been made an
object of thought and reflection, nor to have been honoured with a name
in any language; that philosophers, as well as the vulgar, should have
5   entirely overlooked it, or confounded it with that quality of bodies which
we call *hardness*, to which it hath not the least similitude. May we not
hence conclude, That the knowledge of the human faculties is but in its
infancy? That we have not yet learned to attend to those operations of the
mind, of which we are conscious every hour of our lives? That there are
10   habits of inattention acquired very early, which are as hard to be overcome
as other habits? For I think it is probable, that the novelty of this sensation
will procure some attention to it in children at first; but being in nowise
interesting in itself, as soon as it becomes familiar, it is overlooked, and
the attention turned solely to that which it signifies. Thus, when one is
15   learning a language, he attends to the sounds; but when he is master of it,
he attends only to the sense of what he would express. If this is the case,
we must become as little children again, if we will be philosophers: we
must overcome this habit of inattention which has been gathering strength
ever since we began to think; a habit, the usefulness of which, in common
20   life, atones for the difficulty it creates to the philosopher in discovering
the first principles of the human mind.

The firm cohesion of the parts of a body, is no more like that sensation
by which I perceive it to be hard, than the vibration of a sonorous body
is like the sound I hear: nor can I possibly perceive, by my reason, any
25   connection between the one and the other. No man can give a reason, why
the vibration of a body might not have given the sensation of smelling,
and the effluvia of bodies affected our hearing, if it had so pleased our
Maker. In like manner, no man can give a reason, why the sensations of
smell, or taste, or sound, might not have indicated hardness, as well as
30   that sensation, which, by our constitution, does indicate it. Indeed no man
can conceive any sensation to resemble any known quality of bodies. Nor
can any man show, by any good argument, that all our sensations might
not have been as they are, though no body, nor quality of body, had ever
existed.

35   Here then is a phænomenon of human nature, which comes to be
resolved. Hardness of bodies is a thing that we conceive as distinctly, and
believe as firmly, as any thing in nature. We have no way of coming at
this conception and belief, but by means of a certain sensation of touch,
to which hardness hath not the least similitude; nor can we, by any rules

of reasoning, infer the one from the other. The question is, How we come by this conception and belief?

First, as to the conception: Shall we call it an idea of sensation, or of reflection? The last will not be affirmed; and as little can the first, unless we will call that an idea of sensation, which hath no resemblance to any sensation. So that the origin of this idea of hardness, one of the most common and most distinct we have, is not to be found in all our systems of the mind: not even in those which have so copiously endeavoured to deduce all our notions from sensation and reflection.

But, secondly, supposing we have got the conception of hardness, how come we by the belief of it? Is it self-evident, from comparing the ideas, that such a sensation could not be felt, unless such a quality of bodies existed? No. Can it be proved by probable or certain arguments? No, it cannot. Have we got this belief then by tradition, by education, or by experience? No, it is not got in any of these ways. Shall we then throw off this belief as having no foundation in reason? Alas! it is not in our power; it triumphs over reason, and laughs at all the arguments of a philosopher. Even the author of the *Treatise of human nature*, though he saw no reason for this belief, but many against it, could hardly conquer it in his speculative and solitary moments; at other times he fairly yielded to it, and confesses that he found himself under a necessity to do so.

What shall we say then of this conception, and this belief, which are so unaccountable and untractable? I see nothing left, but to conclude, that, by an original principle of our constitution, a certain sensation of touch both suggests to the mind the conception of hardness, and creates the belief of it: or, in other words, that this sensation is a natural sign of hardness. And this I shall endeavour more fully to explain.

SECT. III.

Of natural signs.

As in artificial signs there is often neither similitude between the sign and thing signified, nor any connection that arises necessarily from the nature of the things; so it is also in natural signs. The word *gold* has no similitude to the substance signified by it; nor is it in its own nature more fit to signify this than any other substance: yet, by habit and custom, it suggests this and no other. In like manner, a sensation of touch suggests hardness, although it hath neither similitude to hardness, nor, as far as we can perceive, any necessary connection with it. The difference betwixt these two signs lies only in this, that, in the first, the suggestion is the effect of habit and custom; in the second, it is not the effect of habit, but of the original constitution of our minds.

5   It appears evident from what hath been said on the subject of language, That there are natural signs, as well as artificial; and particularly, That the thoughts, purposes, and dispositions of the mind, have their natural signs in the features of the face, the modulation of the voice, and the motion and attitude of the body: That without a natural knowledge of the connection

10   between these signs, and the things signified by them, language could never have been invented and established among men: and, That the fine arts are all founded upon this connection, which we may call *the natural language of mankind*. It is now proper to observe, that there are different orders of natural signs, and to point out the different classes into which

15   they may be distinguished, that we may more distinctly conceive the relation between our sensations and the things they suggest, and what we mean by calling sensations signs of external things.

The first class of natural signs comprehends those whose connection with the thing signified is established by nature, but discovered only by

20   experience. The whole of genuine philosophy consists in discovering such connections, and reducing them to general rules. The great Lord Verulam had a perfect comprehension of this, when he called it *an interpretation of nature*. No man ever more distinctly understood, or happily expressed the nature and foundation of the philosophic art. What is all we know

25   of mechanics, astronomy, and optics, but connections established by nature, and discovered by experience or observation, and consequences deduced from them? All the knowledge we have in agriculture, gardening, chemistry, and medicine, is built upon the same foundation. And if ever our philosophy concerning the human mind is carried so far as to deserve

30   the name of science, which ought never to be despaired of, it must be by observing facts, reducing them to general rules, and drawing just conclusions from them. What we commonly call natural *causes* might, with more propriety, be called natural *signs*, and what we call *effects*, the things signified. The causes have no proper efficiency or causality, as far

35   as we know; and all we can certainly affirm, is, that nature hath established a constant conjunction between them and the things called their effects; and hath given to mankind a disposition to observe those connections, to confide in their continuance, and to make use of them for the improvement of our knowledge, and increase of our power.

A second class is that wherein the connection between the sign and thing signified, is not only established by nature, but discovered to us by a natural principle, without reasoning or experience. Of this kind are the natural signs of human thoughts, purposes, and desires, which have been already mentioned as the natural language of mankind. An infant may be put into a fright by an angry countenance, and soothed again by smiles and blandishments. A child that has a good musical ear, may be put to sleep or to dance, may be made merry or sorrowful, by the modulation of musical sounds. The principles of all the fine arts, and of what we call *a fine taste*, may be resolved into connections of this kind. A fine taste may be improved by reasoning and experience; but if the first principles of it were not planted in our minds by nature, it could never be acquired. Nay, we have already made it appear, that a great part of this knowledge, which we have by nature, is lost by the disuse of natural signs, and the substitution of artificial in their place.

A third class of natural signs comprehends those which, though we never before had any notion or conception of the things signified, do suggest it, or conjure it up, as it were, by a natural kind of magic, and at once give us a conception, and create a belief of it. I shewed formerly, that our sensations suggest to us a sentient being or mind to which they belong: a being which hath a permanent existence, although the sensations are transient and of short duration: a being which is still the same, while its sensations and other operations are varied ten thousand ways: a being which hath the same relation to all that infinite variety of thoughts, purposes, actions, affections, enjoyments, and sufferings, which we are conscious of, or can remember. The conception of a mind is neither an idea of sensation nor of reflection; for it is neither like any of our sensations, nor like any thing we are conscious of. The first conception of it, as well as the belief of it, and of the common relation it bears to all that we are conscious of, or remember, is suggested to every thinking being, we do not know how.

The notion of hardness in bodies, as well as the belief of it, are got in a similar manner; being, by an original principle of our nature, annexed to that sensation which we have when we feel a hard body. And so naturally and necessarily does the sensation convey the notion and belief of hardness, that hitherto they have been confounded by the most acute inquirers into the principles of human nature, although they appear, upon accurate reflection, not only to be different things, but as unlike as pain is to the point of a sword.

It may be observed, that as the first class of natural signs I have mentioned, is the foundation of true philosophy, and the second, the foundation of the fine arts, or of taste; so the last is the foundation of common sense; a part of human nature which hath never been explained.

5   I take it for granted, that the notion of hardness, and the belief of it, is first got by means of that particular sensation, which, as far back as we can remember, does invariably suggest it; and that if we had never had such a feeling, we should never have had any notion of hardness. I think it is evident, that we cannot, by reasoning from our sensations, collect

10 the existence of bodies at all, far less any of their qualities. This hath been proved by unanswerable arguments by the Bishop of Cloyne, and by the author of the *Treatise of human nature*. It appears as evident, that this connection between our sensations and the conception and belief of external existences cannot be produced by habit, experience, education,

15 or any principle of human nature that hath been admitted by philosophers. At the same time, it is a fact, that such sensations are invariably connected with the conception and belief of external existences. Hence, by all rules of just reasoning, we must conclude, that this connection is the effect of our constitution, and ought to be considered as an original principle of

20 human nature, till we find some more general principle into which it may be resolved.

S E C T. IV.

25   *Of hardness, and other primary qualities.*

FURTHER I observe, that hardness is a quality, of which we have as clear and distinct a conception as of any thing whatsoever. The cohesion of the parts of a body with more or less force, is perfectly understood, though

30 its cause is not: we know what it is, as well as how it affects the touch. It is therefore a quality of a quite different order from those secondary qualities we have already taken notice of, whereof we know no more naturally, than that they are adapted to raise certain sensations in us. If hardness were a quality of the same kind, it would be a proper inquiry for

35 philosophers, What hardness in bodies is? and we should have had various hypotheses about it, as well as about colour and heat. But it is evident that any such hypothesis would be ridiculous. If any man should say, that hardness in bodies is a certain vibration of their parts, or that it is certain effluvia emitted by them which affect our touch in the manner we feel;

such hypotheses would shock common sense; because we all know, that
if the parts of a body adhere strongly, it is hard, although it should neither
emit effluvia, nor vibrate. Yet at the same time, no man can say, but that
effluvia, or the vibration of the parts of a body, might have affected our
5   touch, in the same manner that hardness now does, if it had so pleased
the Author of our nature: and if either of these hypotheses is applied to
explain a secondary quality, such as smell, or taste, or sound, or colour,
or heat, there appears no manifest absurdity in the supposition.

The distinction betwixt primary and secondary qualities hath had
10   several revolutions. Democritus and Epicurus, and their followers,
maintained it. Aristotle and the Peripatetics abolished it. Des Cartes,
Malebranche, and Locke, revived it, and were thought to have put it in a
very clear light. But Bishop Berkeley again discarded this distinction, by
such proofs as must be convincing to those that hold the received doctrine
15   of ideas. Yet, after all, there appears to be a real foundation for it in the
principles of our nature.

What hath been said of hardness, is so easily applicable, not only to its
opposite, softness, but likewise to roughness and smoothness, to figure
and motion, that we may be excused from making the application, which
20   would only be a repetition of what hath been said. All these, by means of
certain corresponding sensations of touch, are presented to the mind as
real external qualities; the conception and the belief of them are invariably
connected with the corresponding sensations, by an original principle of
human nature. Their sensations have no name in any language; they have
25   not only been overlooked by the vulgar, but by philosophers; or if they
have been at all taken notice of, they have been confounded with the
external qualities which they suggest.

SECT. V.
30

Of extension.

It is further to be observed, that hardness and softness, roughness and
smoothness, figure and motion, do all suppose extension, and cannot be
35   conceived without it; yet I think it must, on the other hand, be allowed,
that if we had never felt any thing hard or soft, rough or smooth, figured
or moved, we should never have had a conception of extension: so that
as there is good ground to believe, that the notion of extension could not
be prior to that of other primary qualities; so it is certain that it could not

be posterior to the notion of any of them, being necessarily implied in them all.

Extension, therefore, seems to be a quality suggested to us, by the very same sensations which suggest the other qualities above mentioned. When I grasp a ball in my hand, I perceive it at once hard, figured, and extended. The feeling is very simple, and hath not the least resemblance to any quality of body. Yet it suggests to us three primary qualities perfectly distinct from one another, as well as from the sensation which indicates them. When I move my hand along the table, the feeling is so simple, that I find it difficult to distinguish it into things of different natures; yet it immediately suggests hardness, smoothness, extension, and motion, things of very different natures, and all of them as distinctly understood as the feeling which suggests them.

We are commonly told by philosophers, that we get the idea of extension by feeling along the extremities of a body, as if there was no manner of difficulty in the matter. I have sought, with great pains, I confess, to find out how this idea can be got by feeling, but I have sought in vain. Yet it is one of the clearest and most distinct notions we have; nor is there any thing whatsoever, about which the human understanding can carry on so many long and demonstrative trains of reasoning.

The notion of extension is so familiar to us from infancy, and so constantly obtruded by every thing we see and feel, that we are apt to think it obvious how it comes into the mind; but upon a narrower examination we shall find it utterly inexplicable. It is true we have feelings of touch, which every moment present extension to the mind; but how they come to do so, is the question; for those feelings do no more resemble extension, than they resemble justice or courage: nor can the existence of extended things be inferred from those feelings by any rules of reasoning: so that the feelings we have by touch, can neither explain how we get the notion, nor how we come by the belief of extended things.

What hath imposed upon philosophers in this matter, is, that the feelings of touch, which suggest primary qualities, have no names, nor are they ever reflected upon. They pass through the mind instantaneously, and serve only to introduce the notion and belief of external things, which by our constitution are connected with them. They are natural signs, and the mind immediately passes to the thing signified, without making the least reflection upon the sign, or observing that there was any such thing. Hence it hath always been taken for granted, that the ideas of extension, figure, and motion, are ideas of sensation, which enter into the mind by the sense of touch, in the same manner as the sensations of sound and smell do by the ear and nose. The sensations of touch are so connected, by our constitution, with the notions of extension, figure, and motion, that philosophers have mistaken the one for the other, and never have been able to discern that they were not only distinct things, but altogether unlike. However, if we will reason distinctly upon this subject, we ought to give names to those feelings of touch; we must accustom ourselves to attend to them, and to reflect upon them, that we may be able to disjoin them from, and to compare them with, the qualities signified or suggested by them.

The habit of doing this is not to be attained without pains and practice; and till a man hath acquired this habit, it will be impossible for him to think distinctly, or to judge right, upon this subject.

Let a man press his hand against the table: *he feels it hard.* But what is the meaning of this? The meaning undoubtedly is, that he hath a certain feeling of touch, from which he concludes, without any reasoning, or comparing ideas, that there is something external really existing, whose parts stick so firmly together, that they cannot be displaced without considerable force.

There is here a feeling, and a conclusion drawn from it, or some way suggested by it. In order to compare these, we must view them separately, and then consider by what tie they are connected, and wherein they resemble one another. The hardness of the table is the conclusion, the feeling is the medium by which we are led to that conclusion. Let a man attend distinctly to this medium, and to the conclusion, and he will perceive them to be as unlike as any two things in nature. The one is a sensation of the mind, which can have no existence but in a sentient being; nor can it exist one moment longer than it is felt; the other is in the table, and we conclude without any difficulty, that it was in the table before it was felt, and continues after the feeling is over. The one implies no kind of extension, nor parts, nor cohesion; the other implies all these. Both indeed admit of degrees, and the feeling, beyond a certain degree, is a species of pain; but adamantine hardness does not imply the least pain.

And as the feeling hath no similitude to hardness, so neither can our reason perceive the least tie or connection between them; nor will the logician ever be able to show a reason why we should conclude hardness from this feeling, rather than softness, or any other quality whatsoever. But in reality all mankind are led by their constitution to conclude hardness from this feeling.

The sensation of heat, and the sensation we have by pressing a hard body, are equally feelings; nor can we by reasoning draw any conclusion from the one, but what may be drawn from the other: but, by our constitution, we conclude from the first an obscure or occult quality, of which we have only this relative conception, that it is something adapted to raise in us the sensation of heat; from the second, we conclude a quality of which we have a clear and distinct conception, to wit, the hardness of the body.

SECT. VI.

Of extension.

To put this matter in another light, it may be proper to try, whether from sensation alone we can collect any notion of extension, figure, motion, and space. I take it for granted, that a blind man hath the same notions of extension, figure, and motion, as a man that sees; that Dr Saunderson had the same notion of a cone, a cylinder, and a sphere, and of the motions and distances of the heavenly bodies, as Sir Isaac Newton.

As sight therefore is not necessary for our acquiring those notions, we shall leave it out altogether in our inquiry into the first origin of them; and shall suppose a blind man, by some strange distemper, to have lost all the experience and habits and notions he had got by touch; not to have the least conception of the existence, figure, dimensions, or extension, either of his own body, or of any other; but to have all his knowledge of external things to acquire anew, by means of sensation, and the power of reason, which we suppose to remain entire.

We shall, first, suppose his body fixed immoveably in one place, and that he can only have the feelings of touch, by the application of other bodies to it. Suppose him first to be pricked with a pin; this will, no doubt, give a smart sensation: he feels pain; but what can he infer from it? Nothing surely with regard to the existence or figure of a pin. He can infer nothing from this species of pain, which he may not as well infer from the gout or sciatica. Common sense may lead him to think that this pain has a cause; but whether this cause is body or spirit, extended or unextended, figured or not figured, he cannot possibly, from any principles he is supposed to have, form the least conjecture. Having had formerly no notion of body or of extension, the prick of a pin can give him none.

Suppose, next, a body not pointed, but blunt, is applied to his body with a force gradually increased until it bruises him. What has he got by this, but another sensation, or train of sensations, from which he is able to conclude as little as from the former? A schirrous tumour in any inward part of the body, by pressing upon the adjacent parts, may give the same kind of sensation as the pressure of an external body, without conveying any notion but that of pain, which surely hath no resemblance to extension.

Suppose, thirdly, that the body applied to him touches a larger or a lesser part of his body. Can this give him any notion of its extension or dimensions? To me it seems impossible that it should, unless he had some previous notion of the dimensions and figure of his own body, to serve him as a measure. When my two hands touch the extremities of a body; if I know them to be a foot asunder, I easily collect that the body is a foot long; and if I know them to be five feet asunder, that it is five feet long: but if I know not what the distance of my hands is, I cannot know the length of the object they grasp; and if I have no previous notion of hands at all, or of distance between them, I can never get that notion by their being touched.

Suppose, again, that a body is drawn along his hands or face, while they are at rest: Can this give him any notion of space or motion? It no doubt gives a new feeling; but how it should convey a notion of space or motion, to one who had none before, I cannot conceive. The blood moves along the arteries and veins, and this motion, when violent, is felt: but I imagine no man, by this feeling, could get the conception of space or motion, if he had it not before. Such a motion may give a certain succession of feelings, as the colic may do; but no feelings, nor any combination of feelings, can ever resemble space or motion.

Let us next suppose, that he makes some instinctive effort to move his head or his hand; but that no motion follows, either on account of external resistance, or of palsy. Can this effort convey the notion of space and motion to one who never had it before? Surely it cannot.

Last of all, let us suppose, that he moves a limb by instinct, without having had any previous notion of space or motion. He has here a new sensation, which accompanies the flexure of joints, and the swelling of muscles. But how this sensation can convey into his mind the idea of space and motion, is still altogether mysterious and unintelligible. The motions of the heart and lungs are all performed by the contraction of muscles, yet give no conception of space or motion. An embryo in the womb has many such motions, and probably the feelings that accompany them, without any idea of space or motion.

Upon the whole, it appears, that our philosophers have imposed upon themselves, and upon us, in pretending to deduce from sensation the first origin of our notions of external existences, of space, motion, and extension, and all the primary qualities of body, that is, the qualities
5   whereof we have the most clear and distinct conception. These qualities do not at all tally with any system of the human faculties that hath been advanced. They have no resemblance to any sensation, or to any operation of our minds; and therefore they cannot be ideas either of sensation, or of reflection. The very conception of them is irreconcileable to the principles
10 of all our philosophic systems of the understanding. The belief of them is no less so.

SECT. VII.

15 *Of the existence of a material world.*

Iᴛ is beyond our power to say, when or in what order we came by our notions of these qualities. When we trace the operations of our minds as far back as memory and reflection can carry us, we find them already in
20 possession of our imagination and belief, and quite familiar to the mind: but how they came first into its acquaintance, or what has given them so strong a hold of our belief, and what regard they deserve, are no doubt very important questions in the philosophy of human nature.

Shall we, with the Bishop of Cloyne, serve them with a *Quo warranto*,
25 and have them tried at the bar of philosophy, upon the statute of the ideal system? Indeed, in this trial they seem to have come off very pitifully. For although they had very able counsel, learned in the law, *viz.* Des Cartes, Malebranche, and Locke, who said every thing they could for their clients; the Bishop of Cloyne, believing them to be aiders and abetters of heresy
30 and schism, prosecuted them with great vigour, fully answered all that had been pleaded in their defence, and silenced their ablest advocates, who seem for half a century past to decline the argument, and to trust to the favour of the jury rather than to the strength of their pleadings.

Thus, the wisdom of *philosophy* is set in opposition to the *common*
35 *sense* of mankind. The first pretends to demonstrate *a priori*, that there can be no such thing as a material world; that sun, moon, stars, and earth, vegetable and animal bodies, are, and can be nothing else, but sensations in the mind, or images of those sensations in the memory and imagination; that, like pain and joy, they can have no existence when they are not

thought of. The last can conceive no otherwise of this opinion, than as a kind of metaphysical lunacy; and concludes, that too much learning is apt to make men mad; and that the man who seriously entertains this belief, though in other respects he may be a very good man, as a man may be who believes that he is made of glass; yet surely he hath a soft place in his understanding, and hath been hurt by much thinking.

This opposition betwixt philosophy and common sense, is apt to have a very unhappy influence upon the philosopher himself. He sees human nature in an odd, unamiable, and mortifying light. He considers himself, and the rest of his species, as born under a necessity of believing ten thousand absurdities and contradictions, and endowed with such a pittance of reason, as is just sufficient to make this unhappy discovery: and this is all the fruit of his profound speculations. Such notions of human nature tend to slacken every nerve of the soul, to put every noble purpose and sentiment out of countenance, and spread a melancholy gloom over the whole face of things.

If this is wisdom, let me be deluded with the vulgar. I find something within me that recoils against it, and inspires more reverent sentiments of the human kind, and of the universal administration. Common sense and reason have both one author; that Almighty author, in all whose other works we observe a consistency, uniformity, and beauty, which charm and delight the understanding: there must therefore be some order and consistency in the human faculties, as well as in other parts of his workmanship. A man that thinks reverently of his own kind, and esteems true wisdom and philosophy, will not be fond, nay, will be very suspicious, of such strange and paradoxical opinions. If they are false, they disgrace philosophy; and if they are true, they degrade the human species, and make us justly ashamed of our frame.

To what purpose is it for philosophy to decide against common sense in this or any other matter? The belief of a material world is older, and of more authority, than any principles of philosophy. It declines the tribunal of reason, and laughs at all the artillery of the logician. It retains its sovereign authority in spite of all the edicts of philosophy, and reason itself must stoop to its orders. Even those philosophers who have disowned the authority of our notions of an external material world, confess, that they find themselves under a necessity of submitting to their power.

Methinks, therefore, it were better to make a virtue of necessity; and, since we cannot get rid of the vulgar notion and belief of an external world, to reconcile our reason to it as well as we can: for if Reason should stomach and fret ever so much at this yoke, she cannot throw it off; if she will not be the servant of Common Sense, she must be her slave.

In order therefore to reconcile reason to common sense in this matter, I beg leave to offer to the consideration of philosophers these two observations. First, That in all this debate about the existence of a material world, it hath been taken for granted on both sides, that this same material world, if any such there be, must be the express image of our sensations; that we can have no conception of any material thing which is not like some sensation in our minds; and particularly, that the sensations of touch are images of extension, hardness, figure, and motion. Every argument brought against the existence of a material world, either by the Bishop of Cloyne, or by the author of the *Treatise of human nature*, supposeth this. If this is true, their arguments are conclusive and unanswerable: but, on the other hand, if it is not true, there is no shadow of argument left. Have those philosophers then given any solid proof of this hypothesis, upon which the whole weight of so strange a system rests? No. They have not so much as attempted to do it. But, because ancient and modern philosophers have agreed in this opinion, they have taken it for granted. But let us, as becomes philosophers, lay aside authority; we need not surely consult Aristotle or Locke, to know whether pain be like the point of a sword. I have as clear a conception of extension, hardness, and motion, as I have of the point of a sword; and, with some pains and practice, I can form as clear a notion of the other sensations of touch, as I have of pain. When I do so, and compare them together, it appears to me clear as day-light, that the former are not of kin to the latter, nor resemble them in any one feature. They are as unlike, yea as certainly and manifestly unlike, as pain is to the point of a sword. It may be true, that those sensations first introduced the material world to our acquaintance; it may be true, that it seldom or never appears without their company; but, for all that, they are as unlike as the passion of anger is to those features of the countenance which attend it.

So that, in the sentence those philosophers have passed against the material world, there is an *error personæ*. Their proof touches not matter, or any of its qualities; but strikes directly against an idol of their own imagination, a material world made of ideas and sensations, which never had nor can have an existence.

Secondly, The very existence of our conceptions of extension, figure, and motion, since they are neither ideas of sensation nor reflection, overturns the whole ideal system, by which the material world hath been tried and condemned: so that there hath been likewise in this sentence an *error juris.*

It is a very fine and a just observation of Locke, That as no human art can create a single particle of matter, and the whole extent of our power over the material world, consists in compounding, combining, and disjoining the matter made to our hands; so in the world of thought, the materials are all made by nature, and can only be variously combined and disjoined by us. So that it is impossible for reason or prejudice, true or false philosophy, to produce one simple notion or conception, which is not the work of nature, and the result of our constitution. The conception of extension, motion, and the other attributes of matter, cannot be the effect of error or prejudice; it must be the work of nature. And the power or faculty, by which we acquire those conceptions, must be something different from any power of the human mind that hath been explained, since it is neither sensation nor reflection.

This I would therefore humbly propose as an *experimentum crucis*, by which the ideal system must stand or fall; and it brings the matter to a short issue: Extension, figure, motion, may, any one, or all of them, be taken for the subject of this experiment. Either they are ideas of sensation, or they are not. If any one of them can be shown to be an idea of sensation, or to have the least resemblance to any sensation, I lay my hand upon my mouth, and give up all pretence to reconcile reason to common sense in this matter, and must suffer the ideal scepticism to triumph. But if, on the other hand, they are not ideas of sensation, nor like to any sensation, then the ideal system is a rope of sand, and all the laboured arguments of the sceptical philosophy against a material world, and against the existence of every thing but impressions and ideas, proceed upon a false hypothesis.

If our philosophy concerning the mind be so lame with regard to the origin of our notions of the clearest, most simple, and most familiar objects of thought, and the powers from which they are derived, can we expect that it should be more perfect in the account it gives of the origin of our opinions and belief? We have seen already some instances of its imperfection in this respect: and perhaps that same nature which hath given us the power to conceive things altogether unlike to any of our sensations, or to any operation of our minds, hath likewise provided for our belief of them, by some part of our constitution hitherto not explained.

Bishop Berkeley hath proved, beyond the possibility of reply, that we cannot by reasoning infer the existence of matter from our sensations: and the author of the *Treatise of human nature* hath proved no less clearly,

that we cannot by reasoning infer the existence of our own or other minds from our sensations. But are we to admit nothing but what can be proved by reasoning? Then we must be sceptics indeed, and believe nothing at all. The author of the *Treatise of human nature* appears to me to be but a half-
5   sceptic. He hath not followed his principles so far as they lead him: but after having, with unparalleled intrepidity and success, combated vulgar prejudices; when he had but one blow to strike, his courage fails him, he fairly lays down his arms, and yields himself a captive to the most common of all vulgar prejudices, I mean the belief of the existence of his
10   own impressions and ideas.

I beg therefore to have the honour of making an addition to the sceptical system, without which I conceive it cannot hang together. I affirm, that the belief of the existence of impressions and ideas, is as little supported by reason, as that of the existence of minds and bodies. No man ever did, or
15   could offer any reason for this belief. Des Cartes took it for granted, that he thought, and had sensations and ideas; so have all his followers done. Even the hero of scepticism hath yielded this point, I crave leave to say, weakly and imprudently. I say so, because I am persuaded that there is no principle of his philosophy that obliged him to make this concession.
20   And what is there in impressions and ideas so formidable, that this all-conquering philosophy, after triumphing over every other existence, should pay homage to them? Besides, the concession is dangerous: for belief is of such a nature, that if you leave any root, it will spread; and you may more easily pull it up altogether, than say, Hitherto shalt thou go
25   and no further: the existence of impressions and ideas I give up to thee; but see thou pretend to nothing more. A thorough and consistent sceptic will never, therefore, yield this point; and while he holds it, you can never oblige him to yield any thing else.

To such a sceptic I have nothing to say; but of the semi-sceptics, I
30   should beg to know, why they believe the existence of their impressions and ideas. The true reason I take to be, because they cannot help it; and the same reason will lead them to believe many other things.

All reasoning must be from first principles; and for first principles no other reason can be given but this, that, by the constitution of our nature,
35   we are under a necessity of assenting to them. Such principles are parts of our constitution, no less than the power of thinking: reason can neither make nor destroy them; nor can it do any thing without them: it is like a telescope, which may help a man to see farther, who hath eyes; but without eyes, a telescope shews nothing at all. A mathematician cannot

prove the truth of his axioms, nor can he prove any thing, unless he takes them for granted. We cannot prove the existence of our minds, nor even of our thoughts and sensations. A historian, or a witness, can prove nothing, unless it is taken for granted, that the memory and senses may be trusted.
5 A natural philosopher can prove nothing, unless it is taken for granted, that the course of nature is steady and uniform.

How or when I got such first principles, upon which I build all my reasoning, I know not; for I had them before I can remember: but I am sure they are parts of my constitution, and that I cannot throw them off. That
10 our thoughts and sensations must have a subject, which we call *ourself*, is not therefore an opinion got by reasoning, but a natural principle. That our sensations of touch indicate something external, extended, figured, hard or soft, is not a deduction of reason, but a natural principle. The belief of it, and the very conception of it, are equally parts of our constitution. If
15 we are deceived in it, we are deceived by Him that made us, and there is no remedy.

I do not mean to affirm, that the sensations of touch do from the very first suggest the same notions of body and its qualities, which they do when we are grown up. Perhaps Nature is frugal in this, as in her other
20 operations. The passion of love, with all its concomitant sentiments and desires, is naturally suggested by the perception of beauty in the other sex. Yet the same perception does not suggest the tender passion, till a certain period of life. A blow given to an infant, raises grief and lamentation; but when he grows up, it as naturally stirs resentment, and prompts him to
25 resistance. Perhaps a child in the womb, or for some short period of its existence, is merely a sentient being: the faculties, by which it perceives an external world, by which it reflects on its own thoughts, and existence, and relation to other things, as well as its reasoning and moral faculties, unfold themselves by degrees; so that it is inspired with the various
30 principles of common sense, as with the passions of love and resentment, when it has occasion for them.

S E C T. VIII.

35 *Of the systems of philosophers concerning the senses.*

ALL the systems of philosophers about our senses and their objects have split upon this rock, of not distinguishing properly sensations, which can have no existence but when they are felt, from the things suggested by

them. Aristotle, with as distinguishing a head as ever applied to philosophical disquisitions, confounds these two; and makes every sensation
to be the form, without the matter, of the thing perceived by it. As the
impression of a seal upon wax has the form of the seal, but nothing of
the matter of it; so he conceived our sensations to be impressions upon
the mind, which bear the image, likeness, or form of the external thing
perceived, without the matter of it. Colour, sound, and smell, as well as
extension, figure, and hardness, are, according to him, various forms of
matter: our sensations are the same forms imprinted on the mind, and
perceived in its own intellect. It is evident from this, that Aristotle made no
distinction between primary and secondary qualities of bodies, although
that distinction was made by Democritus, Epicurus, and others of the
ancients.

Des Cartes, Malebranche, and Locke, revived the distinction between
primary and secondary qualities. But they made the secondary qualities
mere sensations, and the primary ones resemblances of our sensations.
They maintained, that colour, sound, and heat, are not any thing in bodies,
but sensations of the mind: at the same time, they acknowledged some
particular texture or modification of the body, to be the cause or occasion
of those sensations; but to this modification they gave no name. Whereas,
by the vulgar, the names of colour, heat, and sound, are but rarely applied
to the sensations, and most commonly to those unknown causes of them;
as hath been already explained. The constitution of our nature leads
us rather to attend to the things signified by the sensation, than to the
sensation itself, and to give a name to the former rather than to the latter.
Thus we see, that with regard to secondary qualities, these philosophers
thought with the vulgar, and with common sense. Their paradoxes were
only an abuse of words. For when they maintain, as an important modern
discovery, that there is no heat in the fire, they mean no more, than that
the fire does not feel heat, which every one knew before.

With regard to primary qualities, these philosophers erred more
grossly: They indeed believed the existence of those qualities; but they
did not at all attend to the sensations that suggest them, which having
no names, have been as little considered as if they had no existence.
They were aware, that figure, extension, and hardness, are perceived by
means of sensations of touch; whence they rashly concluded, that these
sensations must be images and resemblances of figure, extension, and
hardness.

The received hypothesis of ideas naturally led them to this conclusion;

and indeed cannot consist with any other; for, according to that hypothesis, external things must be perceived by means of images of them in the
mind; and what can those images of external things in the mind be, but
the sensations by which we perceive them?

This however was to draw a conclusion from a hypothesis against
fact. We need not have recourse to any hypothesis to know what our
sensations are, or what they are like. By a proper degree of reflection
and attention we may understand them perfectly, and be as certain that
they are not like any quality of body, as we can be, that the toothach is
not like a triangle. How a sensation should instantly make us conceive
and believe the existence of an external thing altogether unlike to it, I
do not pretend to know; and when I say that the one suggests the other,
I mean not to explain the manner of their connection, but to express a
fact, which every one may be conscious of; namely, that, by a law of our
nature, such a conception and belief constantly and immediately follow
the sensation.

Bishop Berkeley gave new light to this subject, by showing, that the
qualities of an inanimate thing, such as matter is conceived to be, cannot
resemble any sensation; that it is impossible to conceive any thing like the
sensations of our minds, but the sensations of other minds. Every one that
attends properly to his sensations must assent to this; yet it had escaped
all the philosophers that came before Berkeley; it had escaped even the
ingenious Locke, who had so much practised reflection on the operations
of his own mind. So difficult it is to attend properly even to our own
feelings. They are so accustomed to pass through the mind unobserved,
and instantly to make way for that which nature intended them to signify,
that it is extremely difficult to stop, and survey them; and when we think
we have acquired this power, perhaps the mind still fluctuates between the
sensation and its associated quality, so that they mix together, and present
something to the imagination that is compounded of both. Thus in a globe
or cylinder, whose opposite sides are quite unlike in colour, if you turn it
slowly, the colours are perfectly distinguishable, and their dissimilitude
is manifest; but if it is turned fast, they lose their distinction, and seem to
be of one and the same colour.

No succession can be more quick, than that of tangible qualities to the
sensations with which nature has associated them: but when one has once
acquired the art of making them separate and distinct objects of thought,
he will then clearly perceive, that the maxim of Bishop Berkeley above
mentioned, is self-evident; and that the features of the face are not more

unlike to a passion of the mind which they indicate, than the sensations of touch are to the primary qualities of body.

But let us observe what use the Bishop makes of this important discovery: Why, he concludes, that we can have no conception of an inanimate substance, such as matter is conceived to be, or of any of its qualities; and that there is the strongest ground to believe that there is no existence in nature but minds, sensations, and ideas: If there is any other kind of existences, it must be what we neither have nor can have any conception of. But how does this follow? Why thus: We can have no conception of any thing but what resembles some sensation or idea in our minds; but the sensations and ideas in our minds can resemble nothing but the sensations and ideas in other minds; therefore, the conclusion is evident. This argument, we see, leans upon two propositions. The last of them the ingenious author hath indeed made evident to all that understand his reasoning, and can attend to their own sensations: but the first proposition he never attempts to prove; it is taken from the doctrine of ideas, which hath been so universally received by philosophers, that it was thought to need no proof.

We may here again observe, that this acute writer argues from a hypothesis against fact, and against the common sense of mankind. That we can have no conception of any thing, unless there is some impression, sensation, or idea, in our minds which resembles it, is indeed an opinion which hath been very generally received among philosophers; but it is neither self-evident, nor hath it been clearly proved; and therefore it had been more reasonable to call in question this doctrine of philosophers, than to discard the material world, and by that means expose philosophy to the ridicule of all men, who will not offer up common sense as a sacrifice to metaphysics.

We ought, however, to do this justice both to the Bishop of Cloyne and to the author of the *Treatise of human nature*, to acknowledge, that their conclusions are justly drawn from the doctrine of ideas, which has been so universally received. On the other hand, from the character of Bishop Berkeley, and of his predecessors Des Cartes, Locke, and Malebranche, we may venture to say, that if they had seen all the consequences of this doctrine, as clearly as the author before mentioned did, they would have suspected it vehemently, and examined it more carefully than they appear to have done.

The theory of ideas, like the Trojan horse, had a specious appearance both of innocence and beauty; but if those philosophers had known that it carried in its belly death and destruction to all science and common sense, they would not have broken down their walls to give it admittance.

That we have clear and distinct conceptions of extension, figure, motion, and other attributes of body, which are neither sensations, nor like any sensation, is a fact of which we may be as certain, as that we have sensations. And that all mankind have a fixed belief of an external material world, a belief which is neither got by reasoning nor education, and a belief which we cannot shake off, even when we seem to have strong arguments against it, and no shadow of argument for it, is likewise a fact, for which we have all the evidence that the nature of the thing admits. These facts are phænomena of human nature, from which we may justly argue against any hypothesis, however generally received. But to argue from a hypothesis against facts, is contrary to the rules of true philosophy.

CHAP. VI.

Of SEEING.

SECT. I.

The excellence and dignity of this faculty.

THE advances made in the knowledge of optics in the last age, and in the
present, and chiefly the discoveries of Sir Isaac Newton, do honour, not
to philosophy only, but to human nature. Such discoveries ought for ever
to put to shame the ignoble attempts of our modern sceptics to depreciate
the human understanding, and to dispirit men in the search of truth, by
representing the human faculties as fit for nothing, but to lead us into
absurdities and contradictions.

Of the faculties called *the five senses*, sight is without doubt the noblest.
The rays of light, which minister to this sense, and of which, without it,
we could never have had the least conception, are the most wonderful and
astonishing part of the inanimate creation. We must be satisfied of this,
if we consider their extreme minuteness, their inconceivable velocity, the
regular variety of colours which they exhibit, the invariable laws according to which they are acted upon by other bodies, in their reflections,
inflections, and refractions, without the least change of their original
properties, and the facility with which they pervade bodies of great
density, and of the closest texture, without resistance, without crowding
or disturbing one another, without giving the least sensible impulse to the
lightest bodies.

The structure of the eye, and of all its appurtenances, the admirable
contrivances of nature for performing all its various external and internal
motions, and the variety in the eyes of different animals, suited to their
several natures and ways of life, clearly demonstrate this organ to be a
masterpiece of Nature's work. And he must be very ignorant of what hath
been discovered about it, or have a very strange cast of understanding,
who can seriously doubt, whether or not the rays of light and the eye
were made for one another, with consummate wisdom, and perfect skill
in optics.

If we should suppose an order of beings, endued with every human
faculty but that of sight, how incredible would it appear to such beings,
accustomed only to the slow informations of touch, that, by the addition

of an organ, consisting of a ball and socket of an inch diameter, they might be enabled in an instant of time, without changing their place, to perceive the disposition of a whole army, or the order of a battle, the figure of a magnificent palace, or all the variety of a landscape? If a man were by feeling to find out the figure of the peak of Teneriffe, or even of St Peter's church at Rome, it would be the work of a lifetime.

It would appear still more incredible to such beings as we have supposed, if they were informed of the discoveries which may be made by this little organ in things far beyond the reach of any other sense: That by means of it we can find our way in the pathless ocean; that we can traverse the globe of the earth, determine its figure and dimensions, and delineate every region of it: Yea, that we can measure the planetary orbs, and make discoveries in the sphere of the fixed stars.

Would it not appear still more astonishing to such beings, if they should be farther informed, That, by means of this same organ, we can perceive the tempers and dispositions, the passions and affections of our fellow-creatures, even when they want most to conceal them? That when the tongue is taught most artfully to lie and dissemble, the hypocrisy should appear in the countenance to a discerning eye? And that by this organ, we can often perceive what is straight and what is crooked in the mind as well as in the body? How many mysterious things must a blind man believe, if he will give credit to the relations of those that see? Surely he needs as strong a faith as is required of a good Christian.

It is not therefore without reason, that the faculty of seeing is looked upon, not only as more noble than the other senses, but as having something in it of a nature superior to sensation. The evidence of reason is called *seeing*, not *feeling*, *smelling*, or *tasting*. Yea, we are wont to express the manner of the divine knowledge by *seeing*, as that kind of knowledge which is most perfect in us.

SECT. II.

Sight discovers almost nothing which the blind may not comprehend.
The reason of this.

NOTWITHSTANDING what hath been said of the dignity and superior nature of this faculty, it is worthy of our observation, that there is very little of the knowledge acquired by sight, that may not be communicated to a man born blind. One who never saw the light, may be learned and knowing in every science, even in optics; and may make discoveries in every branch of philosophy. He may understand as much as another man, not only of the order, distances, and motions of the heavenly bodies; but of the nature of light, and of the laws of the reflection and refraction of its rays. He may understand distinctly, how those laws produce the phænomena of the rain-bow, the prism, the camera obscura, and the magic lanthorn, and all the powers of the microscope and telescope. This is a fact sufficiently attested by experience.

In order to perceive the reason of it, we must distinguish the appearance that objects make to the eye, from the things suggested by that appearance: and again, in the visible appearance of objects, we must distinguish the appearance of colour from the appearance of extension, figure, and motion. First, then, as to the visible appearance of the figure, and motion, and extension of bodies, I conceive that a man born blind may have a distinct notion, if not of the very things, at least of something extremely like to them. May not a blind man be made to conceive, that a body moving directly from the eye, or directly towards it, may appear to be at rest? and that the same motion may appear quicker or slower, according as it is nearer to the eye or farther off, more direct or more oblique? May he not be made to conceive, that a plain surface, in a certain position, may appear as a straight line, and vary its visible figure, as its position, or the position of the eye, is varied? That a circle seen obliquely will appear an ellipse; and a square, a rhombus, or an oblong rectangle? Dr Saunderson understood the projection of the sphere, and the common rules of perspective; and if he did, he must have understood all that I have mentioned. If there were any doubt of Dr Saunderson's understanding these things, I could mention my having heard him say in conversation, that he found great difficulty in understanding Dr Halley's demonstration of that proposition, That the angles made by the circles of the sphere, are equal to the angles made by their representatives in the stereographic projection: but, said he, when I laid aside that demonstration, and considered the proposition in my own way, I saw clearly that it must be true. Another gentleman, of undoubted credit and judgment in these matters, who had part in this conversation, remembers it distinctly.

As to the appearance of colour, a blind man must be more at a loss; because he hath no perception that resembles it. Yet he may, by a kind of analogy, in part supply this defect. To those who see, a scarlet colour signifies an unknown quality in bodies, that makes to the eye an appearance, which they are well acquainted with, and have often observed: to a blind man, it signifies an unknown quality that makes to the eye an appearance, which he is unacquainted with. But he can conceive the eye to be variously affected by different colours, as the nose is by different smells, or the ear by different sounds. Thus he can conceive scarlet to differ from blue, as the sound of a trumpet does from that of a drum; or as the smell of an orange differs from that of an apple. It is impossible to know whether a scarlet colour has the same appearance to me which it hath to another man; and if the appearances of it to different persons differed as much as colour does from sound, they might never be able to discover this difference. Hence it appears obvious, that a blind man might talk long about colours distinctly and pertinently: and if you were to examine him in the dark about the nature, composition, and beauty of them, he might be able to answer, so as not to betray his defect.

We have seen how far a blind man may go in the knowledge of the appearances which things make to the eye. As to the things which are suggested by them, or inferred from them; although he could never discover them of himself, yet he may understand them perfectly by the information of others. And every thing of this kind that enters into our minds by the eye, may enter into his by the ear. Thus, for instance, he could never, if left to the direction of his own faculties, have dreamed of any such thing as light; but he can be informed of every thing we know about it. He can conceive, as distinctly as we, the minuteness and velocity of its rays, their various degrees of refrangibility and reflexibility, and all the magical powers and virtues of that wonderful element. He could never of himself have found out, that there are such bodies as the sun, moon, and stars; but he may be informed of all the noble discoveries of astronomers about their motions, and the laws of nature by which they are regulated. Thus it appears, that there is very little knowledge got by the eye, which may not be communicated by language to those who have no eyes.

If we should suppose, that it were as uncommon for men to see, as it is to be born blind; would not the few who had this rare gift, appear as prophets and inspired teachers to the many? We conceive inspiration to give a man no new faculty, but to communicate to him in a new way, and by extraordinary means, what the faculties common to mankind can apprehend, and what he can communicate to others by ordinary means. On the supposition we have made, sight would appear to the blind very similar to this: for the few who had this gift, could communicate the knowledge acquired by it to those who had it not. They could not indeed convey to the blind any distinct notion of the manner in which they acquired this knowledge. A ball and socket would seem, to a blind man, in this case, as improper an instrument for acquiring such a variety and extent of knowledge, as a dream or a vision. The manner in which a man who sees, discerns so many things by means of the eye, is as unintelligible to the blind, as the manner in which a man may be inspired with knowledge by the Almighty, is to us. Ought the blind man therefore, without examination, to treat all pretences to the gift of seeing as imposture? Might he not, if he were candid and tractable, find reasonable evidence of the reality of this gift in others, and draw great advantages from it to himself?

The distinction we have made between the visible appearances of the objects of sight, and things suggested by them, is necessary to give us a just notion of the intention of nature in giving us eyes. If we attend duly to the operation of our mind in the use of this faculty, we shall perceive, that the visible appearance of objects is hardly ever regarded by us. It is not at all made an object of thought or reflection, but serves only as a sign to introduce to the mind something else, which may be distinctly conceived by those who never saw.

Thus the visible appearance of things in my room varies almost every hour, according as the day is clear or cloudy, as the sun is in the east, or south, or west, and as my eye is in one part of the room or in another: but I never think of these variations, otherwise than as signs of morning, noon, or night, of a clear or cloudy sky. A book or a chair has a different appearance to the eye, in every different distance and position: yet we conceive it to be still the same; and, overlooking the appearance, we immediately conceive the real figure, distance, and position of the body, of which its visible or perspective appearance is a sign and indication.

When I see a man at the distance of ten yards, and afterwards see him at the distance of a hundred yards, his visible appearance in its length, breadth, and all its linear proportions, is ten times less in the last case than it is in the first: yet I do not conceive him one inch diminished by this diminution of his visible figure. Nay, I do not in the least attend to this diminution, even when I draw from it the conclusion of his being at a greater distance. For such is the subtilty of the mind's operation in this case, that we draw the conclusion, without perceiving that ever the premises entered into the mind. A thousand such instances might be pro-duced, in order to shew that the visible appearances of objects are intended by nature only as signs or indications; and that the mind passes instantly to the things signified, without making the least reflection upon the sign, or even perceiving that there is any such thing. It is in a way somewhat similar, that the sounds of a language, after it is become familiar, are overlooked, and we attend only to the things signified by them.

It is therefore a just and important observation of the Bishop of Cloyne, That the visible appearance of objects is a kind of language used by nature, to inform us of their distance, magnitude, and figure. And this observation hath been very happily applied by that ingenious writer, to the solution of some phænomena in optics, which had before perplexed the greatest masters in that science. The same observation is further improved by the judicious Dr Smith, in his *Optics*, for explaining the apparent figure of the heavens, and the apparent distances and magnitudes of objects seen with glasses, or by the naked eye.

Avoiding as much as possible the repetition of what hath been said by these excellent writers, we shall avail ourselves of the distinction between the signs that nature useth in this visual language, and the things signified by them; and in what remains to be said of sight, shall first make some observations upon the signs.

SECT. III.

Of the visible appearances of objects.

In this section we must speak of things which are never made the object of reflection, though almost every moment presented to the mind. Nature intended them only for signs; and in the whole course of life they are put to no other use. The mind has acquired a confirmed and inveterate habit of inattention to them; for they no sooner appear, than quick as lightning the thing signified succeeds, and ingrosses all our regard. They have no name in language; and although we are conscious of them when they pass through the mind, yet their passage is so quick, and so familiar, that it is absolutely unheeded; nor do they leave any footsteps of themselves, either in the memory or imagination. That this is the case with regard to the sensations of touch, hath been shown in the last chapter; and it holds no less with regard to the visible appearances of objects.

I cannot therefore entertain the hope of being intelligible to those readers who have not, by pains and practice, acquired the habit of distinguishing the appearance of objects to the eye, from the judgment which we form by sight of their colour, distance, magnitude, and figure. The only profession in life wherein it is necessary to make this distinction, is that of painting. The painter hath occasion for an abstraction, with regard to visible objects, somewhat similar to that which we here require: and this indeed is the most difficult part of his art. For it is evident, that if he could fix in his imagination the visible appearance of objects, without confounding it with the things signified by that appearance, it would be as easy for him to paint from the life, and to give every figure its proper shading and relief, and its perspective proportions, as it is to paint from a copy. Perspective, shading, giving relief, and colouring, are nothing else but copying the appearance which things make to the eye. We may therefore borrow some light on the subject of visible appearance from this art.

Let one look upon any familiar object, such as a book, at different distances and in different positions: is he not able to affirm, upon the testimony of his sight, that it is the same book, the same object, whether seen at the distance of one foot or of ten, whether in one position or another; that the colour is the same, the dimensions the same, and the figure the same, as far as the eye can judge? This surely must be acknowledged. The same individual object is presented to the mind, only placed at different distances, and in different positions. Let me ask, in the next place, Whether this object has the same appearance to the eye in these different distances? Infallibly it hath not. For,

First, However certain our judgment may be that the colour is the same, it is as certain that it hath not the same appearance at different distances. There is a certain degradation of the colour, and a certain confusion and indistinctness of the minute parts, which is the natural consequence of the removal of the object to a greater distance. Those that are not painters, or critics in painting, overlook this; and cannot easily be persuaded, that the colour of the same object hath a different appearance at the distance of one foot and of ten, in the shade and in the light. But the masters in painting know how, by the degradation of the colour, and the confusion of the minute parts, figures, which are upon the same canvas, and at the same distance from the eye, may be made to represent objects which are at the most unequal distances. They know how to make the objects appear to be of the same colour, by making their pictures really of different colours, according to their distances or shades.

Secondly, Every one who is acquainted with the rules of perspective, knows that the appearance of the figure of the book must vary in every different position: yet if you ask a man that has no notion of perspective, whether the figure of it does not appear to his eye to be the same in all its different positions? he can with a good conscience affirm, that it does. He hath learned to make allowance for the variety of visible figure arising from the difference of position, and to draw the proper conclusions from it. But he draws these conclusions so readily and habitually, as to lose sight of the premises: and therefore where he hath made the same conclusion, he conceives the visible appearance must have been the same.

Thirdly, Let us consider the apparent magnitude or dimensions of the book. Whether I view it at the distance of one foot or of ten feet, it seems to be about seven inches long, five broad, and one thick. I can judge of these dimensions very nearly by the eye, and I judge them to be the same at both distances. But yet it is certain, that at the distance of one foot, its visible length and breadth is about ten times as great as at the distance of ten feet; and consequently its surface is about a hundred times as great. This great change of apparent magnitude is altogether overlooked, and every man is apt to imagine, that it appears to the eye of the same size at both distances. Further, when I look at the book, it seems plainly to have three dimensions, of length, breadth, and thickness: but it is certain that the visible appearance hath no more than two, and can be exactly represented upon a canvas which hath only length and breadth.

In the last place, Does not every man, by sight, perceive the distance of the book from his eye? Can he not affirm with certainty, that in one case it is not above one foot distant, that in another it is ten? Nevertheless it appears certain, that distance from the eye, is no immediate object of sight. There are certain things in the visible appearance, which are signs of distance from the eye, and from which, as we shall afterwards show, we learn by experience to judge of that distance within certain limits; but it seems beyond doubt, that a man born blind, and suddenly made to see, could form no judgment at first of the distance of the objects which he saw. The young man couched by Cheselden, thought, at first, that every thing he saw touched his eye, and learned only by experience to judge of the distance of visible objects.

I have entered into this long detail, in order to shew, that the visible appearance of an object is extremely different from the notion of it which experience teaches us to form by sight; and to enable the reader to attend to the visible appearance of colour, figure, and extension, in visible things, which is no common object of thought, but must be carefully attended to by those who would enter into the philosophy of this sense, or would comprehend what shall be said upon it. To a man newly made to see, the visible appearance of objects would be the same as to us; but he would see nothing at all of their real dimensions, as we do. He could form no

conjecture, by means of his sight only, how many inches or feet they were
in length, breadth, or thickness. He could perceive little or nothing of their
real figure; nor could he discern, that this was a cube, that a sphere; that
this was a cone, and that a cylinder. His eye could not inform him, that this
object was near, and that more remote. The habit of a man or of a woman,
which appeared to us of one uniform colour, variously folded and shaded,
would present to his eye neither fold nor shade, but variety of colour. In a
word, his eyes, though ever so perfect, would at first give him almost no
information of things without him. They would indeed present the same
appearances to him as they do to us, and speak the same language; but
to him it is an unknown language; and therefore he would attend only to
the signs, without knowing the signification of them: whereas to us it is a
language perfectly familiar; and therefore we take no notice of the signs,
but attend only to the thing signified by them.

SECT. IV.

That colour is a quality of bodies, not a sensation of the mind.

By colour, all men, who have not been tutored by modern philosophy,
understand, not a sensation of the mind, which can have no existence
when it is not perceived, but a quality or modification of bodies, which
continues to be the same, whether it is seen or not. The scarlet-rose, which
is before me, is still a scarlet-rose when I shut my eyes, and was so at
midnight when no eye saw it. The colour remains when the appearance
ceases: it remains the same when the appearance changes. For when I
view this scarlet-rose through a pair of green spectacles, the appearance
is changed, but I do not conceive the colour of the rose changed. To a
person in the jaundice, it has still another appearance; but he is easily
convinced, that the change is in his eye, and not in the colour of the object.
Every different degree of light makes it have a different appearance, and
total darkness takes away all appearance, but makes not the least change
in the colour of the body. We may, by a variety of optical experiments,
change the appearance of figure and magnitude in a body, as well as that
of colour; we may make one body appear to be ten. But all men believe,
that as a multiplying glass does not really produce ten guineas out of one,
nor a microscope turn a guinea into a ten pound piece; so neither does a
coloured glass change the real colour of the object seen through it, when
it changes the appearance of that colour.

The common language of mankind shows evidently, that we ought to distinguish between the colour of a body, which is conceived to be a fixed and permanent quality in the body, and the appearance of that colour to the eye, which may be varied a thousand ways, by a variation of the light, of
5 the medium, or of the eye itself. The permanent colour of the body is the cause, which, by the mediation of various kinds or degrees of light, and of various transparent bodies interposed, produces all this variety of appearances. When a coloured body is presented, there is a certain apparition to the eye, or to the mind, which we have called *the appearance of colour.*
10 Mr Locke calls it *an idea*; and indeed it may be called so with the greatest propriety. This idea can have no existence but when it is perceived. It is a kind of thought, and can only be the act of a percipient or thinking being. By the constitution of our nature, we are led to conceive this idea as a sign of something external, and are impatient till we learn its meaning. A
15 thousand experiments for this purpose are made every day by children, even before they come to the use of reason. They look at things, they handle them, they put them in various positions, at different distances, and in different lights. The ideas of sight, by these means, come to be associated with, and readily to suggest, things external, and altogether
20 unlike them. In particular, that idea which we have called *the appearance of colour*, suggests the conception and belief of some unknown quality in the body, which occasions the idea; and it is to this quality, and not to the idea, that we give the name of *colour*. The various colours, although in their nature equally unknown, are easily distinguished when we think
25 or speak of them, by being associated with the ideas which they excite. In like manner, gravity, magnetism, and electricity, although all unknown qualities, are distinguished by their different effects. As we grow up, the mind acquires a habit of passing so rapidly from the ideas of sight to the external things suggested by them, that the ideas are not in the least
30 attended to, nor have they names given them in common language.

When we think or speak of any particular colour, however simple the notion may seem to be, which is presented to the imagination, it is really in some sort compounded. It involves an unknown cause, and a known effect. The name of *colour* belongs indeed to the cause only, and not to the
35 effect. But as the cause is unknown, we can form no distinct conception of it, but by its relation to the known effect. And therefore both go together in the imagination, and are so closely united, that they are mistaken for one simple object of thought. When I would conceive those colours of bodies which we call *scarlet* and *blue*; if I conceived them only as unknown

qualities, I could perceive no distinction between the one and the other. I must therefore, for the sake of distinction, join to each of them in my imagination some effect or some relation that is peculiar. And the most obvious distinction is, the appearance which one and the other makes to
5   the eye. Hence the appearance is, in the imagination, so closely united with the quality called *a scarlet-colour*, that they are apt to be mistaken for one and the same thing, although they are in reality so different and so unlike, that one is an idea in the mind, the other is a quality of body.

I conclude then, that colour is not a sensation, but a secondary quality
10   of bodies, in the sense we have already explained; that it is a certain power or virtue in bodies, that in fair day-light exhibits to the eye an appearance, which is very familiar to us, although it hath no name. Colour differs from other secondary qualities in this, that whereas the name of the quality is sometimes given to the sensation which indicates it, and is
15   occasioned by it, we never, as far as I can judge, give the name of *colour* to the sensation, but to the quality only. Perhaps the reason of this may be, that the appearances of the same colour are so various and changeable, according to the different modifications of the light, of the medium, and of the eye, that language could not afford names for them. And indeed
20   they are so little interesting, that they are never attended to, but serve only as signs to introduce the things signified by them. Nor ought it to appear incredible, that appearances so frequent and so familiar should have no names, nor be made objects of thought; since we have before shown, that this is true of many sensations of touch, which are no less frequent, nor
25   less familiar.

S E C T. V.

An inference from the preceding.

30

FROM what hath been said about colour, we may infer two things. The first is, that one of the most remarkable paradoxes of modern philosophy, which hath been universally esteemed as a great discovery, is, in reality, when examined to the bottom, nothing else but an abuse of words. The
35   paradox I mean is, That colour is not a quality of bodies, but only an idea in the mind. We have shown, that the word *colour*, as used by the vulgar, cannot signify an idea in the mind, but a permanent quality of body. We have shown, that there is really a permanent quality of body, to which the common use of this word exactly agrees. Can any stronger proof be

desired, that this quality is that to which the vulgar give the name of *colour*? If it should be said, that this quality, to which we give the name of *colour*, is unknown to the vulgar, and therefore can have no name among them; I answer, it is indeed known only by its effects; that is, by
5   its exciting a certain idea in us: but are there not numberless qualities of bodies which are known only by their effects, to which, notwithstanding, we find it necessary to give names? Medicine alone might furnish us with a hundred instances of this kind. Do not the words *astringent, narcotic, epispastic, caustic,* and innumerable others, signify qualities of bodies,
10   which are known only by their effects upon animal bodies? Why then should not the vulgar give a name to a quality, whose effects are every moment perceived by their eyes? We have all the reason therefore that the nature of the thing admits, to think that the vulgar apply the name of *colour* to that quality of bodies which excites in us what the philosophers call the
15   *idea of colour.* And that there is such a quality in bodies, all philosophers allow, who allow that there is any such thing as body. Philosophers have thought fit to leave that quality of bodies which the vulgar call *colour,* without a name, and to give the name of *colour* to the idea or appearance, to which, as we have shown, the vulgar give no name, because they never
20   make it an object of thought or reflection. Hence it appears, that when philosophers affirm that colour is not in bodies, but in the mind; and the vulgar affirm, that colour is not in the mind, but is a quality of bodies; there is no difference between them about things, but only about the meaning of a word.

25   The vulgar have undoubted right to give names to things which they are daily conversant about; and philosophers seem justly chargeable with an abuse of language, when they change the meaning of a common word, without giving warning.

If it is a good rule, to think with philosophers, and speak with the vulgar,
30   it must be right to speak with the vulgar when we think with them, and not to shock them by philosophical paradoxes, which, when put into common language, express only the common sense of mankind.

If you ask a man that is no philosopher, what colour is? or, what makes one body appear white, another scarlet? he cannot tell. He leaves that
35   inquiry to philosophers, and can embrace any hypothesis about it, except that of our modern philosophers, who affirm, that colour is not in body, but only in the mind.

Nothing appears more shocking to his apprehension, than that visible objects should have no colour, and that colour should be in that which he conceives to be invisible. Yet this strange paradox is not only universally received, but considered as one of the noblest discoveries of modern philosophy. The ingenious Addison, in the Spectator, No 413. speaks thus of it. "I have here supposed that my reader is acquainted with that great modern discovery, which is at present universally acknowledged by all the inquirers into natural philosophy, namely, that light and colours, as apprehended by the imagination, are only ideas in the mind, and not qualities that have any existence in matter. As this is a truth which has been proved incontestably by many modern philosophers, and is indeed one of the finest speculations in that science, if the English reader would see the notion explained at large, he may find it in the eighth chapter of the second book of Locke's *Essay on human understanding*."

Mr Locke and Mr Addison are writers who have deserved so well of mankind, that one must feel some uneasiness in differing from them, and would wish to ascribe all the merit that is due to a discovery upon which they put so high a value. And indeed it is just to acknowledge, that Locke, and other modern philosophers, on the subject of secondary qualities, have the merit of distinguishing more accurately than those that went before them, between the sensation in the mind, and that constitution or quality of bodies which gives occasion to the sensation. They have shown clearly, that these two things are not only distinct, but altogether unlike: that there is no similitude between the effluvia of an odorous body, and the sensation of smell, or between the vibrations of a sounding body, and the sensation of sound: that there can be no resemblance between the feeling of heat, and the constitution of the heated body which occasions it; or between the appearance which a coloured body makes to the eye, and the texture of the body which causes that appearance.

Nor was the merit small of distinguishing these things accurately; because, however different and unlike in their nature, they have been always so associated in the imagination, as to coalesce, as it were into one two-faced form, which, from its amphibious nature, could not justly be appropriated either to body or mind; and until it was properly distinguished into its different constituent parts, it was impossible to assign to either their just shares in it. None of the ancient philosophers had made this distinction. The followers of Democritus and Epicurus conceived the forms of heat, and sound, and colour, to be in the mind only, but that our senses fallaciously represented them as being in bodies. The Peripatetics imagined, that those forms are really in bodies; and that the images of them are conveyed to the mind by our senses.

The one system made the senses naturally fallacious and deceitful; the other made the qualities of body to resemble the sensations of the mind. Nor was it possible to find a third, without making the distinction we have mentioned; by which indeed the errors of both these ancient systems are
5   avoided, and we are not left under the hard necessity of believing, either, on the one hand, that our sensations are like to the qualities of body, or, on the other, that God hath given us one faculty to deceive us, and another to detect the cheat.

We desire therefore, with pleasure, to do justice to the doctrine of
10   Locke, and other modern philosophers, with regard to colour, and other secondary qualities, and to ascribe to it its due merit, while we beg leave to censure the language in which they have expressed their doctrine. When they had explained and established the distinction between the appearance which colour makes to the eye, and the modification of the coloured body,
15   which, by the laws of Nature, causes that appearance; the question was, Whether to give the name of *colour* to the cause, or to the effect? By giving it, as they have done, to the effect, they set philosophy apparently in opposition to common sense, and expose it to the ridicule of the vulgar. But had they given the name of *colour* to the cause, as they ought to
20   have done, they must then have affirmed, with the vulgar, that colour is a quality of bodies; and that there is neither colour nor any thing like it in the mind. Their language, as well as their sentiments, would have been perfectly agreeable to the common apprehensions of mankind, and true philosophy would have joined hands with Common Sense. As Locke was
25   no enemy to common sense, it may be presumed that, in this instance, as in some others, he was seduced by some received hypothesis: and that this was actually the case, will appear in the following section.

30   S E C T. VI.

That none of our sensations are resemblances of any of the qualities of bodies.

A SECOND inference is, That although colour is really a quality of body, yet
35   it is not represented to the mind by an idea or sensation that resembles it; on the contrary, it is suggested by an idea which does not in the least resemble it. And this inference is applicable, not to colour only, but to all the qualities of body which we have examined.

It deserves to be remarked, that in the analysis we have hitherto given of the operations of the five senses, and of the qualities of bodies discovered by them, no instance hath occurred, either of any sensation which resembles any quality of body, or of any quality of body whose image or resemblance is conveyed to the mind by means of the senses.

5   There is no phænomenon in nature more unaccountable, than the intercourse that is carried on between the mind and the external world: there is no phænomenon which philosophical spirits have shown greater avidity to pry into, and to resolve. It is agreed by all, that this intercourse is carried on by means of the senses: and this satisfies the vulgar curiosity,

10   but not the philosophic. Philosophers must have some system, some hypothesis, that shews the manner in which our senses make us acquainted with external things. All the fertility of human invention seems to have produced only one hypothesis for this purpose, which therefore hath been universally received; and that is, that the mind, like a mirror, receives the

15   images of things from without, by means of the senses; so that their use must be to convey these images into the mind.

       Whether to these images of external things in the mind, we give the name of *sensible forms*, or *sensible species*, with the Peripatetics, or the name *of ideas of sensation*, with Locke; or whether, with later philoso-

20   phers, we distinguish *sensations*, which are immediately conveyed by the senses, from *ideas of sensation*, which are faint copies of our sensations retained in the memory and imagination; these are only differences about words. The hypothesis I have mentioned is common to all these different systems.

25   The necessary and allowed consequence of this hypothesis is, That no material thing, nor any quality of material things, can be conceived by us, or made an object of thought, until its image is conveyed to the mind by means of the senses. We shall examine this hypothesis particularly after-wards, and at this time only observe, that in consequence of it, one would

30   naturally expect, that to every quality and attribute of body we know or can conceive, there should be a sensation corresponding, which is the image and resemblance of that quality; and that the sensations which have no similitude or resemblance to body, or to any of its qualities, should give us no conception of a material world, or of any thing belonging to it. These

35   things might be expected as the natural consequences of the hypothesis we have mentioned.

       Now, we have considered, in this and the preceding chapters, extension, figure, solidity, motion, hardness, roughness, as well as colour, heat and cold, sound, taste, and smell. We have endeavoured to shew, that our

nature and constitution lead us to conceive these as qualities of body, as all mankind have always conceived them to be. We have likewise examined, with great attention, the various sensations we have by means of the five senses, and are not able to find among them all one single image of body,
5   or of any of its qualities. From whence then come those images of body and of its qualities into the mind? Let philosophers resolve this question. All I can say is, that they come not by the senses. I am sure, that, by proper attention and care, I may know my sensations, and be able to affirm with certainty what they resemble, and what they do not resemble.
10   I have examined them one by one, and compared them with matter and its qualities; and I cannot find one of them that confesses a resembling feature.

A truth so evident as this, That our sensations are not images of matter, or of any of its qualities, ought not to yield to a hypothesis such as that
15   above mentioned, however ancient, or however universally received by philosophers; nor can there be any amicable union between the two. This will appear by some reflections upon the spirit of the ancient and modern philosophy concerning sensation.

During the reign of the Peripatetic philosophy, our sensations were not
20   minutely or accurately examined. The attention of philosophers, as well as of the vulgar, was turned to the things signified by them: therefore, in consequence of the common hypothesis, it was taken for granted, that all the sensations we have from external things, are the forms or images of these external things. And thus the truth we have mentioned yielded
25   entirely to the hypothesis, and was altogether suppressed by it.

Des Cartes gave a noble example of turning our attention inward, and scrutinizing our sensations; and this example hath been very worthily followed by modern philosophers, particularly by Malebranche, Locke, Berkeley, and Hume. The effect of this scrutiny hath been, a gradual
30   discovery of the truth above mentioned, to wit, the dissimilitude between the sensations of our minds, and the qualities or attributes of an insentient, inert substance, such as we conceive matter to be. But this valuable and useful discovery, in its different stages, hath still been unhappily united to the ancient hypothesis: and from this inauspicious match of opinions,
35   so unfriendly and discordant in their natures, have arisen those monsters of paradox and scepticism with which the modern philosophy is too justly chargeable.

Locke saw clearly, and proved incontestably, that the sensations we have by taste, smell, and hearing, as well as the sensations of colour, heat, and cold, are not resemblances of any thing in bodies; and in this he agrees with Des Cartes and Malebranche. Joining this opinion with the hypothesis, it follows necessarily, that three senses of the five are cut off from giving us any intelligence of the material world, as being altogether inept for that office. Smell, and taste, and sound, as well as colour and heat, can have no more relation to body, than anger or gratitude; nor ought the former to be called qualities of body, whether primary or secondary, any more than the latter. For it was natural and obvious to argue thus from that hypothesis: If heat, and colour, and sound, are real qualities of body, the sensations by which we perceive them, must be resemblances of those qualities; but these sensations are not resemblances; therefore those are not real qualities of body.

We see then, that Locke, having found that the ideas of secondary qualities are no resemblances, was compelled, by a hypothesis common to all philosophers, to deny that they are real qualities of body. It is more difficult to assign a reason, why, after this, he should call them *secondary qualities*; for this name, if I mistake not, was of his invention. Surely he did not mean that they were secondary qualities of the mind; and I do not see with what propriety, or even by what tolerable licence, he could call them secondary qualities of body, after finding that they were no qualities of body at all. In this, he seems to have sacrificed to Common Sense, and to have been led by her authority even in opposition to his hypothesis. The same sovereign mistress of our opinions that led this philosopher to call those things secondary qualities of body, which, according to his principles and reasonings, were no qualities of body at all, hath led, not the vulgar of all ages only, but philosophers also, and even the disciples of Locke, to believe them to be real qualities of body: she hath led them to investigate, by experiments, the nature of colour, and sound, and heat, in bodies. Nor hath this investigation been fruitless, as it must have been, if there had been no such thing in bodies: on the contrary, it hath produced very noble and useful discoveries, which make a very considerable part of natural philosophy. If then natural philosophy be not a dream, there is something in bodies which we call *colour*, and *heat*, and *sound*. And if this be so, the hypothesis from which the contrary is concluded, must be false: for the argument, leading to a false conclusion, recoils against the hypothesis from which it was drawn, and thus directs its force backward. If the qualities of body were known to us only by sensations that resemble them, then colour, and sound, and heat, could be no qualities of body; but these are real qualities of body; and therefore the qualities of body are not known only by means of sensations that resemble them.

But to proceed: What Locke had proved with regard to the sensations we have by smell, taste, and hearing, Bishop Berkeley proved no less
5   unanswerably with regard to all our other sensations; to wit, that none of them can in the least resemble the qualities of a lifeless and insentient being, such as matter is conceived to be. Mr Hume hath confirmed this by his authority and reasoning. This opinion surely looks with a very malign aspect upon the old hypothesis; yet that hypothesis hath still been retained,
10   and conjoined with it. And what a brood of monsters hath this produced!

The first-born of this union, and perhaps the most harmless, was, That the secondary qualities of body were mere sensations of the mind. To pass by Malebranche's notion of seeing all things in the ideas of the divine mind, as a foreigner never naturalized in this island; the next was
15   Berkeley's system, That extension, and figure, and hardness, and motion; that land, and sea, and houses, and our own bodies, as well as those of our wives, and children, and friends, are nothing but ideas of the mind; and that there is nothing existing in nature, but minds and ideas.

The progeny that followed, is still more frightful; so that it is surprising,
20   that one could be found who had the courage to act the midwife, to rear it up, and to usher it into the world. No causes nor effects; no substances, material or spiritual; no evidence even in mathematical demonstration; no liberty nor active power; nothing existing in nature, but impressions and ideas, following each other, without time, place, or subject. Surely
25   no age ever produced such a system of opinions, justly deduced with great acuteness, perspicuity, and elegance, from a principle universally received. The hypothesis we have mentioned, is the father of them all. The dissimilitude of our sensations and feelings to external things, is the innocent mother of most of them.

30   As it happens sometimes in an arithmetical operation, that two errors balance one another, so that the conclusion is little or nothing affected by them; but when one of them is corrected, and the other left, we are led farther from the truth, than by both together: so it seems to have happened in the Peripatetic philosophy of sensation, compared with the modern. The
35   Peripatetics adopted two errors; but the last served as a corrective to the first, and rendered it mild and gentle; so that their system had no tendency to scepticism. The moderns have retained the first of those errors, but have gradually detected and corrected the last. The consequence hath been, that the light we have struck out hath created darkness, and scepticism hath

advanced hand in hand with knowledge, spreading its melancholy gloom, first over the material world, and at last over the whole face of nature. Such a phænomenon as this, is apt to stagger even the lovers of light and knowledge, while its cause is latent; but when that is detected, it may
5   give hopes, that this darkness shall not be everlasting, but that it shall be succeeded by a more permanent light.

SECT. VII.

10   *Of visible figure and extension.*

ALTHOUGH there is no resemblance, nor, as far as we know, any necessary connection, between that quality in a body which we call its *colour*, and the appearance which that colour makes to the eye; it is quite otherwise
15   with regard to its figure and magnitude. There is certainly a resemblance, and a necessary connection, between the visible figure and magnitude of a body, and its real figure and magnitude; no man can give a reason why a scarlet colour affects the eye in the manner it does; no man can be sure that it affects his eye in the same manner as it affects the eye of
20   another, and that it has the same appearance to him, as it has to another man; but we can assign a reason why a circle placed obliquely to the eye, should appear in the form of an ellipse. The visible figure, magnitude, and position, may, by mathematical reasoning, be deduced from the real; and it may be demonstrated, that every eye that sees distinctly and perfectly,
25   must, in the same situation, see it under this form, and no other. Nay, we may venture to affirm, that a man born blind, if he were instructed in mathematics, would be able to determine the visible figure of a body, when its real figure, distance, and position, are given. Dr Saunderson understood the projection of the sphere, and perspective. Now, I require
30   no more knowledge in a blind man, in order to his being able to determine the visible figure of bodies, than that he can project the outline of a given body, upon the surface of a hollow sphere, whose centre is in the eye. This projection is the visible figure he wants; for it is the same figure with that which is projected upon the *tunica retina* in vision.
35   A blind man can conceive lines drawn from every point of the object to the centre of the eye, making angles. He can conceive, that the length of the object will appear greater or less, in proportion to the angle which it subtends at the eye; and that, in like manner, the breadth, and in general the distance of any one point of the object from any other point, will

appear greater or less, in proportion to the angles which those distances subtend. He can easily be made to conceive, that the visible appearance has no thickness, any more than a projection of the sphere, or a perspective draught. He may be informed, that the eye, until it is aided by experience, does not represent one object as nearer or more remote than another. Indeed he would probably conjecture this of himself, and be apt to think that the rays of light must make the same impression upon the eye, whether they come from a greater or a less distance.

These are all the principles which we suppose our blind mathematician to have; and these he may certainly acquire by information and reflection. It is no less certain, that from these principles, having given the real figure and magnitude of a body, and its position and distance with regard to the eye, he can find out its visible figure and magnitude. He can demonstrate in general, from these principles, that the visible figure of all bodies will be the same with that of their projection upon the surface of a hollow sphere, when the eye is placed in the centre. And he can demonstrate, that their visible magnitude will be greater or less, according as their projection occupies a greater or less part of the surface of this sphere.

To set this matter in another light, let us distinguish betwixt the *position* of objects with regard to the eye, and their *distance* from it. Objects that lie in the same right line drawn from the centre of the eye, have the same position, however different their distances from the eye may be: but objects which lie in different right lines drawn from the eye's centre, have a different position; and this difference of position is greater or less in proportion to the angle made at the eye by the right lines mentioned. Having thus defined what we mean by the position of objects with regard to the eye, it is evident, that as the real figure of a body consists in the situation of its several parts with regard to one another, so its visible figure consists in the position of its several parts with regard to the eye; and as he that hath a distinct conception of the situation of the parts of the body with regard to one another, must have a distinct conception of its real figure; so he that conceives distinctly the position of its several parts with regard to the eye, must have a distinct conception of its visible figure. Now, there is nothing surely to hinder a blind man from conceiving the position of the several parts of a body with regard to the eye, any more than from conceiving their situation with regard to one another; and therefore I conclude, that a blind man may attain a distinct conception of the visible figure of bodies.

Although we think the arguments that have been offered are sufficient to prove, that a blind man may conceive the visible extension and figure of bodies; yet, in order to remove some prejudices against this truth, it will be of use to compare the notion which a blind mathematician might form to himself of visible figure, with that which is presented to the eye in vision, and to observe wherein they differ.

First, Visible figure is never presented to the eye but in conjunction with colour: and although there be no connection between them from the nature of the things, yet having so invariably kept company together, we are hardly able to disjoin them even in our imagination. What mightily increases this difficulty is, that we have never been accustomed to make visible figure an object of thought. It is only used as a sign, and having served this purpose, passes away, without leaving a trace behind. The drawer or designer, whose business it is to hunt this fugitive form, and to take a copy of it, finds how difficult his task is, after many years labour and practice. Happy! if at last he can acquire the art of arresting it in his imagination, until he can delineate it. For then it is evident, that he must be able to draw as accurately from the life as from a copy. But how few of the professed masters of designing are ever able to arrive at this degree of perfection? It is no wonder, then, that we should find so great difficulty in conceiving this form apart from its constant associate, when it is so difficult to conceive it at all. But our blind man's notion of visible figure will not be associated with colour, of which he hath no conception; but it will perhaps be associated with hardness or smoothness, with which he is acquainted by touch. These different associations are apt to impose upon us, and to make things seem different, which in reality are the same.

Secondly, The blind man forms the notion of visible figure to himself, by thought, and by mathematical reasoning from principles; whereas the man that sees, has it presented to his eye at once, without any labour, without any reasoning, by a kind of inspiration. A man may form to himself the notion of a parabola, or a cycloid, from the mathematical definition of those figures, although he had never seen them drawn or delineated. Another, who knows nothing of the mathematical definition of the figures, may see them delineated on paper, or feel them cut out in wood. Each may have a distinct conception of the figures, one by mathematical reasoning, the other by sense. Now, the blind man forms his notion of visible figure in the same manner as the first of these formed his notion of a parabola or a cycloid, which he never saw.

Thirdly, Visible figure leads the man that sees, directly to the conception of the real figure, of which it is a sign. But the blind man's

thoughts move in a contrary direction. For he must first know the real figure, distance, and situation, of the body, and from thence he slowly traces out the visible figure by mathematical reasoning. Nor does his nature lead him to conceive this visible figure as a sign; it is a creature of
5   his own reason and imagination.

SECT. VIII.

Some queries concerning visible figure answered.

10

IT may be asked, What kind of thing is this visible figure? Is it a sensation, or an idea? If it is an idea, from what sensation is it copied? These questions may seem trivial or impertinent to one who does not know, that there is a tribunal of inquisition erected by certain modern philosophers,
15   before which every thing in nature must answer. The articles of inquisition are few indeed, but very dreadful in their consequences. They are only these: Is the prisoner an impression, or an idea? If an idea, from what impression copied? Now, if it appears that the prisoner is neither an impression, nor an idea copied from some impression, immediately,
20   without being allowed to offer any thing in arrest of judgment, he is sentenced to pass out of existence, and to be, in all time to come, an empty unmeaning sound, or the ghost of a departed entity.

    Before this dreadful tribunal, cause and effect, time and place, matter and spirit, have been tried and cast: How then shall such a poor flimsy
25   form as visible figure stand before it? It must even plead guilty, and confess that it is neither an impression nor an idea. For, alas! it is notorious, that it is extended in length and breadth; it may be long or short, broad or narrow, triangular, quadrangular, or circular: and therefore unless ideas and impressions are extended and figured, it cannot belong
30   to that category.

    If it should still be asked, To what category of beings does visible figure then belong? I can only, in answer, give some tokens, by which those who are better acquainted with the categories, may chance to find its place. It is, as we have said, the position of the several parts of a figured body with
35   regard to the eye. The different positions of the several parts of the body with regard to the eye, when put together, make a real figure, which is truly extended in length and breadth, and which represents a figure that is extended in length, breadth, and thickness. In like manner, a projection of the sphere is a real figure, and hath length and breadth, but represents

the sphere, which hath three dimensions. A projection of the sphere, or a perspective view of a palace, is a representative in the very same sense as visible figure is, and wherever they have their lodgings in the categories, this will be found to dwell next door to them.

5   It may farther be asked, Whether there be any sensation proper to visible figure, by which it is suggested in vision? Or by what means it is presented to the mind? This is a question of some importance, in order to our having a distinct notion of the faculty of seeing: and to give all the light to it we can, it is necessary to compare this sense with other senses, and

10 to make some suppositions, by which we may be enabled to distinguish things that are apt to be confounded, although they are totally different.

    There are three of our senses which give us intelligence of things at a distance: smell, hearing, and sight. In smelling, and in hearing, we have a sensation or impression upon the mind, which, by our constitution,

15 we conceive to be a sign of something external: but the position of this external thing, with regard to the organ of sense, is not presented to the mind along with the sensation. When I hear the sound of a coach, I could not, previous to experience, determine whether the sounding body was above or below, to the right hand or to the left. So that the sensation

20 suggests to me some external object as the cause or occasion of it; but it suggests not the position of that object, whether it lies in this direction or in that. The same thing may be said with regard to smelling. But the case is quite different with regard to seeing. When I see an object, the appearance which the colour of it makes, may be called *the sensation*,

25 which suggests to me some external thing as its cause; but it suggests likewise the individual direction and position of this cause with regard to the eye. I know it is precisely in such a direction, and in no other. At the same time I am not conscious of any thing that can be called *sensation*, but the sensation of colour. The position of the coloured thing is no sensation,

30 but it is by the laws of my constitution presented to the mind along with the colour, without any additional sensation.

    Let us suppose, that the eye were so constituted, that the rays coming from any one point of the object were not, as they are in our eyes, collected in one point of the *retina*, but diffused over the whole: It is evident to

35 those who understand the structure of the eye, that such an eye as we have supposed, would shew the colour of a body as our eyes do, but that it would neither shew figure nor position. The operation of such an eye would be precisely similar to that of hearing and smell; it would give no perception of figure or extension, but merely of colour. Nor is the

supposition we have made altogether imaginary: for it is nearly the case of most people who have cataracts, whose crystalline, as Mr Cheselden observes, does not altogether exclude the rays of light, but diffuses them over the *retina*, so that such persons see things as one does through a glass of broken gelly: they perceive the colour, but nothing of the figure or magnitude of objects.

Again, if we should suppose, that smell and sound were conveyed in right lines from the objects, and that every sensation of hearing and smell suggested the precise direction or position of its object; in this case the operations of hearing and smelling would be similar to that of seeing: we should smell and hear the figure of objects, in the same sense as now we see it; and every smell and sound would be associated with some figure in the imagination, as colour is in our present state.

We have reason to believe, that the rays of light make some impression upon the *retina*; but we are not conscious of this impression; nor have anatomists or philosophers been able to discover the nature and effects of it; whether it produces a vibration in the nerve, or the motion of some subtile fluid contained in the nerve, or something different from either, to which we cannot give a name. Whatever it is, we shall call it the *material impression*; remembering carefully, that it is not an impression upon the mind, but upon the body; and that it is no sensation, nor can resemble sensation, any more than figure or motion can resemble thought. Now, this material impression, made upon a particular point of the *retina*, by the laws of our constitution, suggests two things to the mind, namely, the colour, and the position of some external object. No man can give a reason, why the same material impression might not have suggested sound, or smell, or either of these along with the position of the object. That it should suggest colour and position, and nothing else, we can resolve only into our constitution, or the will of our Maker. And since there is no necessary connection between these two things suggested by this material impression, it might, if it had so pleased our Creator, have suggested one of them without the other. Let us suppose, therefore, since it plainly appears to be possible, that our eyes had been so framed, as to suggest to us the position of the object, without suggesting colour, or any other quality: What is the consequence of this supposition? It is evidently this, that the person endued with such an eye, would perceive the visible figure of bodies, without having any sensation or impression made upon his mind. The figure he perceives is altogether external; and therefore cannot be called an impression upon the mind, without the grossest abuse of language. If it should be said, that it is impossible to perceive a figure, unless there be some impression of it upon the mind; I beg leave not to admit the impossibility of this without some proof; and I can find none. Neither can I conceive what is meant by an impression of figure upon the mind. I can conceive an impression of figure upon wax, or upon any body that is fit to receive it; but an impression of it upon the mind, is to me quite unintelligible; and although I form the most distinct conception of the figure, I cannot, upon the strictest examination, find any impression of it upon my mind.

If we suppose, last of all, that the eye hath the power restored of perceiving colour, I apprehend that it will be allowed, that now it perceives figure in the very same manner as before, with this difference only, that colour is always joined with it.

In answer therefore to the question proposed, there seems to be no sensation that is appropriated to visible figure, or whose office it is to suggest it. It seems to be suggested immediately by the material impression upon the organ, of which we are not conscious: and why may not a material impression upon the *retina* suggest visible figure, as well as the material impression made upon the hand, when we grasp a ball, suggests real figure? In the one case, one and the same material impression, suggests both colour and visible figure; and in the other case, one and the same material impression suggests hardness, heat, or cold, and real figure, all at the same time.

We shall conclude this section with another question upon this subject. Since the visible figure of bodies is a real and external object to the eye, as their tangible figure is to the touch; it may be asked, Whence arises the difficulty of attending to the first, and the facility of attending to the last? It is certain that the first is more frequently presented to the eye, than the last is to the touch: the first is as distinct and determinate an object as the last, and seems in its own nature as proper for speculation. Yet so little hath it been attended to, that it never had a name in any language, until Bishop Berkeley gave it that which we have used after his example, to distinguish it from the figure which is the object of touch.

The difficulty of attending to the visible figure of bodies, and making it an object of thought, appears so similar to that which we find in attending to our sensations, that both have probably like causes. Nature intended the visible figure as a sign of the tangible figure and situation of bodies, and hath taught us by a kind of instinct to put it always to this use. Hence it happens, that the mind passes over it with a rapid motion, to attend to the things signified by it. It is as unnatural to the mind to stop at the visible figure, and attend to it, as it is to a spherical body to stop upon an inclined plane. There is an inward principle, which constantly carries it forward, and which cannot be overcome but by a contrary force.

5   There are other external things which nature intended for signs; and we find this common to them all, that the mind is disposed to overlook them, and to attend only to the things signified by them. Thus there are certain modifications of the human face, which are natural signs of the present disposition of the mind. Every man understands the meaning of

10   these signs, but not one of a hundred ever attended to the signs themselves, or knows any thing about them. Hence you may find many an excellent practical physiognomist, who knows nothing of the proportions of a face, nor can delineate or describe the expression of any one passion.

      An excellent painter or statuary can tell, not only what are the pro-

15   portions of a good face, but what changes every passion makes in it. This, however, is one of the chief mysteries of his art, to the acquisition of which, infinite labour and attention, as well as a happy genius, are required. But when he puts his art in practice, and happily expresses a passion by its proper signs, every one understands the meaning of these

20   signs, without art, and without reflection.

      What has been said of painting, might easily be applied to all the fine arts. The difficulty in them all consists in knowing and attending to those natural signs, whereof every man understands the meaning.

      We pass from the sign to the thing signified, with ease, and by natural

25   impulse; but to go backward from the thing signified to the sign, is a work of labour and difficulty. Visible figure, therefore, being intended by nature to be a sign, we pass on immediately to the thing signified, and cannot easily return to give any attention to the sign.

      Nothing shews more clearly our indisposition to attend to visible figure

30   and visible extension than this, that although mathematical reasoning is no less applicable to them, than to tangible figure and extension, yet they have entirely escaped the notice of mathematicians. While that figure and that extension which are objects of touch, have been tortured ten thousand ways for twenty centuries, and a very noble system of science has been

35   drawn out of them; not a single proposition do we find with regard to the figure and extension which are the immediate objects of sight!

      When the geometrician draws a diagram with the most perfect accuracy; when he keeps his eye fixed upon it, while he goes through a long process of reasoning, and demonstrates the relations of the several parts

of his figure; he does not consider, that the visible figure presented to his eye, is only the representative of a tangible figure, upon which all his attention is fixed; he does not consider that these two figures have really different properties; and that what he demonstrates to be true of the one,
5   is not true of the other.

This perhaps will seem so great a paradox, even to mathematicians, as to require demonstration before it can be believed. Nor is the demonstration at all difficult, if the reader will have patience to enter but a little into the mathematical consideration of visible figure, which we shall call
10   *the geometry of visibles.*

SECT. IX.

Of the geometry of visibles.

15

In this geometry, the definitions of a point; of a line, whether straight or curve; of an angle, whether acute, or right, or obtuse; and of a circle, are the same as in common geometry. The mathematical reader will easily enter into the whole mystery of this geometry, if he attends duly to these
20   few evident principles.

1. Supposing the eye placed in the centre of a sphere, every great circle of the sphere will have the same appearance to the eye as if it was a straight line. For the curvature of the circle being turned directly toward the eye, is not perceived by it. And for the same reason, any line which is drawn
25   in the plane of a great circle of the sphere, whether it be in reality straight or curve, will appear straight to the eye.

2. Every visible right line will appear to coincide with some great circle of the sphere; and the circumference of that great circle, even when it is produced until it returns into itself, will appear to be a
30   continuation of the same visible right line, all the parts of it being visibly *in directum*. For the eye, perceiving only the position of objects with regard to itself, and not their distance, will see those points in the same visible place which have the same position with regard to the eye, how different soever their distances from it may be. Now, since a plane
35   passing through the eye and a given visible right line, will be the plane of some great circle of the sphere, every point of the visible right line will have the same position as some point of the great circle; therefore they will both have the same visible place, and coincide to the eye: and the whole circumference of the great circle continued even until it

returns into itself, will appear to be a continuation of the same visible
right line.

Hence it follows,

3. That every visible right line, when it is continued *in directum*, as far
as it may be continued, will be represented by a great circle of a sphere,
in whose centre the eye is placed. It follows,

4. That the visible angle comprehended under two visible right lines,
is equal to the spherical angle comprehended under the two great
circles which are the representatives of these visible lines. For since the
visible lines appear to coincide with the great circles, the visible angle
comprehended under the former, must be equal to the visible angle
comprehended under the latter. But the visible angle comprehended under
the two great circles, when seen from the centre, is of the same magnitude
with the spherical angle which they really comprehend, as mathematicians
know; therefore the visible angle made by any two visible lines, is equal
to the spherical angle made by the two great circles of the sphere which
are their representatives.

5. Hence it is evident, that every visible right-lined triangle, will coincide in all its parts with some spherical triangle. The sides of the one
will appear equal to the sides of the other, and the angles of the one to
the angles of the other, each to each; and therefore the whole of the one
triangle will appear equal to the whole of the other. In a word, to the eye
they will be one and the same, and have the same mathematical properties.
The properties therefore of visible right-lined triangles, are not the same
with the properties of plain triangles, but are the same with those of
spherical triangles.

6. Every lesser circle of the sphere, will appear a circle to the eye,
placed, as we have supposed all along, in the centre of the sphere. And,
on the other hand, every visible circle will appear to coincide with some
lesser circle of the sphere.

7. Moreover, the whole surface of the sphere will represent the whole
of visible space: for, since every visible point coincides with some point
of the surface of the sphere, and has the same visible place, it follows,
that all the parts of the spherical surface taken together, will represent all
possible visible places, that is, the whole of visible space. And from this
it follows, in the last place,

8. That every visible figure will be represented by that part of the surface
of the sphere, on which it might be projected, the eye being in the centre.
And every such visible figure will bear the same *ratio* to the whole of

visible space, as the part of the spherical surface which represents it, bears to the whole spherical surface.

The mathematical reader, I hope, will enter into these principles with perfect facility, and will as easily perceive, that the following propositions with regard to visible figure and space, which we offer only as a specimen, may be mathematically demonstrated from them, and are not less true nor less evident than the propositions of Euclid, with regard to tangible figures.

Prop. 1. Every right line being produced, will at last return into itself.

2. A right line returning into itself, is the longest possible right line; and all other right lines bear a finite *ratio* to it.

3. A right line returning into itself, divides the whole of visible space into two equal parts, which will both be comprehended under this right line.

4. The whole of visible space bears a finite *ratio* to any part of it.

5. Any two right lines being produced, will meet in two points, and mutually bisect each other.

6. If two lines be parallel, that is, every where equally distant from each other, they cannot both be straight.

7. Any right line being given, a point may be found, which is at the same distance from all the points of the given right line.

8. A circle may be parallel to a right line, that is, may be equally distant from it in all its parts.

9. Right-lined triangles that are similar, are also equal.

10. Of every right-lined triangle, the three angles taken together, are greater than two right angles.

11. The angles of a right-lined triangle, may all be right angles, or all obtuse angles.

12. Unequal circles are not as the squares of their diameters, nor are their circumferences in the *ratio* of their diameters.

This small specimen of the geometry of visibles, is intended to lead the reader to a clear and distinct conception of the figure and extension which is presented to the mind by vision; and to demonstrate the truth of what we have affirmed above, namely, That those figures and that extension which are the immediate objects of sight, are not the figures and the extension about which common geometry is employed; that the geometrician, while he looks at his diagram, and demonstrates a proposition, hath a figure presented to his eye, which is only a sign and representative of a tangible figure; that he gives not the least attention to the first, but attends only to the last; and that these two figures have different properties, so that what he demonstrates of the one, is not true of the other.

It deserves, however, to be remarked, that as a small part of a spherical surface differs not sensibly from a plain surface; so a small part of visible extension differs very little from that extension in length and breadth, which is the object of touch. And it is likewise to be observed, that the human eye is so formed, that an object which is seen distinctly and at one view, can occupy but a small part of visible space: for we never see distinctly what is at a considerable distance from the axis of the eye; and therefore when we would see a large object at one view, the eye must be at so great a distance, that the object occupies but a small part of visible space. From these two observations, it follows, that plain figures which are seen at one view, when their planes are not oblique, but direct to the eye, differ little from the visible figures which they present to the eye. The several lines in the tangible figure have very nearly the same proportion to each other as in the visible; and the angles of the one are very nearly, although not strictly and mathematically, equal to those of the other. Although therefore we have found many instances of natural signs which have no similitude to the things signified, this is not the case with regard to visible figure. It hath in all cases such a similitude to the thing signified by it, as a plan or profile hath to that which it represents; and in some cases the sign and thing signified have to all sense the same figure and the same proportions. If we could find a being endued with sight only, without any other external sense, and capable of reflecting and reasoning upon what he sees, the notions and philosophical speculations of such a being, might assist us in the difficult task of distinguishing the perceptions which we have purely by sight, from those which derive their origin from other senses. Let us suppose such a being, and conceive, as well as we can, what notion he would have of visible objects, and what conclusions he would deduce from them. We must not conceive him disposed by his constitution, as we are, to consider the visible appearance as a sign of something else: it is no sign to him, because there is nothing signified by it; and therefore we must suppose him as much disposed to attend to the visible figure and extension of bodies, as we are disposed to attend to their tangible figure and extension.

If various figures were presented to his sense, he might without doubt, as they grow familiar, compare them together, and perceive wherein they agree, and wherein they differ. He might perceive visible objects to have length and breadth, but could have no notion of a third dimension, any

more than we can have of a fourth. All visible objects would appear to be terminated by lines, straight or curve; and objects terminated by the same visible lines, would occupy the same place, and fill the same part of visible space. It would not be possible for him to conceive one object
5   to be behind another, or one to be nearer, another more distant.

To us, who conceive three dimensions, a line may be conceived straight; or it may be conceived incurvated in one dimension, and straight in another; or, lastly, it may be incurvated in two dimensions. Suppose a line to be drawn upwards and downwards, its length makes one
10   dimension, which we shall call *upwards and downwards*; and there are two dimensions remaining, according to which it may be straight or curve. It may be bent to the right or to the left; and if it has no bending either to right or left, it is straight in this dimension. But supposing it straight in this dimension of right and left, there is still another dimension remaining, in
15   which it may be curve; for it may be bent backwards or forwards. When we conceive a tangible straight line, we exclude curvature in either of these two dimensions: and as what is conceived to be excluded, must be conceived, as well as what is conceived to be included, it follows, that all the three dimensions enter into our conception of a straight line. Its length
20   is one dimension, its straightness in two other dimensions is included, or curvature in these two dimensions excluded, in the conception of it.

The being we have supposed, having no conception of more than two dimensions, of which the length of a line is one, cannot possibly conceive it either straight or curve in more than one dimension: so that
25   in his conception of a right line, curvature to the right hand or left is excluded; but curvature backwards or forwards cannot be excluded, because he neither hath, nor can have any conception of such curvature. Hence we see the reason that a line, which is straight to the eye, may return into itself: for its being straight to the eye, implies only straight-
30   ness in one dimension; and a line which is straight in one dimension, may notwithstanding be curve in another dimension, and so may return into itself.

To us, who conceive three dimensions, a surface is that which hath length and breadth, excluding thickness: and a surface may be either plain
35   in this third dimension, or it may be incurvated: so that the notion of a third dimension enters into our conception of a surface; for it is only by means of this third dimension that we can distinguish surfaces into plain and curve surfaces; and neither one nor the other can be conceived without conceiving a third dimension.

The being we have supposed having no conception of a third dimension, his visible figures have length and breadth indeed; but thickness is neither included nor excluded, being a thing of which he has no conception. And therefore visible figures, although they have length and breadth, as surfaces have, yet they are neither plain surfaces, nor curve surfaces. For a curve surface implies curvature in a third dimension, and a plain surface implies the want of curvature in a third dimension; and such a being can conceive neither of these, because he has no conception of a third dimension. Moreover, although he hath a distinct conception of the inclination of two lines which make an angle, yet he can neither conceive a plain angle nor a spherical angle. Even his notion of a point is somewhat less determined than ours. In the notion of a point we exclude length, breadth, and thickness; he excludes length and breadth, but cannot either exclude or include thickness, because he hath no conception of it.

Having thus settled the notions which such a being as we have supposed might form of mathematical points, lines, angles, and figures, it is easy to see, that by comparing these together, and reasoning about them, he might discover their relations, and form geometrical conclusions built upon self-evident principles. He might likewise, without doubt, have the same notions of numbers as we have, and form a system of arithmetic. It is not material to say in what order he might proceed in such discoveries, or how much time and pains he might employ about them; but what such a being, by reason and ingenuity, without any materials of sensation but those of sight only, might discover.

As it is more difficult to attend to a detail of possibilities, than of facts even of slender authority, I shall beg leave to give an extract from the travels of Johannes Rudolphus Anepigraphus, a Rosicrucian philosopher, who having, by deep study of the occult sciences, acquired the art of transporting himself to various sublunary regions, and of conversing with various orders of intelligences, in the course of his adventures, became acquainted with an order of beings exactly such as I have supposed.

How they communicate their sentiments to one another, and by what means he became acquainted with their language, and was initiated into their philosophy, as well as of many other particulars, which might have gratified the curiosity of his readers, and perhaps added credibility to his relation, he hath not thought fit to inform us; these being matters proper for adepts only to know.

His account of their philosophy is as follows:

"The Idomenians," saith he, "are many of them very ingenious, and much given to contemplation. In arithmetic, geometry, metaphysics, and physics, they have most elaborate systems. In the two latter indeed they have had many disputes carried on with great subtilty, and are divided into various sects; yet in the two former there hath been no less unanimity than among the human species. Their principles relating to numbers and arithmetic, making allowance for their notation, differ in nothing from ours: but their geometry differs very considerably."

As our author's account of the geometry of the Idomenians agrees in every thing with the geometry of visibles, of which we have already given a specimen, we shall pass over it. He goes on thus: "Colour, extension, and figure, are conceived to be the essential properties of body. A very considerable sect maintains, that colour is the essence of body. If there had been no colour, say they, there had been no perception or sensation. Colour is all that we perceive, or can conceive, that is peculiar to body; extension and figure being modes common to body and to empty space. And if we should suppose a body to be annihilated, colour is the only thing in it that can be annihilated; for its place, and consequently the figure and extension of that place, must remain, and cannot be imagined not to exist. These philosophers hold space to be the place of all bodies, immoveable and indestructible, without figure, and similar in all its parts, incapable of increase or diminution, yet not unmeasureable: for every the least part of space bears a finite *ratio* to the whole. So that with them the whole extent of space is the common and natural measure of every thing that hath length and breadth, and the magnitude of every body and of every figure is expressed by its being such a part of the universe. In like manner, the common and natural measure of length, is an infinite right line, which, as hath been before observed, returns into itself, and hath no limits, but bears a finite *ratio* to every other line.

"As to their natural philosophy, it is now acknowledged by the wisest of them to have been for many ages in a very low state. The philosophers observing, that one body can differ from another only in colour, figure, or magnitude, it was taken for granted, that all their particular qualities must arise from the various combinations of these their essential attributes. And therefore it was looked upon as the end of natural philosophy, to shew how the various combinations of these three qualities in different bodies produced all the phænomena of nature. It were endless to enumerate the various systems that were invented with this view, and the disputes that were carried on for ages; the followers of every system exposing the weak sides of other systems, and palliating those of their own, with great art.

"At last, some free and facetious spirits, wearied with eternal disputation, and the labour of patching and propping weak systems, began to
complain of the subtilty of nature; of the infinite changes that bodies
undergo in figure, colour, and magnitude; and of the difficulty of
5   accounting for these appearances, making this a pretence for giving up all
inquiries into the causes of things, as vain and fruitless.

"These wits had ample matter of mirth and ridicule in the systems of
philosophers, and finding it an easier task to pull down than to build
or support, and that every sect furnished them with arms and auxiliaries
10 to destroy another, they began to spread mightily, and went on with
great success. Thus philosophy gave way to scepticism and irony, and
those systems which had been the work of ages, and the admiration of
the learned, became the jest of the vulgar: for even the vulgar readily
took part in the triumph over a kind of learning which they had long
15 suspected, because it produced nothing but wrangling and altercation.
The wits having now acquired great reputation, and being flushed with
success, began to think their triumph incomplete, until every pretence
to knowledge was overturned; and accordingly began their attacks upon
arithmetic, geometry, and even upon the common notions of untaught
20 Idomenians. So difficult it hath always been (says our author) for great
conquerors to know where to stop.

"In the mean time, natural philosophy began to rise from its ashes,
under the direction of a person of great genius, who is looked upon as
having had something in him above Idomenian nature. He observed, that
25 the Idomenian faculties were certainly intended for contemplation, and
that the works of nature were a nobler subject to exercise them upon, than
the follies of systems, or the errors of the learned; and being sensible of
the difficulty of finding out the causes of natural things, he proposed, by
accurate observation of the phænomena of nature, to find out the rules
30 according to which they happen, without inquiring into the causes of those
rules. In this he made considerable progress himself, and planned out
much work for his followers, who call themselves *inductive philosophers*.
The sceptics look with envy upon this rising sect, as eclipsing their
reputation, and threatening to limit their empire; but they are at a loss
35 on what hand to attack it. The vulgar begin to reverence it, as producing
useful discoveries.

"It is to be observed, that every Idomenian firmly believes, that two or
more bodies may exist in the same place. For this they have the testimony
of sense, and they can no more doubt of it, than they can doubt whether

they have any perception at all. They often see two bodies meet, and coincide in the same place, and separate again, without having undergone any change in their sensible qualities by this penetration. When two bodies meet, and occupy the same place, commonly one only appears in that place, and the other disappears. That which continues to appear is said to overcome, the other to be overcome."

To this quality of bodies they gave a name, which our author tells us hath no word answering to it in any human language. And therefore, after making a long apology, which I omit, he begs leave to call it *the overcoming quality of bodies*. He assures us, that "the speculations which had been raised about this single quality of bodies, and the hypotheses contrived to account for it, were sufficient to fill many volumes. Nor have there been fewer hypotheses invented by their philosophers, to account for the changes of magnitude and figure; which, in most bodies that move, they perceive to be in a continual fluctuation. The founder of the inductive sect, believing it to be above the reach of Idomenian faculties, to discover the real causes of these phænomena, applied himself to find from observation, by what laws they are connected together; and discovered many mathematical ratios and relations concerning the motions, magnitudes, figures, and overcoming quality of bodies, which constant experience confirms. But the opposers of this sect chuse rather to content themselves with feigned causes of these phænomena, than to acknowledge the real laws whereby they are governed, which humble their pride, by being confessedly unaccountable."

Thus far Johannes Rudolphus Anepigraphus. Whether this Anepigraphus be the same who is recorded among the Greek alchemistical writers not yet published, by Borrichius, Fabricius, and others, I do not pretend to determine. The identity of their name, and the similitude of their studies, although no slight arguments, yet are not absolutely conclusive. Nor will I take upon me to judge of the narrative of this learned traveller by the *external* marks of his credibility; I shall confine myself to those which the critics call *internal*. It would even be of small importance to inquire, whether the Idomenians have a real, or only an ideal existence; since this is disputed among the learned with regard to things with which we are more nearly connected. The important question is, Whether the account above given, is a just account of their geometry and philosophy? We have all the faculties which they have, with the addition of others which they have not: we may therefore form some judgment of their philosophy and geometry, by separating from all others, the perceptions

we have by sight, and reasoning upon them. As far as I am able to judge in this way after a careful examination, their geometry must be such as Anepigraphus hath described. Nor does his account of their philosophy appear to contain any evident marks of imposture; although here, no
5   doubt, proper allowance is to be made for liberties which travellers take, as well as for involuntary mistakes which they are apt to fall into.

S E C T. X.

10   *Of the parallel motion of the eyes.*

HAVING explained, as distinctly as we can, visible figure, and shewn its connection with the things signified by it, it will be proper next to consider some phænomena of the eyes, and of vision, which have commonly been
15   referred to custom, to anatomical or to mechanical causes; but which, as I conceive, must be resolved into original powers and principles of the human mind; and therefore belong properly to the subject of this inquiry.

The first is, the parallel motion of the eyes; by which, when one eye
20   is turned to the right or to the left, upwards or downwards, or straight forwards, the other always goes along with it in the same direction. We see plainly, when both eyes are open, that they are always turned the same way, as if both were acted upon by the same motive force: and if one eye is shut, and the hand laid upon it, while the other turns various ways, we
25   feel the eye that is shut turn at the same time, and that whether we will or not. What makes this phænomenon surprising is, that it is acknowledged by all anatomists, that the muscles which move the two eyes, and the nerves which serve these muscles, are entirely distinct and unconnected. It would be thought very surprising and unaccountable to see a man, who,
30   from his birth, never moved one arm, without moving the other precisely in the same manner, so as to keep them always parallel: yet it would not be more difficult to find the physical cause of such motion of the arms, than it is to find the cause of the parallel motion of the eyes, which is perfectly similar.
35   The only cause that hath been assigned of this parallel motion of the eyes, is custom. We find by experience, it is said, when we begin to look at objects, that in order to have distinct vision, it is necessary to turn both eyes the same way; therefore we soon acquire the habit of doing it constantly, and by degrees lose the power of doing otherwise.

This account of the matter seems to be insufficient; because habits are not got at once; it takes time to acquire and to confirm them; and if this motion of the eyes were got by habit, we should see children, when they are born, turn their eyes different ways, and move one without the other, as they do their hands or legs. I know some have affirmed that they are apt to do so. But I have never found it true from my own observation, although I have taken pains to make observations of this kind, and have had good opportunities. I have likewise consulted experienced midwives, mothers, and nurses, and found them agree, that they had never observed distortions of this kind in the eyes of children, but when they had reason to suspect convulsions, or some preternatural cause.

It seems therefore to be extremely probable, that, previous to custom, there is something in the constitution, some natural instinct, which directs us to move both eyes always the same way.

We know not how the mind acts upon the body, nor by what power the muscles are contracted and relaxed: but we see that in some of the voluntary, as well as in some of the involuntary motions, this power is so directed, that many muscles which have no material tie or connection, act in concert, each of them being taught to play its part in exact time and measure. Nor doth a company of expert players in a theatrical performance, or of excellent musicians in a concert, or of good dancers in a country-dance, with more regularity and order, conspire and contribute their several parts, to produce one uniform effect, than a number of muscles do, in many of the animal functions, and in many voluntary actions. Yet we see such actions no less skilfully and regularly performed in children, and in those who know not that they have such muscles, than in the most skilful anatomist and physiologist.

Who taught all the muscles that are concerned in sucking, in swallowing our food, in breathing, and in the several natural expulsions, to act their part in such regular order and exact measure? It was not custom surely. It was that same powerful and wise Being who made the fabric of the human body, and fixed the laws by which the mind operates upon every part of it, so that they may answer the purposes intended by them. And when we see, in so many other instances, a system of unconnected muscles conspiring so wonderfully in their several functions, without the aid of habit, it needs not be thought strange, that the muscles of the eyes should, without this aid, conspire to give that direction to the eyes, without which they could not answer their end.

We see a like conspiring action in the muscles which contract the

pupils of the two eyes; and in those muscles, whatever they be, by
which the conformation of the eyes is varied according to the distance of
objects.

5   It ought however to be observed, that although it appears to be by
natural instinct that both eyes are always turned the same way, there is
still some latitude left for custom.

What we have said of the parallel motion of the eyes, is not to be
understood so strictly, as if nature directed us to keep their axes always
precisely and mathematically parallel to each other. Indeed, although they
10   are always nearly parallel, they hardly ever are exactly so. When we look
at an object, the axes of the eyes meet in that object; and therefore make
an angle, which is always small, but will be greater or less, according as
the object is nearer or more remote. Nature hath very wisely left us the
power of varying the parallelism of our eyes a little, so that we can direct
15   them to the same point, whether remote or near. This, no doubt, is learned
by custom; and accordingly we see, that it is a long time before children
get this habit in perfection.

This power of varying the parallelism of the eyes is naturally no more
than is sufficient for the purpose intended by it, but by much practice
20   and straining, it may be increased. Accordingly we see, that some have
acquired the power of distorting their eyes into unnatural directions, as
others have acquired the power of distorting their bodies into unnatural
postures.

Those who have lost the sight of an eye, commonly lose what they
25   had got by custom, in the direction of their eyes, but retain what they
had by nature; that is, although their eyes turn and move always together;
yet, when they look upon an object, the blind eye will often have a very
small deviation from it; which is not perceived by a slight observer, but
may be discerned by one accustomed to make exact observations in these
30   matters.

SECT. XI.

Of our seeing objects erect by inverted images.

35

ANOTHER phænomenon which hath perplexed philosophers, is, our seeing
objects erect, when it is well known that their images or pictures upon the
tunica retina of the eye are inverted.

The sagacious Kepler first made the noble discovery, That distinct but inverted pictures of visible objects, are formed upon the *retina* by the rays of light coming from the object. The same great philosopher demonstrated, from the principles of optics, how these pictures are formed, to wit, That the rays coming from any one point of the object, and falling upon the various parts of the pupil, are, by the *cornea* and crystalline, refracted so as to meet again in one point of the *retina*, and there paint the colour of that point of the object from which they come. As the rays from different points of the object cross each other before they come to the *retina*, the picture they form must be inverted; the upper part of the object being painted upon the lower part of *retina*, the right side of the object upon the left of the *retina*, and so of the other parts.

This philosopher thought that we see objects erect by means of these inverted pictures, for this reason, That as the rays from different points of the object cross each other, before they fall upon the *retina*, we conclude that the impulse which we feel upon the lower part of the *retina*, comes from above; and that the impulse which we feel upon the higher part, comes from below.

Des Cartes afterwards gave the same solution of this phænomenon, and illustrated it by the judgment which we form of the position of objects which we feel with our arms crossed, or with two sticks that cross each other.

But we cannot acquiesce in this solution. First, Because it supposes our seeing things erect, to be a deduction of reason, drawn from certain premises; whereas it seems to be an immediate perception. And, secondly, Because the premises from which all mankind are supposed to draw this conclusion, never entered into the minds of the far greater part, but are absolutely unknown to them. We have no feeling or perception of the pictures upon the *retina*, and as little surely of the position of them. In order to see objects erect, according to the principles of Kepler or Des Cartes, we must previously know, that the rays of light come from the object to the eye in straight lines; we must know, that the rays from different points of the object cross one another, before they form the pictures upon the *retina*; and lastly, we must know that these pictures are really inverted. Now, although all these things are true, and known to philosophers, yet they are absolutely unknown to the far greatest part of mankind: nor is it possible that they who are absolutely ignorant of them, should reason from them, and build conclusions upon them. Since therefore visible objects appear erect to the ignorant as well as to the learned, this cannot be a conclusion drawn from premises which never entered into the minds of the ignorant. We have indeed had occasion to observe many instances of conclusions drawn, either by means of original principles, or by habit, from premises which pass through the mind very quickly, and which are never made the objects of reflection; but surely no man will conceive it possible to draw conclusions from premises which never entered into the mind at all.

Bishop Berkeley having justly rejected this solution, gives one founded upon his own principles; wherein he is followed by the judicious Dr Smith in his *Optics*, and this we shall next explain and examine.

That ingenious writer conceives the ideas of sight to be altogether unlike those of touch. And since the notions we have of an object by these different senses have no similitude, we can learn only by experience how one sense will be affected, by what, in a certain manner, affects the other. Figure, position, and even number, in tangible objects, are ideas of touch; and although there is no similitude between these and the ideas of sight, yet we learn by experience, that a triangle affects the sight in such a manner, and that a square affects it in such another manner: hence we judge that which affects it in the first manner, to be a triangle, and that which affects it in the second, to be a square. In the same way, finding from experience, that an object in an erect position, affects the eye in one manner, and the same object in an inverted position, affects it in another, we learn to judge, by the manner in which the eye is affected, whether the object is erect or inverted. In a word, visible ideas, according to this author, are signs of the tangible; and the mind passeth from the sign to the thing signified, not by means of any similitude between the one and the other, nor by any natural principle; but by having found them constantly conjoined in experience, as the sounds of a language are with the things they signify. So that if the images upon the *retina* had been always erect, they would have shewn the objects erect, in the manner as they do now that they are inverted: nay, if the visible idea which we now have from an inverted object, had been associated from the beginning with the erect position of that object, it would have signified an erect position, as readily as it now signifies an inverted one. And if the visible appearance of two shillings had been found connected from the beginning with the tangible idea of one shilling, that appearance would as naturally and readily have signified the unity of the object, as now it signifies its duplicity.

This opinion is undoubtedly very ingenious; and, if it is just, serves to resolve, not only the phænomenon now under consideration, but likewise that which we shall next consider, our seeing objects single with two eyes.

It is evident, that in this solution it is supposed, that we do not originally, and previous to acquired habits, see things either erect or inverted, of one figure or another, single or double, but learn from experience to judge of their tangible position, figure, and number, by certain visible signs.

Indeed it must be acknowledged to be extremely difficult to distinguish the immediate and natural objects of sight, from the conclusions which we have been accustomed from infancy to draw from them. Bishop Berkeley was the first that attempted to distinguish the one from the other, and to trace out the boundary that divides them. And if, in doing so, he hath gone a little to the right hand or to the left, this might be expected in a subject altogether new, and of the greatest subtilty. The nature of vision hath received great light from this distinction; and many phænomena in optics, which before appeared altogether unaccountable, have been clearly and distinctly resolved by it. It is natural, and almost unavoidable, to one who hath made an important discovery in philosophy, to carry it a little beyond its sphere, and to apply it to the resolution of phænomena which do not fall within its province. Even the great Newton, when he had discovered the universal law of gravitation, and observed how many of the phænomena of nature depend upon this, and other laws of attraction and repulsion, could not help expressing his conjecture, that all the phænomena of the material world depend upon attracting and repelling forces in the particles of matter. And I suspect that the ingenious Bishop of Cloyne, having found so many phænomena of vision reducible to the constant association of the ideas of sight and touch, carried this principle a little beyond its just limits.

In order to judge as well as we can, whether it is so, let us suppose such a blind man as Dr Saunderson, having all the knowledge and abilities which a blind man may have, suddenly made to see perfectly. Let us suppose him kept from all opportunities of associating his ideas of sight with those of touch, until the former become a little familiar; and the first surprise, occasioned by objects so new, being abated, he has time to canvass them, and to compare them, in his mind, with the notions which he formerly had by touch; and in particular to compare, in his mind, that visible extension which his eyes present, with the extension in length and breadth with which he was before acquainted.

We have endeavoured to prove, that a blind man may form a notion of the visible extension and figure of bodies, from the relation which it bears to their tangible extension and figure. Much more, when this visible extension and figure are presented to his eye, will he be able to compare them with tangible extension and figure, and to perceive, that the one has length and breadth as well as the other; that the one may be bounded by lines, either straight or curve, as well as the other. And therefore, he will perceive, that there may be visible, as well as tangible circles, triangles, quadrilateral and multilateral figures. And although the visible figure is coloured, and the tangible is not, they may, notwithstanding, have the same figure; as two objects of touch may have the same figure, although one is hot and the other cold.

We have demonstrated, that the properties of visible figures differ from those of the plain figures which they represent: but it was observed at the same time, that when the object is so small as to be seen distinctly at one view, and is placed directly before the eye, the difference between the visible and the tangible figure is too small to be perceived by the senses. Thus it is true, that of every visible triangle, the three angles are greater than two right angles; whereas in a plain triangle, the three angles are equal to two right angles: but when the visible triangle is small, its three angles will be so nearly equal to two right angles, that the sense cannot discern the difference. In like manner, the circumferences of unequal visible circles are not, but those of plain circles are, in the *ratio* of their diameters; yet in small visible circles, the circumferences are very nearly in the *ratio* of their diameters; and the diameter bears the same *ratio* to the circumference, as in a plain circle, very nearly.

Hence it appears, that small visible figures (and such only can be seen distinctly at one view) have not only a resemblance to the plain tangible figures which have the same name, but are to all sense the same. So that if Dr Saunderson had been made to see, and had attentively viewed the figures of the first book of Euclid, he might, by thought and consideration, without touching them, have found out that they were the very figures he was before so well acquainted with by touch.

When plain figures are seen obliquely, their visible figure differs more from the tangible; and the representation which is made to the eye, of solid figures, is still more imperfect; because visible extension hath not three, but two dimensions only. Yet as it cannot be said that an exact picture of a man hath no resemblance of the man, or that a perspective view of a house hath no resemblance of the house; so it cannot be said, with any propriety, that the visible figure of a man, or of a house, hath no resemblance of the objects which they represent.

Bishop Berkeley therefore proceeds upon a capital mistake, in supposing that there is no resemblance betwixt the extension, figure, and position which we see, and that which we perceive by touch.

We may further observe, that Bishop Berkeley's system, with regard to material things, must have made him see this question, of the erect appearance of objects, in a very different light from that in which it appears to those who do not adopt his system.

In his theory of vision, he seems indeed to allow, that there is an external material world: but he believed that this external world is tangible only, and not visible; and that the visible world, the proper object of sight, is not external, but in the mind. If this is supposed, he that affirms that he sees things erect and not inverted, affirms that there is a top and a bottom, a right and a left in the mind. Now, I confess I am not so well acquainted with the topography of the mind, as to be able to affix a meaning to these words when applied to it.

We shall therefore allow, that if visible objects were not external, but existed only in the mind, they could have no figure, or position, or extension; and that it would be absurd to affirm, that they are seen either erect or inverted; or that there is any resemblance between them and the objects of touch. But when we propose the question, Why objects are seen erect and not inverted? we take it for granted, that we are not in Bishop Berkeley's ideal world, but in that world which men, who yield to the dictates of common sense, believe themselves to inhabit. We take it for granted, that the objects both of sight and touch, are external, and have a certain figure, and a certain position with regard to one another, and with regard to our bodies, whether we perceive it or not.

When I hold my walking-cane upright in my hand, and look at it, I take it for granted, that I see and handle the same individual object. When I say that I feel it erect, my meaning is, that I feel the head directed from the horizon, and the point directed towards it: and when I say that I see it erect, I mean that I see it with the head directed from the horizon, and the point towards it. I conceive the horizon as a fixed object both of sight and touch, with relation to which, objects are said to be high or low, erect or inverted: and when the question is asked, Why I see the object erect, and not inverted? it is the same as if you should ask, Why I see it in that position which it really hath? or, Why the eye shows the real position of objects, and doth not show them in an inverted position, as they are seen by a common astronomical telescope, or as their pictures are seen upon the *retina* of an eye when it is dissected?

S E C T. XII.

The same subject continued.

It is impossible to give a satisfactory answer to this question, otherwise than by pointing out the laws of nature which take place in vision; for by these the phænomena of vision must be regulated.

Therefore I answer, First, That, by a law of nature, the rays of light proceed from every point of the object to the pupil of the eye in straight lines. Secondly, That, by the laws of nature, the rays coming from any one point of the object to the various parts of the pupil, are so refracted, as to meet again in one point of the *retina*; and the rays from different points of the object, first crossing each other, and then proceeding to as many different points of the *retina*, form an inverted picture of the object.

So far the principles of optics carry us; and experience further assures us, that if there is no such picture upon the *retina*, there is no vision; and that such as the picture on the *retina* is, such is the appearance of the object, in colour and figure, distinctness or indistinctness, brightness or faintness.

It is evident, therefore, that the pictures upon the *retina* are, by the laws of nature, a mean of vision; but in what way they accomplish their end, we are totally ignorant. Philosophers conceive, that the impression made on the *retina* by the rays of light, is communicated to the optic nerve, and by the optic nerve conveyed to some part of the brain, by them called the *sensorium*; and that the impression thus conveyed to the *sensorium* is immediately perceived by the mind, which is supposed to reside there. But we know nothing of the seat of the soul: and we are so far from perceiving immediately what is transacted in the brain, that of all parts of the human body we know least about it. It is indeed very probable, that the optic nerve is an instrument of vision no less necessary than the *retina*; and that some impression is made upon it, by means of the pictures on the *retina*. But of what kind this impression is, we know nothing.

There is not the least probability, that there is any picture or image of the object either in the optic nerve or brain. The pictures on the *retina* are formed by the rays of light; and whether we suppose, with some, that their impulse upon the *retina* causes some vibration of the fibres of the optic nerve; or, with others, that it gives motion to some subtile fluid contained in the nerve; neither that vibration, nor this motion, can resemble the visible object which is presented to the mind. Nor is there any probability, that the mind perceives the pictures upon the *retina*. These pictures are no more objects of our perception, than the brain is, or the optic nerve. No man ever saw the pictures in his own eye, nor indeed the pictures in the eye of another, until it was taken out of the head, and duly prepared.

It is very strange, that philosophers, of all ages, should have agreed in this notion, That the images of external objects are conveyed by the organs of sense to the brain, and are there perceived by the mind. Nothing can be more unphilosophical. For, first, This notion hath no foundation in fact and observation. Of all the organs of sense, the eye only, as far as we can discover, forms any kind of image of its object; and the images formed by the eye are not in the brain, but only in the bottom of the eye; nor are they at all perceived or felt by the mind. Secondly, It is as difficult to conceive how the mind perceives images in the brain, as, how it perceives things more distant. If any man will shew how the mind may perceive images in the brain, I will undertake to shew how it may perceive the most distant objects: for if we give eyes to the mind, to perceive what is transacted at home in its dark chamber, why may we not make these eyes a little longer-sighted? and then we shall have no occasion for that unphilosophical fiction of images in the brain. In a word, the manner and mechanism of the mind's perception is quite beyond our comprehension: and this way of explaining it by images in the brain, seems to be founded upon very gross notions of the mind and its operations; as if the supposed images in the brain, by a kind of contact, formed similar impressions or images of objects upon the mind, of which impressions it is supposed to be conscious.

We have endeavoured to shew, throughout the course of this inquiry, that the impressions made upon the mind by means of the five senses, have not the least resemblance to the objects of sense: and therefore, as we see no shadow of evidence, that there are any such images in the brain, so we see no purpose, in philosophy, that the supposition of them can answer. Since the picture upon the *retina* therefore is neither itself seen by the mind, nor produces any impression upon the brain or *sensorium*, which is seen by the mind, nor makes any impression upon the mind that resembles the object, it may still be asked, How this picture upon the *retina* causes vision?

Before we answer this question, it is proper to observe, that in the

operations of the mind, as well as in those of bodies, we must often be satisfied with knowing, that certain things are connected, and invariably follow one another, without being able to discover the chain that goes between them. It is to such connections that we give the name of *laws*
5   *of nature*; and when we say that one thing produces another by a law of nature, this signifies no more, but that one thing, which we call in popular language *the cause*, is constantly and invariably followed by another, which we call *the effect*; and that we know not how they are connected. Thus, we see it is a fact, that bodies gravitate towards bodies; and that this
10   gravitation is regulated by certain mathematical proportions, according to the distances of the bodies from each other, and their quantities of matter. Being unable to discover the cause of this gravitation, and presuming that it is the immediate operation, either of the Author of nature, or of some subordinate cause, which we have not hitherto been able to reach, we call
15   it *a law of nature*. If any philosopher should hereafter be so happy as to discover the cause of gravitation, this can only be done by discovering some more general law of nature, of which the gravitation of bodies is a necessary consequence. In every chain of natural causes, the highest link is a primary law of nature; and the highest link which we can trace, by just
20   induction, is either this primary law of nature, or a necessary consequence of it. To trace out the laws of nature, by induction, from the phænomena of nature, is all that true philosophy aims at, and all that it can ever reach.

There are laws of nature by which the operations of the mind are regulated; there are also laws of nature that govern the material system:
25   and as the latter are the ultimate conclusions which the human faculties can reach in the philosophy of bodies, so the former are the ultimate conclusions we can reach in the philosophy of minds.

To return, therefore, to the question above proposed, we may see, from what hath been just now observed, that it amounts to this, By what law of
30   nature is a picture upon the *retina*, the mean or occasion of my seeing an external object of the same figure and colour, in a contrary position, and in a certain direction from the eye?

It will, without doubt, be allowed, that I see the whole object in the same manner and by the same law by which I see any one point of it.
35   Now, I know it to be a fact, that, in direct vision, I see every point of the object in the direction of the right line that passeth from the centre of the eye to that point of the object; and I know likewise, from optics, that the ray of light that comes to the centre of my eye, passes on to the *retina* in the same direction. Hence it appears to be a fact, that every point of

the object is seen in the direction of a right line passing from the picture of that point on the *retina* through the centre of the eye. As this is a fact that holds universally and invariably, it must either be a law of nature, or the necessary consequence of some more general law of nature. And according to the just rules of philosophizing, we may hold it for a law of nature, until some more general law be discovered, whereof it is a necessary consequence, which I suspect can never be done.

Thus we see, that the phænomena of vision lead us by the hand to a law of nature, or a law of our constitution, of which law our seeing objects erect by inverted images, is a necessary consequence. For it necessarily follows, from the law we have mentioned, that the object whose picture is lowest on the *retina*, must be seen in the highest direction from the eye; and that the object whose picture is on the right of the *retina*, must be seen on the left; so that if the pictures had been erect in the *retina*, we should have seen the object inverted. My chief intention in handling this question, was to point out this law of nature; which, as it is a part of the constitution of the human mind, belongs properly to the subject of this inquiry. For this reason I shall make some farther remarks upon it, after doing justice to the ingenious Dr Porterfield, who, long ago in the Medical Essays, or more lately in his Treatise of the Eye, pointed out, as a primary law of our nature, That a visible object appears in the direction of a right line perpendicular to the *retina* at that point where its image is painted. If lines drawn from the centre of the eye to all parts of the *retina* be perpendicular to it, as they must be very nearly, this coincides with the law we have mentioned, and is the same in other words. In order, therefore, that we may have a more distinct notion of this law of our constitution, we may observe,

1. That we can give no reason why the *retina* is, of all parts of the body, the only one on which pictures made by the rays of light cause vision; and therefore we must resolve this solely into a law of our constitution. We may form such pictures by means of optical glasses, upon the hand, or upon any other part of the body; but they are not felt, nor do they produce any thing like vision. A picture upon the *retina* is as little felt as one upon the hand; but it produces vision; for no other reason that we know, but because it is destined by the wisdom of nature to this purpose. The vibrations of the air strike upon the eye, the palate, and the olfactory membrane, with the same force as upon the *membrana tympani* of the ear: The impression they make upon the last, produces the sensation of sound; but their impression upon any of the former, produces no sensation

at all. This may be extended to all the senses, whereof each hath its
peculiar laws, according to which, the impressions made upon the organ
of that sense, produce sensations or perceptions in the mind, that cannot
be produced by impressions made upon any other organ.

5   2. We may observe, that the laws of perception, by the different senses,
are very different, not only in respect of the nature of the objects perceived
by them, but likewise in respect of the notices they give us of the distance
and situation of the object. In all of them the object is conceived to be
external, and to have real existence, independent of our perception: but

10   in one, the distance, figure, and situation of the object, are all presented
to the mind; in another, the figure and situation, but not the distance; and
in others, neither figure, situation, nor distance. In vain do we attempt to
account for these varieties in the manner of perception by the different
senses, from principles of anatomy or natural philosophy. They must

15   at last be resolved into the will of our Maker, who intended that our
powers of perception should have certain limits, and adapted the organs
of perception, and the laws of nature by which they operate, to his wise
purposes.

      When we hear an unusual sound, the sensation indeed is in the mind,

20   but we know that there is something external that produced this sound.
At the same time our hearing does not inform us, whether the sounding
body is near or at a distance, in this direction or that; and therefore we
look round to discover it.

      If any new phænomenon appears in the heavens, we see exactly its

25   colour, its apparent place, magnitude, and figure, but we see not its
distance. It may be in the atmosphere, it may be among the planets, or it
may be in the sphere of the fixed stars, for any thing the eye can determine.

      The testimony of the sense of touch reaches only to objects that are
contiguous to the organ, but with regard to them, is more precise and

30   determinate. When we feel a body with our hand, we know the figure,
distance, and position of it, as well as whether it is rough or smooth, hard
or soft, hot or cold.

      The sensations of touch, of seeing, and hearing, are all in the mind,
and can have no existence but when they are perceived. How do they all

35   constantly and invariably suggest the conception and belief of external
objects, which exist whether they are perceived or not? No philosopher
can give any other answer to this, but that such is the constitution of our
nature. How do we know, that the object of touch is at the fingers end,
and no where else? that the object of sight is in such a direction from

the eye, and in no other, but may be at any distance? and that the object of hearing may be at any distance, and in any direction? Not by custom surely; not by reasoning, or comparing ideas, but by the constitution of our nature. How do we perceive visible objects in the direction of right lines perpendicular to that part of the *retina* on which the rays strike, while we do not perceive the objects of hearing in lines perpendicular to the *membrana tympani*, upon which the vibrations of the air strike? Because such are the laws of our nature. How do we know the parts of our bodies affected by particular pains? Not by experience or by reasoning, but by the constitution of nature. The sensation of pain is, no doubt, in the mind, and cannot be said to have any relation, from its own nature, to any part of the body: but this sensation, by our constitution, gives a perception of some particular part of the body, whose disorder causes the uneasy sensation. If it were not so, a man who never before felt either the gout or the toothach, when he is first seized with the gout in his toe, might mistake it for the toothach.

Every sense therefore hath its peculiar laws and limits, by the constitution of our nature; and one of the laws of sight is, That we always see an object in the direction of a right line passing from its image on the *retina* through the centre of the eye.

3. Perhaps some readers will imagine, that it is easier, and will answer the purpose as well, to conceive a law of nature, by which we shall always see objects in the place in which they are, and in their true position, without having recourse to images on the *retina*, or to the optical centre of the eye.

To this I answer, That nothing can be a law of nature which is contrary to fact. The laws of nature are the most general facts we can discover in the operations of nature. Like other facts, they are not to be hit upon by a happy conjecture, but justly deduced from observation: Like other general facts, they are not to be drawn from a few particulars, but from a copious, patient, and cautious induction. That we see things always in their true place and position, is not fact; and therefore it can be no law of nature. In a plain mirror, I see myself, and other things, in places very different from those they really occupy. And so it happens in every instance, wherein the rays coming from the object are either reflected or refracted before falling upon the eye. Those who know any thing of optics, know that, in all such cases, the object is seen in the direction of a line passing from the centre of the eye, to the point where the rays were last reflected or refracted; and that upon this all the powers of the telescope and microscope depend.

Shall we say then, that it is a law of nature, that the object is seen in the direction which the rays have when they fall on the eye, or rather in the direction contrary to that of the rays when they fall upon the eye? No. This is not true; and therefore it is no law of nature. For the rays, from
5　　any one point of the object, come to all parts of the pupil; and therefore must have different directions: but we see the object only in one of these directions, to wit, in the direction of the rays that come to the centre of the eye. And this holds true, even when the rays that should pass through the centre are stopt, and the object is seen by rays that pass at a distance
10　　from the centre.

Perhaps it may still be imagined, that although we are not made so as to see objects always in their true place, nor so as to see them precisely in the direction of the rays when they fall upon the *cornea*; yet we may be so made, as to see the object in the direction which the rays have when
15　　they fall upon the *retina*, after they have undergone all their refractions in the eye, that is, in the direction in which the rays pass from the crystalline to the *retina*. But neither is this true; and consequently it is no law of our constitution. In order to see that it is not true, we must conceive all the rays that pass from the crystalline to one point of the *retina*, as forming a small
20　　cone, whose base is upon the back of the crystalline, and whose vertex is a point of the *retina*. It is evident that the rays which form the picture in this point, have various directions, even after they pass the crystalline; yet the object is seen only in one of these directions, to wit, in the direction of the rays that come from the centre of the eye. Nor is this owing to any
25　　particular virtue in the central rays, or in the centre itself; for the central rays may be stopt. When they are stopt, the image will be formed upon the same point of the *retina* as before, by rays that are not central, nor have the same direction which the central rays had: and in this case the object is seen in the same direction as before, although there are now no
30　　rays coming in that direction.

From this induction we conclude, That our seeing an object in that particular direction in which we do see it, is not owing to any law of nature by which we are made to see it in the direction of the rays, either before their refractions in the eye, or after, but to a law of our nature, by which
35　　we see the object in the direction of the right line that passeth from the picture of the object upon the *retina* to the centre of the eye.

The facts upon which I ground this induction, are taken from some curious experiments of Scheiner, in his *Fundament. Optic.* quoted by Dr Porterfield, and confirmed by his experience. I have also repeated these experiments, and found them to answer. As they are easily made, and tend to illustrate and confirm the law of nature I have mentioned, I shall recite them as briefly and distinctly as I can.

Experiment 1. Let a very small object, such as the head of a pin, well illuminated, be fixed at such a distance from the eye, as to be beyond the nearest limit and within the farthest limit of distinct vision. For a young eye, not near-sighted, the object may be placed at the distance of eighteen inches. Let the eye be kept steadily in one place, and take a distinct view of the object. We know from the principles of optics, that the rays from any one point of this object, whether they pass through the centre of the eye, or at any distance from the centre which the breadth of the pupil will permit, do all unite again in one point of the *retina*. We know also, that these rays have different directions, both before they fall upon the eye, and after they pass through the crystalline.

Now we can see the object by any one small parcel of these rays, excluding the rest, by looking through a small pin-hole in a card. Moving this pin-hole over the various parts of the pupil, we can see the object, first by the rays that pass above the centre of the eye, then by the central rays, then by the rays that pass below the centre, and in like manner by the rays that pass on the right and left of the centre. Thus, we view this object, successively, by rays that are central, and by rays that are not central; by rays that have different directions, and are variously inclined to each other, both when they fall upon the *cornea*, and when they fall upon the *retina*; but always, by rays which fall upon the same point of the *retina*. And what is the event? It is this, that the object is seen in the same individual direction, whether seen by all these rays together, or by any one parcel of them.

Experiment 2. Let the object above mentioned be now placed within the nearest limit of distinct vision, that is, for an eye that is not near-sighted, at the distance of four or five inches. We know, that in this case, the rays coming from one point of the object, do not meet in one point of the *retina*, but spread over a small circular spot of it; the central rays occupying the centre of this circle, the rays that pass above the centre occupying the upper part of the circular spot, and so of the rest. And we know that the object is in this case seen confused, every point of it being seen, not in one, but in various directions. To remedy this confusion, we look at the object through the pin-hole, and while we move the pin-hole over the various parts of the pupil, the object does not keep its place, but seems to move in a contrary direction.

It is here to be observed, that when the pin-hole is carried upwards over the pupil, the picture of the object is carried upwards upon the *retina*, and the object at the same time seems to move downwards, so as to be always in the right line passing from the picture through the centre of the

5 eye. It is likewise to be observed, that the rays which form the upper and the lower pictures upon the *retina*, do not cross each other as in ordinary vision; yet still the higher picture shews the object lower, and the lower picture shews the object higher, in the same manner as when the rays cross each other. Whence we may observe, by the way, that this phænomenon

10 of our seeing objects in a position contrary to that of their pictures upon the *retina*, does not depend upon the crossing of the rays, as Kepler and Des Cartes conceived.

Experiment 3. Other things remaining as in the last experiment, make three pinholes in a straight line, so near, that the rays coming from the

15 object through all the holes, may enter the pupil at the same time. In this case we have a very curious phænomenon; for the object is seen triple with one eye. And if you make more holes within the breadth of the pupil, you will see as many objects as there are holes. However, we shall suppose them only three; one on the right, one in the middle, and one

20 on the left; in which case you see three objects standing in a line from right to left.

It is here to be observed, that there are three pictures on the *retina*; that on the left being formed by the rays which pass on the left of the eye's centre; the middle picture being formed by the central rays, and

25 the right-hand picture by the rays which pass on the right of the eye's centre. It is farther to be observed, that the object which appears on the right, is not that which is seen through the hole on the right, but that which is seen through the hole on the left; and in like manner, the left-hand object is seen through the hole on the right, as is easily proved by

30 covering the holes successively. So that, whatever is the direction of the rays which form the right-hand and left-hand pictures, still the right-hand picture shows a left-hand object, and the left-hand picture shows a right-hand object.

Experiment 4. It is easy to see how the two last experiments may be

35 varied, by placing the object beyond the farthest limit of distinct vision. In order to make this experiment, I looked at a candle at the distance of ten feet, and put the eye of my spectacles behind the card, that the rays from the same point of the object might meet, and cross each other, before they reached the *retina*. In this case, as in the former, the candle was seen

triple through the three pin-holes; but the candle on the right, was seen through the hole on the right; and, on the contrary, the left-hand candle was seen through the hole on the left. In this experiment it is evident from the principles of optics, that the rays forming the several pictures on the *retina*, cross each other a little before they reach the *retina*; and therefore the left-hand picture is formed by the rays which pass through the hole on the right: so that the position of the pictures is contrary to that of the holes by which they are formed; and therefore is also contrary to that of their objects, as we have found it to be in the former experiments.

These experiments exhibit several uncommon phænomena, that regard the apparent place, and the direction of visible objects from the eye; phænomena that seem to be most contrary to the common rules of vision. When we look at the same time through three holes that are in a right line, and at certain distances from each other, we expect, that the objects seen through them should really be, and should appear to be, at a distance from each other: Yet, by the first experiment, we may, through three such holes, see the same object, and the same point of that object; and through all the three it appears in the same individual place and direction.

When the rays of light come from the object in right lines to the eye, without any reflection, inflection, or refraction, we expect, that the object should appear in its real and proper direction from the eye; and so it commonly does: but in the second, third, and fourth experiments, we see the object in a direction which is not its true and real direction from the eye, although the rays come from the object to the eye, without any inflection, reflection, or refraction.

When both the object and the eye are fixed without the least motion, and the medium unchanged, we expect, that the object should appear to rest, and keep the same place: Yet in the second and fourth experiments, when both the eye and the object are at rest, and the medium unchanged, we make the object appear to move upwards or downwards, or in any direction we please.

When we look at the same time, and with the same eye, through holes that stand in a line from right to left, we expect, that the object seen through the left-hand hole should appear on the left, and the object seen through the right-hand hole, should appear on the right: Yet in the third experiment, we find the direct contrary.

Although many instances occur of seeing the same object double with two eyes, we always expect, that it should appear single when seen only by one eye: Yet in the second and fourth experiments, we have instances wherein the same object may appear double, triple, or quadruple to one eye, without the help of a polyhedron or multiplying glass.

All these extraordinary phænomena, regarding the direction of visible objects from the eye, as well as those that are common and ordinary, lead us to that law of nature which I have mentioned, and are the necessary consequences of it. And, as there is no probability that we shall ever be able to give a reason, why pictures upon the *retina* make us see external objects, any more than pictures upon the hand or upon the cheek; or, that we shall ever be able to give a reason, why we see the object in the direction of a line passing from its picture through the centre of the eye, rather than in any other direction; I am therefore apt to look upon this law as a primary law of our constitution.

To prevent being misunderstood, I beg the reader to observe, that I do not mean to affirm, that the picture upon the *retina* will make us see an object in the direction mentioned, or in any direction, unless the optic nerve, and the other more immediate instruments of vision, be sound, and perform their function. We know not well what is the office of the optic nerve, nor in what manner it performs that office; but that it hath some part in the faculty of seeing, seems to be certain; because in an *amaurosis*, which is believed to be a disorder of the optic nerve, the pictures on the *retina* are clear and distinct, and yet there is no vision.

We know still less of the use and function of the choroid membrane; but it seems likewise to be necessary to vision: for it is well known, that pictures upon that part of the *retina* where it is not covered by the choroid, I mean at the entrance of the optic nerve, produce no vision, any more than a picture upon the hand. We acknowledge, therefore, that the *retina* is not the last and most immediate instrument of the mind in vision. There are other material organs, whose operation is necessary to seeing, even after the pictures upon the *retina* are formed. If ever we come to know the structure and use of the choroid membrane, the optic nerve, and the brain, and what impressions are made upon them by means of the pictures on the *retina*, some more links of the chain may be brought within our view, and a more general law of vision discovered: but while we know so little of the nature and office of these more immediate instruments of vision, it seems to be impossible to trace its laws beyond the pictures upon the *retina*.

Neither do I pretend to say, that there may not be diseases of the eye, or accidents, which may occasion our seeing objects in a direction somewhat different from that mentioned above. I shall beg leave to mention one instance of this kind that concerns myself.

In May 1761, being occupied in making an exact meridian, in order to observe the transit of Venus, I rashly directed to the sun, by my right eye, the cross hairs of a small telescope. I had often done the like in my younger days with impunity; but I suffered by it at last, which I mention as a warning to others.

I soon observed a remarkable dimness in that eye; and for many weeks, when I was in the dark, or shut my eyes, there appeared before the right eye a lucid spot, which trembled much like the image of the sun seen by reflection from water. This appearance grew fainter, and less frequent by degrees; so that now there are seldom any remains of it. But some other very sensible effects of this hurt still remain. For, first, The sight of the right eye continues to be more dim than that of the left. Secondly, The nearest limit of distinct vision is more remote in the right eye than in the other; although, before the time mentioned, they were equal in both these respects, as I had found by many trials. But, thirdly, what I chiefly intended to mention is, That a straight line, in some circumstances, appears to the right eye to have a curvature in it. Thus, when I look upon a music-book, and, shutting my left eye, direct the right to a point of the middle line of the five which compose the staff of music; the middle line appears dim indeed, at the point to which the eye is directed, but straight; at the same time the two lines above it, and the two below it, appear to be bent outwards, and to be more distant from each other, and from the middle line, than at other parts of the staff, to which the eye is not directed. Fourthly, Although I have repeated this experiment times innumerable, within these sixteen months, I do not find that custom and experience takes away this appearance of curvature in straight lines. Lastly, This appearance of curvature is perceptible when I look with the right eye only, but not when I look with both eyes; yet I see better with both eyes together, than even with the left eye alone.

I have related this fact minutely as it is, without regard to any hypothesis; because I think such uncommon facts deserve to be recorded. I shall leave it to others to conjecture the cause of this appearance. To me it seems most probable, that a small part of the *retina* towards the centre is shrunk, and that thereby the contiguous parts are drawn nearer to the centre, and to one another, than they were before; and that objects whose images fall on these parts, appear at that distance from each other which corresponds, not to the interval of the parts in their present preternatural contraction, but to their interval in their natural and sound state.

Of seeing objects single with two eyes.

ANOTHER phænomenon of vision which deserves attention, is our seeing
objects single with two eyes. There are two pictures of the object, one on
each *retina*; and each picture by itself makes us see an object in a certain
direction from the eye: yet both together commonly make us see only
one object. All the accounts or solutions of this phænomenon given by
anatomists and philosophers, seem to be unsatisfactory. I shall pass over
the opinions of Galen, of Gassendus, of Baptista Porta, and of Rohault.
The reader may see these examined and refuted by Dr Porterfield. I shall
examine Dr Porterfield's own opinion, Bishop Berkeley's, and some
others. But it will be necessary first to ascertain the facts; for if we
mistake the phænomena of single and double vision, it is ten to one but
this mistake will lead us wrong in assigning the causes. This likewise
we ought carefully to attend to, which is acknowledged in theory by all
who have any true judgment or just taste in inquiries of this nature, but is
very often overlooked in practice, namely, That in the solution of natural
phænomena, all the length that the human faculties can carry us, is only
this, that from particular phænomena, we may, by induction, trace out
general phænomena, of which all the particular ones are necessary consequences. And when we have arrived at the most general phænomena we
can reach, there we must stop. If it is asked, Why such a body gravitates
towards the earth? all the answer that can be given is, Because all bodies
gravitate towards the earth. This is resolving a particular phænomenon
into a general one. If it should again be asked, Why do all bodies gravitate
towards the earth? we can give no other solution of this phænomenon, but
that all bodies whatsoever gravitate towards each other. This is resolving
a general phænomenon into a more general one. If it should be asked,
Why all bodies gravitate to one another? we cannot tell; but if we could
tell, it could only be by resolving this universal gravitation of bodies into
some other phænomenon still more general, and of which the gravitation
of all bodies is a particular instance. The most general phænomena we
can reach, are what we call *laws of nature*. So that the laws of nature
are nothing else but the most general facts relating to the operations of
nature, which include a great many particular facts under them. And if
in any case we should give the name of a law of nature to a general
phænomenon, which human industry shall afterwards trace to one more

general, there is no great harm done. The most general assumes the name
of a law of nature, when it is discovered; and the less general is contained
and comprehended in it. Having premised these things, we proceed to
consider the phænomena of single and double vision, in order to discover
some general principle to which they all lead, and of which they are the
necessary consequences. If we can discover any such general principle, it
must either be a law of nature, or the necessary consequence of some law
of nature; and its authority will be equal, whether it is the first or the last.

1. We find, that when the eyes are sound and perfect, and the axes of
both directed to one point, an object placed in that point is seen single:
and here we observe, that in this case the two pictures which show the
object single, are in the centres of the *retinæ*. When two pictures of a small
object are formed upon points of the *retinæ*, if they show the object single,
we shall, for the sake of perspicuity, call such two points of the *retinæ*,
corresponding points; and where the object is seen double, we shall call
the points of the *retinæ* on which the pictures are formed, *points that do
not correspond*. Now, in this first phænomenon it is evident, that the two
centres of the *retinæ* are corresponding points.

2. Supposing the same things as in the last phænomenon, other objects
at the same distance from the eyes as that to which their axes are directed,
do also appear single. Thus, if I direct my eyes to a candle placed at the
distance of ten feet; and, while I look at this candle, another stands at the
same distance from my eyes, within the field of vision; I can, while I look
at the first candle, attend to the appearance which the second makes to the
eye; and I find that in this case it always appears single. It is here to be
observed, that the pictures of the second candle do not fall upon the centres
of the *retinæ*, but they both fall upon the same side of the centres, that
is, both to the right, or both to the left, and both are at the same distance
from the centres. This might easily be demonstrated from the principles of
optics. Hence it appears, that in this second phænomenon of single vision,
the corresponding points are points of the two *retinæ*, which are similarly
situate with respect to the two centres, being both upon the same side of
the centre, and at the same distance from it. It appears likewise from this
phænomenon, that every point in one *retina* corresponds with that which
is similarly situate in the other.

3. Supposing still the same things, objects which are much nearer to the
eyes, or much more distant from them, than that to which the two eyes are
directed, appear double. Thus, if the candle is placed at the distance of ten
feet, and I hold my finger at arms-length between my eyes and the candle;

when I look at the candle, I see my finger double; and when I look at my finger, I see the candle double: and the same thing happens with regard to all other objects at like distances which fall within the sphere of vision. In this phænomenon, it is evident to those who understand the principles of optics, that the pictures of the objects which are seen double, do not fall upon points of the *retinæ* which are similarly situate, but that the pictures of the objects seen single do fall upon points similarly situate. Whence we infer, that as the points of the two *retinæ*, which are similarly situate with regard to the centres, do correspond, so those which are dissimilarly situate, do not correspond.

4. It is to be observed, that although, in such cases as are mentioned in the last phænomenon, we have been accustomed from infancy to see objects double which we know to be single; yet custom, and experience of the unity of the object, never take away this appearance of duplicity.

5. It may however be remarked, that the custom of attending to visible appearances has a considerable effect, and makes the phænomenon of double vision to be more or less observed and remembered. Thus you may find a man that can say with a good conscience, that he never saw things double all his life; yet this very man, put in the situation above mentioned, with his finger between him and the candle, and desired to attend to the appearance of the object which he does not look at, will, upon the first trial, see the candle double, when he looks at his finger; and his finger double, when he looks at the candle. Does he now see otherwise than he saw before? No, surely; but he now attends to what he never attended to before. The same double appearance of an object hath been a thousand times presented to his eye before now; but he did not attend to it; and so it is as little an object of his reflection and memory, as if it had never happened.

When we look at an object, the circumjacent objects may be seen at the same time, although more obscurely and indistinctly: for the eye hath a considerable field of vision, which it takes in at once. But we attend only to the object we look at. The other objects which fall within the field of vision, are not attended to; and therefore are as if they were not seen. If any of them draws our attention, it naturally draws the eyes at the same time: for in the common course of life, the eyes always follow the attention: or if at any time, in a reverie, they are separated from it, we hardly at that time see what is directly before us. Hence we may see the reason, why the man we are speaking of, thinks that he never before saw an object double. When he looks at any object, he sees it single, and takes no notice of other visible objects at that time, whether they appear single or double. If any of them draws his attention, it draws his eyes at the same time; and as soon as the eyes are turned towards it, it appears single. But in order to see things double, at least in order to have any reflection

5   or remembrance that he did so, it is necessary that he should look at one object, and at the same time attend to the faint appearance of other objects which are within the field of vision. This is a practice which perhaps he never used, nor attempted; and therefore he does not recollect that ever he saw an object double. But when he is put upon giving this attention, he

10 immediately sees objects double in the same manner, and with the very same circumstances, as they who have been accustomed, for the greatest part of their lives, to give this attention.

There are many phænomena of a similar nature, which shew, that the mind may not attend to, and thereby, in some sort, not perceive objects

15 that strike the senses. I had occasion to mention several instances of this in the second chapter; and I have been assured, by persons of the best skill in music, that in hearing a tune upon the harpsichord, when they give attention to the treble, they do not hear the bass; and when they attend to the bass, they do not perceive the air of the treble. Some persons are

20 so near-sighted, that, in reading, they hold the book to one eye, while the other is directed to other objects. Such persons acquire the habit of attending in this case to the objects of one eye, while they give no attention to those of the other.

6. It is observable, that in all cases wherein we see an object double, the

25 two appearances have a certain position with regard to one another, and a certain apparent or angular distance. This apparent distance is greater or less in different circumstances; but in the same circumstances, it is always the same, not only to the same, but to different persons.

Thus, in the experiment above mentioned, if twenty different persons,

30 who see perfectly with both eyes, shall place their finger and the candle at the distances above expressed, and hold their heads upright; looking at the finger, they will see two candles, one on the right, another on the left. That which is seen on the right, is seen by the right eye, and that which is seen on the left, by the left eye; and they will see them at the same apparent

35 distance from each other. If again they look at the candle, they will see two fingers, one on the right, and the other on the left; and all will see them at the same apparent distance; the finger towards the left being seen by the right eye, and the other by the left. If the head is laid horizontally to one side, other circumstances remaining the same, one appearance of

the object seen double, will be directly above the other. In a word, vary the circumstances as you please, and the appearances are varied to all the spectators in one and the same manner.

7. Having made many experiments in order to ascertain the apparent distance of the two appearances of an object seen double, I have found that in all cases this apparent distance is proportioned to the distance between the point of the *retina*, where the picture is made in one eye, and the point which is situated similarly to that on which the picture is made on the other eye. So that as the apparent distance of two objects seen with one eye, is proportioned to the arch of the *retina*, which lies between their pictures; in like manner, when an object is seen double with the two eyes, the apparent distance of the two appearances is proportioned to the arch of either *retina*, which lies between the picture in that *retina*, and the point corresponding to that of the picture in the other *retina*.

8. As in certain circumstances we invariably see one object appear double, so in others we as invariably see two objects unite into one; and, in appearance, lose their duplicity. This is evident in the appearance of the binocular telescope. And the same thing happens when any two similar tubes are applied to the two eyes in a parallel direction; for in this case we see only one tube. And if two shillings are placed at the extremities of the two tubes, one exactly in the axis of one eye, and the other in the axis of the other eye, we shall see but one shilling. If two pieces of coin, or other bodies, of different colour, and of different figure, be properly placed in the two axes of the eyes, and at the extremities of the tubes, we shall see both the bodies in one and the same place, each as it were spread over the other, without hiding it; and the colour will be that which is compounded of the two colours.

9. From these phænomena, and from all the trials I have been able to make, it appears evidently, that in perfect human eyes, the centres of the two *retinæ* correspond and harmonize with one another; and that every other point in one *retina*, doth correspond and harmonize with the point which is similarly situate in the other; in such manner, that pictures falling on the corresponding points of the two *retinæ*, shew only one object, even when there are really two; and pictures falling upon points of the *retinæ* which do not correspond, shew us two visible appearances, although there be but one object. So that pictures, upon corresponding points of the two *retinæ* present the same appearance to the mind as if they had both fallen upon the same point of one *retina*; and pictures upon points of the two *retinæ*, which do not correspond, present to the mind the same apparent

distance and position of two objects, as if one of those pictures was carried to the point corresponding to it in the other *retina*. This relation and sympathy between corresponding points of the two *retinæ*, I do not advance as a hypothesis, but as a general fact or phænomenon of vision. All the phænomena before mentioned, of single or double vision, lead to it, and are necessary consequences of it. It holds true invariably in all perfect human eyes, as far as I am able to collect from innumerable trials of various kinds made upon my own eyes, and many made by others at my desire. Most of the hypotheses that have been contrived to resolve the phænomena of single and double vision, suppose this general fact, while their authors were not aware of it. Sir Isaac Newton, who was too judicious a philosopher, and too accurate an observer, to have offered even a conjecture which did not tally with the facts that had fallen under his observation, proposes a query with respect to the cause of it, *Optics, quer.* 15. The judicious Dr Smith, in his *Optics, lib.* 1. § 137. hath confirmed the truth of this general phænomenon from his own experience, not only as to the apparent unity of objects whose pictures fall upon the corresponding points of the *retinæ*, but also as to the apparent distance of the two appearances of the same object when seen double.

This general phænomenon appears therefore to be founded upon a very full induction, which is all the evidence we can have for a fact of this nature. Before we make an end of this subject, it will be proper to inquire, first, Whether those animals whose eyes have an adverse position in their heads, and look contrary ways, have such corresponding points in their *retinæ*? Secondly, What is the position of the corresponding points in imperfect human eyes, I mean in those that squint? And, in the last place, Whether this harmony of the corresponding points in the *retinæ*, be natural and original, or the effect of custom? And if it is original, Whether it can be accounted for by any of the laws of nature already discovered? or whether it is itself to be looked upon as a law of nature, and a part of the human constitution?

SECT. XIV.

Of the laws of vision in brute animals.

It is the intention of nature, in giving eyes to animals, that they may perceive the situation of visible objects, or the direction in which they are placed: it is probable, therefore, that, in ordinary cases, every animal,

whether it has many eyes or few, whether of one structure or of another, sees objects single, and in their true and proper direction. And since there is a prodigious variety in the structure, the motions, and the number of eyes in different animals and insects, it is probable that the laws by which
5   vision is regulated, are not the same in all, but various, adapted to the eyes which nature hath given them.

Mankind naturally turn their eyes always the same way, so that the axes of the two eyes meet in one point. They naturally attend to, or look at that object only which is placed in the point where the axes meet. And
10   whether the object be more or less distant, the configuration of the eye is adapted to the distance of the object, so as to form a distinct picture of it.

When we use our eyes in this natural way, the two pictures of the object we look at, are formed upon the centres of the two *retinæ*; and the two pictures of any contiguous object are formed upon the points of the
15   *retinæ* which are similarly situate with regard to the centres. Therefore, in order to our seeing objects single, and in their proper direction, with two eyes, it is sufficient that we be so constituted, that objects whose pictures are formed upon the centres of the two *retinæ*, or upon points similarly situate with regard to these centres, shall be seen in the same
20   visible place. And this is the constitution which nature hath actually given to human eyes.

When we distort our eyes from their parallel direction, which is an unnatural motion, but may be learned by practice; or when we direct the axes of the two eyes to one point, and at the same time direct our attention
25   to some visible object much nearer or much more distant than that point, which is also unnatural, yet may be learned; in these cases, and in these only, we see one object double, or two objects confounded in one. In these cases, the two pictures of the same object are formed upon points of the *retinæ* which are not similarly situate, and so the object is seen double; or
30   the two pictures of different objects are formed upon points of the *retinæ* which are similarly situate, and so the two objects are seen confounded in one place.

Thus it appears, that the laws of vision in the human constitution are wisely adapted to the natural use of human eyes, but not to that use of
35   them which is unnatural. We see objects truly when we use our eyes in the natural way; but have false appearances presented to us when we use them in a way that is unnatural. We may reasonably think, that the case is the same with other animals. But is it not unreasonable to think, that those animals which naturally turn one eye towards one object, and another

eye towards another object, must thereby have such false appearances presented to them, as we have when we do so against nature?

Many animals have their eyes by nature placed adverse and immoveable, the axes of the two eyes being always directed to opposite points. Do objects painted on the centres of the two *retinæ* appear to such animals as they do to human eyes, in one and the same visible place? I think it is highly probable that they do not; and that they appear, as they really are, in opposite places.

If we judge from analogy in this case, it will lead us to think that there is a certain correspondence between points of the two *retinæ* in such animals, but of a different kind from that which we have found in human eyes. The centre of one *retina* will correspond with the centre of the other, in such manner, that the objects whose pictures are formed upon these corresponding points, shall appear not to be in the same place, as in human eyes, but in opposite places. And in the same manner will the superior part of one *retina* correspond with the inferior part of the other, and the anterior part of one with the posterior part of the other.

Some animals, by nature, turn their eyes with equal facility, either the same way, or different ways, as we turn our hands and arms. Have such animals corresponding points in their *retinæ*, and points which do not correspond, as the human kind has? I think it is probable that they have not; because such a constitution in them could serve no other purpose but to exhibit false appearances.

If we judge from analogy, it will lead us to think, that as such animals move their eyes in a manner similar to that in which we move our arms, they have an immediate and natural perception of the direction they give to their eyes, as we have of the direction we give to our arms; and perceive the situation of visible objects by their eyes, in a manner similar to that in which we perceive the situation of tangible objects with our hands.

We cannot teach brute animals to use their eyes in any other way than in that which nature hath taught them; nor can we teach them to communicate to us the appearances which visible objects make to them, either in ordinary or in extraordinary cases. We have not therefore the same means of discovering the laws of vision in them, as in our own kind, but must satisfy ourselves with probable conjectures: and what we have said upon this subject, is chiefly intended to shew, that animals to which nature hath given eyes differing in their number, in their position, and in their natural motions, may very probably be subjected to different laws of vision, adapted to the peculiarities of their organs of vision.

SECT. XV.

Squinting considered hypothetically.

WHETHER there be corresponding points in the *retinæ*, of those who have an involuntary squint? and if there are, whether they be situate in the same manner as in those who have no squint? are not questions of mere curiosity. They are of real importance to the physician who attempts the cure of a squint, and to the patient who submits to the cure. After so much has been said of the *strabismus*, or squint, both by medical and by optical writers, one might expect to find abundance of facts for determining these questions. Yet I confess I have been disappointed in this expectation, after taking some pains both to make observations, and to collect those which have been made by others.

Nor will this appear very strange, if we consider that to make the observations which are necessary for determining these questions, knowledge of the principles of optics, and of the laws of vision, must concur with opportunities rarely to be met with.

Of those who squint, the far greater part have no distinct vision with one eye. When this is the case, it is impossible, and indeed of no importance, to determine the situation of the corresponding points. When both eyes are good, they commonly differ so much in their direction, that the same object cannot be seen by both at the same time; and in this case it will be very difficult to determine the situation of the corresponding points; for such persons will probably attend only to the objects of one eye, and the objects of the other will be as little regarded as if they were not seen.

We have before observed, that when we look at a near object, and attend to it, we do not perceive the double appearances of more distant objects, even when they are in the same direction, and are presented to the eye at the same time. It is probable that a squinting person, when he attends to the objects of one eye, will, in like manner, have his attention totally diverted from the objects of the other; and that he will perceive them as little as we perceive the double appearances of objects when we use our eyes in the natural way. Such a person, therefore, unless he is so much a philosopher as to have acquired the habit of attending very accurately to the visible appearances of objects, and even of objects which he does not look at, will not be able to give any light to the questions now under consideration.

It is very probable that hares, rabbits, birds, and fishes, whose eyes

are fixed in an adverse position, have the natural faculty of attending at
the same time to visible objects placed in different, and even in contrary
directions; because, without this faculty, they could not have those advantages from the contrary direction of their eyes, which nature seems to have
intended. But it is not probable that those who squint have any such natural
faculty; because we find no such faculty in the rest of the species. We
naturally attend to objects placed in the point where the axes of the two
eyes meet, and to them only. To give attention to an object in a different
direction is unnatural, and not to be learned without pains and practice.

A very convincing proof of this may be drawn from a fact now well
known to philosophers: When one eye is shut, there is a certain space
within the field of vision, where we can see nothing at all; the space which
is directly opposed to that part of the bottom of the eye where the optic
nerve enters. This defect of sight, in one part of the eye, is common to all
human eyes, and hath been so from the beginning of the world; yet it was
never known, until the sagacity of the Abbé Mariotte discovered it in the
last century. And now when it is known, it cannot be perceived, but by
means of some particular experiments, which require care and attention
to make them succeed.

What is the reason that so remarkable a defect of sight, common to
all mankind, was so long unknown, and is now perceived with so much
difficulty? It is surely this, That the defect is at some distance from the
axis of the eye, and consequently in a part of the field of vision to which
we never attend naturally, and to which we cannot attend at all, without
the aid of some particular circumstances.

From what we have said, it appears, that, to determine the situation of
the corresponding points in the eyes of those who squint, is impossible, if
they do not see distinctly with both eyes; and that it will be very difficult,
unless the two eyes differ so little in their direction, that the same object
may be seen with both at the same time. Such patients I apprehend are
rare; at least there are very few of them with whom I have had the fortune
to meet: and therefore, for the assistance of those who may have happier
opportunities, and inclination to make the proper use of them, we shall
consider the case of squinting hypothetically, pointing out the proper
articles of inquiry, the observations that are wanted, and the conclusions
that may be drawn from them.

1. It ought to be inquired, Whether the squinting person sees equally
well with both eyes? and, if there be a defect in one, the nature and degree
of that defect ought to be remarked. The experiments by which this may

be done, are so obvious, that I need not mention them. But I would advise the observer to make the proper experiments, and not to rely upon the testimony of the patient; because I have found many instances, both of persons that squinted, and others, who were found, upon trial, to have a
5   great defect in the sight of one eye, although they were never aware of it before. In all the following articles, it is supposed that the patient sees with both eyes so well, as to be able to read with either, when the other is covered.

2. It ought to be inquired, Whether, when one eye is covered, the
10   other is turned directly to the object? This ought to be tried in both eyes successively. By this observation, as a touchstone, we may try the hypothesis concerning squinting, invented by M. de la Hire, and adopted by Boerhaave, and many others of the medical faculty.

The hypothesis is, That in one eye of a squinting person, the greatest
15   sensibility and the most distinct vision is not, as in other men, in the centre of the *retina*, but upon one side of the centre; and that he turns the axis of this eye aside from the object, in order that the picture of the object may fall upon the most sensible part of the *retina*, and thereby give the most distinct vision. If this is the cause of squinting, the squinting eye will be
20   turned aside from the object, when the other eye is covered, as well as when it is not.

A trial so easy to be made, never was made for more than forty years; but the hypothesis was very generally received. So prone are men to invent hypotheses, and so backward to examine them by facts. At last Dr Jurin
25   having made the trial, found that persons who squint, turn the axis of the squinting eye directly to the object, when the other eye is covered. This fact is confirmed by Dr Porterfield; and I have found it verified in all the instances that have fallen under my observation.

3. It ought to be inquired, Whether the axes of the two eyes follow
30   one another, so as to have always the same inclination, or make the same angle, when the person looks to the right or to the left, upward or downward, or straight forward. By this observation we may judge, whether a squint is owing to any defect in the muscles which move the eye, as some have supposed. In the following articles we suppose that the
35   inclination of the axes of the eyes is found to be always the same.

4. It ought to be inquired, Whether the person that squints sees an object single or double?

If he sees the object double; and if the two appearances have an angular distance equal to the angle which the axes of his eyes make with each other, it may be concluded that he hath corresponding points in the *retinæ* of his eyes, and that they have the same situation as in those who have no squint. If the two appearances should have an angular distance which is always the same, but manifestly greater or less than the angle contained under the optic axes, this would indicate corresponding points in the *retinæ*, whose situation is not the same as in those who have no squint; but it is difficult to judge accurately of the angle which the optic axes make.

A squint too small to be perceived, may occasion double vision of objects: for if we speak strictly, every person squints more or less, whose optic axes do not meet exactly in the object which he looks at. Thus, if a man can only bring the axes of his eyes to be parallel, but cannot make them converge in the least, he must have a small squint in looking at near objects, and will see them double, while he sees very distant objects single. Again, if the optic axes always converge, so as to meet eight or ten feet before the face at farthest, such a person will see near objects single; but when he looks at very distant objects, he will squint a little, and see them double.

An instance of this kind is related by Aguilonius in his *Optics*; who says, that he had seen a young man to whom near objects appeared single, but distant objects appeared double.

Dr Briggs, in his *Nova visionis theoria*, having collected from authors several instances of double vision, quotes this from Aguilonius, as the most wonderful and unaccountable of all, in so much that he suspects some imposition on the part of the young man: but to those who understand the laws by which single and double vision are regulated, it appears to be the natural effect of a very small squint.

Double vision may always be owing to a small squint, when the two appearances are seen at a small angular distance, although no squint was observed: and I do not remember any instances of double vision recorded by authors, wherein any account is given of the angular distance of the appearances.

In almost all the instances of double vision, there is reason to suspect a squint or distortion of the eyes, from the concomitant circumstances, which we find to be one or other of the following, the approach of death, or of a *deliquium*, excessive drinking, or other intemperance, violent headach, blistering the head, smoking tobacco, blows or wounds in the head. In all these cases, it is reasonable to suspect a distortion of the eyes, either from spasm, or paralysis in the muscles that move them. But although it be probable that there is always a squint greater or less where there is double vision; yet it is certain that there is not double vision always where there is a squint. I know no instance of double vision that continued for life, or even for a great number of years. We shall therefore suppose, in the following articles, that the squinting person sees objects single.

5. The next inquiry then ought to be, Whether the object is seen with both eyes at the same time, or only with the eye whose axis is directed to it? It hath been taken for granted, by the writers upon the *strabismus*, before Dr Jurin, that those who squint, commonly see objects single with both eyes at the same time; but I know not one fact advanced by any writer which proves it. Dr Jurin is of a contrary opinion; and as it is of consequence, so it is very easy to determine this point in particular instances, by this obvious experiment. While the person that squints looks steadily at an object, let the observer carefully remark the direction of both his eyes, and observe their motions; and let an opaque body be interposed between the object and the two eyes successively. If the patient, notwithstanding this interposition, and without changing the direction of his eyes, continues to see the object all the time, it may be concluded that he saw it with both eyes at once. But if the interposition of the body between one eye and the object, makes it disappear, then we may be certain, that it was seen by that eye only. In the two following articles, we shall suppose the first to happen, according to the common hypothesis.

6. Upon this supposition, it ought to be inquired, Whether the patient sees an object double in those circumstances wherein it appears double to them who have no squint? Let him, for instance, place a candle at the distance of ten feet; and holding his finger at arm's length between him and the candle, let him observe, when he looks at the candle, whether he sees his finger with both eyes, and whether he sees it single or double; and when he looks at his finger, let him observe whether he sees the candle with both eyes, and whether single or double.

By this observation, it may be determined, whether to this patient, the phænomena of double as well as of single vision are the same as to them who have no squint. If they are not the same; if he sees objects single with two eyes, not only in the cases wherein they appear single, but in those also wherein they appear double to other men; the conclusion to be drawn from this supposition is, that his single vision does not arise from corresponding points in the *retinæ* of his eyes; and that the laws of vision are not the same in him as in the rest of mankind.

7. If, on the other hand, he sees objects double in those cases wherein they appear double to others, the conclusion must be, that he hath

corresponding points in the *retinæ* of his eyes, but unnaturally situate; and their situation may be thus determined.

When he looks at an object, having the axis of one eye directed to it, and the axis of the other turned aside from it; let us suppose a right line to pass from the object through the centre of the diverging eye. We shall, for the sake of perspicuity, call this right line *the natural axis of the eye*: and it will make an angle with the real axis, greater or less, according as his squint is greater or less. We shall also call that point of the *retina* in which the natural axis cuts it, *the natural centre of the retina*; which will be more or less distant from the real centre, according as the squint is greater or less.

Having premised these definitions, it will be evident to those who understand the principles of optics, that in this person the natural centre of one *retina* corresponds with the real centre of the other, in the very same manner as the two real centres correspond in perfect eyes; and that the points similarly situate with regard to the real centre in one *retina*, and the natural centre in the other, do likewise correspond, in the very same manner as the points similarly situate with regard to the two real centres correspond in perfect eyes.

If it is true, as has been commonly affirmed, that one who squints sees an object with both eyes at the same time, and yet sees it single, the squint will most probably be such as we have described in this article. And we may further conclude, that if a person affected with such a squint as we have supposed, could be brought to the habit of looking straight, his sight would thereby be greatly hurt. For he would then see every thing double which he saw with both eyes at the same time; and objects distant from one another, would appear to be confounded together. His eyes are made for squinting, as much as those of other men are made for looking straight; and his sight would be no less injured by looking straight, than that of another man by squinting. He can never see perfectly when he does not squint, unless the corresponding points of his eyes should by custom change their place; but how small the probability of this is, will appear in the 17th section.

Those of the medical faculty who attempt the cure of a squint, would do well to consider, whether it is attended with such symptoms as are above described. If it is, the cure would be worse than the malady: for every one will readily acknowledge, that it is better to put up with the deformity of a squint, than to purchase the cure by the loss of perfect and distinct vision.

8. We shall now return to Dr Jurin's hypothesis, and suppose that our

patient, when he saw objects single notwithstanding his squint, was found, upon trial, to have seen them only with one eye.

We would advise such a patient, to endeavour, by repeated efforts, to lessen his squint, and to bring the axes of his eyes nearer to a parallel direction. We have naturally the power of making small variations in the inclination of the optic axes; and this power may be greatly increased by exercise.

In the ordinary and natural use of our eyes, we can direct their axes to a fixed star; in this case they must be parallel: we can direct them also to an object six inches distant from the eye; and in this case the axes must make an angle of fifteen or twenty degrees. We see young people in their frolics learn to squint, making their eyes either converge or diverge, when they will, to a very considerable degree. Why should it be more difficult for a squinting person to learn to look straight when he pleases? If once, by an effort of his will, he can but lessen his squint, frequent practice will make it easy to lessen it, and will daily increase his power. So that if he begins this practice in youth, and perseveres in it, he may probably, after some time, learn to direct both his eyes to one object.

When he hath acquired this power, it will be no difficult matter to determine, by proper observations, whether the centres of the *retinæ*, and other points similarly situate with regard to the centres, correspond, as in other men.

9. Let us now suppose that he finds this to be the case; and that he sees an object single with both eyes, when the axes of both are directed to it. It will then concern him to acquire the habit of looking straight, as he hath got the power, because he will thereby not only remove a deformity, but improve his sight: and I conceive this habit, like all others, may be got by frequent exercise. He may practise before a mirror when alone, and in company he ought to have those about him, who will observe and admonish him when he squints.

10. What is supposed in the 9th article is not merely imaginary; it is really the case of some squinting persons, as will appear in the next section. Therefore it ought further to be inquired, How it comes to pass, that such a person sees an object which he looks at, only with one eye, when both are open? In order to answer this question, it may be observed, first, Whether, when he looks at an object, the diverging eye is not drawn so close to the nose, that it can have no distinct images? Or, secondly, Whether the pupil of the diverging eye is not covered wholly, or in part, by the upper eye-lid? Dr Jurin observed instances of these cases in persons

that squinted, and assigns them as causes of their seeing the object only with one eye. Thirdly, it may be observed, Whether the diverging eye is not so directed, that the picture of the object falls upon that part of the *retina* where the optic nerve enters, and where there is no vision? This will probably happen in a squint wherein the axes of the eyes converge so as to meet about six inches before the nose.

11. In the last place, it ought to be inquired, Whether such a person hath any distinct vision at all with the diverging eye, at the time he is looking at an object with the other?

It may seem very improbable, that he should be able to read with the diverging eye when the other is covered, and yet, when both are open, have no distinct vision with it at all. But this perhaps will not appear so improbable, if the following considerations are duly attended to.

Let us suppose that one who saw perfectly, gets, by a blow on the head, or some other accident, a permanent and involuntary squint. According to the laws of vision, he will see objects double, and will see objects distant from one another, confounded together: but such vision being very disagreeable, as well as inconvenient, he will do every thing in his power to remedy it. For alleviating such distresses, nature often teaches men wonderful expedients, which the sagacity of a philosopher would be unable to discover. Every accidental motion, every direction or conformation of his eyes, which lessens the evil, will be agreeable; it will be repeated, until it be learned to perfection, and become habitual, even without thought or design. Now, in this case, what disturbs the sight of one eye, is the sight of the other; and all the disagreeable appearances in vision would cease, if the light of one eye was extinct: The sight of one eye will become more distinct and more agreeable, in the same proportion as that of the other becomes faint and indistinct. It may therefore be expected, that every habit will, by degrees, be acquired, which tends to destroy distinct vision in one eye, while it is preserved in the other. These habits will be greatly facilitated, if one eye was at first better than the other; for in that case the best eye will always be directed to the object which he intends to look at, and every habit will be acquired which tends to hinder his seeing it at all, or seeing it distinctly by the other at the same time.

I shall mention one or two habits that may probably be acquired in such a case; perhaps there are others which we cannot so easily conjecture. First, By a small increase or diminution of his squint, he may bring it to correspond with one or other of the cases mentioned in the last article. Secondly, The diverging eye may be brought to such a conformation as

to be extremely short-sighted, and consequently to have no distinct vision
of objects at a distance. I knew this to be the case of one person that
squinted; but cannot say whether the short-sightedness of the diverging
eye was original, or acquired by habit.

5   We see, therefore, that one who squints, and originally saw objects
double by reason of that squint, may acquire such habits, that when he
looks at an object, he shall see it only with one eye: nay, he may acquire
such habits, that when he looks at an object with his best eye, he shall
have no distinct vision with the other at all. Whether this is really the
10   case, being unable to determine in the instances that have fallen under my
observation, I shall leave to future inquiry.

I have endeavoured, in the foregoing articles, to delineate such a process as is proper in observing the phænomena of squinting. I know well
by experience, that this process appears more easy in theory, than it will
15   be found to be in practice; and that in order to carry it on with success,
some qualifications of mind are necessary in the patient, which are not
always to be met with. But if those who have proper opportunities, and
inclination, to observe such phænomena, attend duly to this process, they
may be able to furnish facts less vague and uninstructive than those we
20   meet with, even in authors of reputation. By such facts, vain theories may
be exploded, and our knowledge of the laws of nature, which regard the
noblest of our senses, enlarged.

25   S E C T. XVI.

                    Facts relating to squinting.

HAVING considered the phænomena of squinting hypothetically, and their
connection with corresponding points in the *retinæ*; I shall now mention
30   the facts I have had occasion to observe myself, or have met with in
authors, that can give any light to this subject.

Having examined above twenty persons that squinted, I found in all of
them a defect in the sight of one eye. Four only had so much of distinct
vision in the weak eye, as to be able to read with it, when the other was
35   covered. The rest saw nothing at all distinctly with one eye.

Dr Porterfield says, that this is generally the case of people that squint:
and I suspect it is so more generally than is commonly imagined. Dr Jurin,
in a very judicious dissertation upon squinting, printed in Dr Smith's
Optics, observes, that those who squint, and see with both eyes, never see

the same object with both at the same time; that when one eye is directed straight forward to an object, the other is drawn so close to the nose, that the object cannot at all be seen by it, the images being too oblique and too indistinct to affect the eye. In some squinting persons, he observed the diverging eye drawn under the upper eye-lid while the other was directed to the object. From these observations he concludes, that "the eye is thus distorted, not for the sake of seeing better with it, but rather to avoid seeing at all with it as much as possible." From all the observations he had made, he was satisfied that there is nothing peculiar in the structure of a squinting eye; that the fault is only in its wrong direction; and that this wrong direction is got by habit. Therefore he proposes that method of cure which we have described in the 8th and 9th articles of the last section. He tells us, that he had attempted a cure after this method, upon a young gentleman, with promising hopes of success; but was interrupted by his falling ill of the small-pox, of which he died.

It were to be wished that Dr Jurin had acquainted us, whether he ever brought the young man to direct the axes of both eyes to the same object, and whether, in that case, he saw the object single, and saw it with both eyes; and that he had likewise acquainted us, whether he saw objects double when his squint was diminished. But as to these facts he is silent.

I wished long for an opportunity of trying Dr Jurin's method of curing a squint, without finding one; having always, upon examination, discovered so great a defect in the sight of one eye of the patient as discouraged the attempt.

But I have lately found three young Gentlemen, with whom I am hopeful this method may have success, if they have patience and per-severance in using it. Two of them are brothers, and, before I had access to examine them, had been practising this method by the direction of their tutor, with such success, that the elder looks straight when he is upon his guard: the younger can direct both his eyes to one object; but they soon return to their usual squint.

A third young Gentleman, who had never heard of this method before, by a few days practice, was able to direct both his eyes to one object, but could not keep them long in that direction. All the three agree in this, that when both eyes are directed to one object, they see it and the adjacent objects single; but when they squint, they see objects sometimes single and sometimes double. I observed of all the three, that when they squinted most, that is, in the way they had been accustomed to, the axes of their eyes converged so as to meet five or six inches before the nose.

It is probable that in this case the picture of the object in the diverging eye, must fall upon that part of the *retina* where the optic nerve enters; and therefore the object could not be seen by that eye.

All the three have some defect in the sight of one eye, which none of them knew until I put them upon making trials; and when they squint, the best eye is always directed to the object, and the weak eye is that which diverges from it. But when the best eye is covered, the weak eye is turned directly to the object. Whether this defect of sight in one eye, be the effect of its having been long disused, as it must have been when they squinted; or whether some original defect in one eye might be the occasion of their squinting, time may discover. The two brothers have found the sight of the weak eye improved by using to read with it while the other is covered. The elder can read an ordinary print with the weak eye; the other, as well as the third Gentleman, can only read a large print with the weak eye. I have met with one other person only who squinted, and yet could read a large print with the weak eye. He is a young man, whose eyes are both tender and weak-sighted, but the left much weaker than the right. When he looks at any object, he always directs the right eye to it, and then the left is turned towards the nose so much, that it is impossible for him to see the same object with both eyes at the same time. When the right eye is covered, he turns the left directly to the object; but he sees it indistinctly, and as if it had a mist about it.

I made several experiments, some of them in the company and with the assistance of an ingenious physician, in order to discover, whether objects that were in the axes of the two eyes, were seen in one place confounded together, as in those who have no involuntary squint. The object placed in the axis of the weak eye was a lighted candle, at the distance of eight or ten feet. Before the other eye was placed a printed book, at such a distance as that he could read upon it. He said, that while he read upon the book, he saw the candle but very faintly. And from what we could learn, these two objects did not appear in one place, but had all that angular distance in appearance which they had in reality.

If this was really the case, the conclusion to be drawn from it is, that the corresponding points in his eyes are not situate in the same manner as in other men; and that if he could be brought to direct both eyes to one object, he would see it double. But considering that the young man had never been accustomed to observations of this kind, and that the sight of one eye was so imperfect, I do not pretend to draw this conclusion with certainty from this single instance.

All that can be inferred from these facts is, that of four persons who squint, three appear to have nothing preternatural in the structure of their eyes. The centres of their *retinæ*, and the points similarly situate with regard to the centres, do certainly correspond in the same manner as in
5   other men. So that if they can be brought to the habit of directing their eyes right to an object, they will not only remove a deformity, but improve their sight. With regard to the fourth, the case is dubious, with some probability of a deviation from the usual course of nature in the situation of the corresponding points of his eyes.
10

S E C T. XVII.

Of the effect of custom in seeing objects single.

15   IT appears from the phænomena of single and double vision, recited in Sect. 13. that our seeing an object single with two eyes, depends upon these two things. First, Upon that mutual correspondence of certain points of the *retinæ* which we have often described. Secondly, Upon the two eyes being directed to the object so accurately, that the two images of it
20   fall upon corresponding points. These two things must concur in order to our seeing an object single with two eyes; and as far as they depend upon custom, so far only can single vision depend upon custom.

With regard to the second, that is, the accurate direction of both eyes to the object, I think it must be acknowledged that this is only learned by
25   custom. Nature hath wisely ordained the eyes to move in such manner, that their axes shall always be nearly parallel; but hath left it in our power to vary their inclination a little, according to the distance of the object we look at. Without this power, objects would appear single at one particular distance only; and, at distances much less, or much greater, would always
30   appear double. The wisdom of nature is conspicuous in giving us this power, and no less conspicuous in making the extent of it exactly adequate to the end.

The parallelism of the eyes, in general, is therefore the work of nature; but that precise and accurate direction, which must be varied according to
35   the distance of the object, is the effect of custom. The power which nature hath left us of varying the inclination of the optic axes a little, is turned into a habit of giving them always that inclination which is adapted to the distance of the object.

But it may be asked, What gives rise to this habit? The only answer

that can be given to this question is, that it is found necessary to perfect
and distinct vision. A man who hath lost the sight of one eye, very often
loses the habit of directing it exactly to the object he looks at, because
that habit is no longer of use to him. And if he should recover the sight of
5   his eye, he would recover this habit, by finding it useful. No part of the
human constitution is more admirable than that whereby we acquire habits
which are found useful, without any design or intention. Children must
see imperfectly at first; but, by using their eyes, they learn to use them in
the best manner, and acquire, without intending it, the habits necessary
10 for that purpose. Every man becomes most expert in that kind of vision
which is most useful to him in his particular profession and manner of
life. A miniature painter, or an engraver, sees very near objects better than
a sailor; but the sailor sees very distant objects much better than they. A
person that is short-sighted, in looking at distant objects, gets the habit of
15 contracting the aperture of his eyes, by almost closing his eye-lids. Why?
For no other reason, but because this makes him see the object more
distinct. In like manner, the reason why every man acquires the habit of
directing both eyes accurately to the object, must be, because thereby he
sees it more perfectly and distinctly.

20   It remains to be considered, whether that correspondence between
certain points of the *retinæ*, which is likewise necessary to single vision,
be the effect of custom, or an original property of human eyes.

A strong argument for its being an original property, may be drawn
from the habit just now mentioned of directing the eyes accurately to an
25 object. This habit is got by our finding it necessary to perfect and distinct
vision. But why is it necessary? For no other reason but this, because
thereby the two images of the object falling upon corresponding points,
the eyes assist each other in vision, and the object is seen better by both
together, than it could be by one; but when the eyes are not accurately
30 directed, the two images of an object fall upon points that do not
correspond, whereby the sight of one eye disturbs the sight of the other,
and the object is seen more indistinctly with both eyes, than it would be
with one. Whence it is reasonable to conclude, that this correspondence
of certain points of the *retinæ*, is prior to the habits we acquire in vision,
35 and consequently is natural and original. We have all acquired the habit
of directing our eyes always in a particular manner, which causes single
vision. Now, if nature hath ordained that we should have single vision
only, when our eyes are thus directed, there is an obvious reason why all
mankind should agree in the habit of directing them in this manner. But if

single vision is the effect of custom, any other habit of directing the eyes
would have answered the purpose; and no account can be given why this
particular habit should be so universal; and it must appear very strange,
that no one instance hath been found of a person who had acquired the
5   habit of seeing objects single with both eyes, while they were directed in
any other manner.

The judicious Dr Smith, in his excellent system of optics, maintains
the contrary opinion, and offers some reasonings and facts in proof of it.
He agrees with Bishop Berkeley in attributing it entirely to custom, that
10   we see objects single with two eyes, as well as that we see objects erect
by inverted images. Having considered Bishop Berkeley's reasonings in
the 11th section, we shall now beg leave to make some remarks on what
Dr Smith hath said upon this subject, with the respect due to an author to
whom the world owes, not only many valuable discoveries of his own, but
15   those of the brightest mathematical genius of this age, which, with great
labour, he generously redeemed from oblivion.

He observes, that the question, Why we see objects single with two
eyes? is of the same sort with this, Why we hear sounds single with two
ears? and that the same answer must serve both. The inference intended to
20   be drawn from this observation is, that as the second of these phænomena
is the effect of custom, so likewise is the first.

Now I humbly conceive that the questions are not so much of the same
sort, that the same answer must serve for both; and moreover, that our
hearing single with two ears, is not the effect of custom.

25   Two or more visible objects, although perfectly similar, and seen at
the very same time, may be distinguished by their visible places; but
two sounds perfectly similar, and heard at the same time, cannot be
distinguished; for from the nature of sound, the sensations they occasion
must coalesce into one, and lose all distinction. If therefore it is asked,
30   Why we hear sounds single with two ears? I answer, Not from custom;
but because two sounds which are perfectly like and synchronous, have
nothing by which they can be distinguished. But will this answer fit the
other question? I think not.

The object makes an appearance to each eye, as the sound makes an
35   impression upon each ear; so far the two senses agree. But the visible
appearances may be distinguished by place, when perfectly like in other
respects; the sounds cannot be thus distinguished; and herein the two
senses differ. Indeed, if the two appearances have the same visible place,
they are, in that case, as incapable of distinction as the sounds were, and

we see the object single. But when they have not the same visible place, they are perfectly distinguishable, and we see the object double. We see the object single only, when the eyes are directed in one particular manner; while there are many other ways of directing them within the sphere of our power, by which we see the object double.

It may be taken for a general rule, That things which are produced by custom, may be undone or changed by disuse, or by a contrary custom. On the other hand, it is a strong argument, that an effect is not owing to custom, but to the constitution of nature, when a contrary custom, long continued, is found neither to change nor weaken it. I take this to be the best rule by which we can determine the question presently under consideration. I shall therefore mention two facts brought by Dr Smith, to prove that the corresponding points of the *retinæ* have been changed by custom; and then I shall mention some facts tending to prove, that there are corresponding points of the *retinæ* of the eyes originally, and that custom produces no change in them.

Dr Smith justly attributes to custom that well-known fallacy in feeling, whereby a button pressed with two opposite sides of two contiguous fingers laid across, is felt double. I agree with him, that the cause of this appearance is, that those opposite sides of the fingers have never been used to feel the same object, but two different objects, at the same time. And I beg leave to add, that as custom produces this phænomenon, so a contrary custom destroys it: for if a man frequently accustoms himself to feel the button with his fingers across, it will at last be felt single; as I have found by experience.

One fact is related upon the authority of Martin Folkes, Esq; "who was informed by Dr Hepburn of Lynn, that the Reverend Mr Foster of Clinchwharton, in that neighbourhood, having been blind for some years of a *gutta serena*, was restored to sight by salivation: and that upon his first beginning to see, all objects appeared to him double; but afterwards the two appearances approaching by degrees, he came at last to see single, and as distinctly as he did before he was blind."

Upon this case I observe, first, That it does not prove any change of the corresponding points of the eyes, unless we suppose, what is not affirmed, that Mr Foster directed his eyes to the object at first, when he saw double, with the same accuracy, and in the same manner, that he did afterwards when he saw single. Secondly, If we should suppose this, no account can be given, why at first the two appearances should be seen at one certain angular distance rather than another; or why this angular distance should

gradually decrease, until at last the appearances coincided. How could this effect be produced by custom? But, thirdly, Every circumstance of this case may be accounted for on the supposition that Mr Foster had corresponding points in the *retinæ* of his eyes from the time he began
5   to see, and that custom made no change with regard to them. We need only further suppose, what is common in such cases, that by some years blindness, he had lost the habit of directing his eyes accurately to an object, and that he gradually recovered this habit when he came to see.

The second fact mentioned by Dr Smith, is taken from Mr Cheselden's
10   anatomy; and is this, "A gentleman who, from a blow on the head, had one eye distorted, found every object appear double; but by degrees the most familiar ones became single; and in time all objects became so, without any amendment of the distortion."

I observe here, that it is not said that the two appearances gradually
15   approached, and at last united, without any amendment of the distortion. This would indeed have been a decisive proof of a change in the corresponding points of the *retinæ*; and yet of such a change as could not be accounted for from custom. But this is not said; and if it had been observed, a circumstance so remarkable would have been mentioned
20   by Mr Cheselden, as it was in the other case by Dr Hepburn. We may therefore take it for granted, that one of the appearances vanished by degrees, without approaching to the other. And this I conceive might happen several ways. First, The sight of the distorted eye might gradually decay by the hurt; so the appearances presented by that eye would gradu-
25   ally vanish. Secondly, A small and unperceived change in the manner of directing the eyes, might occasion his not seeing the object with the distorted eye, as appears from Sect. 15. Art. 10. Thirdly, By acquiring the habit of directing one and the same eye always to the object, the faint and oblique appearance, presented by the other eye, might be so little attended
30   to when it became familiar, as not to be perceived. One of these causes, or more of them concurring, might produce the effect mentioned, without any change of the corresponding points of the eyes.

For these reasons, the facts mentioned by Dr Smith, although curious, seem not to be decisive.
35   The following facts ought to be put in the opposite scale. First, In the famous case of the young gentleman couched by Mr Cheselden, after having had cataracts on both eyes until he was thirteen years of age, it appears, that he saw objects single from the time he began to see with both eyes. Mr Cheselden's words are, "And now being lately couched of his

other eye, he says, that objects at first appeared large to this eye, but not so large as they did at first to the other; and looking upon the same object with both eyes, he thought it looked about twice as large as with the first couched eye only, but not double, that we can any ways discover."

5   Secondly, The three young Gentlemen mentioned in the last section, who had squinted, as far as I know, from infancy; as soon as they learned to direct both eyes to an object, saw it single. In these four cases, it appears evident, that the centres of the *retinæ* corresponded originally, and before custom could produce any such effect: for Mr Cheselden's young 10   gentleman had never been accustomed to see at all before he was couched; and the other three had never been accustomed to direct the axes of both eyes to the object.

Thirdly, From the facts recited in Sect. 13. it appears, That from the time we are capable of observing the phænomena of single and double 15   vision, custom makes no change in them.

I have amused myself with such observations for more than thirty years; and in every case wherein I saw the object double at first, I see it so to this day, notwithstanding the constant experience of its being single. In other cases where I know there are two objects, there appears only one, 20   after thousands of experiments.

Let a man look at a familiar object through a polyhedron or multiplying-glass every hour of his life, the number of visible appearances will be the same at last as at first: nor does any number of experiments, or length of time, make the least change.

25   Effects produced by habit, must vary according as the acts by which the habit is acquired are more or less frequent: but the phænomena of single and double vision are so invariable and uniform in all men, and so exactly regulated by mathematical rules, that I think we have good reason to conclude, that they are not the effect of custom, but of fixed and 30   immutable laws of nature.

SECT. XVIII.

Of Dr Porterfield's account of single and double vision.

35

BISHOP BERKELEY and Dr Smith seem to attribute too much to custom in vision, Dr Porterfield too little.

This ingenious writer thinks, that, by an original law of our nature, antecedent to custom and experience, we perceive visible objects in their

true place, not only as to their direction, but likewise as to their distance
from the eye: and therefore he accounts for our seeing objects single, with
two eyes, in this manner. Having the faculty of perceiving the object with
each eye in its true place, we must perceive it with both eyes in the same
5   place; and consequently must perceive it single.

He is aware, that this principle, although it accounts for our seeing
objects single with two eyes, yet does not at all account for our seeing
objects double: and whereas other writers on this subject take it to be
a sufficient cause for double vision, that we have two eyes, and only
10   find it difficult to assign a cause for single vision; on the contrary, Dr
Porterfield's principle throws all the difficulty on the other side.

Therefore, in order to account for the phænomena of double vision, he
advances another principle, without signifying whether he conceives it to
be an original law of our nature, or the effect of custom. It is, That our
15   natural perception of the distance of objects from the eye, is not extended
to all the objects that fall within the field of vision, but limited to that
which we directly look at; and that the circumjacent objects, whatever be
their real distance, are seen at the same distance with the object we look at;
as if they were all in the surface of a sphere whereof the eye is the centre.
20   Thus, single vision is accounted for by our seeing the true distance of
an object which we look at; and double vision, by a false appearance of
distance in objects which we do not directly look at.

We agree with this learned and ingenious author, that it is by a natural
and original principle that we see visible objects in a certain direction from
25   the eye, and honour him as the author of this discovery: but we cannot
assent to either of those principles by which he explains single and double
vision, for the following reasons.

1. Our having a natural and original perception of the distance of objects
from the eye, appears contrary to a well-attested fact: for the young
30   gentleman couched by Mr Cheselden, imagined at first, that whatever he
saw, touched his eye, as what he felt, touched his hand.

2. The perception we have of the distance of objects from the eye,
whether it be from nature or custom, is not so accurate and determinate
as is necessary to produce single vision. A mistake of the twentieth or
35   thirtieth part of the distance of a small object, such as a pin, ought, according to Dr Porterfield's hypothesis, to make it appear double. Very few can
judge of the distance of a visible object with such accuracy. Yet we never
find double vision produced by mistaking the distance of the object. There
are many cases in vision, even with the naked eye, wherein we mistake

the distance of an object by one half or more: why do we see such objects single? When I move my spectacles from my eyes toward a small object, two or three feet distant, the object seems to approach, so as to be seen at last at about half its real distance; but it is seen single at that apparent distance, as well as when we see it with the naked eye at its real distance. And when we look at an object with a binocular telescope, properly fitted to the eyes, we see it single, while it appears fifteen or twenty times nearer than it is. There are then few cases wherein the distance of an object from the eye is seen so accurately as is necessary for single vision, upon this hypothesis: This seems to be a conclusive argument against the account given of single vision. We find likewise, that false judgments or fallacious appearances of the distance of an object, do not produce double vision. This seems to be a conclusive argument against the account given of double vision.

3. The perception we have of the linear distance of objects, seems to be wholly the effect of experience. This I think hath been proved by Bishop Berkeley and by Dr Smith; and when we come to point out the means of judging of distance by sight, it will appear that they are all furnished by experience.

4. Supposing that by a law of our nature, the distance of objects from the eye were perceived most accurately, as well as their direction, it will not follow that we must see the object single. Let us consider what means such a law of nature would furnish for resolving the question, Whether the objects of the two eyes are in one and the same place, and consequently are not two, but one?

Suppose then two right lines, one drawn from the centre of one eye to its object, the other drawn, in like manner, from the centre of the other eye to its object. This law of nature gives us the direction or position of each of these right lines, and the length of each; and this is all that it gives. These are geometrical *data*, and we may learn from geometry what is determined by their means. Is it then determined by these *data*, Whether the two right lines terminate in one and the same point, or not? No truly. In order to determine this, we must have three other *data*. We must know whether the two right lines are in one plane: we must know what angle they make, and we must know the distance between the centres of the eyes. And when these things are known, we must apply the rules of trigonometry, before we can resolve the question, Whether the objects of the two eyes are in one and the same place; and consequently whether they are two or one?

5. That false appearance of distance into which double vision is re-solved, cannot be the effect of custom; for constant experience contradicts it: Neither hath it the features of a law of nature; because it does not answer any good purpose, nor indeed any purpose at all but to deceive us. But why should we seek for arguments, in a question concerning what appears to us, or does not appear? The question is, At what distance do the objects now in my eye appear? Do they all appear at one distance, as if placed in the concave surface of a sphere, the eye being in the centre? Every man surely may know this with certainty; and, if he will but give attention to the testimony of his eyes, needs not ask a philosopher, how visible objects appear to him. Now, it is very true, that if I look up to a star in the heavens, the other stars that appear at the same time, do appear in this manner: Yet this phænomenon does not favour Dr Porterfield's hypothesis; for the stars and heavenly bodies, do not appear at their true distances when we look directly to them, any more than when they are seen obliquely: and if this phænomenon be an argument for Dr Porterfield's second principle, it must destroy the first.

The true cause of this phænomenon will be given afterwards; therefore setting it aside for the present, let us put another case. I sit in my room, and direct my eyes to the door, which appears to be about sixteen feet distant: at the same time I see many other objects faintly and obliquely; the floor, floor-cloth, the table which I write upon, papers, standish, candle, &c. Now, do all these objects appear at the same distance of sixteen feet? Upon the closest attention, I find they do not.

S E C T. XIX.

Of Dr Briggs's theory, and Sir Isaac Newton's conjecture on this subject.

I AM afraid the reader, as well as the writer, is already tired of the subject of single and double vision. The multitude of theories advanced by authors of great name, and the multitude of facts, observed without sufficient skill in optics, or related without attention to the most material and decisive circumstances, have equally contributed to perplex it.

In order to bring it to some issue, I have, in the 13th section, given a more full and regular deduction than had been given heretofore, of the phænomena of single and double vision, in those whose sight is perfect; and have traced them up to one general principle, which appears to be a law of vision in human eyes that are perfect and in their natural state.

In the 14th section I have made it appear, that this law of vision, although excellently adapted to the fabric of human eyes, cannot answer the purposes of vision in some other animals; and therefore, very probably, is not common to all animals. The purpose of the 15th and 16th

5   sections is, to inquire, Whether there be any deviation from this law of vision in those who squint? a question which is of real importance in the medical art, as well as in the philosophy of vision; but which, after all that hath been observed and written on the subject, seems not to be ripe for a determination, for want of proper observations. Those who have had skill

10 to make proper observations, have wanted opportunities; and those who have had opportunities, have wanted skill or attention. I have therefore thought it worth while to give a distinct account of the observations necessary for the determination of this question, and what conclusions may be drawn from the facts observed. I have likewise collected, and set

15 in one view, the most conclusive facts that have occurred in authors, or have fallen under my own observation.

It must be confessed that these facts, when applied to the question in hand, make a very poor figure; and the gentlemen of the medical faculty are called upon, for the honour of their profession, and for the benefit of

20 mankind, to add to them.

All the medical, and all the optical writers, upon the *strabismus*, that I have met with, except Dr Jurin, either affirm, or take it for granted, that squinting persons see the object with both eyes, and yet see it single. Dr Jurin affirms, that squinting persons never see the object with both eyes;

25 and that if they did, they would see it double. If the common opinion be true, the cure of a squint would be as pernicious to the sight of the patient, as the causing of a permanent squint would be to one who naturally had no squint: and therefore no physician ought to attempt such a cure; no patient ought to submit to it. But if Dr Jurin's opinion be true, most young

30 people that squint may cure themselves, by taking some pains; and may not only remove the deformity, but at the same time improve their sight. If the common opinion be true, the centres and other points of the two *retinæ* in squinting persons do not correspond as in other men, and nature in them deviates from her common rule. But if Dr Jurin's opinion be true,

35 there is reason to think, that the same general law of vision which we have found in perfect human eyes, extends also to those which squint.

It is impossible to determine, by reasoning, which of these opinions is true; or whether one may not be found true in some patients, and the other in others. Here, experience and observation are our only guides; and a deduction of instances is the only rational argument. It might therefore have been expected, that the patrons of the contrary opinions should have given instances, in support of them, that are clear and indisputable: but I have not found one such instance on either side of the question, in all the authors I have met with. I have given three instances from my own observation, in confirmation of Dr Jurin's opinion, which admit of no doubt; and one which leans rather to the other opinion, but is dubious. And here I must leave the matter to further observation.

In the 17th section, I have endeavoured to shew, that the correspondence and sympathy of certain points of the two *retinæ*, into which we have resolved all the phænomena of single and double vision, is not, as Dr Smith conceived, the effect of custom, nor can be changed by custom, but is a natural and original property of human eyes: and in the last section, that it is not owing to an original and natural perception of the true distance of objects from the eye, as Dr Porterfield imagined. After this recapitulation, which is intended to relieve the attention of the reader, shall we enter into more theories upon this subject?

That of Dr Briggs, first published in English, in the Philosophical Transactions, afterwards in Latin, under the title of *Nova visionis theoria*, with a prefatory epistle of Sir Isaac Newton to the author, amounts to this, That the fibres of the optic nerves passing from corresponding points of the *retinæ* to the *thalami nervorum opticorum*, having the same length, the same tension, and a similar situation, will have the same tone; and therefore their vibrations, excited by the impression of the rays of light, will be like unisons in music, and will present one and the same image to the mind: but the fibres passing from parts of the *retinæ* which do not correspond, having different tensions and tones, will have discordant vibrations; and therefore present different images to the mind.

I shall not enter upon a particular examination of this theory. It is enough to observe in general, that it is a system of conjectures concerning things of which we are entirely ignorant; and that all such theories in philosophy deserve rather to be laughed at, than to be seriously refuted.

From the first dawn of philosophy to this day, it hath been believed that the optic nerves are intended to carry the images of visible objects from the bottom of the eye to the mind; and that the nerves belonging to the organs of the other senses have a like office. But how do we know this? We conjecture it: and taking this conjecture for a truth, we consider how the nerves may best answer this purpose. The system of the nerves, for many ages, was taken to be a hydraulic engine, consisting of a bundle of pipes which carry to and fro a liquor called *animal spirits*. About the time of Dr Briggs, it was thought rather to be a stringed instrument, composed of vibrating chords, each of which had its proper tension and tone. But some, with as great probability, conceived it to be a wind instrument, which played its part by the vibrations of an elastic æther in the nervous fibrils.

These, I think, are all the engines into which the nervous system hath been moulded by philosophers, for conveying the images of sensible things from the organ to the *sensorium*. And for all that we know of the matter, every man may freely chuse which he thinks fittest for the purpose; for, from fact and experiment, no one of them can claim preference to another. Indeed, they all seem so unhandy engines for carrying images, that a man would be tempted to invent a new one.

Since, therefore, a blind man may guess as well in the dark as one that sees, I beg leave to offer another conjecture touching the nervous system, which I hope will answer the purpose as well as those we have mentioned, and which recommends itself by its simplicity. Why may not the optic nerves, for instance, be made up of empty tubes, opening their mouths wide enough to receive the rays of light which form the image upon the *retina*, and gently conveying them safe, and in their proper order, to the very seat of the soul, until they flash in her face? It is easy for an ingenious philosopher to fit the caliber of these empty tubes to the diameter of the particles of light, so as they shall receive no grosser kind of matter. And if these rays should be in danger of mistaking their way, an expedient may also be found to prevent this. For it requires no more than to bestow upon the tubes of the nervous system a peristaltic motion, like that of the alimentary tube.

It is a peculiar advantage of this hypothesis, that, although all philosophers believe that the species or images of things are conveyed by the nerves to the soul, yet none of their hypotheses shew how this may be done. For how can the images of sound, taste, smell, colour, figure, and all sensible qualities, be made out of the vibrations of musical chords, or the undulations of animal spirits, or of æther? We ought not to suppose means inadequate to the end. Is it not as philosophical, and more intelligible, to conceive, that as the stomach receives its food, so the soul receives her images by a kind of nervous deglutition? I might add, that we need only continue this peristaltic motion of the nervous tubes from the *sensorium* to the extremities of the nerves that serve the muscles, in order to account for muscular motion.

Thus nature will be consonant to herself; and as sensation will be the conveyance of the ideal aliment to the mind, so muscular motion will be the expulsion of the recrementitious part of it. For who can deny, that the images of things conveyed by sensation, may, after due concoction, become fit to be thrown off by muscular motion? I only give hints of these things to the ingenious, hoping that in time this hypothesis may be wrought up into a system as truly philosophical, as that of animal spirits, or the vibration of nervous fibres.

To be serious: In the operations of nature, I hold the theories of a philosopher, which are unsupported by fact, in the same estimation with the dreams of a man asleep, or the ravings of a madman. We laugh at the Indian philosopher, who, to account for the support of the earth, contrived the hypothesis of a huge elephant, and to support the elephant, a huge tortoise. If we will candidly confess the truth, we know as little of the operation of the nerves, as he did of the manner in which the earth is supported; and our hypotheses about animal spirits, or about the tension and vibrations of the nerves, are as like to be true, as his about the support of the earth. His elephant was a hypothesis, and our hypotheses are elephants. Every theory in philosophy, which is built on pure conjecture, is an elephant; and every theory that is supported partly by fact, and partly by conjecture, is like Nebuchadnezzar's image, whose feet were partly of iron, and partly of clay.

The great Newton first gave an example to philosophers, which always ought to be, but rarely hath been followed, by distinguishing his conjectures from his conclusions, and putting the former by themselves, in the modest form of queries. This is fair and legal; but all other philosophical traffick in conjecture, ought to be held contraband and illicit. Indeed his conjectures have commonly more foundation in fact, and more verisimilitude, than the dogmatical theories of most other philosophers; and therefore we ought not to omit that which he hath offered concerning the cause of our seeing objects single with two eyes, in the 15th query annexed to his *Optics*.

"Are not the species of objects seen with both eyes, united where the optic nerves meet before they come into the brain, the fibres on the right side of both nerves uniting there, and after union going thence into the brain in the nerve which is on the right side of the head, and the fibres on the left side of both nerves uniting in the same place, and after union going into the brain in the nerve which is on the left side of the head, and these two nerves meeting in the brain in such a manner that their fibres

make but one entire species or picture, half of which on the right side of
the *sensorium* comes from the right side of both eyes through the right
side of both optic nerves, to the place where the nerves meet, and from
thence on the right side of the head into the brain, and the other half on
5   the left side of the *sensorium* comes, in like manner, from the left side
of both eyes? For the optic nerves of such animals as look the same way
with both eyes (as men, dogs, sheep, oxen, &c.) meet before they come
into the brain; but the optic nerves of such animals as do not look the same
way with both eyes (as of fishes and of the chameleon) do not meet, if I
10   am rightly informed."

I beg leave to distinguish this query into two, which are of very different
natures; one being purely anatomical, the other relating to the carrying
species or pictures of visible objects to the *sensorium*.

The first question is, Whether the fibres coming from corresponding
15   points of the two *retinæ*, do not unite at the place where the optic nerves
meet, and continue united from thence to the brain; so that the right optic
nerve, after the meeting of the two nerves, is composed of the fibres
coming from the right side of both *retinæ*, and the left, of the fibres coming
from the left side of both *retinæ*?

20   This is undoubtedly a curious and rational question; because if we
could find ground from anatomy to answer it in the affirmative, it would
lead us a step forward in discovering the cause of the correspondence
and sympathy which there is between certain points of the two *retinæ*.
For although we know not what is the particular function of the optic
25   nerves, yet it is probable that some impression made upon them, and
communicated along their fibres, is necessary to vision: and whatever
be the nature of this impression, if two fibres are united into one, an
impression made upon one of them, or upon both, may probably produce
the same effect. Anatomists think it a sufficient account of a sympathy
30   between two parts of the body, when they are served by branches of the
same nerve: we should therefore look upon it as an important discovery
in anatomy, if it were found that the same nerve sent branches to the
corresponding points of the *retinæ*.

But hath any such discovery been made? No, not so much as in one
35   subject, as far as I can learn. But in several subjects, the contrary seems
to have been discovered. Dr Porterfield hath given us two cases at length
from Vesalius, and one from Cæsalpinus, wherein the optic nerves, after
touching one another as usual, appeared to be reflected back to the same
side whence they came, without any mixture of their fibres. Each of these

persons had lost an eye some time before his death, and the optic nerve belonging to that eye was shrunk, so that it could be distinguished from the other at the place where they met. Another case which the same author gives from Vesalius, is still more remarkable; for in it the optic nerves did not touch at all; and yet, upon inquiry, those who were most familiar with the person in his lifetime, declared that he never complained of any defect of sight, or of his seeing objects double. Diemerbroeck tells us, that Aquapendens and Valverda likewise affirm, that they have met with subjects wherein the optic nerves did not touch.

As these observations were made before Sir Isaac Newton put this query, it is uncertain whether he was ignorant of them, or whether he suspected some inaccuracy in them, and desired that the matter might be more carefully examined. But from the following passage of the most accurate Winslow, it does not appear, that later observations have been more favourable to his conjecture. "The union of these [optic] nerves, by the small curvatures of their *cornua*, is very difficult to be unfolded in human bodies. This union is commonly found to be very close, but in some subjects it seems to be no more than a strong adhesion, in others to be partly made by an intersection or crossing of fibres. They have been found quite separate; and in other subjects, one of them has been found to be very much altered both in size and colour through its whole passage, the other remaining in its natural state."

When we consider this conjecture of Sir Isaac Newton by itself, it appears more ingenious, and to have more verisimilitude, than any thing that has been offered upon the subject; and we admire the caution and modesty of the author, in proposing it only as a subject of inquiry: but when we compare it with the observations of anatomists which contradict it, we are naturally led to this reflection, That if we trust to the conjectures of men of the greatest genius in the operations of nature, we have only the chance of going wrong in an ingenious manner.

The second part of the query is, Whether the two species of objects from the two eyes are not, at the place where the optic nerves meet, united into one species or picture, half of which is carried thence to the *sensorium* in the right optic nerve, and the other half in the left? and whether these two halves are not so put together again at the *sensorium*, as to make one species or picture?

Here it seems natural to put the previous question, What reason have we to believe, that pictures of objects are at all carried to the *sensorium*, either by the optic nerves, or by any other nerves? Is it not possible, that this great philosopher, as well as many of a lower form, having been led into this opinion at first by education, may have continued in it, because he never thought of calling it in question? I confess this was my own case for a considerable part of my life. But since I was led by accident to think seriously what reason I had to believe it, I could find none at all. It seems to be a mere hypothesis, as much as the Indian philosopher's elephant. I am not conscious of any pictures of external objects in my *sensorium*, any more than in my stomach: the things which I perceive by my senses, appear to be external, and not in any part of the brain; and my sensations, properly so called, have no resemblance of external objects.

The conclusion from all that hath been said, in no less than seven sections, upon our seeing objects single with two eyes, is this, That, by an original property of human eyes, objects painted upon the centres of the two *retinæ*, or upon points similarly situate with regard to the centres, appear in the same visible place; that the most plausible attempts to account for this property of the eyes, have been unsuccessful; and, therefore, that it must be either a primary law of our constitution, or the consequence of some more general law which is not yet discovered.

We have now finished what we intended to say, both of the visible appearances of things to the eye, and of the laws of our constitution by which those appearances are exhibited. But it was observed, in the beginning of this chapter, that the visible appearances of objects serve only as signs of their distance, magnitude, figure, and other tangible qualities. The visible appearance is that which is presented to the mind by nature, according to those laws of our constitution which have been explained. But the thing signified by that appearance, is that which is presented to the mind by custom.

When one speaks to us in a language that is familiar, we hear certain sounds, and this is all the effect that his discourse has upon us by nature: but by custom we understand the meaning of these sounds; and therefore we fix our attention, not upon the sounds, but upon the things signified by them. In like manner, we see only the visible appearance of objects by nature; but we learn by custom to interpret these appearances, and to understand their meaning. And when this visual language is learned, and becomes familiar, we attend only to the things signified; and cannot, without great difficulty, attend to the signs by which they are presented. The mind passes from one to the other so rapidly, and so familiarly, that no trace of the sign is left in the memory, and we seem immediately, and without the intervention of any sign, to perceive the thing signified.

When I look at the apple-tree which stands before my window, I perceive, at the first glance, its distance and magnitude, the roughness of its trunk, the disposition of its branches, the figure of its leaves and fruit. I seem to perceive all these things immediately. The visible appearance which presented them all to the mind, has entirely escaped me; I cannot, without great difficulty, and painful abstraction, attend to it, even when it stands before me. Yet it is certain that this visible appearance only, is presented to my eye by nature, and that I learned by custom to collect all the rest from it. If I had never seen before now, I should not perceive either the distance or tangible figure of the tree, and it would have required the practice of seeing for many months, to change that original perception which nature gave me by my eyes, into that which I now have by custom.

The objects which we see naturally and originally, as hath been before observed, have length and breadth, but no thickness, nor distance from the eye. Custom, by a kind of legerdemain, withdraws gradually these original and proper objects of sight, and substitutes in their place objects of touch, which have length, breadth, and thickness, and a determinate distance from the eye. By what means this change is brought about, and what principles of the human mind concur in it, we are next to inquire.

SECT. XX.

Of perception in general.

SENSATION, and the perception of external objects by the senses, though very different in their nature, have commonly been considered as one and the same thing. The purposes of common life do not make it necessary to distinguish them, and the received opinions of philosophers tend rather to confound them: but, without attending carefully to this distinction, it is impossible to have any just conception of the operations of our senses. The most simple operations of the mind, admit not of a logical definition: all we can do is to describe them, so as to lead those who are conscious of them in themselves, to attend to them, and reflect upon them: and it is often very difficult to describe them so as to answer this intention.

The same mode of expression is used to denote sensation and perception; and therefore we are apt to look upon them as things of the same nature. Thus, *I feel a pain; I see a tree*: the first denoteth a sensation, the last a perception. The grammatical analysis of both expressions is the same: for both consist of an active verb and an object. But, if we attend to the things signified by these expressions, we shall find, that in the first, the distinction between the act and the object is not real but grammatical; in the second, the distinction is not only grammatical but real.

5 The form of the expression, *I feel pain*, might seem to imply, that the feeling is something distinct from the pain felt; yet, in reality, there is no distinction. As *thinking a thought* is an expression which could signify no more than *thinking*, so *feeling a pain* signifies no more than *being pained*. What we have said of pain is applicable to every other mere sensation.

10 It is difficult to give instances, very few of our sensations having names; and where they have, the name being common to the sensation, and to something else which is associated with it. But when we attend to the sensation by itself, and separate it from other things which are conjoined with it in the imagination, it appears to be something which can have no

15 existence but in a sentient mind, no distinction from the act of the mind by which it is felt.

Perception, as we here understand it, hath always an object distinct from the act by which it is perceived; an object which may exist whether it be perceived or not. I perceive a tree that grows before my window;

20 there is here an object which is perceived, and an act of the mind by which it is perceived; and these two are not only distinguishable, but they are extremely unlike in their natures. The object is made up of a trunk, branches, and leaves; but the act of the mind by which it is perceived, hath neither trunk, branches, nor leaves. I am conscious of this act of

25 my mind, and I can reflect upon it; but it is too simple to admit of an analysis, and I cannot find proper words to describe it. I find nothing that resembles it so much as the remembrance of the tree, or the imagination of it. Yet both these differ essentially from perception; they differ likewise one from another. It is in vain that a philosopher assures me, that the

30 imagination of the tree, the remembrance of it, and the perception of it, are all one, and differ only in degree of vivacity. I know the contrary; for I am as well acquainted with all the three, as I am with the apartments of my own house. I know this also, that the perception of an object implies both a conception of its form, and a belief of its present existence. I know

35 moreover, that this belief is not the effect of argumentation and reasoning; it is the immediate effect of my constitution.

I am aware, that this belief which I have in perception, stands exposed to the strongest batteries of scepticism. But they make no great impression upon it. The sceptic asks me, Why do you believe the existence of

the external object which you perceive? This belief, Sir, is none of my
manufacture; it came from the mint of Nature; it bears her image and
superscription; and, if it is not right, the fault is not mine: I even took it
upon trust, and without suspicion. Reason, says the sceptic, is the only
5   judge of truth, and you ought to throw off every opinion and every belief
that is not grounded on reason. Why, Sir, should I believe the faculty of
reason more than that of perception; they came both out of the same shop,
and were made by the same artist; and if he puts one piece of false ware
into my hands, what should hinder him from putting another?

10   Perhaps the sceptic will agree to distrust reason, rather than give any
credit to perception. For, says he, since, by your own concession, the
object which you perceive, and that act of your mind, by which you
perceive it, are quite different things, the one may exist without the other;
and as the object may exist without being perceived, so the perception may
15   exist without an object. There is nothing so shameful in a philosopher as
to be deceived and deluded; and therefore you ought to resolve firmly to
with-hold assent, and to throw off this belief of external objects, which
may be all delusion. For my part, I will never attempt to throw it off; and
although the sober part of mankind will not be very anxious to know my
20   reasons, yet if they can be of use to any sceptic, they are these.

First, Because it is not in my power: why then should I make a vain
attempt? It would be agreeable to fly to the moon, and to make a visit
to Jupiter and Saturn; but when I know that Nature has bound me down
by the law of gravitation to this planet which I inhabit, I rest contented,
25   and quietly suffer myself to be carried along in its orbit. My belief is
carried along by perception, as irresistibly as my body by the earth. And
the greatest sceptic will find himself to be in the same condition. He may
struggle hard to disbelieve the informations of his senses, as a man does
to swim against a torrent; but ah! it is in vain. It is in vain that he strains
30   every nerve, and wrestles with nature, and with every object that strikes
upon his senses. For after all, when his strength is spent in the fruitless
attempt, he will be carried down the torrent with the common herd of
believers.

Secondly, I think it would not be prudent to throw off this belief, if it
35   were in my power. If Nature intended to deceive me, and impose upon
me by false appearances, and I, by my great cunning and profound logic,
have discovered the imposture; prudence would dictate to me in this case,
even to put up this indignity done me, as quietly as I could, and not to call
her an impostor to her face, lest she should be even with me in another

way. For what do I gain by resenting this injury? You ought at least not to believe what she says. This indeed seems reasonable, if she intends to impose upon me. But what is the consequence? I resolve not to believe my senses. I break my nose against a post that comes in my way; I step into a dirty kennel; and, after twenty such wise and rational actions, I am taken up and clapt into a mad-house. Now, I confess I would rather make one of the credulous fools whom Nature imposes upon, than of those wise and rational philosophers who resolve to with-hold assent at all this expence. If a man pretends to be a sceptic with regard to the informations of sense, and yet prudently keeps out of harm's way as other men do, he must excuse my suspicion, that he either acts the hypocrite, or imposes upon himself. For if the scale of his belief were so evenly poised, as to lean no more to one side than to the contrary, it is impossible that his actions could be directed by any rules of common prudence.

Thirdly, Although the two reasons already mentioned are perhaps two more than enough, I shall offer a third. I gave implicit belief to the informations of Nature by my senses, for a considerable part of my life, before I had learned so much logic as to be able to start a doubt concerning them. And now, when I reflect upon what is past, I do not find that I have been imposed upon by this belief. I find, that without it I must have perished by a thousand accidents. I find, that without it I should have been no wiser now than when I was born. I should not even have been able to acquire that logic which suggests these sceptical doubts with regard to my senses. Therefore, I consider this instinctive belief as one of the best gifts of Nature. I thank the Author of my being who bestowed it upon me, before the eyes of my reason were opened, and still bestows it upon me to be my guide, where reason leaves me in the dark. And now I yield to the direction of my senses, not from instinct only, but from confidence and trust in a faithful and beneficent Monitor, grounded upon the experience of his paternal care and goodness.

In all this, I deal with the Author of my being, no otherwise than I thought it reasonable to deal with my parents and tutors. I believed by in-stinct whatever they told me, long before I had the idea of a lie, or thought of the possibility of their deceiving me. Afterwards, upon reflection, I found they had acted like fair and honest people who wished me well. I found, that if I had not believed what they told me, before I could give a reason of my belief, I had to this day been little better than a changeling. And although this natural credulity hath sometimes occasioned my being imposed upon by deceivers, yet it hath been of infinite advantage to me upon the whole; therefore I consider it as another good gift of Nature. And I continue to give that credit, from reflection, to those of whose integrity and veracity I have had experience, which before I gave from instinct.

There is a much greater similitude than is commonly imagined, between the testimony of nature given by our senses, and the testimony of men given by language. The credit we give to both is at first the effect of instinct only. When we grow up, and begin to reason about them, the credit given to human testimony is restrained, and weakened, by the experience we have of deceit. But the credit given to the testimony of our senses, is established and confirmed by the uniformity and constancy of the laws of Nature.

Our perceptions are of two kinds: some are natural and original, others acquired, and the fruit of experience. When I perceive that this is the taste of cyder, that of brandy; that this is the smell of an apple, that of an orange; that this is the noise of thunder, that the ringing of bells; this the sound of a coach passing, that the voice of such a friend; these perceptions, and others of the same kind, are not original, they are acquired. But the perception which I have by touch, of the hardness and softness of bodies, of their extension, figure, and motion, is not acquired, it is original.

In all our senses, the acquired perceptions are many more than the original, especially in sight. By this sense we perceive originally the visible figure and colour of bodies only, and their visible place: but we learn to perceive by the eye, almost every thing which we can perceive by touch. The original perceptions of this sense, serve only as signs to introduce the acquired.

The signs by which objects are presented to us in perception, are the language of Nature to man; and as, in many respects, it hath great affinity with the language of man to man; so particularly in this, that both are partly natural and original, partly acquired by custom. Our original or natural perceptions are analogous to the natural language of man to man, of which we took notice in the 4th chapter; and our acquired perceptions are analogous to artificial language, which, in our mother-tongue, is got very much in the same manner with our acquired perceptions, as we shall afterwards more fully explain.

Not only men, but children, idiots, and brutes, acquire by habit many perceptions which they had not originally. Almost every employment in life, hath perceptions of this kind that are peculiar to it. The shepherd knows every sheep of his flock, as we do our acquaintance, and can pick them out of another flock one by one. The butcher knows by sight the weight and quality of his beeves and sheep before they are killed. The farmer perceives by his eye, very nearly, the quantity of hay in a rick, or of corn in a heap. The sailor sees the burthen, the built, and the distance of a ship at sea, while she is a great way off. Every man accustomed to writing, distinguishes his acquaintance by their hand-writing, as he does by their faces. And the painter distinguishes in the works of his art, the style of all the great masters. In a word, acquired perception is very different in different persons, according to the diversity of objects about which they are employed, and the application they bestow in observing them.

Perception ought not only to be distinguished from sensation, but likewise from that knowledge of the objects of sense which is got by reasoning. There is no reasoning in perception, as hath been observed. The belief which is implied in it, is the effect of instinct. But there are many things, with regard to sensible objects, which we can infer from what we perceive; and such conclusions of reason ought to be distinguished from what is merely perceived. When I look at the moon, I perceive her to be sometimes circular, sometimes horned, and sometimes gibbous. This is simple perception, and is the same in the philosopher, and in the clown: but from these various appearances of her enlightened part, I infer that she is really of a spherical figure. This conclusion is not obtained by simple perception, but by reasoning. Simple perception has the same relation to the conclusions of reason drawn from our perceptions, as the axioms in mathematics have to the propositions. I cannot demonstrate, that two quantities which are equal to the same quantity, are equal to each other; neither can I demonstrate, that the tree which I perceive, exists. But, by the constitution of my nature, my belief is irresistibly carried along by my apprehension of the axiom; and, by the constitution of my nature, my belief is no less irresistibly carried along by my perception of the tree. All reasoning is from principles. The first principles of mathematical reasoning are mathematical axioms and definitions; and the first principles of all our reasoning about existences, are our perceptions. The first principles of every kind of reasoning are given us by Nature, and are of equal authority with the faculty of reason itself, which is also the gift of Nature. The conclusions of reason are all built upon first principles, and can have no other foundation. Most justly, therefore, do such principles disdain to be tried by reason, and laugh at all the artillery of the logician, when it is directed against them.

When a long train of reasoning is necessary in demonstrating a mathematical proposition, it is easily distinguished from an axiom, and they seem to be things of a very different nature. But there are some propositions which lie so near to axioms, that it is difficult to say, whether they ought to be held as axioms, or demonstrated as propositions. The same thing holds with regard to perception, and the conclusions drawn from it. Some of these conclusions follow our perceptions so easily, and are so immediately connected with them, that it is difficult to fix the limit which divides the one from the other.

Perception, whether original or acquired, implies no exercise of reason; and is common to men, children, idiots, and brutes. The more obvious conclusions drawn from our perceptions, by reason, make what we call *common understanding*; by which men conduct themselves in the common affairs of life, and by which they are distinguished from idiots. The more remote conclusions which are drawn from our perceptions, by reason, make what we commonly call *science* in the various parts of nature, whether in agriculture, medicine, mechanics, or in any part of natural philosophy. When I see a garden in good order, containing a great variety of things of the best kinds, and in the most flourishing condition, I immediately conclude from these signs, the skill and industry of the gardener. A farmer, when he rises in the morning, and perceives that the neighbouring brook overflows his field, concludes that a great deal of rain hath fallen in the night. Perceiving his fence broken, and his corn trodden down, he concludes that some of his own or his neighbours cattle have broke loose. Perceiving that his stable-door is broke open, and some of his horses gone, he concludes that a thief has carried them off. He traces the prints of his horses feet in the soft ground, and by them discovers which road the thief hath taken. These are instances of common understanding, which dwells so near to perception, that it is difficult to trace the line which divides the one from the other. In like manner, the science of nature dwells so near to common understanding, that we cannot discern where the latter ends and the former begins. I perceive that bodies lighter than water swim in water, and that those which are heavier sink. Hence I conclude, that if a body remains wherever it is put under water, whether at the top or bottom, it is precisely of the same weight with water. If it will rest only when part of it is above water, it is lighter than water. And the greater the part above water is, compared with the whole, the lighter is the body. If it had no gravity at all, it would make no impression upon the water, but stand wholly above it. Thus, every man, by common understanding, has a rule by which he judges of the specific gravity of bodies which swim in water; and a step or two more leads him into the science of hydrostatics.

All that we know of nature, or of existences, may be compared to a tree, which hath its root, trunk, and branches. In this tree of knowledge, perception is the root, common understanding is the trunk, and the sciences are the branches.

S E C T. XXI.

Of the process of nature in perception.

ALTHOUGH there is no reasoning in perception, yet there are certain means and instruments, which, by the appointment of Nature, must intervene between the object and our perception of it; and, by these, our perceptions are limited and regulated. First, If the object is not in contact with the organ of sense, there must be some medium which passes between them. Thus, in vision, the rays of light; in hearing, the vibrations of elastic air; in smelling, the effluvia of the body smelled, must pass from the object to the organ; otherwise we have no perception. Secondly, There must be some action or impression upon the organ of sense, either by the immediate application of the object, or by the medium that goes between them. Thirdly, The nerves which go from the brain to the organ, must receive some impression by means of that which was made upon the organ; and, probably, by means of the nerves, some impression must be made upon the brain. Fourthly, The impression made upon the organ, nerves, and brain, is followed by a sensation. And, last of all, This sensation is followed by the perception of the object.

Thus our perception of objects is the result of a train of operations; some of which affect the body only, others affect the mind. We know very little of the nature of some of these operations; we know not at all how they are connected together, or in what way they contribute to that perception which is the result of the whole: but, by the laws of our constitution, we perceive objects in this, and in no other way.

There may be other beings, who can perceive external objects without rays of light, or vibrations of air, or effluvia of bodies, without impressions on bodily organs, or even without sensations: but we are so framed by the Author of Nature, that even when we are surrounded by external objects, we may perceive none of them. Our faculty of perceiving an object lies dormant, until it is roused and stimulated by a certain corresponding sensation. Nor is this sensation always at hand to perform its office; for it enters into the mind only in consequence of a certain corresponding impression made on the organ of sense by the object.

Let us trace this correspondence of impressions, sensations, and perceptions, as far as we can; beginning with that which is first in order, the impression made upon the bodily organ. But, alas! we know not of what nature these impressions are, far less how they excite sensations in the mind.

We know that one body may act upon another by pressure, by percussion, by attraction, by repulsion, and probably in many other ways which we neither know, nor have names to express. But in which of these ways objects, when perceived by us, act upon the organs of sense, these organs upon the nerves, and the nerves upon the brain, we know not. Can any man tell me how, in vision, the rays of light act upon the *retina*, how the *retina* acts upon the optic nerve, and how the optic nerve acts upon the brain? No man can. When I feel the pain of the gout in my toe, I know that there is some unusual impression made upon that part of my body. But of what kind is it? Are the small vessels distended with some redundant elastic, or unelastic fluid? Are the fibres unusually stretched? Are they torn asunder by force, or gnawed and corroded by some acrid humour? I can answer none of these questions. All that I feel is pain, which is not an impression upon the body, but upon the mind; and all that I perceive by this sensation is, that some distemper in my toe occasions this pain. But as I know not the natural temper and texture of my toe when it is at ease, I know as little what change or disorder of its parts occasions this uneasy sensation. In like manner, in every other sensation there is, without doubt, some impression made upon the organ of sense; but an impression of which we know not the nature. It is too subtile to be discovered by our senses, and we may make a thousand conjectures without coming near the truth. If we understood the structure of our organs of sense so minutely, as to discover what effects are produced upon them by external objects, this knowledge would contribute nothing to our perception of the object; for they perceive as distinctly who know least about the manner of perception, as the greatest adepts. It is necessary that the impression be made upon our organs, but not that it be known. Nature carries on this part of the process of perception, without our consciousness or concurrence.

But we cannot be unconscious of the next step in this process, the sensation of the mind, which always immediately follows the impression made upon the body. It is essential to a sensation to be felt, and it can be nothing more than we feel it to be. If we can only acquire the habit of attending to our sensations, we may know them perfectly. But how are the sensations of the mind produced by impressions upon the body? Of this we are absolutely ignorant, having no means of knowing how the body acts upon the mind, or the mind upon the body. When we consider the nature and attributes of both, they seem to be so different, and so unlike, that we can find no handle by which the one may lay hold of the other. There is a deep and a dark gulf between them, which our understanding cannot pass; and the manner of their correspondence and intercourse is absolutely unknown.

Experience teaches us, that certain impressions upon the body are constantly followed by certain sensations of the mind; and that, on the other hand, certain determinations of the mind are constantly followed by certain motions in the body: but we see not the chain that ties these things together. Who knows but their connection may be arbitrary, and owing to the will of our Maker? Perhaps the same sensations might have been connected with other impressions, or other bodily organs. Perhaps we might have been so made, as to taste with our fingers, to smell with our ears, and to hear by the nose. Perhaps we might have been so made, as to have all the sensations and perceptions which we have, without any impression made upon our bodily organs at all.

However these things may be, if Nature had given us nothing more than impressions made upon the body, and sensations in our minds corresponding to them, we should in that case have been merely sentient, but not percipient beings. We should never have been able to form a conception of any external object, far less a belief of its existence. Our sensations have no resemblance to external objects; nor can we discover, by our reason, any necessary connection between the existence of the former, and that of the latter.

We might perhaps have been made of such a constitution, as to have our present perceptions connected with other sensations. We might perhaps have had the perception of external objects, without either impressions upon the organs of sense, or sensations. Or lastly, The perceptions we have, might have been immediately connected with the impressions upon our organs, without any intervention of sensations. This last seems really to be the case in one instance, to wit, in our perception of the visible figure of bodies, as was observed in the 8th section of this chapter.

The process of Nature in perception by the senses, may therefore be conceived as a kind of drama, wherein some things are performed behind the scenes, others are represented to the mind in different scenes, one succeeding another. The impression made by the object upon the organ, either by immediate contact, or by some intervening medium, as well as the impression made upon the nerves and brain, is performed behind the scenes, and the mind sees nothing of it. But every such impression, by the laws of the drama, is followed by a sensation, which is the first scene exhibited to the mind; and this scene is quickly succeeded by another, which is the perception of the object.

In this drama, Nature is the actor, we are the spectators. We know nothing of the machinery by means of which every different impression upon the organ, nerves, and brain, exhibits its corresponding sensation; or of the machinery by means of which each sensation exhibits its corresponding perception. We are inspired with the sensation, and we are inspired with the corresponding perception, by means unknown. And because the mind passes immediately from the sensation to that conception and belief of the object which we have in perception, in the same manner as it passes from signs to the things signified by them, we have therefore called our sensations *signs of external objects*; finding no word more proper to express the function which Nature hath assigned them in perception, and the relation which they bear to their corresponding objects.

There is no necessity of a resemblance between the sign and the thing signified: and indeed no sensation can resemble any external object. But there are two things necessary to our knowing things by means of signs. First, That a real connection between the sign and thing signified be established, either by the course of nature, or by the will and appointment of men. When they are connected by the course of nature, it is a natural sign; when by human appointment, it is an artificial sign. Thus, smoke is a natural sign of fire; certain features are natural signs of anger: but our words, whether expressed by articulate sounds or by writing, are artificial signs of our thoughts and purposes.

Another requisite to our knowing things by signs is, that the appearance of the sign to the mind, be followed by the conception and belief of the thing signified. Without this the sign is not understood or interpreted; and therefore is no sign to us, however fit in its own nature for that purpose.

Now, there are three ways in which the mind passes from the appearance of a natural sign to the conception and belief of the thing signified; by original principles of our constitution, by custom, and by reasoning.

Our original perceptions are got in the first of these ways, our acquired perceptions in the second, and all that reason discovers of the course of

nature, in the third. In the first of these ways, Nature, by means of the sensations of touch, informs us of the hardness and softness of bodies; of their extension, figure, and motion; and of that space in which they move and are placed, as hath been already explained in the fifth chapter of this
5   inquiry. And in the second of these ways she informs us, by means of our eyes, of almost all the same things which originally we could perceive only by touch.

In order, therefore, to understand more particularly how we learn to perceive so many things by the eye, which originally could be perceived
10   only by touch, it will be proper, first, To point out the signs by which those things are exhibited to the eye, and their connection with the things signified by them; and, secondly, To consider how the experience of this connection produces that habit by which the mind, without any reasoning or reflection, passes from the sign to the conception and belief of the thing
15   signified.

Of all the acquired perceptions which we have by sight, the most remarkable is the perception of the distance of objects from the eye; we shall therefore particularly consider the signs by which this perception is exhibited, and only make some general remarks with regard to the signs
20   which are used in other acquired perceptions.

S E C T. XXII.

Of the signs by which we learn to perceive distance from the eye.

25
It was before observed in general, That the original perceptions of sight are signs which serve to introduce those that are acquired: but this is not to be understood as if no other signs were employed for that purpose. There are several motions of the eyes, which, in order to distinct vision, must be
30   varied, according as the object is more or less distant; and such motions being by habit connected with the corresponding distances of the object, become signs of those distances. These motions were at first voluntary and unconfined; but as the intention of Nature was, to produce perfect and distinct vision by their means, we soon learn by experience to regulate
35   them according to that intention only, without the least reflection.

A ship requires a different trim for every variation of the direction and strength of the wind: and, if we may be allowed to borrow that word, the eyes require a different trim for every degree of light, and for every variation of the distance of the object, while it is within certain limits. The eyes are trimmed for a particular object, by contracting certain muscles, and relaxing others; as the ship is trimmed for a particular wind, by drawing certain ropes, and slackening others. The sailor learns the trim of his ship, as we learn the trim of our eyes, by experience. A ship, although the noblest machine that human art can boast, is far inferior to the eye in this respect, that it requires art and ingenuity to navigate her; and a sailor must know what ropes he must pull, and what he must slacken, to fit her to a particular wind: but with such superior wisdom is the fabric of the eye, and the principles of its motion contrived, that it requires no art nor ingenuity to see by it. Even that part of vision which is got by experience, is attained by idiots. We need not know what muscles we are to contract, and what we are to relax, in order to fit the eye to a particular distance of the object.

But although we are not conscious of the motions we perform, in order to fit the eyes to the distance of the object, we are conscious of the effort employed in producing these motions; and probably have some sensation which accompanies them, to which we give as little attention as to other sensations. And thus, an effort consciously exerted, or a sensation consequent upon that effort, comes to be conjoined with the distance of the object which gave occasion to it, and by this conjunction becomes a sign of that distance. Some instances of this will appear in considering the means or signs by which we learn to see the distance of objects from the eye. In the enumeration of these, we agree with Dr Porterfield, notwithstanding that distance from the eye, in his opinion, is perceived originally, but in our opinion, by experience only.

In general, when a near object affects the eye in one manner, and the same object, placed at a greater distance, affects it in a different manner; these various affections of the eye become signs of the corresponding distances. The means of perceiving distance by the eye, will therefore be explained, by shewing in what various ways objects affect the eye differently, according to their proximity or distance.

1. It is well known, that to see objects distinctly at various distances, the form of the eye must undergo some change. And Nature hath given us the power of adapting it to near objects, by the contraction of certain muscles, and to distant objects, by the contraction of other muscles. As to the manner in which this is done, and the muscular parts employed, anatomists do not altogether agree. The ingenious Dr Jurin, in his excellent essay on distinct and indistinct vision, seems to have given the most probable account of this matter; and to him I refer the reader.

But whatever be the manner in which this change of the form of the eye is effected, it is certain that young people have commonly the power of adapting their eyes to all distances of the object, from six or seven inches, to fifteen or sixteen feet; so as to have perfect and distinct vision at any distance within these limits. From this it follows, that the effort we consciously employ to adapt the eye to any particular distance of objects within these limits, will be connected and associated with that distance, and will become a sign of it. When the object is removed beyond the farthest limit of distinct vision, it will be seen indistinctly; but more or less so, according as its distance is greater or less: so that the degrees of indistinctness of the object may become the signs of distances considerably beyond the farthest limit of distinct vision.

If we had no other mean but this, of perceiving the distance of visible objects, the most distant would not appear to be above twenty or thirty feet from the eye, and the tops of houses and trees would seem to touch the clouds; for in that case the signs of all greater distances being the same, they have the same signification, and give the same perception of distance.

But it is of more importance to observe, that because the nearest limit of distinct vision in the time of youth, when we learn to perceive distance by the eye, is about six or seven inches, no object seen distinctly, ever appears to be nearer than six or seven inches from the eye. We can, by art, make a small object appear distinct, when it is in reality not above half an inch from the eye; either by using a single microscope, or by looking through a small pin-hole in a card. When, by either of these means, an object is made to appear distinct, however small its distance is in reality, it seems to be removed at least to the distance of six or seven inches, that is, within the limits of distinct vision.

This observation is the more important, because it affords the only reason we can give why an object is magnified either by a single microscope, or by being seen through a pin-hole; and the only mean by which we can ascertain the degree in which the object will be magnified by either. Thus, if the object is really half an inch distant from the eye, and appears to be seven inches distant, its diameter will seem to be enlarged in the same proportion as its distance, that is, fourteen times.

2. In order to direct both eyes to an object, the optic axes must have a greater or less inclination, according as the object is nearer or more distant. And although we are not conscious of this inclination, yet we are conscious of the effort employed in it. By this mean we perceive small

distances more accurately than we could do by the conformation of the
eye only. And therefore we find, that those who have lost the sight of one
eye, are apt, even within arm's-length, to make mistakes in the distance of
objects, which are easily avoided by those who see with both eyes. Such
mistakes are often discovered in snuffing a candle, in threading a needle,
or in filling a tea-cup.

When a picture is seen with both eyes, and at no great distance, the
representation appears not so natural as when it is seen only with one. The
intention of painting being to deceive the eye, and to make things appear
at different distances which in reality are upon the same piece of canvas,
this deception is not so easily put upon both eyes as upon one; because we
perceive the distance of visible objects more exactly and determinately
with two eyes than with one. If the shading and relief be executed in the
best manner, the picture may have almost the same appearance to one
eye as the objects themselves would have, but it cannot have the same
appearance to both. This is not the fault of the artist, but an unavoidable
imperfection in the art. And it is owing to what we just now observed,
that the perception we have of the distance of objects by one eye is more
uncertain, and more liable to deception, than that which we have by both.

The great impediment, and I think the only invincible impediment,
to that agreeable deception of the eye which the painter aims at, is the
perception which we have of the distance of visible objects from the eye,
partly by means of the conformation of the eye, but chiefly by means of
the inclination of the optic axes. If this perception could be removed, I see
no reason why a picture might not be made so perfect as to deceive the eye
in reality, and to be mistaken for the original object. Therefore, in order to
judge of the merit of a picture, we ought, as much as possible, to exclude
these two means of perceiving the distance of the several parts of it.

In order to remove this perception of distance, the connoisseurs in
painting use a method which is very proper. They look at the picture with
one eye, through a tube which excludes the view of all other objects.
By this method, the principal mean whereby we perceive the distance of
the object, to wit, the inclination of the optic axes, is entirely excluded.
I would humbly propose, as an improvement of this method of viewing
pictures, that the aperture of the tube next to the eye should be very small.
If it is as small as a pin-hole, so much the better, providing there be light
enough to see the picture clearly. The reason of this proposal is, that when
we look at an object through a small aperture, it will be seen distinctly
whether the conformation of the eye be adapted to its distance or not, and

we have no mean left to judge of the distance, but the light and colouring, which are in the painter's power. If, therefore, the artist performs his part properly, the picture will by this method affect the eye in the same manner that the object represented would do, which is the perfection of this art.

Although this second mean of perceiving the distance of visible objects be more determinate and exact than the first, yet it hath its limits, beyond which it can be of no use. For when the optic axes directed to an object are so nearly parallel, that in directing them to an object yet more distant, we are not conscious of any new effort, nor have any different sensation, there our perception of distance stops; and as all more distant objects affect the eye in the same manner, we perceive them to be at the same distance. This is the reason why the sun, moon, planets, and fixed stars, when seen not near the horizon, appear to be all at the same distance, as if they touched the concave surface of a great sphere. The surface of this celestial sphere is at that distance beyond which all objects affect the eye in the same manner. Why this celestial vault appears more distant towards the horizon, than towards the zenith, will afterwards appear.

3. The colours of objects, according as they are more distant, become more faint and languid, and are tinged more with the azure of the intervening atmosphere: to this we may add, that their minute parts become more indistinct, and their outline less accurately defined. It is by these means chiefly, that painters can represent objects at very different distances, upon the same canvas. And the diminution of the magnitude of an object, would not have the effect of making it appear to be at a great distance, without this degradation of colour, and indistinctness of the outline, and of the minute parts. If a painter should make a human figure ten times less than other human figures that are in the same piece, having the colours as bright, and the outline and minute parts as accurately defined, it would not have the appearance of a man at a great distance, but of a pigmy or Lilliputian.

When an object hath a known variety of colours, its distance is more clearly indicated by the gradual dilution of the colours into one another, than when it is of one uniform colour. In the steeple which stands before me, at a small distance the joinings of the stones are clearly perceptible; the gray colour of the stone and the white cement are distinctly limited: when I see it at a greater distance, the joinings of the stones are less distinct, and the colours of the stone and of the cement begin to dilute into one another: at a distance still greater, the joinings disappear altogether, and the variety of colour vanishes.

In an apple-tree which stands at the distance of about twelve feet, covered with flowers, I can perceive the figure and the colour of the leaves and petals; pieces of branches, some larger, others smaller, peeping through the intervals of the leaves, some of them enlightened by the sun's rays, others shaded; and some openings of the sky are perceived through the whole. When I gradually remove from this tree, the appearance, even as to colour, changes every minute. First, the smaller parts, then the larger, are gradually confounded and mixed. The colours of leaves, petals, branches, and sky, are gradually diluted into each other, and the colour of the whole becomes more and more uniform. This change of appearance, corresponding to the several distances, marks the distance more exactly than if the whole object had been of one colour.

Dr Smith, in his *Optics*, gives us a very curious observation made by Bishop Berkeley, in his travels through Italy and Sicily. He observed, That in those countries, cities and palaces seen at a great distance, appeared nearer to him by several miles than they really were: and he very judiciously imputed it to this cause, That the purity of the Italian and Sicilian air, gave to very distant objects, that degree of brightness and distinctness, which, in the grosser air of his own country, was to be seen only in those that are near. The purity of the Italian air hath been assigned as the reason why the Italian painters commonly give a more lively colour to the sky, than the Flemish. Ought they not, for the same reason, to give less degradation of the colours, and less indistinctness of the minute parts, in the representation of very distant objects?

It is very certain, that as in air uncommonly pure, we are apt to think visible objects nearer, and less than they really are; so, in air uncommonly foggy, we are apt to think them more distant and larger than the truth. Walking by the sea-side in a thick fog, I see an object which seems to me to be a man on horseback, and at the distance of about half a mile. My companion, who has better eyes, or is more accustomed to see such objects in such circumstances, assures me, that it is a sea-gull, and not a man on horseback. Upon a second view, I immediately assent to his opinion; and now it appears to me to be a sea-gull, and at the distance only of seventy or eighty yards. The mistake made on this occasion, and the correction of it, are both so sudden, that we are at a loss whether to call them by the name of *judgment*, or by that of *simple perception*.

It is not worth while to dispute about names; but it is evident, that my belief, both first and last, was produced rather by signs than by arguments; and that the mind proceeded to the conclusion in both cases by habit, and not by ratiocination. And the process of the mind seems to have been this. First, Not knowing, or not minding, the effect of a foggy air on the visible appearance of objects, the object seems to me to have that degradation of colour, and that indistinctness of the outline, which objects have at the distance of half a mile; therefore, from the visible appearance as a sign, I immediately proceed to the belief that the object is half a mile distant. Then, this distance, together with the visible magnitude, signify to me the real magnitude, which, supposing the distance to be half a mile, must be equal to that of a man on horseback; and the figure, considering the indistinctness of the outline, agrees with that of a man on horseback. Thus the deception is brought about. But when I am assured that it is a sea-gull, the real magnitude of a sea-gull, together with the visible magnitude presented to the eye, immediately suggest the distance, which in this case cannot be above seventy or eighty yards: the indistinctness of the figure likewise suggests the fogginess of the air as its cause: and now the whole chain of signs, and things signified, seems stronger and better connected than it was before; the half-mile vanishes to eighty yards; the man on horseback dwindles to a sea-gull; I get a new perception, and wonder how I got the former, or what is become of it; for it is now so entirely gone, that I cannot recover it.

It ought to be observed, that in order to produce such deceptions from the clearness or fogginess of the air, it must be uncommonly clear, or uncommonly foggy: for we learn from experience, to make allowance for that variety of constitutions of the air which we have been accustomed to observe, and of which we are aware. Bishop Berkeley therefore committed a mistake, when he attributed the large appearance of the horizontal moon to the faintness of her light, occasioned by its passing through a larger tract of atmosphere: for we are so much accustomed to see the moon in all degrees of faintness and brightness, from the greatest to the least, that we learn to make allowance for it; and do not imagine her magnitude increased by the faintness of her appearance. Besides, it is certain that the horizontal moon seen through a tube which cuts off the view of the interjacent ground, and of all terrestrial objects, loses all that unusual appearance of magnitude.

4. We frequently perceive the distance of objects, by means of intervening or contiguous objects, whose distance or magnitude is otherwise known. When I perceive certain fields or tracts of ground to lie between me and an object, it is evident that these may become signs of its distance. And although we have no particular information of the dimensions of such

fields or tracts, yet their similitude to others which we know, suggests their dimensions.

We are so much accustomed to measure with our eye the ground which we travel, and to compare the judgments of distances formed by sight, with our experience or information, that we learn by degrees, in this way, to form a more accurate judgment of the distance of terrestrial objects, than we could do by any of the means before mentioned. An object placed upon the top of a high building, appears much less than when placed upon the ground at the same distance. When it stands upon the ground, the intervening tract of ground serves as a sign of its distance; and the distance, together with the visible magnitude, serves as a sign of its real magnitude. But when the object is placed on high, this sign of its distance is taken away: the remaining signs lead us to place it at a less distance; and this less distance, together with the visible magnitude, becomes a sign of a less real magnitude.

The two first means we have mentioned, would never of themselves make a visible object appear above a hundred and fifty or two hundred feet distant; because, beyond that, there is no sensible change, either of the conformation of the eyes, or of the inclination of their axes. The third mean, is but a vague and undeterminate sign, when applied to distances above two or three hundred feet, unless we know the real colour and figure of the object; and the fifth mean, to be afterwards mentioned, can only be applied to objects which are familiar, or whose real magnitude is known. Hence it follows, that when unknown objects, upon, or near the surface of the earth, are perceived to be at the distance of some miles, it is always by this fourth mean that we are led to that conclusion.

Dr Smith hath observed, very justly, that the known distance of the terrestrial objects which terminate our view, makes that part of the sky which is towards the horizon, appear more distant than that which is towards the zenith. Hence it comes to pass, that the apparent figure of the sky is not that of a hemisphere, but rather a less segment of a sphere. And hence likewise it comes to pass, that the diameter of the sun or moon, or the distance between two fixed stars, seen contiguous to a hill, or to any distant terrestrial object, appears much greater than when no such object strikes the eye at the same time.

These observations have been sufficiently explained and confirmed by Dr Smith. I beg leave to add, that when the visible horizon is terminated by very distant objects, the celestial vault seems to be enlarged in all its dimensions. When I view it from a confined street or lane, it bears some proportion to the buildings that surround me: but when I view it from a large plain, terminated on all hands by hills which rise one above another, to the distance of twenty miles from the eye, methinks I see a new heaven, whose magnificence declares the greatness of its Author, and puts every human edifice out of countenance; for now the lofty spires and the gorgeous palaces shrink into nothing before it, and bear no more proportion to the celestial dome, than their makers bear to its Maker.

5. There remains another mean by which we perceive the distance of visible objects, and that is, the diminution of their visible or apparent magnitude. By experience, I know what figure a man, or any other known object, makes to my eye, at the distance of ten feet: I perceive the gradual and proportional diminution of this visible figure, at the distance of twenty, forty, a hundred feet, and at greater distances, until it vanish altogether. Hence a certain visible magnitude of a known object, becomes the sign of a certain determinate distance, and carries along with it the conception and belief of that distance.

In this process of the mind, the sign is not a sensation; it is an original perception. We perceive the visible figure and visible magnitude of the object, by the original powers of vision; but the visible figure is used only as a sign of the real figure, and the visible magnitude is used only as a sign either of the distance, or of the real magnitude, of the object; and therefore these original perceptions, like other mere signs, pass through the mind without any attention or reflection.

This last mean of perceiving the distance of known objects, serves to explain some very remarkable phænomena in optics, which would otherwise appear very mysterious. When we view objects of known dimensions through optical glasses, there is no other mean left of determining their distance, but this fifth. Hence it follows, that known objects seen through glasses, must seem to be brought nearer, in proportion to the magnifying power of the glass, or to be removed to a greater distance, in proportion to the diminishing power of the glass.

If a man who had never before seen objects through a telescope, were told, that the telescope, which he is about to use, magnifies the diameter of the object ten times; when he looks through this telescope at a man six feet high, what would he expect to see? Surely he would very naturally expect to see a giant sixty feet high. But he sees no such thing. The man appears no more than six feet high, and consequently no bigger than he really is; but he appears ten times nearer than he is. The telescope indeed magnifies the image of this man upon the *retina* ten times in diameter,

and must therefore magnify his visible figure in the same proportion; and as we have been accustomed to see him of this visible magnitude when he was ten times nearer than he is presently, and in no other case; this visible magnitude, therefore, suggests the conception and belief of that
5   distance of the object with which it hath been always connected. We have been accustomed to conceive this amplification of the visible figure of a known object, only as the effect or sign of its being brought nearer: and we have annexed a certain determinate distance to every degree of visible magnitude of the object; and therefore, any particular degree of visible
10   magnitude, whether seen by the naked eye or by glasses, brings along with it the conception and belief of the distance which corresponds to it. This is the reason why a telescope seems not to magnify known objects, but to bring them nearer to the eye.

When we look through a pin-hole, or a single microscope, at an object
15   which is half an inch from the eye, the picture of the object upon the *retina* is not enlarged, but only rendered distinct; neither is the visible figure enlarged: yet the object appears to the eye twelve or fourteen times more distant, and as many times larger in diameter, than it really is. Such a telescope as we have mentioned, amplifies the image on the *retina*, and
20   the visible figure of the object, ten times in diameter, and yet makes it seem no bigger, but only ten times nearer. These appearances had been long observed by the writers on optics; they tortured their invention to find the causes of them from optical principles; but in vain: they must be resolved into habits of perception, which are acquired by custom, but are
25   apt to be mistaken for original perceptions. The Bishop of Cloyne first furnished the world with the proper key for opening up these mysterious appearances; but he made considerable mistakes in the application of it. Dr Smith, in his elaborate and judicious treatise of *Optics*, hath applied it to the apparent distance of objects seen with glasses, and to the apparent
30   figure of the heavens, with such happy success, that there can be no more doubt about the causes of these phænomena.

SECT. XXIII.

35   *Of the signs used in other acquired perceptions.*

THE distance of objects from the eye, is the most important lesson in vision. Many others are easily learned in consequence of it. The distance of the object, joined with its visible magnitude, is a sign of its real magnitude:

and the distance of the several parts of an object, joined with its visible
figure, becomes a sign of its real figure. Thus, when I look at a globe
which stands before me, by the original powers of sight I perceive only
something of a circular form, variously coloured. The visible figure hath
5   no distance from the eye, no convexity, nor hath it three dimensions; even
its length and breadth are incapable of being measured by inches, feet, or
other linear measures. But when I have learned to perceive the distance of
every part of this object from the eye, this perception gives it convexity,
and a spherical figure; and adds a third dimension to that which had but
10   two before. The distance of the whole object makes me likewise perceive
the real magnitude; for being accustomed to observe how an inch or a
foot of length affects the eye at that distance, I plainly perceive by my eye
the linear dimensions of the globe, and can affirm with certainty that its
diameter is about one foot and three inches.
15   It was shewn in the seventh section of this chapter, that the visible
figure of a body may, by mathematical reasoning, be inferred from its real
figure, distance, and position, with regard to the eye: in like manner, we
may, by mathematical reasoning, from the visible figure, together with the
distance of the several parts of it from the eye, infer the real figure and
20   position. But this last inference is not commonly made by mathematical
reasoning, nor indeed by reasoning of any kind, but by custom.
          The original appearance which the colour of an object makes to the eye,
is a sensation for which we have no name, because it is used merely as
a sign, and is never made an object of attention in common life: but this
25   appearance, according to the different circumstances, signifies various
things. If a piece of cloth, of one uniform colour, is laid so that part of
it is in the sun, and part in the shade; the appearance of colour, in these
different parts, is very different: yet we perceive the colour to be the same;
we interpret the variety of appearance as a sign of light and shade, and
30   not as a sign of real difference in colour. But if the eye could be so far
deceived, as not to perceive the difference of light in the two parts of the
cloth, we should, in that case, interpret the variety of appearance to signify
a variety of colour in the parts of the cloth.
          Again, if we suppose a piece of cloth placed as before, but having
35   the shaded part so much brighter in the colour, that it gives the same
appearance to the eye as the more enlightened part; the sameness of
appearance will here be interpreted to signify a variety of colour, because
we shall make allowance for the effect of light and shade.
          When the real colour of an object is known, the appearance of it

indicates, in some circumstances, the degree of light or shade; in others, the colour of the circumambient bodies, whose rays are reflected by it; and in other circumstances it indicates the distance or proximity of the object, as was observed in the last section; and by means of these, many other things are suggested to the mind. Thus, an unusual appearance in the colour of familiar objects, may be the diagnostic of a disease in the spectator. The appearance of things in my room, may indicate sunshine or cloudy weather, the earth covered with snow, or blackened with rain. It hath been observed, that the colour of the sky, in a piece of painting, may indicate the country of the painter, because the Italian sky is really of a different colour from the Flemish.

It was already observed, that the original and acquired perceptions which we have by our senses, are the language of nature to man, which, in many respects, hath a great affinity to human languages. The instances which we have given of acquired perceptions, suggest this affinity, that as, in human languages, ambiguities are often found, so this language of nature in our acquired perceptions is not exempted from them. We have seen, in vision particularly, that the same appearance to the eye, may, in different circumstances, indicate different things. Therefore, when the circumstances are unknown upon which the interpretation of the signs depends, their meaning must be ambiguous; and when the circumstances are mistaken, the meaning of the signs must also be mistaken.

This is the case in all the phænomena which we call *fallacies of the senses*; and particularly, in those which are called *fallacies in vision*. The appearance of things to the eye, always corresponds to the fixed laws of Nature; therefore, if we speak properly, there is no fallacy in the senses. Nature always speaketh the same language, and useth the same signs in the same circumstances: but we sometimes mistake the meaning of the signs, either through ignorance of the laws of Nature, or through ignorance of the circumstances which attend the signs.

To a man unacquainted with the principles of optics, almost every experiment that is made with the prism, with the magic lanthorn, with the telescope, with the microscope, seems to produce some fallacy in vision. Even the appearance of a common mirror, to one altogether unacquainted with the effects of it, would seem most remarkably fallacious. For how can a man be more imposed upon, than in seeing that before him which is really behind him? How can he be more imposed upon, than in being made to see himself several yards removed from himself? Yet children, even before they can speak their mother-tongue, learn not to be deceived by these appearances. These, as well as all the other surprising appearances produced by optical glasses, are a part of the visual language; and, to those who understand the laws of Nature concerning light and colours, are in no wise fallacious, but have a distinct and true meaning.

S E C T. XXIV.

Of the analogy between perception,
and the credit we give to human testimony.

THE objects of human knowledge are innumerable, but the channels by which it is conveyed to the mind are few. Among these, the perception of external things by our senses, and the informations which we receive upon human testimony, are not the least considerable: and so remarkable is the analogy between these two, and the analogy between the principles of the mind which are subservient to the one and those which are subservient to the other, that, without further apology, we shall consider them together.

In the testimony of nature given by the senses, as well as in human testimony given by language, things are signified to us by signs: and in one as well as the other, the mind, either by original principles, or by custom, passes from the sign to the conception and belief of the thing signified.

We have distinguished our perceptions into original and acquired; and language, into natural and artificial. Between acquired perception, and artificial language, there is a great analogy; but still a greater between original perception and natural language.

The signs in original perception are sensations, of which nature hath given us a great variety, suited to the variety of the things signified by them. Nature hath established a real connection between the signs and the things signified; and nature hath also taught us the interpretation of the signs; so that, previous to experience, the sign suggests the thing signified, and creates the belief of it.

The signs in natural language are features of the face, gestures of the body, and modulations of the voice; the variety of which is suited to the variety of the things signified by them. Nature hath established a real connection between these signs, and the thoughts and dispositions of the mind which are signified by them; and nature hath taught us the interpretation of these signs; so that, previous to experience, the sign suggests the thing signified, and creates the belief of it.

A man in company, without doing good or evil, without uttering an articulate sound, may behave himself gracefully, civilly, politely; or, on the contrary, meanly, rudely, and impertinently. We see the dispositions of his mind, by their natural signs in his countenance and behaviour, in the same manner as we perceive the figure and other qualities of bodies by the sensations which nature hath connected with them.

The signs in the natural language of the human countenance and behaviour, as well as the signs in our original perceptions, have the same signification in all climates and in all nations; and the skill of interpreting them is not acquired, but innate.

In acquired perception, the signs are either sensations, or things which we perceive by means of sensations. The connection between the sign, and the thing signified, is established by nature: and we discover this connection by experience; but not without the aid of our original perceptions, or of those which we have already acquired. After this connection is discovered, the sign, in like manner as in original perception, always suggests the thing signified, and creates the belief of it.

In artificial language, the signs are articulate sounds, whose connection with the things signified by them is established by the will of men: and in learning our mother-tongue, we discover this connection by experience; but not without the aid of natural language, or of what we had before attained of artificial language. And after this connection is discovered, the sign, as in natural language, always suggests the thing signified, and creates the belief of it.

Our original perceptions are few, compared with the acquired; but without the former, we could not possibly attain the latter. In like manner, natural language is scanty, compared with artificial; but without the former, we could not possibly attain the latter.

Our original perceptions, as well as the natural language of human features and gestures, must be resolved into particular principles of the human constitution. Thus, it is by one particular principle of our constitution, that certain features express anger; and by another particular principle, that certain features express benevolence. It is in like manner, by one particular principle of our constitution, that a certain sensation signifies hardness in the body which I handle; and it is by another particular principle, that a certain sensation signifies motion in that body.

But our acquired perceptions, and the information we receive by means of artificial language, must be resolved into general principles of the human constitution. When a painter perceives, that this picture is the work of Raphael, that the work of Titian; a jeweller, that this is a true diamond, that

a counterfeit; a sailor, that this is a ship of five hundred ton, that of four hundred: these different acquired perceptions are produced by the same general principles of the human mind, which have a different operation in the same person according as they are variously applied, and in different
5   persons, according to the diversity of their education and manner of life. In like manner, when certain articulate sounds convey to my mind the knowledge of the battle of Pharsalia, and others, the knowledge of the battle of Poltowa; when a Frenchman and an Englishman receive the same information by different articulate sounds; the signs used in these different
10   cases, produce the knowledge and belief of the things signified, by means of the same general principles of the human constitution.

Now, if we compare the general principles of our constitution, which fit us for receiving information from our fellow-creatures by language, with the general principles which fit us for acquiring the perception of things
15   by our senses, we shall find them to be very similar in their nature and manner of operation.

When we begin to learn our mother-tongue, we perceive by the help of natural language, that they who speak to us, use certain sounds to express certain things: we imitate the same sounds when we would express the
20   same things, and find that we are understood.

But here a difficulty occurs which merits our attention, because the solution of it leads to some original principles of the human mind, which are of great importance, and of very extensive influence. We know by experience, that men *have* used such words to express such things. But all
25   experience is of the *past*, and can, of itself, give no notion or belief of what is *future*. How come we then to believe, and to rely upon it with assurance, that men who have it in their power to do otherwise, will continue to use the same words when they think the same things? Whence comes this knowledge and belief, this foresight we ought rather to call it, of the future
30   and voluntary actions of our fellow-creatures? Have they promised that they will never impose upon us by equivocation or falsehood? No, they have not. And if they had, this would not solve the difficulty: for such promise must be expressed by words, or by other signs; and before we can rely upon it, we must be assured that they put the usual meaning upon the
35   signs which express that promise. No man of common sense ever thought of taking a man's own word for his honesty; and it is evident that we take his veracity for granted, when we lay any stress upon his word or promise. I might add, that this reliance upon the declarations and testimony of men, is found in children long before they know what a promise is.

There is therefore in the human mind an early anticipation, neither derived from experience, nor from reason, nor from any compact or promise, that our fellow-creatures will use the same signs in language, when they have the same sentiments.

This is, in reality, a kind of prescience of human actions; and it seems to me to be an original principle of the human constitution, without which we should be incapable of language, and consequently incapable of instruction.

The wise and beneficent Author of Nature, who intended that we should be social creatures, and that we should receive the greatest and most important part of our knowledge by the information of others, hath, for these purposes, implanted in our natures two principles that tally with each other.

The first of these principles is, a propensity to speak truth, and to use the signs of language, so as to convey our real sentiments. This principle has a powerful operation, even in the greatest liars; for where they lie once, they speak truth a hundred times. Truth is always uppermost, and is the natural issue of the mind. It requires no art or training, no inducement or temptation, but only that we yield to a natural impulse. Lying, on the contrary, is doing violence to our nature; and is never practised, even by the worst men, without some temptation. Speaking truth is like using our natural food, which we would do from appetite, although it answered no end; but lying is like taking physic, which is nauseous to the taste, and which no man takes but for some end which he cannot otherwise attain.

If it should be objected, That men may be influenced by moral or political considerations to speak truth, and therefore, that their doing so, is no proof of such an original principle as we have mentioned; I answer, first, That moral or political considerations can have no influence, until we arrive at years of understanding and reflection; and it is certain from experience, that children keep to truth invariably, before they are capable of being influenced by such considerations. Secondly, When we are influenced by moral or political considerations, we must be conscious of that influence, and capable of perceiving it upon reflection. Now, when I reflect upon my actions most attentively, I am not conscious that in speaking truth, I am influenced on ordinary occasions by any motive moral or political. I find, that truth is always at the door of my lips, and goes forth spontaneously, if not held back. It requires neither good nor bad intention to bring it forth, but only that I be artless and undesigning. There may indeed be temptations to falsehood, which would be too strong

for the natural principle of veracity, unaided by principles of honour or
virtue; but where there is no such temptation, we speak truth by instinct;
and this instinct is the principle I have been explaining.

By this instinct, a real connection is formed between our words and our
thoughts, and thereby the former become fit to be signs of the latter, which
they could not otherwise be. And although this connection is broken
in every instance of lying and equivocation, yet these instances being
comparatively few, the authority of human testimony is only weakened
by them, but not destroyed.

Another original principle implanted in us by the Supreme Being, is a
disposition to confide in the veracity of others, and to believe what they
tell us. This is the counter-part to the former; and as that may be called
the principle of veracity, we shall, for want of a more proper name, call
this *the principle of credulity*. It is unlimited in children, until they meet
with instances of deceit and falsehood: and it retains a very considerable
degree of strength through life.

If nature had left the mind of the speaker *in æquilibrio*, without any
inclination to the side of truth more than to that of falsehood; children
would lie as often as they speak truth, until reason was so far ripened,
as to suggest the imprudence of lying, or conscience, as to suggest its
immorality. And if nature had left the mind of the hearer *in æquilibrio*,
without any inclination to the side of belief more than to that of disbelief,
we should take no man's word until we had positive evidence that he
spoke truth. His testimony would, in this case, have no more authority
than his dreams; which may be true or false, but no man is disposed to
believe them, on this account, that they were dreamed. It is evident, that,
in the matter of testimony, the balance of human judgment is by nature
inclined to the side of belief; and turns to that side of itself, when there is
nothing put into the opposite scale. If it was not so, no proposition that is
uttered in discourse would be believed, until it was examined and tried by
reason; and most men would be unable to find reasons for believing the
thousandth part of what is told them. Such distrust and incredulity would
deprive us of the greatest benefits of society, and place us in a worse
condition than that of savages.

Children, on this supposition, would be absolutely incredulous; and
therefore absolutely incapable of instruction: those who had little knowledge of human life, and of the manners and characters of men, would be in
the next degree incredulous: and the most credulous men would be those
of greatest experience, and of the deepest penetration; because, in many

cases, they would be able to find good reasons for believing testimony, which the weak and the ignorant could not discover.

In a word, if credulity were the effect of reasoning and experience, it must grow up and gather strength, in the same proportion as reason and experience do. But if it is the gift of nature, it will be strongest in child-hood, and limited and restrained by experience; and the most superficial view of human life shows, that the last is really the case, and not the first.

It is the intention of nature, that we should be carried in arms before we are able to walk upon our legs; and it is likewise the intention of nature, that our belief should be guided by the authority and reason of others, before it can be guided by our own reason. The weakness of the infant, and the natural affection of the mother, plainly indicate the former; and the natural credulity of youth, and authority of age, as plainly indicate the latter. The infant, by proper nursing and care, acquires strength to walk without support. Reason hath likewise her infancy, when she must be carried in arms: then she leans entirely upon authority, by natural instinct, as if she was conscious of her own weakness; and without this support, she becomes vertiginous. When brought to maturity by proper culture, she begins to feel her own strength, and leans less upon the reason of others; she learns to suspect testimony in some cases, and to disbelieve it in others; and sets bounds to that authority to which she was at first entirely subject. But still, to the end of life, she finds a necessity of borrowing light from testimony, where she has none within herself, and of leaning in some degree upon the reason of others, where she is conscious of her own imbecillity.

And as in many instances, Reason, even in her maturity, borrows aid from testimony; so in others she mutually gives aid to it, and strengthens its authority. For as we find good reason to reject testimony in some cases, so in others we find good reason to rely upon it with perfect security, in our most important concerns. The character, the number, and the disinterestedness of witnesses, the impossibility of collusion, and the incredibility of their concurring in their testimony without collusion, may give an irresistible strength to testimony, compared to which its native and intrinsic authority is very inconsiderable.

Having now considered the general principles of the human mind which fit us for receiving information from our fellow-creatures, by the means of language; let us next consider the general principles which fit us for receiving the information of nature by our acquired perceptions.

It is undeniable, and indeed is acknowledged by all, that when we

have found two things to have been constantly conjoined in the course
of nature, the appearance of one of them is immediately followed by the
conception and belief of the other. The former becomes a natural sign of
the latter; and the knowledge of their constant conjunction in time past,
whether got by experience or otherwise, is sufficient to make us rely with
assurance upon the continuance of that conjunction.

This process of the human mind is so familiar, that we never think
of inquiring into the principles upon which it is founded. We are apt to
conceive it as a self-evident truth, that what is to come must be similar to
what is past. Thus, if a certain degree of cold freezes water to-day, and
has been known to do so in all time past, we have no doubt but the same
degree of cold will freeze water to-morrow, or a year hence. That this
is a truth which all men believe as soon as they understand it, I readily
admit; but the question is, Whence does its evidence arise? Not from
comparing the ideas, surely. For when I compare the idea of cold with
that of water hardened into a transparent solid body, I can perceive no
connection between them: no man can show the one to be the necessary
effect of the other: no man can give a shadow of reason why nature hath
conjoined them. But do we not learn their conjunction from experience?
True; experience informs us that they have been conjoined in time *past*:
but no man ever had any experience of what is *future*: and this is the
very question to be resolved, How we come to believe that the *future* will
be like the *past*? Hath the Author of nature promised this? Or were we
admitted to his council, when he established the present laws of nature,
and determined the time of their continuance? No, surely. Indeed, if we
believe that there is a wise and good Author of nature, we may see a good
reason, why he should continue the same laws of nature, and the same
connections of things, for a long time: because, if he did otherwise, we
could learn nothing from what is past, and all our experience would be of
no use to us. But though this consideration, when we come to the use of
reason, may confirm our belief of the continuance of the present course
of nature, it is certain that it did not give rise to this belief; for children
and idiots have this belief as soon as they know that fire will burn them.
It must therefore be the effect of instinct, not of reason.

The wise Author of our nature intended, that a great and necessary
part of our knowledge should be derived from experience, before we are
capable of reasoning, and he hath provided means perfectly adequate to
this intention. For, first, He governs nature by fixed laws, so that we
find innumerable connections of things which continue from age to age.

Without this stability of the course of nature, there could be no experience; or, it would be a false guide, and lead us into error and mischief. If there were not a principle of veracity in the human mind, mens words would not be signs of their thoughts: and if there were no regularity in the course of nature, no one thing could be a natural sign of another. Secondly, He hath implanted in human minds an original principle by which we believe and expect the continuance of the course of nature, and the continuance of those connections which we have observed in time past. It is by this general principle of our nature, that when two things have been found connected in time past, the appearance of the one produces the belief of the other.

I think the ingenious author of the *Treatise of human nature* first observed, That our belief of the continuance of the laws of nature cannot be founded either upon knowledge or probability: but, far from conceiving it to be an original principle of the mind, he endeavours to account for it from his favourite hypothesis, That belief is nothing but a certain degree of vivacity in the idea of the thing believed. I made a remark upon this curious hypothesis in the second chapter, and shall now make another.

The belief which we have in perception, is a belief of the present existence of the object; that which we have in memory, is a belief of its past existence; the belief of which we are now speaking, is a belief of its future existence, and in imagination there is no belief at all. Now, I would gladly know of this author, how one degree of vivacity fixes the existence of the object to the present moment; another carries it back to time past; a third, taking a contrary direction, carries it into futurity; and a fourth carries it out of existence altogether. Suppose, for instance, that I see the sun rising out of the sea; I remember to have seen him rise yesterday; I believe he will rise to-morrow near the same place; I can likewise imagine him rising in that place, without any belief at all. Now, according to this sceptical hypothesis, this perception, this memory, this foreknowledge, and this imagination, are all the same idea, diversified only by different degrees of vivacity. The perception of the sun rising, is the most lively idea; the memory of his rising yesterday, is the same idea a little more faint; the belief of his rising to-morrow, is the same idea yet fainter; and the imagination of his rising, is still the same idea, but faintest of all. One is apt to think, that this idea might gradually pass through all possible degrees of vivacity, without stirring out of its place. But if we think so, we deceive ourselves; for no sooner does it begin to grow languid, than it moves backward into time past. Supposing this to be granted, we expect

at least that as it moves backward by the decay of its vivacity, the more
that vivacity decays, it will go back the farther, until it remove quite out of
sight. But here we are deceived again; for there is a certain period of this
declining vivacity, when, as if it had met an elastic obstacle in its motion
5   backward, it suddenly rebounds from the past to the future, without taking
the present in its way. And now having got into the regions of futurity, we
are apt to think, that it has room enough to spend all its remaining vigour:
but still we are deceived; for, by another sprightly bound, it mounts up into
the airy region of imagination. So that ideas, in the gradual declension of
10 their vivacity, seem to imitate the inflection of verbs in grammar. They
begin with the present, and proceed in order to the preterite, the future,
and the indefinite. This article of the sceptical creed is indeed so full of
mystery, on whatever side we view it, that they who hold that creed, are
very injuriously charged with incredulity: for to me it appears to require
15 as much faith as that of St Athanasius.

However, we agree with the author of the *Treatise of human nature*
in this, That our belief of the continuance of nature's laws is not derived
from reason. It is an instinctive prescience of the operations of nature,
very like to that prescience of human actions which makes us rely upon
20 the testimony of our fellow-creatures; and as, without the latter, we should
be incapable of receiving information from men by language; so, without
the former, we should be incapable of receiving the information of nature
by means of experience.

All our knowledge of nature, beyond our original perceptions, is got
25 by experience, and consists in the interpretation of natural signs. The
constancy of nature's laws connects the sign with the thing signified, and,
by the natural principle just now explained, we rely upon the continuance
of the connections which experience hath discovered; and thus the
appearance of the sign, is followed by the belief of the thing signified.

30 Upon this principle of our constitution, not only acquired perception,
but all inductive reasoning, and all our reasoning from analogy, is
grounded: and therefore, for want of another name, we shall beg leave to
call it *the inductive principle*. It is from the force of this principle, that
we immediately assent to that axiom upon which all our knowledge of
35 nature is built, That effects of the same kind must have the same cause.
For *effects* and *causes*, in the operations of nature, mean nothing but signs,
and the things signified by them. We perceive no proper causality or
efficiency in any natural cause; but only a connection established by the
course of nature between it and what is called its effect. Antecedently to

all reasoning, we have, by our constitution, an anticipation, that there is a fixed and steady course of nature; and we have an eager desire to discover this course of nature. We attend to every conjunction of things which presents itself, and expect the continuance of that conjunction. And when such a conjunction has been often observed, we conceive the things to be naturally connected, and the appearance of one, without any reasoning or reflection, carries along with it the belief of the other.

If any reader should imagine that the inductive principle may be resolved into what philosophers usually call the *association of ideas*, let him observe, that, by this principle, natural signs are not associated with the idea only, but with the belief of the things signified. Now, this can with no propriety be called an association of ideas, unless ideas and belief be one and the same thing. A child has found the prick of a pin conjoined with pain; hence he believes, and knows, that these things are naturally connected; he knows that the one will always follow the other. If any man will call this only an association of ideas, I dispute not about words, but I think he speaks very improperly. For if we express it in plain English, it is a prescience, that things which he hath found conjoined in time past, will be conjoined in time to come. And this prescience is not the effect of reasoning, but of an original principle of human nature, which I have called *the inductive principle*.

This principle, like that of credulity, is unlimited in infancy, and gradually restrained and regulated as we grow up. It leads us often into mistakes, but is of infinite advantage upon the whole. By it the child once burnt shuns the fire; by it, he likewise runs away from the surgeon by whom he was inoculated. It is better that he should do the last, than that he should not do the first.

But the mistakes we are led into by these two natural principles, are of a different kind. Men sometimes lead us into mistakes, when we perfectly understand their language, by speaking lies. But Nature never misleads us in this way: her language is always true; and it is only by misinterpreting it that we fall into error. There must be many accidental conjunctions of things, as well as natural connections; and the former are apt to be mistaken for the latter. Thus, in the instance above mentioned, the child connected the pain of inoculation with the surgeon; whereas it was really connected with the incision only. Philosophers, and men of science, are not exempted from such mistakes; indeed all false reasoning in philosophy is owing to them: it is drawn from experience and analogy, as well as just reasoning, otherwise it could have no verisimilitude: but the one is an unskilful and rash, the other a just and legitimate interpretation of natural signs. If a child, or a man of common understanding, were put to interpret a book of science, wrote in his mother-tongue, how many blunders and mistakes would he be apt to fall into? Yet he knows as much of this language as is necessary for his manner of life.

The language of nature is the universal study; and the students are of different classes. Brutes, idiots, and children, employ themselves in this study, and owe to it all their acquired perceptions. Men of common understanding make a greater progress, and learn, by a small degree of reflection, many things of which children are ignorant.

Philosophers fill up the highest form in this school, and are critics in the language of nature. All these different classes have one teacher, Experience, enlightened by the inductive principle. Take away the light of this inductive principle, and Experience is as blind as a mole: she may indeed feel what is present, and what immediately touches her; but she sees nothing that is either before or behind, upon the right hand or upon the left, future or past.

The rules of inductive reasoning, or of a just interpretation of nature, as well as the fallacies by which we are apt to misinterpret her language, have been, with wonderful sagacity, delineated by the great genius of Lord Bacon: so that his *Novum organum* may justly be called *a grammar of the language of Nature*. It adds greatly to the merit of this work, and atones for its defects, that, at the time it was written, the world had not seen any tolerable model of inductive reasoning, from which the rules of it might be copied. The arts of poetry and eloquence were grown up to perfection when Aristotle described them; but the art of interpreting nature was yet *in embryo* when Bacon delineated its manly features and proportions. Aristotle drew his rules from the best models of those arts that have yet appeared; but the best models of inductive reasoning that have yet appeared, which I take to be the third book of the *Principia* and the *Optics* of Newton, were drawn from Bacon's rules. The purpose of all those rules, is to teach us to distinguish seeming or apparent connections of things in the course of nature, from such as are real.

They that are unskilful in inductive reasoning, are more apt to fall into error in their *reasonings* from the phænomena of nature, than in their *acquired perceptions*; because we often reason from a few instances, and thereby are apt to mistake accidental conjunctions of things for natural connections: but that habit of passing, without reasoning, from the sign to the thing signified, which constitutes acquired perception, must be learned by many instances or experiments; and the number of experiments serves to disjoin those things which have been accidentally conjoined, as well as to confirm our belief of natural connections.

From the time that children begin to use their hands, nature directs them to handle every thing over and over, to look at it while they handle it, and to put it in various positions, and at various distances from the eye. We are apt to excuse this as a childish diversion, because they must be doing something, and have not reason to entertain themselves in a more manly way. But if we think more justly, we shall find, that they are engaged in the most serious and important study; and if they had all the reason of a philosopher, they could not be more properly employed. For it is this childish employment that enables them to make the proper use of their eyes. They are thereby every day acquiring habits of perception, which are of greater importance than any thing we can teach them. The original perceptions which Nature gave them are few, and insufficient for the purposes of life; and therefore she made them capable of acquiring many more perceptions by habit. And to complete her work, she hath given them an unwearied assiduity in applying to the exercises by which those perceptions are acquired.

This is the education which Nature gives to her children. And since we have fallen upon this subject, we may add, that another part of Nature's education is, That, by the course of things, children must often exert all their muscular force, and employ all their ingenuity, in order to gratify their curiosity, and satisfy their little appetites. What they desire is only to be obtained at the expence of labour and patience, and many disappointments. By the exercise of body and mind necessary for satisfying their desires, they acquire agility, strength, and dexterity in their motions, as well as health and vigour to their constitutions; they learn patience and perseverance; they learn to bear pain without dejection, and disappointment without despondence. The education of Nature is most perfect in savages, who have no other tutor: and we see, that, in the quickness of all their senses, in the agility of their motions, in the hardiness of their constitutions, and in the strength of their minds to bear hunger, thirst, pain, and disappointment, they commonly far exceed the civilized. A most ingenious writer, on this account, seems to prefer the savage life to that of society. But the education of Nature could never of itself produce a Rousseau. It is the intention of Nature, that human education should be joined to her institution, in order to form the man. And she hath fitted us for human education, by the natural principles of imitation and credulity, which discover themselves almost in infancy, as well as by others which are of later growth.

When the education which we receive from men, does not give scope to the education of Nature, it is wrong directed; it tends to hurt our faculties of perception, and to enervate both the body and mind. Nature hath her way of rearing men, as she hath of curing their diseases. The art of medicine is to follow Nature, to imitate and to assist her in the cure of diseases; and the art of education is to follow Nature, to assist and to imitate her in her way of rearing men. The ancient inhabitants of the Baleares followed Nature in the manner of teaching their children to be good archers, when they hung their dinner aloft by a thread, and left the younkers to bring it down by their skill in archery.

The education of Nature, without any more human care than is necessary to preserve life, makes a perfect savage. Human education, joined to that of Nature, may make a good citizen, a skilful artisan, or a well-bred man. But Reason and Reflection must superadd their tutory, in order to produce a Rousseau, a Bacon, or a Newton.

Notwithstanding the innumerable errors committed in human education, there is hardly any education so bad, as to be worse than none. And I apprehend, that if even Rousseau were to chuse whether to educate a son among the French, the Italians, the Chinese, or among the Eskimaux, he would not give the preference to the last.

When Reason is properly employed, she will confirm the documents of Nature, which are always true and wholesome; she will distinguish, in the documents of human education, the good from the bad, rejecting the last with modesty, and adhering to the first with reverence.

Most men continue all their days to be just what Nature and human education made them. Their manners, their opinions, their virtues, and their vices, are all got by habit, imitation, and instruction; and Reason has little or no share in forming them.

CONCLUSION.

THERE are two ways in which men may form their notions and opinions concerning the mind, and concerning its powers and operations. The first is the only way that leads to truth; but it is narrow and rugged, and few have entered upon it. The second is broad and smooth, and hath been much beaten, not only by the vulgar, but even by philosophers: it is sufficient for common life, and is well adapted to the purposes of the poet and orator: but, in philosophical disquisitions concerning the mind, it leads to error and delusion.

We may call the first of these ways, *the way of reflection.* When the operations of the mind are exerted, we are conscious of them; and it is in our power to attend to them, and to reflect upon them, until they become familiar objects of thought. This is the only way in which we can form just and accurate notions of those operations. But this attention and reflection is so difficult to man, surrounded on all hands by external objects which constantly solicit his attention, that it has been very little practised, even by philosophers. In the course of this inquiry, we have had many occasions to show, how little attention hath been given to the most familiar operations of the senses.

The second, and the most common way, in which men form their opinions concerning the mind and its operations, we may call *the way of analogy.* There is nothing in the course of nature so singular, but we can find some resemblance, or at least some analogy, between it and other things with which we are acquainted. The mind naturally delights in hunting after such analogies, and attends to them with pleasure. From them, poetry and wit derive a great part of their charms; and eloquence, not a little of its persuasive force.

Besides the pleasure we receive from analogies, they are of very considerable use, both to facilitate the conception of things, when they are not easily apprehended without such a handle, and to lead us to probable conjectures about their nature and qualities, when we want the means of more direct and immediate knowledge. When I consider that the planet Jupiter, in like manner as the earth, rolls round his own axis, and revolves round the sun, and that he is enlightened by several secondary planets, as the earth is enlightened by the moon; I am apt to conjecture from analogy, that as the earth by these means is fitted to be the habitation of various orders of animals, so the planet Jupiter is, by the like means, fitted for the same purpose: and having no argument more direct and conclusive to determine me in this point, I yield, to this analogical reasoning, a degree of assent proportioned to its strength. When I observe, that the potatoe plant very much resembles the *solanum* in its flower and fructification, and am informed, that the last is poisonous, I am apt from analogy to have some suspicion of the former: but in this case, I have access to more direct and certain evidence; and therefore ought not to trust to analogy, which would lead me into an error.

Arguments from analogy are always at hand, and grow up sponta-neously in a fruitful imagination, while arguments that are more direct, and more conclusive, often require painful attention and application: and therefore mankind in general have been very much disposed to trust to the former. If one attentively examines the systems of the ancient phi-losophers, either concerning the material world, or concerning the mind, he will find them to be built solely upon the foundation of analogy. Lord Bacon first delineated the strict and severe method of induction; since his time it has been applied with very happy success in some parts of natural philosophy; and hardly in any thing else. But there is no subject in which mankind are so much disposed to trust to the analogical way of thinking and reasoning, as in what concerns the mind and its operations; because, to form clear and distinct notions of those operations in the direct and proper way, and to reason about them, requires a habit of attentive reflection, of which few are capable, and which, even by those few, cannot be attained without much pains and labour.

Every man is apt to form his notions of things difficult to be apprehended, or less familiar, from their analogy to things which are more familiar. Thus, if a man bred to the seafaring life, and accustomed to think and talk only of matters relating to navigation, enters into discourse upon any other subject; it is well known, that the language and the notions proper to his own profession are infused into every subject, and all things are measured by the rules of navigation: and if he should take it into his head to philosophize concerning the faculties of the mind, it cannot be doubted, but he would draw his notions from the fabric of his ship, and would find in the mind, sails, masts, rudder, and compass.

Sensible objects of one kind or other, do no less occupy and ingross the rest of mankind, than things relating to navigation, the seafaring man. For a considerable part of life, we can think of nothing but the objects of sense; and to attend to objects of another nature, so as to form clear and distinct notions of them, is no easy matter, even after we come to years of reflection. The condition of mankind, therefore, affords good reason to apprehend, that their language, and their common notions, concerning the mind and its operations, will be analogical, and derived from the objects of sense; and that these analogies will be apt to impose upon philosophers, as well as upon the vulgar, and to lead them to materialize the mind and its faculties: and experience abundantly confirms the truth of this.

How generally men of all nations, and in all ages of the world, have conceived the soul, or thinking principle in man, to be some subtile matter, like breath or wind, the names given to it almost in all languages sufficiently testify. We have words which are proper, and not analogical, to express the various ways in which we perceive external objects by the senses; such as *feeling, sight, taste*: but we are often obliged to use these words analogically, to express other powers of the mind which are of a very different nature. And the powers which imply some degree of reflection, have generally no names but such as are analogical. The objects of thought are said to be *in the mind*, to be *apprehended, comprehended, conceived, imagined, retained, weighed, ruminated.*

It does not appear that the notions of the ancient philosophers, with regard to the nature of the soul, were much more refined than those of the vulgar, or that they were formed in any other way. We shall distinguish the philosophy that regards our subject into the *old* and the *new.* The old reached down to Des Cartes, who gave it a fatal blow, of which it has been gradually expiring ever since, and is now almost extinct. Des Cartes is the father of the new philosophy that relates to this subject; but it hath been gradually improving since his time, upon the principles laid down by him. The old philosophy seems to have been purely analogical: the new is more derived from reflection, but still with a very considerable mixture of the old analogical notions.

Because the objects of sense consist of *matter* and *form*, the ancient philosophers conceived every thing to belong to one of these, or to be made up of both. Some therefore thought, that the soul is a particular kind of subtile matter, separable from our gross bodies; others thought that it is only a particular form of the body, and inseparable from it. For there seem to have been some among the ancients, as well as among the moderns, who conceived that a certain structure, or organization of the body, is all that is necessary to render it sensible and intelligent. The different powers of the mind were, accordingly, by the last sect of philosophers, conceived to belong to different parts of the body, as the heart, the brain, the liver, the stomach, the blood.

5   They who thought that the soul is a subtile matter separable from the body, disputed to which of the four elements it belongs, whether to earth, water, air, or fire. Of the three last, each had its particular advocates. But some were of opinion, that it partakes of all the elements; that it must have something in its composition similar to every thing we perceive; and

10 that we perceive earth by the earthly part; water, by the watery part; and fire, by the fiery part of the soul. Some philosophers, not satisfied with determining of what kind of matter the soul is made, inquired likewise into its figure, which they determined to be spherical, that it might be the more fit for motion. The most spiritual and sublime notion concerning

15 the nature of the soul, to be met with among the ancient philosophers, I conceive to be that of the Platonists, who held that it is made of that celestial and incorruptible matter of which the fixed stars were made, and therefore has a natural tendency to rejoin its proper element. I am at a loss to say, in which of these classes of philosophers Aristotle ought to be

20 placed. He defines the soul to be, The first ἐντελεχεια of a natural body which has potential life. I beg to be excused from translating the Greek word, because I know not the meaning of it.

The notions of the ancient philosophers with regard to the operations of the mind, particularly with regard to perception and ideas, seem likewise

25 to have been formed by the same kind of analogy.

Plato, of the writers that are extant, first introduced the word *idea* into philosophy; but his doctrine upon this subject had somewhat peculiar. He agreed with the rest of the ancient philosophers in this, that all things consist of matter and form; and that the matter of which all things were

30 made, existed from eternity, without form: but he likewise believed, that there are eternal forms of all possible things which exist, without matter; and to these eternal and immaterial forms he gave the name of *ideas*; maintaining, that they are the only object of true knowledge. It is of no great moment to us, whether he borrowed these notions from Parmenides,

35 or whether they were the issue of his own creative imagination. The later Platonists seem to have improved upon them, in conceiving those ideas, or eternal forms of things, to exist, not of themselves, but in the Divine Mind, and to be the models and patterns according to which all things were made:

Then liv'd th' Eternal One, then, deep retir'd
In his unfathom'd essence, view'd at large
The uncreated images of things.

5   To these Platonic notions, that of Malebranche is very nearly allied. This author seems, more than any other, to have been aware of the difficulties attending the common hypothesis concerning ideas, to wit, That ideas of all objects of thought are in the human mind; and therefore, in order to avoid those difficulties, makes the ideas which are the immediate objects
10   of human thought, to be the ideas of things in the Divine Mind; who being intimately present to every human mind, may discover his ideas to it, as far as pleaseth him.

The Platonists and Malebranche excepted, all other philosophers, as far as I know, have conceived that there are ideas or images of every object
15   of thought in the human mind, or at least in some part of the brain, where the mind is supposed to have its residence.

Aristotle had no good affection to the word *idea*, and seldom or never uses it but in refuting Plato's notions about ideas. He thought that matter may exist without form; but that forms cannot exist without matter. But at
20   the same time he taught, That there can be no sensation, no imagination, nor intellection, without forms, phantasms, or species in the mind; and that things sensible are perceived by sensible species, and things intelligible by intelligible species. His followers taught more explicitly, that those sensible and intelligible species are sent forth by the objects, and make
25   their impressions upon the passive intellect; and that the active intellect perceives them in the passive intellect. And this seems to have been the common opinion while the Peripatetic philosophy retained its authority.

The Epicurean doctrine, as explained by Lucretius, though widely different from the Peripatetic in many things, is almost the same in this.
30   He affirms, that slender films or ghosts (*tenuia rerum simulacra*) are still going off from all things, and flying about; and that these being extremely subtile, easily penetrate our gross bodies, and striking upon the mind, cause thought and imagination.

After the Peripatetic system had reigned above a thousand years in
35   the schools of Europe, almost without a rival, it sunk before that of Des Cartes; the perspicuity of whose writings and notions, contrasted with the obscurity of Aristotle and his commentators, created a strong prejudice in favour of this new philosophy. The characteristic of Plato's genius was sublimity, that of Aristotle's, subtilty; but Des Cartes far excelled both in

perspicuity, and bequeathed this spirit to his successors. The system which is now generally received, with regard to the mind and its operations, derives not only its spirit from Des Cartes, but its fundamental principles; and after all the improvements made by Malebranche, Locke, Berkeley,

5 and Hume, may still be called *the Cartesian system*: we shall therefore make some remarks upon its spirit and tendency in general, and upon its doctrine concerning ideas in particular.

1. It may be observed, That the method which Des Cartes pursued, naturally led him to attend more to the operations of the mind by accurate

10 reflection, and to trust less to analogical reasoning upon this subject, than any philosopher had done before him. Intending to build a system upon a new foundation, he began with a resolution to admit nothing but what was absolutely certain and evident. He supposed that his senses, his memory, his reason, and every other faculty to which we trust in common life,

15 might be fallacious; and resolved to disbelieve every thing, until he was compelled by irresistible evidence to yield assent.

In this method of proceeding, what appeared to him, first of all, certain and evident, was, That he thought, that he doubted, that he deliberated. In a word, the operations of his own mind, of which he was conscious, must

20 be real, and no delusion; and though all his other faculties should deceive him, his consciousness could not. This therefore he looked upon as the first of all truths. This was the first firm ground upon which he set his foot, after being tossed in the ocean of scepticism; and he resolved to build all knowledge upon it, without seeking after any more first principles.

25 As every other truth, therefore, and particularly the existence of the objects of sense, was to be deduced by a train of strict argumentation from what he knew by consciousness, he was naturally led to give attention to the operations of which he was conscious, without borrowing his notions of them from external things.

30 It was not in the way of analogy, but of attentive reflection, that he was led to observe, That thought, volition, remembrance, and the other attributes of the mind, are altogether unlike to extension, to figure, and to all the attributes of body; that we have no reason, therefore, to conceive thinking substances to have any resemblance to extended substances; and

35 that, as the attributes of the thinking substance are things of which we are conscious, we may have a more certain and immediate knowledge of them by reflection, than we can have of external objects by our senses.

These observations, as far as I know, were first made by Des Cartes; and they are of more importance, and throw more light upon the subject, than all that had been said upon it before. They ought to make us diffident and jealous of every notion concerning the mind and its operations, which is drawn from sensible objects in the way of analogy, and to make us rely only upon accurate reflection, as the source of all real knowledge upon this subject.

2. I observe, That as the Peripatetic system has a tendency to materialize the mind, and its operations; so the Cartesian has a tendency to spiritualize body, and its qualities. One error, common to both systems, leads to the first of these extremes in the way of analogy, and to the last, in the way of reflection. The error I mean is, That we can know nothing about body, or its qualities, but as far as we have sensations which resemble those qualities. Both systems agreed in this: but according to their different methods of reasoning, they drew very different conclusions from it; the Peripatetic drawing his notions of sensation from the qualities of body; the Cartesian, on the contrary, drawing his notions of the qualities of body from his sensations.

The Peripatetic, taking it for granted that bodies and their qualities do really exist, and are such as we commonly take them to be, inferred from them the nature of his sensations, and reasoned in this manner: Our sensations are the impressions which sensible objects make upon the mind, and may be compared to the impression of a seal upon wax; the impression is the image or form of the seal, without the matter of it: in like manner, every sensation is the image or form of some sensible quality of the object. This is the reasoning of Aristotle, and it has an evident tendency to materialize the mind, and its sensations.

The Cartesian, on the contrary, thinks, that the existence of body, or of any of its qualities, is not to be taken as a first principle; and that we ought to admit nothing concerning it, but what, by just reasoning, can be deduced from our sensations; and he knows, that by reflection we can form clear and distinct notions of our sensations, without borrowing our notions of them by analogy from the objects of sense. The Cartesians, therefore, beginning to give attention to their sensations, first discovered that the sensations corresponding to secondary qualities, cannot resemble any quality of body. Hence Des Cartes and Locke inferred, that sound, taste, smell, colour, heat, and cold, which the vulgar took to be qualities of body, were not qualities of body, but mere sensations of the mind. Afterwards the ingenious Berkeley, considering more attentively the nature of sensation in general, discovered, and demonstrated, that no sensation whatever could possibly resemble any quality of an insentient being, such as body is supposed to be: and hence he inferred, very justly, that there is the same reason to hold extension, figure, and all the primary qualities, to be mere sensations, as there is to hold the secondary qualities to be mere sensations. Thus, by just reasoning upon the Cartesian principles, matter was stript of all its qualities; the new system, by a kind of metaphysical sublimation, converted all the qualities of matter into sensations, and spiritualized body, as the old had materialized spirit.

The way to avoid both these extremes, is, to admit the existence of what we see and feel as a first principle, as well as the existence of things whereof we are conscious; and to take our notions of the qualities of body, from the testimony of our senses, with the Peripatetics; and our notions of our sensations, from the testimony of consciousness, with the Cartesians.

3. I observe, That the modern scepticism is the natural issue of the new system; and that, although it did not bring forth this monster until the year 1739, it may be said to have carried it in its womb from the beginning.

The old system admitted all the principles of common sense as first principles, without requiring any proof of them; and therefore, though its reasoning was commonly vague, analogical, and dark, yet it was built upon a broad foundation, and had no tendency to scepticism. We do not find that any Peripatetic thought it incumbent upon him to prove the existence of a material world; but every writer upon the Cartesian system attempted this, until Berkeley clearly demonstrated the futility of their arguments; and thence concluded, that there was no such thing as a material world; and that the belief of it ought to be rejected as a vulgar error.

The new system admits only one of the principles of common sense as a first principle; and pretends, by strict argumentation, to deduce all the rest from it. That our thoughts, our sensations, and every thing of which we are conscious, hath a real existence, is admitted in this system as a first principle; but every thing else must be made evident by the light of reason. Reason must rear the whole fabric of knowledge upon this single principle of consciousness.

There is a disposition in human nature to reduce things to as few principles as possible; and this, without doubt, adds to the beauty of a system, if the principles are able to support what rests upon them. The mathematicians glory, very justly, in having raised so noble and magnificent a system of science, upon the foundation of a few axioms and definitions. This love of simplicity, and of reducing things to few principles, hath produced many a false system; but there never was any system in which it appears so remarkably as that of Des Cartes. His whole system concerning matter and spirit is built upon one axiom, expressed in one word, *cogito*. Upon the foundation of conscious thought, with ideas for his materials, he builds his system of the human understanding, and attempts to account for all its phænomena: and having, as he imagined, from his consciousness, proved the existence of matter; upon the existence of matter, and of a certain quantity of motion originally impressed upon it, he builds his system of the material world, and attempts to account for all its phænomena.

These principles, with regard to the material system, have been found insufficient; and it has been made evident, that besides matter and motion, we must admit gravitation, cohesion, corpuscular attraction, magnetism, and other centripetal and centrifugal forces, by which the particles of matter attract and repel each other. Newton, having discovered this, and demonstrated, that these principles cannot be resolved into matter and motion, was led by analogy, and the love of simplicity, to conjecture, but with a modesty and caution peculiar to him, that all the phænomena of the material world depended upon attracting and repelling forces in the particles of matter. But we may now venture to say, that this conjecture fell short of the mark. For, even in the unorganized kingdom, the powers by which salts, crystals, spars, and many other bodies, concrete into regular forms, can never be accounted for by attracting and repelling forces in the particles of matter. And in the vegetable and animal kingdoms, there are strong indications of powers of a different nature from all the powers of unorganized bodies. We see then, that although in the structure of the material world there is, without doubt, all the beautiful simplicity consistent with the purposes for which it was made, it is not so simple as the great Des Cartes determined it to be: nay, it is not so simple as the greater Newton modestly conjectured it to be. Both were misled by analogy, and the love of simplicity. One had been much conversant about extension, figure, and motion; the other had enlarged his views to attracting and repelling forces; and both formed their notions of the unknown parts of nature, from those with which they were acquainted, as the shepherd Tityrus formed his notion of the city of Rome from his country village:

Urbem quam dicunt Romam, Melibœe, putavi
Stultus ego, huic nostræ similem, quò sæpe solemus
Pastores ovium teneros depellere fœtus.

Sic canibus catulos similes, sic matribus hædos
Nôram: sic parvis componere magna solebam.

This is a just picture of the analogical way of thinking.

But to come to the system of Des Cartes, concerning the human understanding; it was built, as we have observed, upon consciousness as its sole
foundation, and with ideas as its materials; and all his followers have built
upon the same foundation and with the same materials. They acknowledge
that nature hath given us various simple ideas: These are analogous to
the matter of Des Cartes's physical system. They acknowledge likewise
a natural power by which ideas are compounded, disjoined, associated,
compared: This is analogous to the original quantity of motion in Des
Cartes's physical system. From these principles they attempt to explain
the phænomena of the human understanding, just as in the physical system
the phænomena of nature were to be explained by matter and motion. It
must indeed be acknowledged, that there is great simplicity in this system
as well as in the other. There is such a similitude between the two, as may
be expected between children of the same father: but as the one has been
found to be the child of Des Cartes, and not of Nature, there is ground to
think that the other is so likewise.

That the natural issue of this system is scepticism with regard to every
thing except the existence of our ideas, and of their necessary relations
which appear upon comparing them, is evident: for ideas being the only
objects of thought, and having no existence but when we are conscious
of them, it necessarily follows, that there is no object of our thought
which can have a continued and permanent existence. Body and spirit,
cause and effect, time and space, to which we were wont to ascribe an
existence independent of our thought, are all turned out of existence by
this short dilemma: Either these things are ideas of sensation or reflection,
or they are not: if they are ideas of sensation or reflection, they can have
no existence but when we are conscious of them; if they are not ideas of
sensation or reflection, they are words without any meaning.

Neither Des Cartes nor Locke perceived this consequence of their
system concerning ideas. Bishop Berkeley was the first who discovered it.
And what followed upon this discovery? Why, with regard to the material
world, and with regard to space and time, he admits the consequence,
That these things are mere ideas, and have no existence but in our minds:
but with regard to the existence of spirits or minds, he does not admit the
consequence; and if he had admitted it, he must have been an absolute

sceptic. But how does he evade this consequence with regard to the existence of spirits? The expedient which the good Bishop uses on this occasion is very remarkable, and shows his great aversion to scepticism. He maintains, that we have no ideas of spirits; and that we can think, and speak, and reason about them, and about their attributes, without having any ideas of them. If this is so, my Lord, what should hinder us from thinking and reasoning about bodies, and their qualities, without having ideas of them? The Bishop either did not think of this question, or did not think fit to give any answer to it. However, we may observe, that in order to avoid scepticism, he fairly starts out of the Cartesian system, without giving any reason why he did so in this instance, and in no other. This indeed is the only instance of a deviation from Cartesian principles which I have met with in the successors of Des Cartes; and it seems to have been only a sudden start, occasioned by the terror of scepticism; for in all other things Berkeley's system is founded upon Cartesian principles.

Thus we see, that Des Cartes and Locke take the road that leads to scepticism, without knowing the end of it; but they stop short for want of light to carry them farther. Berkeley, frighted at the appearance of the dreadful abyss, starts aside, and avoids it. But the author of the *Treatise of human nature*, more daring and intrepid, without turning aside to the right hand or to the left, like Virgil's Alecto, shoots directly into the gulf:

Hic specus horrendum, et sævi spiracula Ditis
Monstrantur: ruptoque ingens Acheronte vorago
Pestiferas aperit fauces.

4. We may observe, That the account given by the new system, of that furniture of the human understanding which is the gift of nature, and not the acquisition of our own reasoning faculty, is extremely lame and imperfect.

The natural furniture of the human understanding is of two kinds; First, The *notions* or simple apprehensions which we have of things; and, Secondly, The *judgments* or the belief which we have concerning them. As to our notions, the new system reduces them to two classes; *ideas of sensation*, and *ideas of reflection*: the first are conceived to be copies of our sensations, retained in the memory or imagination; the second, to be copies of the operations of our minds whereof we are conscious, in like manner retained in the memory or imagination: and we are taught, that these two comprehend all the materials about which the human

understanding is, or can be employed. As to our judgment of things, or
the belief which we have concerning them, the new system allows no part
of it to be the gift of nature, but holds it to be the acquisition of reason,
and to be got by comparing our ideas, and perceiving their agreements or
5   disagreements. Now I take this account, both of our notions, and of our
judgments or belief, to be extremely imperfect; and I shall briefly point
out some of its capital defects.

The division of our notions into ideas of sensation, and ideas of
reflection, is contrary to all rules of logic; because the second member
10 of the division includes the first. For, can we form clear and just notions
of our sensations any other way than by reflection? Surely we cannot.
Sensation is an operation of the mind of which we are conscious; and we
get the notion of sensation, by reflecting upon that which we are conscious
of. In like manner, doubting and believing are operations of the mind
15 whereof we are conscious; and we get the notion of them by reflecting
upon what we are conscious of. The ideas of sensation, therefore, are ideas
of reflection, as much as the ideas of doubting, or believing, or any other
ideas whatsoever.

But to pass over the inaccuracy of this division, it is extremely
20 incomplete. For, since sensation is an operation of the mind, as well as
all the other things of which we form our notions by reflection; when it
is asserted, that all our notions are either ideas of sensation, or ideas of
reflection, the plain English of this is, That mankind neither do, nor can
think of any thing but of the operations of their own minds. Nothing can
25 be more contrary to truth, or more contrary to the experience of mankind.
I know that Locke, while he maintained this doctrine, believed the notions
which we have of body and of its qualities, and the notions which we have
of motion and of space, to be ideas of sensation. But why did he believe
this? Because he believed those notions to be nothing else but images of
30 our sensations. If therefore the notions of body and its qualities, of motion
and space, be not images of our sensations, will it not follow, that those
notions are not ideas of sensation? Most certainly.

There is no doctrine in the new system which more directly leads to
scepticism than this. And the author of the *Treatise of human nature* knew
35 very well how to use it for that purpose: for, if you maintain that there
is any such existence as body or spirit, time or place, cause or effect, he
immediately catches you between the horns of this dilemma: Your notions
of these existences are either ideas of sensation, or ideas of reflection; if
of sensation, from what sensation are they copied? if of reflection, from

what operation of the mind are they copied?

It is indeed to be wished, that those who have written much about sensation, and about the other operations of the mind, had likewise thought and reflected much, and with great care, upon those operations: but is it not very strange, that they will not allow it to be possible for mankind to think of any thing else?

The account which this system gives of our judgment and belief concerning things, is as far from the truth as the account it gives of our notions or simple apprehensions. It represents our senses as having no other office, but that of furnishing the mind with notions or simple apprehensions of things; and makes our judgment and belief concerning those things to be acquired by comparing our notions together, and perceiving their agreements or disagreements.

We have shown, on the contrary, that every operation of the senses, in its very nature, implies judgment or belief, as well as simple apprehension. Thus, when I feel the pain of the gout in my toe, I have not only a notion of pain, but a belief of its existence, and a belief of some disorder in my toe which occasions it; and this belief is not produced by comparing ideas, and perceiving their agreements and disagreements; it is included in the very nature of the sensation. When I perceive a tree before me, my faculty of seeing gives me not only a notion or simple apprehension of the tree, but a belief of its existence, and of its figure, distance, and magnitude; and this judgment or belief is not got by comparing ideas, it is included in the very nature of the perception. We have taken notice of several original principles of belief in the course of this inquiry; and when other faculties of the mind are examined, we shall find more, which have not occurred in the examination of the five senses.

Such original and natural judgments are therefore a part of that furniture which nature hath given to the human understanding. They are the inspiration of the Almighty, no less than our notions or simple apprehensions. They serve to direct us in the common affairs of life, where our reasoning faculty would leave us in the dark. They are a part of our constitution, and all the discoveries of our reason are grounded upon them. They make up what is called *the common sense of mankind*; and what is manifestly contrary to any of those first principles, is what we call *absurd*. The strength of them is *good sense*, which is often found in those who are not acute in reasoning. A remarkable deviation from them, arising from a disorder in the constitution, is what we call *lunacy*; as when a man believes that he is made of glass. When a man suffers himself to be reasoned out

of the principles of common sense, by metaphysical arguments, we may
call this *metaphysical lunacy*; which differs from the other species of the
distemper in this, that it is not continued, but intermittent: it is apt to
seize the patient in solitary and speculative moments; but when he enters
into society, Common Sense recovers her authority. A clear explication
and enumeration of the principles of common sense, is one of the chief
desiderata in logic. We have only considered such of them as occurred
in the examination of the five senses.

5. The last observation that I shall make upon the new system is, That,
although it professes to set out in the way of reflection, and not of
analogy, it hath retained some of the old analogical notions concerning the
operations of the mind; particularly, That things which do not now exist
in the mind itself, can only be perceived, remembered, or imagined, by
means of ideas or images of them in the mind, which are the immediate
objects of perception, remembrance, and imagination. This doctrine
appears evidently to be borrowed from the old system; which taught, that
external things make impressions upon the mind, like the impressions of
a seal upon wax; that it is by means of those impressions that we perceive,
remember, or imagine them; and that those impressions must resemble
the things from which they are taken. When we form our notions of the
operations of the mind by analogy, this way of conceiving them seems to
be very natural, and offers itself to our thoughts: for as every thing which
is felt must make some impression upon the body, we are apt to think,
that every thing which is understood must make some impression upon
the mind.

From such analogical reasoning, this opinion of the existence of ideas
or images of things in the mind, seems to have taken its rise, and to
have been so universally received among philosophers. It was observed
already, that Berkeley, in one instance, apostatizes from this principle of
the new system, by affirming, that we have no ideas of spirits, and that we
can think of them immediately, without ideas. But I know not whether in
this he has had any followers. There is some difference likewise among
modern philosophers, with regard to the ideas or images by which we
perceive, remember, or imagine sensible things. For, though all agree in
the existence of such images, they differ about their place; some placing
them in a particular part of the brain, where the soul is thought to have
her residence, and others placing them in the mind itself. Des Cartes
held the first of these opinions; to which Newton seems likewise to have
inclined; for he proposes this query in his *Optics*: "Annon sensorium

animalium est locus cui substantia sentiens adest, et in quem sensibiles rerum species per nervos et cerebrum deferuntur, ut ibi præsentes a præsente sentiri possint?" But Locke seems to place the ideas of sensible things in the mind: and that Berkeley, and the author of the *Treatise of human nature*, were of the same opinion, is evident. The last makes a very curious application of this doctrine, by endeavouring to prove from it, That the mind either is no substance, or that it is an extended and divisible substance; because the ideas of extension cannot be in a subject which is indivisible and unextended.

I confess I think his reasoning in this, as in most cases, is clear and strong. For whether the idea of extension be only another name for extension itself, as Berkeley and this author assert; or whether the idea of extension be an image and resemblance of extension, as Locke conceived; I appeal to any man of common sense, whether extension, or any image of extension, can be in an unextended and indivisible subject. But while I agree with him in his reasoning, I would make a different application of it. He takes it for granted, that there are ideas of extension in the mind; and thence infers, that if it is at all a substance, it must be an extended and divisible substance. On the contrary, I take it for granted, upon the testimony of common sense, that my mind is a substance, that is, a permanent subject of thought; and my reason convinces me, that it is an unextended and indivisible substance; and hence I infer, that there cannot be in it any thing that resembles extension. If this reasoning had occurred to Berkeley, it would probably have led him to acknowledge, that we may think and reason concerning bodies, without having ideas of them in the mind, as well as concerning spirits.

I intended to have examined more particularly and fully this doctrine of the existence of ideas or images of things in the mind; and likewise another doctrine, which is founded upon it, to wit, That judgment or belief is nothing but a perception of the agreement or disagreement of our ideas: but having already shewn, through the course of this inquiry, that the operations of the mind which we have examined, give no countenance to either of these doctrines, and in many things contradict them, I have thought it proper to drop this part of my design. It may be executed with more advantage, if it is at all necessary, after inquiring into some other powers of the human understanding.

Although we have examined only the five senses, and the principles of the human mind which are employed about them, or such as have fallen in our way in the course of this examination; we shall leave the further prosecution of this inquiry to future deliberation. The powers of memory, of imagination, of taste, of reasoning, of moral perception, the will, the passions, the affections, and all the active powers of the soul, present a vast and boundless field of philosophical disquisition, which the author of this inquiry is far from thinking himself able to survey with accuracy. Many authors of ingenuity, ancient and modern, have made excursions into this vast territory, and have communicated useful observations: but there is reason to believe, that those who have pretended to give us a map of the whole, have satisfied themselves with a very inaccurate and incomplete survey. If Galileo had attempted a complete system of natural philosophy, he had, probably, done little service to mankind: but by confining himself to what was within his comprehension, he laid the foundation of a system of knowledge, which rises by degrees, and does honour to the human understanding. Newton, building upon this foundation, and in like manner, confining his inquiries to the law of gravitation and the properties of light, performed wonders. If he had attempted a great deal more, he had done a great deal less, and perhaps nothing at all. Ambitious of following such great examples, with unequal steps, alas! and unequal force, we have attempted an inquiry only into one little corner of the human mind; that corner which seems to be most exposed to vulgar observation, and to be most easily comprehended; and yet, if we have delineated it justly, it must be acknowledged, that the accounts heretofore given of it, were very lame, and wide of the truth.

THE END.

EXPLANATORY NOTES

The *Explanatory Notes* contain bibliographical details for quotations and allusions, translations, references to secondary literature, and selections from Reid's manuscripts (see *Manuscripts* for MS editorial principles and symbols). The notes are referenced to the *Inquiry* by page and line number and the relevant portion of text. For example, on page 3 line 10, where Reid gives the biblical reference 'JOB', the explanatory note supplies the chapter and verse.

3/10   JOB] Job 32: 8.

5/4–5   *And . . . behind.*] William Shakespeare, *The Tempest*, IV, i, 151–6. 'And like the baseless fabric of this vision, . . . Leave not a rack behind.' *William Shakespeare: The Complete Works*, eds. S. Wells and G. Taylor (Oxford, Clarendon Press, 1986): p. 1335. Reid uses these lines in writing on Descartes: 'his Successors seem neither to have carefully examined his Principles in this Part of Philosophy nor made any considerable add{ition to} the foundation he has laid down but have built upon it very curious [Fabricks] Structures, which however at last {have been dissolved by the breath of Scepticism and} like the baseless Fabric of a [Dream] {Vision} left not a tract behind' (AUL MS 1/I/3, 33; see *Manuscripts* § 2.1, p. 286.)

5/24   academical life] For an account of Reid's academic environs, see Paul B. Wood, *The Aberdeen Enlightenment: The Arts Curriculum in the Eighteenth Century* (Aberdeen, Aberdeen University Press, 1993).

5/31   philosophical society] For a detailed account of this society, see *The Minutes of the Aberdeen Philosophical Society 1758–1773*, edited by H. Lewis Ulman (Aberdeen, Aberdeen University Press, 1990). Reid's discourses to the Society are presented in *Manuscripts* § 2.

5/29–36   My . . . public.] For a detailed account of the events leading up to the publication of the *Inquiry*, see Paul B. Wood's Introduction in the Thoemmes reprint of the 1785 edition of the *Inquiry*.

11/17   *The importance of the subject*] The only extant MS version of this section heading reads: 'The Importance of an Enquiry into this Subject, & the means of prosecuting it' (AUL MS 1/I/1, 1).

11/25–6   the extensive influence] This view was incorporated, with the assistance of Reid, into the curriculum of King's College, Aberdeen. Reid served on the committee which drafted the new curriculum submitted on 17 August 1753. It states that in the third and final year, students would 'be employed in the Philosophy of the Human Mind and the Sciences that depend on it.' A supplementary regulation, drafted in 1754, reads: 'By the *Philosophy of the Mind*, is understood, An Account of the Constitution of the human Mind, and all of its Powers and Faculties, whether Sensitive, Intellectual, or Moral; the Improvements these are capable of, and the Means of their Improvement; of the mutual Influences of Body and Mind on each other; and of the Knowledge we may acquire of other Minds, and particularly of the Supreme Mind. And the *Sciences depending on the Philosophy of the Mind*, are understood to be Logic, Rhetoric, the Laws of Nature and Nations, Politicks, Oeconomicks, the fine Arts and natural Religion.' Wood, *The Aberdeen Enlightenment,* p. 67.

12/19   *regulæ philosophandi*] The earliest extant Reidian statement of Newton's 'Rules of Philosophizing' is found in student notes taken from Reid's King's College lectures (Session 1757–58): 'Rule Ist. More causes of Natural things are not to be admitted, than are both true & sufficient for explaining their Phænomena. Rule IId. Like effects have the same or like Causes. . . . Rule IIId. These qualities of Bodies which cannot be increased or diminished, & agree in all Bodies, on which Experiments have been made are to be reckoned as qualities of {all} Bodies whatsoever. For the qualities of Bodies are not known but by experiments, & therefore as many are to be reckoned general as generally agree with experiments. Rule IVth. In Experimental Philosophy, Propositions collected from the Phænomena by induction are to be deemed notwithstanding contrary Hypothesis, either accurate or very nearly true, till other Phænomema occur by which they may be rendred more accurate or less liable to exceptions.' (AUL MS K.160, 8) See also Reid's 'Of Newton's Rules of Philosophizing', in Paul B. Wood, *Thomas Reid on the Animate Creation* (Edinburgh, Edinburgh University Press, 1995): pp. 182–92 (AUL 3061/1/4, 12–23); and L. L. Laudan, 'Thomas Reid and the Newtonian turn of British Methodological thought', in *The Methodological Heritage of Newton*, ed. R. E. Butts and J. W. Davis (Oxford, Basil Blackwell, 1970): pp. 103–31.

12/20   animals] Paul Wood suggests that Reid's criticism of 'curious theories . . . of the generation of animals' is directed against Buffon's *Histoire Naturelle. Thomas Reid on the Animate Creation*, p. 59, n. 24.

12/22   Archæus of Paracelsus] Paracelsus (1490–1541) held that the life of every individual thing depends on its possession of a spiritual agent or 'Archæus'. See Henry M. Pachter, *Magic into Science: The Story of Paracelsus* (New York, Henry Schuman, 1951).

16/25–6 Des Cartes . . . deep] Cf. 'I realized that it was necessary, once in the course of my life, to demolish everything completely and start again right from the foundations if I wanted to establish anything at all in the sciences that was stable and likely to last.' René Descartes, 'Meditations on First Philosophy', in *The Philosophical Writings of Descartes*, translated by J. Cottingham, R. Stoothoff and D. Murdoch (Cambridge, Cambridge University Press, 1984): p. 17.

17/29 personal identity] Cf. 'For since consciousness always accompanies thinking, and 'tis that, that makes every one to be, what he calls *self*; and thereby distinguishes himself from all other thinking things, in this alone consists *personal Identity, i.e.* the sameness of a rational Being: And as far as this consciousness can be extended backwards to any past Action or Thought, so far reaches the Identity of that *Person*'. John Locke, *An Essay Concerning Human Understanding*, ed. P. H. Nidditch (Oxford, Clarendon Press, 1975): II.xxvii.9. See D. P. Behan, 'Locke on Persons and Personal Identity', *Canadian Journal of Philosophy* 9 (1979): pp. 53–75; R. Gallie, 'The Same Self', *Locke News* 18 (1987): pp. 45–62.

17/34–5 consequently . . . forgets] The following MS passage occurs immediately above and on the same page as a different work dated 'Dec 1 1758' (see *Manuscripts*, § 3.2); hence it must have been written prior to that date. 'An Argument to prove that the Identity of a person does not consist in Consciousness against Mr Locke by M G Campbel. One was flogged at school for breaking an Orchard, he gained a premium at College by making a copy of verses and afterwards in a battle takes a Standard from the Enemy. When he gained the premium he remembred distinctly his breaking the Orchard & therefore was the same {identical} person that broke it. When he took a Standard he remembred distinctly his gaining the præmium & so was the Identical person who gained it but had at that time quite forgot the breaking of the Orchard and so was not the same person that broke it. Yet it is evident from the case that he must be the same person for the Man that took the Standard is the same with him that gained the premium the man that gained the premium is the same that broke the Orchard therefore the Man that took the Standard is the same that broke the Orchard.' (AUL MS 6/III/5, 2r). Locke considers the objection from forgetfulness in the *Essay*, II.xxvii.20.

18/13–14 Admired Philosophy!] Cf. 'O philosophy, thou guide of life, o thou explorer of virtue and expeller of vice! . . . to thee I fly for refuge, from thee I look for aid, to thee I entrust myself, as once in ample measure, so now wholly and entirely.' Cicero, *Tusculan Disputations*, trans. J. E. King (London, William Heinemann, 1945): V.ii.5.

20/11–12   **in his introduction**] 'In pretending therefore to explain the principles of human nature, we in effect propose a compleat system of the sciences, built on a foundation almost entirely new and the only one upon which they can stand with any security.' David Hume, *A Treatise of Human Nature*, ed. L. A. Selby-Bigge and P. H. Nidditch, 2d ed. (Oxford, Clarendon Press, 1978): p. xvi. In an MS draft of the *Intellectual Powers*, Reid writes: 'as Mr Humes sceptical System is all built upon a wrong & mistaken Account of the intellectual Powers of Man, so it can onely be refuted by giving a true Account of them.' (AUL MS 7/V/4, 4).

20/22–3   **he ingenuously acknowledges**] Hume, *Treatise*, I.iv.7, p. 269.

20/32   **quoted by Diogenes Laertius**] Diogenes Laertius, *Lives of Eminent Philosophers*, with an English translation by R. D. Hicks, 2 vols, Loeb Classical Library (Cambridge, Mass., Harvard University Press, 1979): Bk. 9, Ch. 11, p. 475.

21/6   **is said**] According to Laertius, it was a pupil of Pyrrho, Eurylochus, who was guilty of this unfortunate lapse (Laertius, *Lives*, p. 481).

21/27   **Yahoos**] Cf. Swift's *Gulliver's Travels*, Part IV.

22/37   **my very self**] See H. Lesser, 'Reid's Criticism of Hume's Theory of Personal Identity', *Hume Studies* 4 (1978): pp. 41–63; D. N. Robinson and T. Beauchamp, 'Personal Identity: Reid's Answer to Hume', *Monist* 61 (1978): pp. 326–39.

22/38   **Epicurus's atoms**] See note below (34/26–9).

25/3   **Of SMELLING**] The following undated Reid MS appears to be an early outline of Chapter II: '1 Describe the Organ of Smell | 2 The perceptions we have by it. These are all called by the same Name as the Power itself Smells. They have but few Specific Names. Musty {Stinking} Putrid Cadaverous. Sweet Aromatic But for more Distinction different Smells are distinguished by the bodies that yield them. | 3 Compare this Sense in {different} Men [with the same] {and} in Other Animals | 4 The Uses of it | 5 The situation of the Organ & the degree of its acuteness is suited to the State of the Several Animals endowed with it | Cor. Most bodies emit Effluvia of extream Minuteness and to a Vast Distance | Relig Philosoph Cont 8 § 7. Derham Physico Theology Lib 4 Ch 4 | Pope Essay on Man Ep 1 line 200 Or quick Effluvia darting thro' If Brain | Die of a Rose in Aromatic Pain.' (AUL MS 6/I/20, 3).

7/18   *Sensation*] See P. Bourdillon, 'Thomas Reid's Account of Sensation as a Natural Principle of Belief', *Philosophical Studies* 27 (1975): pp. 19–36.

8/24–5   system of ideas] See A. Broadie, 'Medieval Notions and the Theory of Ideas', *Proceedings of the Aristotelian Society* 87 (1986–7): pp. 153–67; S. A. Grave, 'The 'Theory of Ideas', *Philosophical Monographs* 3 (1976): pp. 55–61; K. Lehrer, 'Beyond Impressions and Ideas: Hume *vs.* Reid', *Monist* 70 (1988): pp. 383–97; D. Palmer, 'Locke and the 'Ancient Hypothesis', *Canadian Journal of Philosophy* Supp. 1, (1974): pp. 41–8; R. C. Sleigh, 'Reid and the Ideal Theory of Conception and Perception', *Philosophical Monographs* 3 (1976): pp. 77–85; R. Stecker, 'Does Reid Reject/Refute the Representational Theory of Mind?', *Pacific Philosophical Quarterly* 73 (1992): pp. 174–84; J. W. Yolton, *Perceptual Acquaintance: From Descartes to Reid.* (Minneapolis, University of Minnesota, 1984).

0/15–16   that modern discovery] Hume, *Treatise*, I.iii.7.

1/9   Locke's notion of belief or knowledge] Locke, *Essay*, IV.i.2.

3/3   No disparagement is meant] This may be a response to Hume's comment on an early draft of the *Inquiry*: 'As to one particular Insinuation, I rather choose not to take notice of it at all because I could not properly reply to it without employing a Style, which I would not willingly use towards one for whom I have otherwise a great Regard and who has the Honour of bearing the Name of your Friend. I wish the Parsons wou'd confine themselves to their old Occupation of worrying one another; & leave Philosophers to argue with Temper, Moderation & good Manners.' (AUL MS 2814/1/39, 2r; see *Manuscripts* § 1.1).

4/26–9   *Principio . . . veniunt.*] Lucretius, *De Rerum Natura*, Bk IV, 724–7. Trans. 'First then, thin *Images* fill all the *Air*, / Thousands on *every* side, and wander there: / These, as they meet in *various dance*, will twine . . .' *Titus Lucretius Carus, His Six Books of Epicurean Philosophy, Done Into English Verse, With Notes*, By T. Creech, 5th ed. (London, Printed for George Sawbridge, at the Three Golden Flower-de-Luces in Little-Britain, 1712): p. 123.

5/8   Plato required] The curriculum and requirements of the Academy are described in Book VII of Plato's *Republic*.

7/10   nay, it is impossible to show] Cf. what appears to be a pre-*Inquiry* MS: 'Mix and compound and divide & compare your Sensations as long as you please. You can never make a Subject of Sensation {out} of these ingredients. It is absolutely a simple thing of an entirely diffrent nature from sensation remembrance passion and every one of its Operations. And one may as well think by compounding the notions of Sounds and tastes to acquire the notion of Colour As by compounding the {Sensations & thoughts} we are conscious of to frame the Notion of Mind or Subject of thought. The notion of it is got by a kind of Natural Inspiration or by some particular faculty which conveys this Notion to us as hearing conveys Sounds.' (AUL MS 1/I/4, 6).

38/3   *suggestion*] Cf. Berkeley's use of the term in his 'Three Dialogues between Hylas and Philonous', in *The Works of George Berkeley*, ed. A. A. Luce and T. E. Jessop, 9 vols, (Edinburgh, Nelson and Sons, 1948–57): Vol. 2, p. 204. See R. Beanblossom, 'In Defense of Thomas Reid's Use of Suggestion', *Grazer Philosophische Studien* 1 (1975): pp. 19–24; P. G. Winch, 'The Notion of "Suggestion" in Thomas Reid's Theory of Perception', *Philosophical Quarterly* 3 (1953): pp. 327–41.

42/8   three of his definitions] 'Definition VI The absolute quantity of a centripetal force is the measure of the same, proportional to the efficacy of the cause that propagates it from the centre, through the spaces round about'; 'Definition VII The accelerative quantity of a centripetal force is the measure of the same, proportional to the velocity which it generates in a given time.'; 'Definition VIII The motive quantity of a centripetal force is the measure of the same, proportional to the motion which it generates in a given time.' (Italicization removed) *Sir Issac Newton's Mathematical Principles of Natural Philosophy and His System of the World*, trans. A. Motte, rev. trans. F. Cajori, ed. T. R. Crawford, 2 vols (Berkeley and Los Angeles, University of California Press, 1962): Bk I.

46/3   Of TASTING] The following undated Reid MS appears to be an early outline of Chap. III: 'Taste 1 Describe its Organ | The Perceptions we have by it. called Tastes. We have perhaps more Specific Names for tasts than Smells. Sweet Acid. Stiptic Salt. Hot Cooling {Oily} Fat. Vinous. Nauseous Vapid. Musty. Acrid. Aromatic Alkaline or Putrid | But as these are far from exhausting all the Variety of Tastes there are many distinguished onely by the Names of the Bodies that Yield them. | 3 Compare Taste in Different Men & other Animals | 4 The Uses of it | 5 Its Situation and Acuteness proportioned to the State of Animals endued with it. See Nirwenlyt & Derham | Tho there are not very many Tastes or Smells that have distinguishing Names yet there are a vast Number of Modifications of these perceptions which are of Considerable Use to enable us to distinguish bodies [by]' (AUL MS 6/I/20, 3).

48/18–19   in a discourse] Dr. Nehemiah Grew, 'A Discourse Of The Diversities

And Causes Of Tasts Chiefly In Plants. Read before the *Royal Society, March* 25. 1675.'

Lord Verulam] See A. W. Davenport, 'Reid's Indebtedness to Bacon', *Monist* 70 (1988): pp. 496–507.

primary and secondary qualities] See A. R. Greenberg, 'Reid on Primary & Secondary Qualities', *Canadian Journal of Philosophy* Supp. vol. 4 (1977): pp. 207–18; K. Lehrer, 'Reid on Primary and Secondary Qualities', *Monist* 61 (1978): pp. 184–91; B. Silver, 'A Note on Berkeley's *New Theory of Vision* and Thomas Reid's Distinction between Primary and Secondary Qualities', *Southern Journal of Philosophy*, 12 (1974): pp. 253–63.

Saunderson] Dr. Nicholas Saunderson was the blind Lucasian Professor of Mathematics at Cambridge. See Diderot's description of Saunderson's method of representing figures to himself by means of tactile imagery, in *Lettre sur les aveugles . . .* (9 June 1749), in M. J. Morgan, *Molyneux's Question* (Cambridge, Cambridge University Press, 1977): pp. 42ff.

common sense] See G. Ardley, 'Hume's Common Sense Critics', *Revue International de Philosophie* 30 (1976): pp. 104–25; G. E. Davie, 'Hume and the Origins of the Common Sense School', *Revue International de Philosophie* 6 (1952): pp. 213–21; J. H. Faurot, 'Common Sense in the Philosophy of Thomas Reid', *The Modern Schoolman*, 33 (1956): pp. 182–89; W. P. Krolikowski, 'The Starting-Point in Scottish Common Sense Realism', *The Modern Schoolman,* 33, (1956): pp. 139–53; G. S. Pappas, 'Common Sense in Berkeley and Reid' *Revue International de Philosophie* 40 (1986): pp. 292–303; J. Somerville, 'Reid's Conception of Common Sense', *Monist* 70 (1988): pp. 418–29; N. W. Thompson, 'Aristotle as a Predecessor to Reid's Common Sense', *Speech Monographs* (Iowa) 43, no.3 (1974): pp. 209–20; G. E. Davie, *The Social Significance of the Philosophy of Common Sense* (Dow Lecture, University of Dundee. Dundee, 1973); S. A. Grave, *The Scottish Philosophy of Common Sense* (Westport, Conn., Greenwood Press, 1977); M. Kuehn, *Scottish Common Sense in Germany, 1768–1800: A Contribution to the History of Critical Philosophy* (Kingston and Montreal, McGill-Queen's University Press, 1987); E. Lobkowicz, *Common Sense und Skeptizismus. Studien zur Philosophie von Thomas Reid und David Hume* (Weinheim, 1986); L. Marcil-Lacoste, *Claude Buffier and Thomas Reid. Two Common-Sense Philosophers* (Canada, McGill-Queen's University Press, 1982); D. F. Norton, *From Moral Sense to Common Sense*, Ph.D. Dissertation, Department of Philosophy, University of California, 1966.

69/3   to reconcile reason to common sense] See S. C. Rome, 'The Scottish
          Refutation of Berkeley's Immaterialism', *Philosophy and
          Phenomenological Research* 3 (1943): pp. 313–23.

70/3   observation of Locke] 'It is not in the Power of the most exalted Wit,
          or enlarged Understanding, by any quickness or variety of Thought, to
          invent or frame one new simple Idea in the mind . . . nor can any force of
          the Understanding, *destroy* those that are there.' Locke, *Essay*, II.ii.2.

79/6   camera obscura] See J. H. Hammond, *The Camera Obscura: A Chronicle*
          (Bristol, Adam Hilger Ltd.,1981).

79/27   my having heard him say] Reid visited Saunderson in 1736.

79/32   Another gentleman] The witness is likely to have been John Stewart, who
          accompanied Reid on his visit to England in 1736. Stewart later became
          Professor of Mathematics in Marischal College. See 'Account of the Life
          and Writings of Thomas Reid . . .', in *The Works of Thomas Reid*, ed. W.
          Hamilton, 8th ed., (Edinburgh, J. Thin, 1895, reprint with introduction
          by H. M. Bracken, Hildesheim, Georg Olms Verlag, 1985): p. 13. In an
          autobiographical MS, Reid describes his visit to England thus: 'Mr. Reid
          . . . & Mr Stewart . . . visited the Universities of Oxford & Cambridge &
          found Acquaintance wt. some of the most distinguished Literary Men of
          that time' (AUL MS 2814/I/50, fol. 1r-v).

82/3   observation of the Bishop of Cloyne] Regarding 'the proper objects of
          vision', Berkeley writes: 'the manner wherein they signify and mark unto
          us the objects which are at a distance is the same with that of languages
          and signs of human appointment, which do not suggest the things signified
          by any likeness or identity of nature, but only by an habitual connexion
          that experience has made us to observe between them.' 'A New Theory
          of Vision', in *The Works of George Berkeley*, p. 231.

82/9   *Optics*] Cf. 'From what has been said it appears that our perception of
          things by sight is no more than this: by memory of former perceptions by
          sight and other senses compared together, we collect in an instant that the
          thing we now perceive by sight only will affect our other senses, upon
          trial, as it formerly used to do. I say in an instant, which will less surprize
          us, when we consider how quick the characters or sounds of words, whose
          signification we could hardly remember at first, do excite in our minds
          the ideas of things they are constantly used to signify: so great is the
          force of habits in bringing our ideas together. And so it appears at the
          last, that the manner, wherein external objects are signified to us, by the
          sensations of light and colours, is the same with that of languages and
          signs of human appointment: which do not suggest the things signified by

any likeness or identity of nature, but only by an habitual connection that constant experience has made us observe between them.' (*Smith gives a reference here to the passage from Berkeley quoted in the note for 82/3 above*). Dr. Robert Smith, *A Complete System Of Opticks in Four Books, viz. A Popular, a Mathematical, a Mechanical, and a Philosophical Treatise. To which are added Remarks upon the Whole*. 2 Vols. (Cambridge, Printed for the Author, and sold there by Cornelius Crownfield, and at London by Stephen Austen at the Angel and Bible in St. Paul's Churchyard, and Robert Dodsley at Tully's Head in Pall Mall, 1738): Vol. I, § 135, pp. 44–6.

28–30 The young man . . . objects.] 'An account of some observations made by a young gentleman, who was born blind, or lost his sight so early, that he had no remembrance of ever having seen, and was couch'd between 13 and 14 years of age. By Mr. Will. Cheselden, F. R. S. Surgeon to Her Majesty, and to St. Thomas's Hospital', in *Philosophical Transactions* (1728), 402, pp. 447–50; and in *The Anatomy of the Human Body* By W. Cheselden (London, Printed for H. Woodfell, *et al.*, 1763): p. 301

4–12 "I have . . . *understanding.*"] Joseph Addison, *The Spectator*, No. 413, June 24, 1712.
Variants between the critical text and the *Spectator*:
89/6   inquirers] Enquirers
89/6   philosophy,] philosophy:
89/8   which] that
89/12   Locke's] Mr Locke's **1** || Mr. *Lock*'s

7 *secondary qualities*] Cf. what appears to be a pre-*Inquiry* MS: 'There is another Class of Sensations which by our Constitution we are led to consider onely as the Signs of certain qualities in bodys which {since} Mr Lock {invented the Name have been called} Secondary Qualities. I would rather chuse to call them relative Qualities, because all we know of them is their Relation to certain Sensations in us which they are adapted to raise ⟨⟨Or if the word was not in disgrace I would call them Occult Qualities. Meaning by that word Such Qualities which are known onely by their Effects.⟩⟩' (AUL MS 1/I/4, 1)

3 Malebranche's notion] Nicolas Malebranche, *The Search After Truth* trans. T. M. Lennon and P. J. Olscamp, (Columbus, Ohio State University Press, 1980): Bk. III, Part II, Ch. 6. See J. W. Yolton, 'Malbranche on Perception and Knowledge', in *Perceptual Acquaintance*, Chapter II.

2 Cheselden] W. Cheselden, 'An account', p. 447; *Anatomy,* p. 300.

14 *Of the geometry of visibles*] See R. B. Angell, 'The Geometry of

Visibles', *Nous* 8 (1974): pp. 87–117; G. N. Cantor, 'Berkeley, Reid, and the Mathematization of Mid Eighteenth-Century Optics', *Journal of the History of Ideas* 38 (1977): pp. 429–48; N. Daniels, *Thomas Reid's Inquiry: The Geometry of Visibles and the Case for Realism* (New York, Burt Franklin & Co., 1974); S. Weldon, 'Direct Realism and Visual Distortion: A Development of Arguments from Thomas Reid', *Journal of the History of Philosophy* 20 (1982): pp. 355–68.

111/27   Borrichius, Fabricius] Presumably, Reid is referring to Johannes Fabricius (1587–1615), a Dutch astronomer who was the first to publish information on sunspots in his *de maculis in sole observatis et apparente earum cum sole conversione, narratio* (Witebergæ, 1611); and the same Borrichius who is mentioned in William Briggs, 'A new Theory of Vision presented to the Royal Society by William Briggs Dr. of Physick, and fellow of the college of Physicians.' in *Philosophical Collections*. Numb. 6. March 1681/2. pp. 167–77, ed. Robert Hooke (London, Printed for Richard Chismel, Printer to the Royal Society, at the Rose and Crown in St. Pauls's Church-yard, 1682): p. 174. (Originally published in Latin).

114/39   Kepler] See Johannes Kepler, *Dioptrice*, (Augsburg, 1611; rpt. Cambridge, W. Heffer & Sons, 1962): §XIX.

115/19   Des Cartes] See René Descartes, 'Dioptrique', in *Oeuvres de Descartes*, ed. C. Adam and P. Tannery, 13 vols (Paris, Leopold, Cerf., 1897–1913): Vol. 6.

116/9   Dr. Smith] See note for 82/9.

121/27–8   of which impressions it is supposed to be conscious] In an MS dated 1748, Reid argues that the mind's consciousness of impressions would lead to an infinite regress: 'I know nothing that is meant . . . by Consciousness of Present Perceptions but the perceiving that we perceive them. I cannot imagine there is any thing more in perceiving that I perceive a Star than in perceiving a Star Simply otherwise there might be perceptions of perceptions in Infinitum' (AUL MS 6/I/18, 1; see *Manuscripts* § 3.1). See K. Lehrer, 'Reid on Consciousness', *Reid Studies* 1 (1986–87): pp. 1–9; K. Lehrer, 'Metamind: Belief, Consciousness, and Intentionality', in *Belief*, ed., R. J. Bogdan (Oxford, Clarendon Press, 1986): pp. 37–59.

123/19   Medical Essays] Dr. William Porterfield, 'An Essay concerning the Motions of our Eyes', in *Medical Essays and Observations*, 3 (1735), pp. 160–261, 4 (1737), pp. 124–294. See also, *A Treatise on the Eye, the Manner and Phaenomena of Vision,* 2 vols, (Edinburgh, Printed for A. Millar at London, and for G. Hamilton and J. Balfour at Edinburgh, 1759).

126/38   Scheiner] Scheiner, Christophorus, *Oculus; hoc est, fundamentum opticum*   [etc.] (Oeniponti, 1619). Quoted in Porterfield, *A Treatise*, Vol. II, Bk. V, Ch. I, § 10.

1/1 May 1761] Cf. 'An observation of the Transit of Venus June 6th 1761 Made at Kings College Aberdeen' (AUL MS 2/I/7, 1). See H. Woolf, *The Transits of Venus: A Study of Eighteenth-Century Science* (Princeton, Princeton University Press, 1959).

2/1 SECT. XIII] See *Manuscripts* § 3.3.

2/11 Galen . . . Rohault] Porterfield, *A Treatise*, Vol. II, Bk. V, Ch. I, § 1–2.

3/36f. 3. . . .] See T. Duggan and R. Taylor, 'On Seeing Double', *Philosophical Quarterly* 8 (1958): pp. 171–74; D. C. Blumenfeld, 'On Not Seeing Double', *Philosophical Quarterly* 9 (1959): pp. 264–66.

7/15 Dr. Smith] Smith, *Opticks*, Vol. I, § 137, pp. 48–9.

0/3 *Squinting*] Cf. Student notes from Reid's Lectures on optics in King's College: 'Prop. XXXV To explain the ordinary causes of a Strabisumus or squint of the eye.' (AUL MS K.160, 305). See M. J. Morgan, *Molyneux's Question*, pp. 118f.

1/16 Abbé Mariotte] See Porterfield, *A Treatise*, Vol. II, II.ix.10.

2/12 M. de la Hire . . .] Presumably, Reid is referring to Philippe de La Hire, author of *Mémoires de Mathématique et de Physique* [etc.] (Paris, 1694); and Herman Boerhaave (1668–1738), Dutch professor of medicine at the University of Leiden, and author of *Aphorisms concerning the Knowledge and Cure of Diseases* [trans.] (London, B. Cowse & W. Innys, 1715) and *Academical lectures on the Theory of Physic* [trans.] (London, W. Innys, 1742–46).

3/21 Dr. Briggs] 'But the oddest case of all is mentioned by *Aguilonius* [*Optic.* p. 346.], who affirms, he saw a young person to whom an object *near hand appeared single* and well enough, but *double afar off*, and further sayes, that he observed no defect in his Eyes, but that they were troubled with *moisture*. I am loth to question the integrity of the Author, and therefore (if he were not imposed upon by the party herein) this *odd accident* might proceed also from the *tension* of the Muscles being *weakned* by the *humour* in such a measure, that they could not keep the Eye *steady* in discerning *afar off*, to which is required a greater *Firmness* of the Muscles (our Eyes being *tired* sooner with looking on *remote* than *vicine* objects) than in viewing an object *near hand*, to which there is not so much *stress* required.' William Briggs, 'A new Theory of Vision', p. 176. See Franciscus Aguilonius, OPTICORVM LIBRI SEX Philosophis iuxta ac Mathematicis utiles FRANCISCI AGVILONII E SOCIETATE IESV ANTVERPÆ, EX OFFICINA PLANTINIANA, (Apud Viduam et Filios Io. Moreti. 1613).

146/23–30   Let us . . . squints.] 'The true method of cure I take to be this. When the
             child is arrived at such an age as to be capable of observing directions,
             place him directly before you, and let him close the undistorted eye and
             look at you with the other. When you find the axis of this eye fixt directly
             upon you, bid him endeavour to keep it in that situation, and open his
             other eye. You will now immediately see the distorted eye turn away
             from you towards his nose, and the axis of the other will be pointed at
             you. But with patience and repeated tryals he will by degrees be able to
             keep his distorted eye fixt upon you, at least for some little time, after the
             other is opened. And when you have brought him to continue the axes of
             both eyes fixt upon you, as you stand directly before him, it will be time
             to change his posture, and to set him first a little to one side of you, and
             then to the other, and so to practise the same thing: and when in all these
             situations he can perfectly and readily turn the axes of both eyes towards
             you, the cure is effected. An adult person may practise all this by a glass,
             without any director; though not so easily as with one. But the older he is,
             the more patience will be necessary.' Smith, *Opticks*, Vol. 2. *Remarks*, §
             192, p. 31.

146/39   Dr. Jurin observed] in Smith, *Opticks*, Vol. 2, § 183, p. 30b.

149/6–8   "the . . . possible."] in Smith, *Opticks*, Vol. 2, § 183, p. 30a.

149/13–15   attempted . . . died.] direct quote from Smith, *Opticks*, Vol. 2, § 193, p. 31.
             Variations between critical text and Smith's *Opticks*:
             method] manner
             gentleman] gentleman about nine years of age

153/17   He observes . . .] 'Now, if it be asked why in seeing with both eyes we do
             not always see double, because of a double sensation; I think it is sufficient
             to say that in the ordinary use of our eyes, in which the pictures of an
             object are constantly painted upon corresponding places of the retinas,
             the predominant sense of feeling has originally and constantly informed
             us that the object is single. By this means our idea of its outward place is
             connected with both those sensations, as is manifest by its appearing in
             two places when its pictures are not painted upon corresponding places
             of the retinas in the extraordinary circumstances above mentioned; which
             is only a direct consequence arising from our general habit of seeing.
             Besides, whatever answer is sufficient to this question, must equally serve
             by the rules of philosophy, for an answer to all others of the same sort:
             as how it happens that in hearing with two ears we do not hear double;
             that in feeling with two feet or two hands or two fingers, we do not feel
             double; as we really do in the dark, when a button is pressed with two

opposite sides of two contiguous fingers laid across; for this reason, that those opposite sides of the fingers have never been used to feel one but always two things at a time. We have learned therefore by experience of both senses compared together, to make their informations consistent with each other.' Smith, *Opticks*, Vol. 1, § 137, pp. 48–9.

54/29   salivation] Morgan describes salivation as 'Mercury therapy involving excess production of saliva'. M. J. Morgan, *Molyneux's Question*, p. 122.

54/26–32   "who . . . blind."] Quoted from Smith, *Opticks*, Vol. 2, § 195, p. 31a-b. Variation: Reverend] late Reverend

55/10–13   "A . . . distortion."] in Smith, *Opticks*, Vol. 1, § 137, p. 49.

55/39–156/4   "And . . . discover."] in Smith, *Opticks*, Vol. 1, § 132, p. 44. See M. J. Morgan, 'Cataract Operations', in *Molyneux's Question*, Ch. 2.

58/13   conclusive argument] In the margin of Reid's Glasgow lecture notes: 'The most decisive Argument against Porterfields Theory of Single and double Vision (omitted in the Inquiry into the human Mind) is that one who has learned to Squint voluntarily can make any Object appear double by directing one Eye to it and making the other to diverge a little from it' (AUL MS 4/II/17, 6)

61/18–28   Dr. Briggs . . . mind.] 'Another instance or two of this kind may be seen in Dr. Briggs's *Nova Visionis Theoria*. pag. 25; wherein he proposes a theory, or rather an hypothesis, to account for the single and double appearances of an object, by means of equal degrees of tension of the fibres, of both the optick nerves, continued from the brain to corresponding parts of the two retinas; in which parts the two pictures of an object usually fall. So that the isochronous vibrations of these corresponding fibres agitated by the rays, may stir up a single sensation in the mind; in like manner as unisons in musick are hardly distinguished from one sound. But when the two pictures of an object fall upon parts of the retina, where the tensions of the fibres are different; their discording vibrations may stir up two distinct sensations in the mind; as in musical concords and discords. But for a fuller account of this hypothesis I chuse to refer the reader to the author himself; because there are several hints and observations in that little treatise, and in his *Anatomy of the Eye*, which may be useful and entertaining to the curious.' Smith, *Opticks*, Vol. 2, *Remarks* § 196, p. 31b.

163/33–164/10   "Are. . . informed."] Sir Isaac Newton, *Opticks: Or, A Treatise of the Reflections, Refractions, Inflections and Colours of Light*, 4th ed. (London, Printed for William Innys at the West-End of St. Paul's, 1730): pp. 320–21.

164/36   Dr. Porterfield] Porterfield, *A Treatise*, Vol. II, V.i.4.

165/15–22   "The union . . . state."] See '*An Anatomical Exposition of the Structure of the Human Body* By James Benignus Winslow Professor of Physick, Anatomy and Surgury in the University of Paris, Member of the Royal Sciences, and of the Royal Society at Berlin', &c. Translated from the French original, By G. Douglas, M.D. (London, Printed for A. Bettersworth, *et.al.,* 1733*)*. The 1768 French edition of the *Inquiry* has the following footnote: 'L'Auteur ne citant point l'endroit des Ouvrages de Winslow où se trouve ce passage, je l'ai cherché en vain sans le trouver: ce qui fait que je n'ai pu rapporter ses propres termes. *Note de Traducteur.*' (Vol. 2, p. 157)

165/30   going . . . manner.] Cf. Student notes for Reid's lectures on Optics, in which Reid referred to Fermat's and Leibniz's derivation of the sine law of refraction in order 'to show that the most ingenious men when they trust to Hypothesis . . . have only the chance of going wrong in a more ingenious way' (AUL MS K.160, 263).

167/24   *Of perception*] For a discussion of Reid's account of the role of sensations in perception, see the debate between Cummins and Pappas in the following articles: P. D. Cummins, 'Reid's Realism', *Journal of the History of Philosophy* 12 (1974): pp. 317–40; G. S. Pappas, 'Sensation and Perception in Reid', *Nous* 23 (1989): pp. 155–67; P. D. Cummins, 'Pappas on the Role of Sensations in Reid's Theory of Perception', *Philosophy and Phenomenological Research* 1 (1990): pp. 755–62; G. S. Pappas, 'Causation and Perception in Reid', *Philosophy and Phenomenological Research* 1 (1990): pp. 763–66. See also K. DeRose, 'Reid's Anti-Sensationalism and His Realism', *The Philosophical Review* 98 (1989): pp. 313–48; T. Duggan, 'Thomas Reid's Theory of Sensation', *Philosophical Review* 69 (1960): pp. 90–100; W. J. Ellos, 'Analysis of sensation, Thomas Reid', *New Scholasticism* 57 (1983): pp. 107–14; E. H. Madden, 'Was Reid a Natural Realist?', *Philosophy and Phenomenological Research* 47 (1986): pp. 255–76; J-C. Smith, 'Reid's Functional Explanation of Sensation', *History of Philosophy Quarterly* 3 (1986): pp. 175–93.

168/38ff.   scepticism . . .] For a discussion of Reid's meta-epistemological response to scepticism, see W. P. Alston, 'Thomas Reid on Epistemic Principles', *History of Philosophy Quarterly* 2 (1985): pp. 435–52; and N. Wolterstorff, 'Hume and Reid', *Monist* 70 (1988): pp. 398–417. For a recent Reidian theory of epistemic warrant, see A. Plantinga, *Warrant and Proper Function* (Oxford, Oxford University Press, 1993).

179/23	we agree with Dr. Porterfield] See *'Of the Distance of Objects'*, Porterfield, *A Treatise*, Vol. II, V.iv.
179/39	to him I refer the reader.] Smith, *Opticks*, Vol. 2, p. 136ff.
182/18–26	The colours . . . parts.] Smith, *Opticks*, Vol. 2, *Remarks*, § 241, p. 40a.
183/13	Dr. Smith] Smith, *Opticks*, Vol. 2, *Remarks*, § 241, p. 40.
185/27	Dr. Smith] Smith, *Opticks*, Vol. 1, p. 60ff.
190/26	signs in original perception are sensations] See B. E. Rollin, 'Thomas Reid and the Semiotics of Perception', *Monist* 61 (1978): pp. 257–70.
201/37	human education] See J. C. Robertson, 'The Well-principled Savage, or The Child of The Scottish Enlightenment', *Journal of the History of Ideas* 42 (1981): pp. 503–25.
206/20	ἐντελέχεια] See Aristotle's *De Anima*, Bk. II, Ch. 1, 412a, 27–8. The Greek word is standardly translated as 'actuality'. Liddell-Scott give the definition: *'full, complete reality'*. H. Liddell and R. Scott, *A Greek-English Lexicon* (Oxford, Oxford University Press, 1968): p. 575b.
206/34	Parmenides] See W. C. K. Guthrie: 'Parmenides', in *A History of Greek Philosophy: The Presocratic Tradition from Parmenides to Democritus*, Vol. II (Cambridge, Cambridge University Press, 1980): pp. 1–80.
207/1–3	*Then . . . things.*] Mark Akenside, *The Pleasures of Imagination, A Poem in Three Books* (London, Printed for R. Dodsley at Tully's-Head in Pall-Mall, 1744): Bk I., lines 64–6.
211/37–212/2	*Urbem . . . solebam.*] Virgil, *Eclogues*, Bk. 1.19–23. Trans. 'Fool that I was, I thought imperial Rome / Like Mantua, where on market-days we come, / And thither drive our tender lambs from home. / So kids and whelps their sires and dams express, / And so the great I measured by the less.' *The Works of Virgil, Translated by John Dryden* (Oxford, Oxford University Press, 1961): p. 4.
213/4	He maintains] Berkeley, *Principles*, § 27, § 140.
213/23–5	*Hic . . . fauces.*] Virgil, *Aeneid*, Bk. 7, 568–70. Trans. 'To this infernal lake the Fury flies; / Here hides her hated head, and frees the labouring skies.' *The Works of Virgil, Translated by John Dryden* (Oxford, Oxford University Press, 1961): p. 321.
216/39–217/3	"Annon . . . possint."] Sir Isaac Newton, *Optice: sive de Reflexionibus, Refractionibus, Inflexionibus & Coloribus Lucis*, Libri Tres, Latine reddidit Samuel Clarke, S.T.P. Editio Secunda, auctior. (Londini, Impensis Gul. & Joh. Innys Regiæ Societatis Typographorum ad Insignia Principis in Area Occidentali D. Pauli, 1719): p. 373. Trans. 'Is not the Sensory of Animals that place to which the sensitive Substance is present, and into which the sensible Species of Things are carried through the

Nerves and Brain, that there they may be perceived by their immediate presence to that Substance?' Newton, *Opticks*, pp. 344–5; See IP, p. 100.

217/6   curious application] Hume, *Treatise*, I.iv.V.

218/1   further prosecution of this inquiry] On the strength of the following MS, it appears that Reid, at some stage, intended to include this 'further prosecution' in the *Inquiry*. 'An Inquiry into the human Mind / on the Principles of Common Sense / Book 2d Chap 1 / Of Memory / {Next to the external Senses,} There is no faculty of the Mind whose Operations are more familiar or seem to be better understood than that of Memory. {for this Reason, having in the former Book inquired into the operations of the ⟨external⟩ Sense⟨s⟩ we proceed next to consider the faculty of Memory.} Our Senses give us [the] immediate Knowledge of things present; Memory an immediate Knowledge of things Past. We have endeavoured to trace the process of Nature in communicating the knowledge of things by the Senses, as far as it is open to our View. We have seen that objects make certain impressions upon the Organs of Sense either by immediate application [to those] or by means of some intervenient medium, that the impression upon the organ is accompanied by some corresponding impression upon the Nerves and brain, that these impressions upon the material part are by the laws of Nature connected with corresponding sensations and the Sensations with corresponding perceptions of objects. But we are not able to discover the connection of any one Step of this process with another. And that perception of external Objects which is the result of the whole is as mysterious & unaccountable as if we had it by immediate inspiration without any of those preliminary means and instruments. ¶ In Memory the process of Nature is shorter but no less unaccountable. In the operations of this Faculty we cannot' (*MS ends*) (AUL MS 1/I/2, 1)

TEXTUAL NOTES

The *Textual Notes* contain a record of variations between the critical text and copies of the four editions of the *Inquiry* published in Reid's lifetime.

1. Copy Text

The copy text for the present critical edition is a copy of the fourth edition of the *Inquiry* (1785), located in Glasgow University Library (see below for details). The final wording of a critical text is not based on the copy text alone, but rather on an evaluation of all the textual evidence available to the editor, including authorial manuscripts and every edition prepared within the author's lifetime. Thus, if, at any point, substantive wording of the copy text contradicts the total evidence, the critical text should diverge from it accordingly. The primary purpose of a copy text is to function as a default text in respect of compositorial style: that is, in matters of spelling, punctuation, capitalisation and italicisation, where there is insufficient evidence regarding authorial intention, and no evidence of compositorial inconsistency, then the critical text should reproduce the copy text reading.

Reid's extant manuscripts suggest that he did not prepare his texts with a view to ensuring that his accidentals would be suitable for publication purposes; and there is no evidence, either way, of Reid's views on the accidentals apparently imposed upon his text by the printer. In short, we can take no account of Reid's intentions in respect of compositorial style, other than that (i) he would have wished his meaning to be conveyed to the reader perspicuously and unambiguously; and that (ii) whatever intentions he might have expressed are likely to have affected only those editions published within his lifetime.

The compositors responsible for the fourth edition, appear to have taken greater care in their attempt to establish a consistent set of compositorial practices than those of the previous editions. It must be made clear, however, that the critical editor's role is not to reproduce the copy text in every detail; rather it is (i) to exercise editorial judgment regarding those instances in which there is reasonable evidence for a failure to maintain compositorial consistency, and (ii) to provide the reader with a clear and accurate record of any subsequent decision to diverge from the copy text.

For these reasons, the critical text has been established in accordance with the compositorial style reflected in the fourth edition.

2. Collation Procedure

The collation was made as follows: An initial visual comparison was made between one copy of the fourth edition and one copy of each of the first three editions. A second visual comparison was later made between a draft of the critical text and two copies of the fourth edition, one of which was the copy text. This second comparison was performed so as to ensure that the critical text conforms exactly to the copy text, except in so far as the editor has deliberately deviated from the latter. Finally, a visual comparison was made between systematically selected portions of the draft of the critical text and copies of the first three editions. The variations thereby identified were then organised into substantives and accidentals. Upon an analysis of the results, the editor judged that the effort involved in a further comparison between different copies of the same editions would not be commensurate with the likely results, given the paucity of substantive variations identified between the copies of the four editions examined.

3. Textual Record

The results of the collation are recorded in two tables. Table 1 provides a record of every substantive reading which deviates from the critical text, identified in the copies of the four editions examined. Table 2 provides a record of every accidental which deviates from the critical text, identified in the copy text. It should be emphasised that, in respect of accidentals, the copies of the four editions examined differ among themselves to a far greater extent than the copy text differs from the critical text. The editor has worked from a comprehensive tabulation of every accidental variant (not here published). This has made possible a meticulous appraisal of the compositorial practices adopted in each edition, and was instrumental in the decision to be guided by the compositorial style of the fourth edition. Where the textual evidence seemed inconclusive, account has also been taken of other records of late eighteenth-century usage.

4. Copies of the Editions Examined

1 EDINBURGH : Printed for A. MILLAR, *London*, and A. KINCAID & J. BELL, *Edinburgh*. MDCCLXIV [1764] pp. xvi, 541, errata, 4°. Location: British Library, 8464.bbb.22.

2 The SECOND EDITION Corrected. EDINBURGH : Printed for A. MILLAR, *London*, and A. KINCAID and J. BELL, *Edinburgh*. MDCCLXV [1765] pp. xvi, 383, 8°. Location: British Library, 1609/2645.

3 The THIRD EDITION Corrected. LONDON: Printed for T. CADELL, (Successor to A. MILLAR) in the Strand, and T. LONGMAN, in Pater-Noster Row, London; and KINCAID & J. BELL, Edinburgh. MDCCLXIX [1769] pp. xvi, 383, 8°. Location: Aberdeen University Library, Special Collections, HN.2.89.

4 The FOURTH EDITION Corrected. LONDON: Printed for T. CADELL in the Strand, London; and J. BELL and W. CREECH, Edinburgh. M,DCC,LXXXV. [1785] pp. xvi, 488, 8°. Location: Glasgow University Library, NM.5.11 (copy text); University of Sydney, Fisher Library, Research Collection, 152/12 (corroborative copy).

5. Collation Format

The variant is referenced to the critical text by page and line number (e.g.). The symbol] separates critical text and variant readings. Editorial comments are italicised and placed between parentheses. For example:

15/39   some] the envious blast of some **1** (*corrected in Errata*)

This means that, on page 15, line 39, where the critical text has 'some', it shares this reading with **2, 3** and **4**; whereas **1** reads 'the envious blast of some'.

The symbol ‖ separates variant readings. For example,

190/17   that,] that **3** ‖ (*omitted*) **4**

Thus, on page 190, line 17, where the critical text has 'that,', it shares this reading with **1** and **2**; whereas **3** reads 'that', and, in **4**, the reading is omitted.

TABLE 1

SUBSTANTIVE VARIANTS

In this category are included (i) all divergences in wording between **1**, **2**, **3** and **4**, whether or not these also constitute a change in sense; and (ii) a small number of divergences in punctuation which might be judged to affect the sense (e.g. by changing the grammatical dependency of subordinate clauses). Forms which are similar in pronunciation but differ in etymology (or vice versa) are treated as variants in wording.

2/8	Moral . . . GLASGOW] Philosophy in King's college, Aberdeen **1**
2/11–16	(*Printer and bookseller details for all editions are recorded in the listing of the editions above.*)
3/6–7	JAMES . . . SEAFIELD] JAMES Lord DESKFOORD **1** ‖ JAMES Earl of FINDLATER and SEAFIELD **2 3**
3/28	conviction] connection **2** (*misprint*)
4/5	ingenuous] ingenious **3 4**
4/33	exist] exist presently **1**
5/5	*track*] *tract* **2 3**
5/19	rank] ranks **2** (*catchword*)
6/1–2	your . . . for] the respect which your Lordship puts upon **1**
6/4	leave] leaves **1**
6/6	was] am **1**
6/16	servant,] servant, King's College, Nov. 9. 1763. **1**
8/3	*as*] *as of* **1 2 3**
9/18	*and*] *and of* **1 2 3**
14/32	a chemist,] chymist; **1**
15/39	some] the envious blast of some **1** (*corrected in the Errata*)
17/2	likewise] likeways **2 3**
17/28	Locke] Mr Locke **1**
17/33	Locke's] Mr Locke's **1**
24/15	the human] human **3 4**
28/3	I . . . reason] is what I believe no philosopher can give a shadow of reason for **1**
28/11	Further] Farther **1**
28/18	now] presently **1**

29/7	shall] will **2 3**
30/13–5	some . . . light] we had wanted some of those paradoxes of the ideal philosophy, which will always to sensible men appear as incredible as any thing that ever enthusiasm dreamed or superstition swallowed **1**
30/17	when] where **1**
31/9	Locke's] Mr Locke's **1**
31/13	Locke's] Mr Locke's **1**
31/14	he] Mr Locke **1**
31/19	Locke's] Mr Locke's **1**
32/2	art] airth **2 3**
32/9–10	depends . . . another] is dependent upon, or resolvable into any of the rest **1**
35/16	track] tract **2**
38/18	now] presently **1**
38/21	and of its] and **1**
38/39–39/1	the . . . odours] odoriferous plants spreading their fragrance **1**
40/7	noways] nowise **1**
40/20	further] farther **1**
41/5	finds] find **1**
41/7	this] the **1**
41/25	further] farther **1**
41/32–3	having . . . and] is common to all languages, having the same causes, and which **1**
43/18	readily] immediately and readily **1**
50/16–17	I conclude . . . reasoning] immediately, without reasoning, I conclude **1**
51/25	affections] and affections **1**
56/7	or by] or **1**
56/38	time] time that **1**
57/18	this . . . has] habits which have **1** (*corrected in Errata*)
57/19	a habit] habits **1** (*corrected in Errata*)
61/38	is] is a **3**
61/39	affect] effect **3 4**
62/5	it] (*omitted*) **3**
65/33	may] might **1**
65/34	has] had **1**
65/35	is] was **1**

65/36	cannot] could not **1**
65/38	can] could **1**
66/2	is] will be **1**
66/8	touches] touched **1**
66/9	Can] Could **1**
70/29	our notions of] (*omitted*) **1** (*corrected in Errata*)
72/29	unfold] do possibly unfold **1**
74/1	cannot] could not **1**
75/9	thus:] thus? **4**
75/24	had] hath **4**
77/31	clearly] do clearly **1**
77/37	should] shall **3 4**
78/5	peak] pike **1**
79/37	those] these **2 3 4**
80/24	could] would **1**
81/7	Might] Would **1**
81/38	things] thing **1**
88/8	a] an **1**
89/3	Addison] Mr Addison **1**
89/16	Locke] Mr Locke **1**
89/23	smell, or] smell which they occasion; nor **1**
89/25	or] nor **1**
89/38	are really] were really **1**
89/39	are conveyed] were conveyed **1**
90/10	Locke] Mr Locke **1**
90/24	Locke] Mr Locke **1**
91/6	external] external material **1**
91/19	Locke] Mr Locke **1**
92/23	are] were **1**
92/38	Locke] Mr Locke **1**
93/13	Locke] Mr Locke **1**
93/21	he] Mr Locke **1**
93/24	this philosopher] Mr Locke **1**
93/27	Locke] Mr Locke **1**
94/3	Locke] Mr Locke **1**
94/17	of] in **1 2 3**
96/34	from conceiving] to conceive **1** (*corrected in Errata*)
96/36	from conceiving] to conceive **1** (*corrected in Errata*)
97/1	man] (*omitted*) **1** (*corrected in Errata*)

100/27	either] any **1**
101/20	In . . . impression] One and the same material impression, in one case **1**
102/26	Visible figure, therefore,] So visible figure **1**
102/34	has been] (*omitted*) **1**
107/27	neither hath] hath not **1**
108/10	make] makes **1 2**
111/7	gave] give **1 2**
112/39	lose] loose **3 4**
118/13	demonstrated] shown above **1**
119/26	and touch] and of touch **1 2 3**
123/19	or] and **1 2**
125/5	the rays] their rays **1 2**
128/4–5	the eye] eye **1**
129/37	of] in **3 4**
130/7	make] should make **1**
130/9	see] should see **1**
132/29	is] again is **1**
133/12	*retinæ*] retinæ **1** ‖ *retina* **3 4**
133/13	*retinæ*] retinæ **1** ‖ *retina* **3 4**
133/14	*retinæ,*] retinæ, **1** ‖ *retina* **3 4**
133/16	*retinæ*] retinæ **1** ‖ *retina* **3 4**
133/18	*retinæ*] retinæ **1** ‖ *retina* **3 4**
137/4	a hypothesis] an hypothesis **4**
138/13	upon the] upon **1 2**
138/39–139/1	another eye] another **1**
139/1	object] (*omitted*) **1**
141/27	who] that **3**
145/23	further] farther **1**
145/26–7	objects . . . another,] distant objects **1 2 3**
148/30	have met] to meet **1**
148/36	Dr] (*no new paragraph*) **1 2**
149/36	objects] object **1** (*corrected in Errata*)
150/14	I] (*new paragraph*) **1**
150/28	was] we **1 2 3**
151/19	object] objects **1** (*corrected in Errata*)
155/6	further] farther **1**
156/4	any ways] anywise **4**
156/27–8	and so] are so **4**

159/6	distance] distances **1**
159/7	now] presently **1**
159/19	in] presently in **1**
160/11	had] had the **1**
161/8	further] farther **1**
169/14	exist] be **1**
176/37	8th] 4th **1**
180/5	we] which we **1**
180/13	the] (*omitted*) **3 4**
182/34	me, . . . distance] me . . . distance, **2 3 4**
185/20	undeterminate] indeterminate **1**
190/17	that,] that **3** ‖ (*omitted*) **4**
190/17	further] farther **1**
190/21	thing] things **2 3 4**
190/30	sign suggests] signs suggest **2 3 4**
191/16	thing] things **2 3 4**
192/34–5	usual . . . promise] same meaning upon those signs as they have used to do **1**
201/11	a philosopher] philosophers **1 2**
202/9–10	inhabitants of the Baleares] Balearides **1** ‖ Baleares **2 3**
202/12	archery] arching **1**
206/10	earthly] earthy **1 2**
206/35	later] latter **4**
207/19	may] might **1**
207/19	cannot] could not **1**
207/20	can] could **1**
207/22	are] were **1**
207/23	those] these **1**
211/34	of Rome] Rome **1 2**
212/33	Locke] Mr Locke **1**
214/33	in] of **1 2**
216/12	now] presently **1**
217/12	this] his **4** (*misprint*)
217/14	appeal] appeal it **1**
218/1	further] farther **1**

TABLE 2

ACCIDENTAL VARIANTS

Listed below are divergences between the critical text and the copy text in either spelling, punctuation, capitalisation or italicisation, which do not change the sense.

5/4	*And,*] *And* **3 4**
9/19	*Briggs's*] *Brigg's* **4**
9/22	*nature*] *Nature* **4**
11/8	MIND.] MIND **4**
11/27	connection] connexion **3 4**
12/8	gravitation] gravitation, **2 3 4**
12/11	philosophizes] philosophises **4**
13/27	these,] these **2 3 4**
16/15	sciences,] sciences **4**
17/31	twelve-month (*line-end hyphenation*)] twelvemonth **4**
22/20	candle-light] candle light **3 4**
23/3	*same,*] *same* **4**
23/32	By] by **3 4**
23/37	suspicion,] suspicion **3 4**
25/29	and] And **2 3 4**
26/9	Yet,] Yet **4**
27/2	: it] : It **2 3 4**
27/10	*genera*] *genera,* **2 3 4**
27/27	be perceived] be perceived, **4**
29/5	There was] there was **2 3 4**
31/4	tell;] tell: **2 3 4**
31/5	but] But **3 4**
31/33	faculties;] faculties: **2 3 4**
32/10	nay,] nay **3 4**
32/25	mind,] mind **3 4**
32/38	impressions,] impressions **3 4**
33/4	Indeed,] Indeed **1 4**
34/36	*minds*;] *minds?* **4**
35/10	connection] connexion **3 4**
35/27	breach.] breach? **3 4**
36/2	fellow-citizen] fellow citizen **3 4**
36/6	closet-belief] closet belief **3 4**

37/23	fairies;] fairies, **3 4**
39/1	deserts] desarts **2 3 4**
39/36	finding,] finding **3 4**
40/7	nowise] noway **2 3 4**
40/28	sense,] sense: **3 4**
43/5	which,] which **2 3 4**
43/10	languages:] languages; **4**
45/4	this,] this **4**
47/22	agreeable;] agreeable, **3 4**
47/24	followed,] followed **4**
47/34	How] how **3 4**
47/36	one,] one **3 4**
48/1	that,] that **3 4**
55/28	bodies,] bodies **4**
55/30	firmly,] firmly **3 4**
56/10	introduce] introduce, **4**
56/29	thing,] thing **4**
57/4	philosophers,] philosophers **4**
58/23	that,] that **4**
59/6	That there] that there **4**
59/34	causality] casuality **3 4**
60/33	being, . . . nature,] being . . . nature **1** ‖ being . . . nature, **3 4**
61/14	education,] education **3 4**
64/15	The] the **3 4**
65/2	feelings;] feelings: **2 3 4**
65/17	figure,] figure **4**
65/19	bodies,] bodies **4**
70/13	or] of **4**
70/16	propose] propose, **4**
70/30	thought,] thought **4**
74/36	but] But **2 3 4**
77/31	to] to, **4**
78/12	Yea,] Yea **4**
79/30	but,] but **4**
79/33	conversation,] conversation **4**
80/37	this:] this, **2 3 4**
81/23	position:] position; **2 3 4**
82/9	*Optics*] Optics **1 2 3 4**
85/3	discern,] discern **4**

85/25	midnight] mid-night (*line-end hyphenation in* **2 3**) **4**
88/34	he] He **2 3 4**
89/17	philosophers,] philosophers **4**
90/25	presumed] presumed, **4**
91/38	heat] heat, **3 4**
92/31	insentient,] insentient **4**
93/10	sensations] sensations, **4**
94/21	up,] up **4**
94/24	ideas,] ideas **2 3 4**
95/29	Now,] Now **3 4**
97/19	It] it **3 4**
98/24	How] how **3 4**
100/27	these] these, **2 3 4**
101/3	proof;] proof: **2 3 4**
101/29	touch:] touch; **4**
104/3	follows,] follows. **2 3** ‖ follows: **4**
104/32	for,] for **1 4**
113/9	mothers,] mothers **3 4**
114/11	therefore] therefore, **4**
115/3	demonstrated,] demonstrated **2 3 4**
115/25	premises;] premises: **3 4**
115/34	lastly,] lastly **3 4**
116/10	*Optics*] Optics **1 2 3 4**
117/13	And if,] And, if **3 4**
118/8	visible,] visible **4**
118/18	Thus] Thus, **2 3 4**
119/28	bodies,] bodies **4**
120/2	dissected?] dissected. **4**
120/11	nature,] nature **3 4**
120/13	That,] That **4**
121/7	head,] head **4**
122/19	nature;] nature, **4**
122/37	object;] object: **4**
123/5	philosophizing] philosophising **4**
123/16	which,] which **3 4**
123/37	*membrana*] *membrani* **3 4**
124/39	that] That **3 4**
125/18	That] that **4**
125/26	That] that **4**

126/4	true;] true, **2 3 4**
127/8	inches. Let] inches, let **4**
129/22	but] But **1 2 3 4**
130/7	reason,] reason **2 3 4**
134/2	and] And **2 3 4**
134/10	situate,] situate **2 3 4**
134/36	reverie] revery **4**
136/34	two;] two: **3 4**
140/32	other;] other: **2 3 4**
141/11	When] when **2 3 4**
141/16	Abbé] Abbe **2 3 4**
141/27	squint] quint **4**
142/11	touchstone] touch-stone (*line-end hyphenation*) **2 3** ‖ touch-stone **4**
145/35	consider,] consider **2 3 4**
145/39	suppose] suppose, **2 3 4**
148/39	*Optics*] Optics **1 2 3 4**
149/14	gentleman] Gentleman **2 3 4**
151/35	object,] object **4**
152/5	eye,] eye **4**
152/9	acquire,] acquire **4**
152/32	eyes,] eyes **2 3 4**
153/7	optics] Optics **4**
154/26	One] "One **1 2 3 4**
154/26	"who] who **1 2 3 4**
154/37	Secondly] 2dly **2 3 4**
155/7	blindness,] blindness **3 4**
156/1	objects] objects, **4**
156/5	Gentleman] gentlemen **1 2 3 4**
157/9	vision,] vision **3 4**
157/31	felt,] felt **4**
159/28	*Briggs's*] *Brigg's* **4**
160/5	Whether] whether **3 4**
160/18	gentlemen] Gentlemen **2 3 4**
161/1	instances] instances, **4**
161/3	them,] them **1 4**
164/9	eyes] eyes, **2 3 4**
164/26	and] And **2 3 4**
168/6	yet,] yet **4**

171/9	testimony] testimony, **2 3 4**
172/28	and,] and **3 4**
174/1	water;] water: **2 3 4**
174/10	*nature*] *Nature* **4**
174/15	If] if **3 4**
174/19	There] there **4**
174/25	The] the **4**
174/26	This sensation] This sensation, **4**
179/2	wind,] wind **2 3 4**
179/3	ropes,] ropes **4**
180/35	is,] is **2 3 4**
182/4	do,] do; **2 3 4**
182/9	sensation,] sensation; **2 3 4**
182/24	distance,] distance **2 3 4**
182/34	me,] me **2 3 4**
183/13	*Optics*] Optics **1 2 3 4**
183/15	distance,] distance **4**
184/17	half-mile] half mile **2 3 4**
185/17-18	fifty . . . feet] fifty, . . . feet, **2 3 4**
185/18	that,] that **3 4**
185/25	some] same **4**
186/11	object,] object **4**
186/28	through] thro' **2 3 4**
187/28	*Optics*] Optics **1 2 3 4**
188/2	Thus,] Thus **3 4**
189/6	objects,] objects **4**
196/10	Thus,] Thus **3 4**
198/24	nature,] nature **4**
198/37	causality] casualty **4** (*misprint*)
199/31	way:] way; **2 3 4**
200/23	that,] that **1 4**
203/23	inquiry] Inquiry **4**
207/1	*th'*] *the* **4**
207/31	things,] things **4**
209/6	That] that **4**
211/3	word,] word **3 4**
211/5	and] And **1 2 3 4**
212/9	ideas:] ideas; **3 4**
213/32	things;] things: **2 3 4**

214/37   dilemma:] dilemma; **1 2 3 4** (*cf. 212/29*)
214/37   Your] your **3 4**
216/29   apostatizes] apostatises **4**
216/39   *Optics*] Optics **2 3 4** ‖ optics **1**

RECURRENT ACCIDENTAL VARIANTS

Italicisation or romanisation of the copy text punctuation has been silently revised to conform to the structure of the sentence: e.g.,

    4/10   *just*;] *just;*

Capitalisation of the first word of every paragraph in the *Dedication*, except the first, has been silently removed.

MANUSCRIPTS

EDITORIAL PRINCIPLES

The editorial conventions adopted for the transcription of the manuscripts presented below are as follows. Spelling, grammar and punctuation are not normalised or modernised. All punctuation is original, except where it has been silently supplied to mark a sentence that the author marks by using alternative conventions: for example, a flourish to fill out a line, an excessive space between sentences, or a paragraph break. Authorial corrections to spelling and punctuation are not normally recorded. Non-standard contractions are expanded only if (i) they would not have remained were the MS to have been converted into printing in the eighteenth century; or (ii) there is a reasonable likelihood that the author would have pronounced the expanded form to himself, or at least expected the reader to do so. Superscripts are silently relocated (e.g. from 'Mr', '1ly' to 'Mr', '1ly'). Overlined words or phrases (used for emphasis) are reproduced in italics. The underlining of a word or phrase is retained. Duplicated wording is silently omitted, and deleted false starts (i.e. fragmentary phrases that were never part of a completed sentence) are not recorded.

Text placed between angle brackets ⟨ ⟩ is the restoration of characters which the editor judges it was the author's intention to write, but for which he does not have the visual evidence: that is, (a) where the MS is frayed and the editor supplies what has been lost; (b) where the MS survives and appears to contain a mistaken character or word, or to omit a necessary character or word. (Angle brackets are not used to indicate expanded contractions.) Text placed between square brackets [ ] is an authorial deletion. An ellipsis placed between square brackets [. . .] indicates an illegible authorial deletion. Text placed between braces { } is an interlinear insertion. Text placed between the symbols ⟪ ⟫ is an authorial addition to the original writing that was placed either in the margin, or late on the page, or on another page.

MS variations are recorded as in the *Textual Notes*, with the following additions: An ellipsis in the recording of a variant is used to indicate that the variant is a piece of expanded writing, curtailed in the copy text (e.g. judgment] . . . and). A full-stop is included in the lemma where expanded writing begins a new sentence (e.g. judgment.] . . . By). Punctuation is included in the variant reading where it begins the expanded writing (e.g.

judgment] . . . ; and). The symbol ¶ indicates a paragraph break (e.g. judgment.] . . . ¶ By). The symbol | indicates a page break (e.g. and | by).

Unless otherwise indicated, manuscripts are from Aberdeen University Library, and referenced by giving the MS catalogue number, followed by a comma and the MS page or folio number (e.g. 4/I/27, 2r). The prefix '2131' for MSS from the Birkwood Collecton is not recorded.

INDEX OF MANUSCRIPTS

The following index is a complete list of the manuscripts reproduced, in whole or in part, in this edition. In subsequent references, the prefix '2131' for the MSS from the Birkwood Collection is not recorded.

Aberdeen University Library Manuscripts

National Library of Scotland Manuscript

1 THE HUME–REID EXCHANGE

Presented below is a transcription of the complete set of extant manuscripts recording the correspondence between David Hume and Thomas Reid. The exchange appears to have been initiated by Hugh Blair, no doubt at the prompting of Reid. Blair evidently delivered to Hume an early draft of part of the *Inquiry*, accompanied by a request that Hume give his 'Judgement of the Argument and of the Piece in general'. Hume's response is contained in a letter addressed to Blair, dated 4 July 1762. One way in which Reid tried to address Hume's criticisms was by producing an abstract of the *Inquiry* which he sent to Hume, again via Blair, along with a more complete version of the *Inquiry*. Hume responded to this material in a letter addressed directly to Reid, dated 25 Feb 1763, to which Reid replied in a letter of 18 March 1763. Each of these letters, along with Reid's abstract, is provided below.

A transcription of Hume's first letter is also published in Paul B. Wood, 'David Hume on Thomas Reid's *An Inquiry into the Human Mind on the Principles of Common Sense*: A New Letter to Hugh Blair from July 1762', *Mind* 95 (1986): pp. 411–16. A transcription of Reid's abstract has been published in David Fate Norton, 'Reid's Abstract of the *Inquiry into the Human Mind*', *Philosophical Monographs* 3 (1976): pp. 125–32.

1.1 David Hume to Hugh Blair (4 July 1762)

2814/1/39, 1r   Sir

I have read over your Friend's Performance & read it over with
5   Pleasure, because it has a Quality seldom to be met with in Performances
of that Nature; which is that it is wrote in a lively entertaining manner
& will be able to fix the Attention even of those who are the {least}
curious about metaphysical Reasonings. You desire me also to give my
Judgement of the Argument and of {the} Piece in general: I own this
10   is not easy, unless one had seen the whole; because the Scope [of] and
Tendency of the Parts is not other wise easily discover'd. However, such
an imperfect Judgement as I can form, I shall very candidly deliver {to
you} leaving you to [deliver] {transmit} what part of it you think proper
to the ingenious Author. I believe the whole of what I can say may be
15   compriz'd in two or three Remarks.

First As far as I can judge, there seems to be some Defect in Method; at
least, I do not find the Subject open up gradually, and one part throwing
light upon another: The Author digresses frequently: For Instance, under
the Article of Smelling, he gives you a Glimpse of all the Depths of his
20   Philosophy. I own, however, that this Censure of mine is premature, on
account of my not having seen the whole.

Secondly. The Author supposes, that the Vulgar do not believe the
sensible Qualities of Heat, Smell, Sound, & probably Colour to be really
[1v]   in the Bodies, but only their Causes or something capable of producing
25   them in the | Mind. But this is imagining the Vulgar to be Philosophers
& Corpuscularians from their Infancy. You know what pains it cost
Malebranche & Locke to establish that Principle. There are but obscure
Traces of it among the Antients viz in the Epicurean School. The Peripatetics maintaind opposite Principles. And indeed Philosophy scarce
30   ever advances a greater Paradox in the Eyes of the People, than when it
affirms that Snow is neither cold nor white: Fire hot nor red.

Thirdly. It surpriz'd me to find the Author affirm, that our Idea of
Extension is nothing like the Objects of Touch. He certainly knows, that
People born blind have very compleat Ideas of Extension[s]; & some of
35   them have even been great Geometers. Touch alone gives us an Idea of
three Dimensions.

Fourthly. If I comprehend the Author's Doctrine, which, I own, I can
hitherto do but imperfectly, it leads us back to innate Ideas. This I do not
advance as an Objection: For nothing ought ever to be supposd finally

decided in Philosophy, so as not to admit of a new Scrutiny; but only
that, I think, the Author affirms I had been hasty, & not supported by any
Colour of Argument when I affirm, that all our Ideas are copy'd from
Impressions. I have endeavourd to build that Principle on two Arguments.
5 The first is desiring any one to make a particular Detail of all his Ideas,
where he woud always find that every Idea had a correspondent & preceding Impression. If no Exception can ever be found, the Principle must
remain incontestible. The second is, that if you exclude any particular
Impression, [. . .] as Colours to the blind, Sound to the Deaf, you also
10 exclude the Ideas. |

These were the most material Remarks, which occurd to me. As to
one particular Insinuation, I rather choose not to take notice of it {at all}
because I could not properly reply to it without employing a Style, which
I woud not willingly use towards one {for whom I have otherwise a great
15 Regard and} who has the Honour of bearing the Name of your Friend. I
wish the Parsons wou'd [. . .] confine themselves to their old Occupation
of worrying one another; & leave Philosophers to argue with Temper,
Moderation & good Manners. I am Sir

Your most obedient Servant

David Hume

⟨Edin⟩burgh
4 July 1762

Address: To The Revd Doctor Blair Professor of Rhetorick in the Uni-
25 versity of Edinburgh

1.2 Thomas Reid: an Abstract of the *Inquiry* (undated)

Ever since the treatise of human Nature was published I respected Mr
Hume as the greatest Metaphysician of the Age, and have learned more
from his writings in matters of that kind than from all others put together.
I read that treatise over and over with great care, made an abstract of it and
wrote my observations upon it. I perceived that his System is all founded
upon one principle, from which his conclusions, however extraordinary,
35 are deduced with irresistible Evidence. The principle I mean is, That all
the objects of human thought are either Impressions or Ideas: which I was
very much disposed to believe untill I read that Treatise; but finding that
if this is true I must be an absolute Sceptic, I thought that it deserved a
carefull Examination.

For this purpose I entered into a Strict Examination of my Impressions that I might know whether all my Thoughts & Conceptions were images and copies of them or not; taking it for granted that if any object of thought was not like any impression it could not be an Idea, because Ideas in his

5   System are faint copies of preceeding impressions.

I have perhaps taken more pains in this Enquiry than perhaps any man ever did, being heartily concerned to know whether there was any such thing as truth within the reach of the human faculties, and imagining that the examination of this principle upon which that System of Scepticism

10   depended would not be very difficult.

For I thus reasoned with my self, My impressions especially those of Sensation I can raise when I please, & continue as long as I please by the presence of the Objects. I can attend to what I feel, & the Sensation is nothing else, nor has any other qualities than what I feel it to have. Its

15   *esse* is *sentiri*, and nothing can be in it that is not felt. So that I concluded I might know perfectly what my Sensations are. Then I can surely attend to sensible Objects, I can compare them with my sensations and see whether they are like or unlike. But however easy this task of attending to my sensations appeared in Theory, I found it very difficult in the Practice. I

[2]   Indeed it is easy to attend to those Sensations which are either very painfull or very pleasant, and it is acknowledged on all hands that they are not like any of those things that we call external objects. But it is extreamly difficult to attend to the sensations that are neither pleasant nor painfull, such as those we have when we feel a body hard or soft, rough

25   or smooth of this or the other figure.

This difficulty arises from our being determined by our Constitution to pass instantaneously from the sensation to the quality which corresponds to it, and to attend only to the latter. One that attends carefully to such sensations will soon be sensible that the most painfull abstraction is not

30   more difficult. And therefore as no philosopher as far as I know hath taken notice of this difficulty, it is probable they never attended to their sensations with sufficient care.

I flatter myself that by much pains and practice I have overcome this difficulty in some degree. When I present an Object to any of my Senses in

35   order to attend to the impression that is made upon the mind, I endeavour to withdraw my thoughts from every thing external, to turn them inward and consider purely what I feel. I suppose every external existence anni- hilated, every impression and thought I ever had before quite obliterated, and that I begin a new Scene of Existence with this single Impression.

What is it? To what is it like? I view it narrowly on every side, and resist every thought that would divert my Attention untill I be well acquainted with it, and able to make it an object of thought.

When I had acquired the power of thus attending to my Sensations, I was soon perswaded that I had never made them objects of thought before & that those Sensations which I had felt every day, perhaps every hour of my life, had notwithstanding been as much unknown to me as if I had never felt them, because I had never given any attention to them. I found in a word that hardness and softness, roughness and smoothness, figure extention and motion had not the least resemblance to those Sensations that correspond to them & by which we are made acquainted with them.

This enquiry into the fundamental Article of Mr Humes System led me I gradually into my present way of thinking with regard to the human Mind: And in what I have wrote concerning the five Senses, I have always had Mr Humes System and particularly this fundamental Article of it in my View.

In treating of the several Senses my Intentions are

1 To lead the reader, To form a clear and distinct conception of the several Sensations which each of them exhibit, To distinguish these Sensations from the things that are constantly associated, and are apt to be confounded with them. And to lead the reader to attend to them so as to be able to make them objects of thought, without which it is impossible that he can enter into my reasoning or understand my principles.

2 To form distinct Notions of the several Sensible qualities which we are acquainted with by means of our Sensations. There is not the same Difficulty in attending to these as to the Sensations; they are indeed the most common objects of thought. It is easy to have the clearest & most distinct Notions of the primary Qualities. But our Notions of secondary qualities are obscure and relative, so that it requires great attention to analyse them; and in this I have done my best, in treating of Smell, of Heat, & chiefly in treating of Colour.

3 To compare our Sensations with the sensible qualities corresponding: and in this comparison I always find a total dissimilitude. This dissimilitude betwixt our Sensations and the sensible qualities known to us by their means, is the Foundation of my System, as their Similitude is the Foundation of all the Systems that went before. Aristotle makes all our Sensations to be Forms or Images of the sensible qualities that correspond to them. Locke makes the Sensations we have by primary Qualities to be resemblances, but not the sensations of the secondary. Berkley and

Hume do not indeed admit the existence of external sensible things, but they affirm that all the Notions we have of what we call sensible qualities are nothing else but copies & images of our Sensations. I have therefore [4] proposed this as an *Experimentum | Crucis* by which these Systems must 5 stand or fall. If what we call Extension, Figure, Motion, Hardness or Softness, Roughness or Smoothness have any Resemblance to the Sensations that correspond to them, then I must Subscribe to Mr Humes Creed and cannot avoid it. But if there is no such resemblance then his System falls to pieces as well as all the other System⟨s⟩ I have named and we are to 10 seek for a new one. The last Appeal in a Question of this kind must be to a mans own Perceptions. He that can attend to his {sensations} so far as to make them an object of thought, and can compare them with sensible qualities can be at no loss to judge in this question. And if he is at any loss this is an evident proof that he has not clear and distinct notions of 15 the things he would compare. After taking much pains to attend to my Sensations and to form clear and distinct conceptions of them, it appears to me as clear and as certain that they are not like to sensible qualities, as that the pain of the toothach is not like to a triangle.

4 Supposing the dissimilitude betwixt our Sensations and sen⟨s⟩ible 20 things established, and of consequence all the former Systems about the senses laid aside; the Question naturally occurs. How Sensations in the mind give us the notions of Sensible things which are no ways like them, and not onely give us the Notions of these things but the firm belief of their real Existence. This Question can be no way resolved but by finding 25 out those laws of our Constitution by which our Sensations are connected with the conception and belief of external Objects. Now I take it for a Rule in Philosophizing That wherever two things are constantly and invariably connected in the course of Nature, and where at the same time this connection cannot be accounted for by any known law of Nature: We 30 ought to consider such connexion as being itself a primary Law of Nature, or else a consequence of some law of nature hitherto undiscovered. Thus when I observe that cold in a certain degree freezes water. If I cannot account for this by any known law of Nature, I hold it for a law of Nature itself. For if it is not a primary law of Nature it must be the consequence 35 of some primary law of Nature, and therefore has the same Authority, and may be taken for a principle in the resolution of other Phænomena in the same manner as if it was a law of Nature. |

[5]   In like manner when certain sensations of my Mind are invariably accompanied with the conception and belief of certain external objects,

when the same connection is found in the minds of all men at all times,
when it can be shewn that this connexion does not arise from Custom
or Education, nor can be accounted for by any Law of the human mind
hitherto known and received; We ought to hold this Connexion to be itself
a Law of the human Mind, untill we find some more general Law of which
it is the consequence.

For aught we know Nature might have given us Sensations of Mind
such as we have without connecting them invariably with certain material
Impressions made upon {the} bodily organs. In like manner for aught we
know, Nature might have given us both the conception and belief of external things, without connecting them invariably with certain Sensations.
For no man can give a shadow of reason why the later should always
precede the former.

This Connexion which Nature hath established betwixt our Sensations
and the conception and belief of external Objects, I express two ways:
Either by saying that the Sensations suggest the objects by a natural
principle of the Mind; or by saying that the Sensations are natural Signs of
the Objects. These Expressions signify one and the same thing, and I do
not pretend by them to account for this Connexion, but onely to affirm it
as a fact that by the constitution of our nature there is such a Connexion.

5 As our Sensations are natural Signs of some External things and many
of them are intended for no other purpose. So some External Things are
natural Signs of Others, & are intended for that Purpose. It is here very
observable that when this is the case, it ⟨is⟩ almost as difficult to attend
to external Natural Signs, as to the internal. We always fix our attention
upon the thing Signified and overlook the Sign. This is fully explained in
treating of Vision which affords the most remarkable instances of it.

6 Many of our Sensations and of their various Modifications, by custom
& habit come to signify things which they did not signify by nature and I
Constitution. In Vision it is very difficult to trace the boundary betwixt
what the Eye presents to us by our Constitution, and what we learn from
custom and habit to discern by it. I have endeavoured to set this matter in
as clear a light as I could.

7 This power of the Mind whereby things are suggested or signified by
means of custom and habit, by such si{g}ns as did not suggest them by
Nature deserves to be analysed. It is {so} similar in many respects to that
power by which we learn language at first, that I have endeavoured to
explain both and reduce them to first principles in the Chapter of Vision.

If these things are understood the whole of my plan will be easily

comprehended. In a word wherever I can find any principle of the human
Mind which is employed in forming our Notions and opinions about
sensible things, I think it falls within my province. And now I shall onely
add a few things concerning the Method and Order of the Performance.

5   I thought it most decent and proper to write not in the Synthetical but in
the Analytical Method; That is, not to lay down my conclusions first and
then to seek for facts to confirm them; But to take the facts in the Order
that the Senses present them & consider what may be inferred from them.
I rather chuse the Character of an Enquirer than of a Doctor and therefore
10   as becomes a fair Enquirer take a precognition of facts before I draw my
conclusions. You have seen the Examination of four of the Witnesses, &
may Judge whether their testimony is fairly and distinctly taken down. A
fifth is to be examined, and when that is done it will be time to sum up
the Evidence.

15   I think nothing a Digression which any of the Senses offer to my consideration, and which tends either to give any new light to the Operations
of the human Mind, or to correct any of the received opinions concerning
it. And in this view I am not sensible that I have made many digressions.
[7]   It is unavoidable in this Method to treat of things under one | Sense which
20   belong equally to another. To avoid repetitions I have thrown several such
things under the first of the Senses I consider, which I supposes gives
occasion to Mr Hume to say that on that Article I have given a glimpse
of all the depths of my Philosophy.

            I have not indeed affected to shew my Method in the tittles of the
25   several Sections, so that those tittles may be onely considered as pointing
to some principal Subject of the Section nor have I taken any pains to point
out my Method by tedious transitions, conceiving it Essential to a Philosophical work to have method but not essential to make ostentation of it.

1.3 David Hume to Thomas Reid (25 Feb 1763)

2814/I/42, 1r   Sir

            By Dr Blair's means, I have been favour'd with the Perusal of your
Performance, which I have read with great Pleasure & Attention. It is
35   certainly very rare that a Piece so deeply philosophical is wrote with
so much Spirit and affords so much Entertainment to the Reader; tho'
I must still regreat the Disadvantages under which I read it, as I never
had the whole Performance at once before me, and could not be able
fully to compare one Part with another. To this Reason chiefly I ascribe

some Obscurities, which, in spite of your short Analysis or Abstract, still seems to hang over your System. For I must do you the Justice to own, that, where I enter into your Ideas, no Man appears to express himself with greater Perspicuity than you do; a Talent, which, above all others, is requisite in that Species of Literature, which you have cultivated. There are some Objections, which I would willingly propose to this fourth Chapter of Sight, did I not suspect that they proceed [chiefly] from my not sufficiently understanding it: And I am the more confirm'd in this Suspicion, as Dr Blair tells me, that the former Objections I made had been deriv'd chiefly from that Cause. I shall therefore forbear till the whole can be before me, and shall not at present propose any farther Difficulties to your Reasonings. I shall only say, that if you have been able to clear up these [Difficult] {abstruse} & important I Subjects, instead of being mortifyd, I shall be so vain as to pretend to a share of the Praise, and shall think, that my Errors, by having at least some Coherence, had led you to make a more strict Review of my Principles which were the common ones, and to perceive their Futility. As I was desirous to be of some Use to you, I kept a watchful Eye all along, over your Style; but it is really so correct and so good English, that I found not any thing worth the remarking. There is only one Passage in this Chapter, where you make use of the Phraze hinder to do instead of hinder from doing, which is the English one; but I could not find the Passage when I sought for it.[1] You may judge how unexceptional the whole appeard to me, when I could remark so small a Blemish. I beg my Compliments to my friendly Adversaries, Dr Campbell & Dr Gerard; and also to Dr Gregory, whom I suspect to be of the same Disposition, tho' he has not openly declard himself such.

I am with Sincerity Sir
Your most obedient humble Servant
David Hume
Edinburgh
25 Feby 1763

---

[1] Neither phrase is to be found in the *Inquiry*.

1.4 Thomas Reid to David Hume (18 March 1763)

23157.
Letter 3, 1r

Kings Coll 18 March 1763

5   Sir

On Monday last Mr John Farquhar brought me your letter of Feb 25th inclosed in one from Dr Blair. I thought my self very happy in having the means of obtaining at second hand, through the friendship of Dr Blair, your Opinion of my performance; and you have been pleased to 10 communicate it directly, in so polite & friendly a manner as merits great acknowledgements on my part.

Your keeping a watchfull Eye over my Style with a view to be of use to me, is an Instance of Candour and Generosity to an Antagonist, which would affect me very sensibly although I had no personal concern in it. 15 And I shall always be proud to follow so amiable an Example. Your Judgment of the Style indeed gives me great consolation, as I was very diffident of my self in regard to English, & have been indebted to Drs Campbell & Gerard for many corrections of that kind.

In attempting to throw some new light upon these abtruse Subjects, 20 I wish to preserve the due mean betwixt Confidence and Despair. But whether I have any Success in this Attempt or not, I shall always avow my self your Disciple in Metaphysicks. I have learned more from your writings in this kind than from all others put together. Your System appears to me not onely coherent in all its parts, but likeways justly deduced | from 25 principles commonly received among Philosophers: Principles, which I never thought of calling in Question, untill the conclusions you draw from them in the treatise of humane Nature made me suspect them. If these principles are Solid your System must stand; And whether they are or not, can better be judged after you have brought to Light the whole System 30 that grows out of them, than when the greater part of it was wrapped up in clouds and darkness. I agree with you therefore that if this System shall ever be demolished, you have a just claim to a great share of the Praise, both because you have made it a distinct and determinate mark to be aimed at, and have furnished proper artillery for the purpose.

35   When you have seen the whole of my performance I shall take it as a very great favour to have your opinion upon it, from which I make no doubt of receiving light, whether I receive conviction or not.

Your Friendly Adversaries Drs Campbel & Gerard as well as Dr Gregory return their Compliments to you respectfully. A little Philosophical Society {here} of which all the three are members, is much indebted to you for its Entertainment. Your Company would, although we are all good Christians, be more acceptable than that of Saint Athanasius. And since we cannot have you upon the bench, you are brought oftner than any other man, to the bar, accused and defended with great Zeal but without bitterness. If you write no more in morals politicks or metaphysicks, I am affraid we shall be at a loss for Subjects. I am respectfully Sir,

Your most obliged
humble Servant
Tho. Reid

Address: To David Hume Esqr   Edinburgh

2 THE ABERDEEN PHILOSOPHICAL SOCIETY

2.1 Reid's Discourses, 1758–1763.

In his *Inquiry*, Reid states that his 'thoughts upon this subject were, a good many years ago, put together in another form, for the use of my pupils; and afterwards were submitted to the judgment of a private philosophical society, of which I have the honour to be a member' (HM, 5/29–32). Reid is referring here to seven discourses he delivered before the Aberdeen Philosophical Society.[1]

NO.	DATE	TITLE	MS
1.	14 June 1758	'The difficulty of a just philosophy of the human mind; General prejudices against David Humes system of the mind; & some observations on the perceptions we have by sight'	3107/1/1, 17–30
2.	14 March 1759	'Analysis of the Sensations of smell and Taste'	3107/1/3, 58–72
3.	15 March 1760	'Analysis of our sensations continued'	3107/1/5, 12r–15r
4.	23 Sept 1760	'Of the sense of touch'	3107/1/6, 29r–37r
5.	8 Sept 1761	'on the sense of seeing'	539/1 (title only)
6.	11 Oct 1762	No source gives the subject matter of the sixth discourse. However, the society Minutes record that Reid 'proposed soon to send it to the press along with the other discourses which he had read before the society'	539/1 (record only).
7.	13 Sept 1763	'upon Perception'	539/1 (title only)

---

[1] Members of this society included James Beattie, Alexander Gerard, George Campbell, James Dunbar, John Farquar, Thomas Gordon, John Gregory, William Ogilvie, Thomas Reid, John Ross, David Skene, George Skene, John Stewart, and Robert Traill. For further detail see *The Minutes of the Aberdeen Philosophical Society 1758–1773*, edited by H. Lewis Ulman (Aberdeen: Aberdeen University Press, 1990).

The first four of Reid's discourses survive in finished form only in transcriptions by his colleague, Thomas Gordon. There is, however, what appears to be an early draft of the second and third discourses in Reid's own hand (undated, 1/I/3, 7–33). In addition, there exists a manuscript that corresponds to various parts of the discourses (undated, 1/I/4, 1–8). It is a self-contained paper, the aim of which, Reid writes, is to consider "the various kinds of Sensations we have by these faculties called the five Senses" and "other Simple Notions or Objects of Thought we have by their Means" (1/I/4, 5).[2]

It would be optimal for a critical edition of the *Inquiry* to present these manuscripts in their entirety. However, a complete reproduction would involve extensive duplication. On the other hand, a simple collation of variants would eliminate several hermeneutically significant features, such as the original sequence of material, omitted portions of text, the immediate context of variants, and so on. By way of a workable alternative, then, Reid's discourses are presented in a combination of transcript and collation formats. Where a portion of a discourse is sufficiently divergent from the *Inquiry* in matters of sequence and substantives, it is fully transcribed. Where the discourse is sufficiently close to the published text to make this unnecessary, the record is limited to a listing of substantive variants only. Variants are located within the manuscript by page or folio number only (e.g. 'p. 17', or 'fo. 12r').

Discourse 1.

'The difficulty of a just philosophy of the human mind; General prejudices against David Humes system of the mind; & some observations on the perceptions we have by sight', delivered 14 June 1758, (MS 3107/1/1, 17–30, in Gordon's hand).

(The following is a record of substantive variants between portions of HM, pp. 10–25, and MS, pp. 17–19.)

2/37–13/20 BUT . . . species.] (*MS begins*) The anatomy of the human mind – curious & useful – hath greater variety & attended with more difficulty than that of the body:- A man hath but one subject to examine in the mental anatomy viz his own mind – what he can collect concerning others from outward signs is of ambiguous interpretation. p. 17

---

[2] Selections from this MS are given in *Explanatory Notes* 37/10 and 93/17.

13/29   exalt and dignify] make the perfection of p. 17
13/31–9   The two-legged . . . others.] Man in a savage state, like a tree in the forest
             is purely of nature's growth: but contains in him the seeds of learning,
             virtue & religion, which must be buried without culture & exercise, hardly
             perceivable either by himself or others. p. 17
14/12   species] . . . & the natural structure of the human mind. p. 17
14/13–25   The language . . . title.] (*omitted*) p. 17
14/31–15/15 The mind . . . perfection.] (*omitted*) p. 17
15/22–3   powers and laws] perceptions p. 18
15/25–19/19 Success . . . rots.] (*omitted*) p. 18
19/20–5   The philosophers . . . Jove.] A prejudice against this Philosopher, that
             there are so many things in his plan which shock the common sense of
             mankind. A Philosopher can never be matched with a harder adversary
             than common sense, who never fails at last to triumph over those who
             wage war with her. p. 18
19/31–21/9   THE present . . . market-place.] (*omitted*) p. 18
21/33–22/3   THERE are . . . America] Presumption in D.H to pretend to give an entire
             system – probably he (*sic*) some parts of it have escaped him, & others
             have been mangled & distorted to ply to his system. p. 18
22/7–14   One may . . . difficult?] (*omitted*) p. 18
22/17–18   I suspect . . . work.] (*omitted*) p. 18
22/20–1   taken . . . trowel] its defects appear p. 18
22/23–6   The little . . . power.] (*omitted*) p. 18
22/32–5   expostulating . . . secrets] expostulating &c p. 18
22/38   shrink into] reduced to a jumble of p. 18
23/6–24/32   plunge . . . infidelity.] lead a man into such determined & dogma | tical
             scepticism. Tho' we have some examples of this in great wits, I am
             not apt to believe that it must necessarly be so. I have always found
             Philosophy an agreeable companion, a kind & benevolent guide, a friend
             to common sense & to the happiness of mankind. ¶ Fortified with these
             maxims I design now & then to make an excursion into human nature
             to observe what offers & to examine the accounts given by others.
             pp. 18–19
25/9–17   IT . . . things.] The perceptions we have by the external senses seem to
             be the first, the simplest, & the most distinct operations of the mind, &
             therefore proper to be first considered in an analysis of it. I shall therefore
             at this time make some observations on the perceptions we have by <u>sight</u>,
             which may be reduced to these three Colour, visible figure, & visible
             extension. p. 19

(The record below is a full transcription of MS, *pp. 19–25, which corresponds to portions of* HM, *pp. 85–166, as indicated in the left margin.)*

5/20–90/27   Mr Locke observed, that if a man had never seen any one distinct colour, he could never by any effort of his mind conceive an idea of it, though he was well acquainted with all the rest. It is a matter more of curiosity than use, to inquire whether this observation may be extended even to shades of the same colour. But it is a phænomenon worthy of our observation, that colours mixed together compound a colour, which seems to the eye as simple as any of the ingredients, & shews as little the marks of composition.

Primary colours are red, orange, yellow green, blue, indigo, violet: all these compounded in a certain proportion make white: taking any three of them in their natural order, the two extremes will compound the middle one; not by the eye distinguishable from the primary colour. – Suppose a piece of cloth stript yellow & blue, very bright & in due proportion; let the breadth of these stripes be diminished more & more, till they are too narrow to be distinguished; the cloth will appear of an uniform & simple green. This green colour, is not only made out of yellow & blue when they come to the eye at the same time in due proportion, but when they come successively. Thus if a body should appear for a small space of time bright yellow then bright blue & so on alternately; let the succession become more & more quick, & the body will at last appear of an uniform & simple green. In like manner a quick succession of all the primary colours will make white. | Taking the facts for granted, let us make some observations upon them.

20]

Does it not appear, that the white & green colours produced in the manner above related, are really compound perceptions, but compounded so nicely as to have the appearance of the most simple ones? Would not the colour of white have forever passed for one of the most simple & elementary perceptions, if we had not by Philosophy aided by other senses discovered it to be a compound?

It is commonly taken for granted, that when several simple perceptions which we are acquainted with, are joined together, we can easily conceive the compound, tho it had never actually been presented to the sense. Yet in colours we seem to have an instance to the contrary. If we should suppose a person well acquainted with all the primary colours, but who had never seen white, let him work upon the primary colours as long as he will in his imagination, let him combine them either by contiguity or succession; he could never be able to imagine a white colour. And yet this same white colour is only a set of primary colours combined by contiguity or succession.

If ever Philosophy should again catch the itch of disputation, might it not be a fit question for ingenious men to display their talents upon Whether the idea of white be a simple or mixed mode? What if ideas of different senses should in some cases be thus combined into one idea, to appearance perfectly simple & indivisible? Would it not be difficult to find out to which sense such an idea belonged? Perhaps one Philosopher would contrive a new sense for it: Another would not admit that there were such an idea, because he could not find what class in his division to refer it to. Whether this may actually be the case in any instance, I do not presently enquire, but there seems so much reason to suspect that it may, as ought to make us sensible of the intricacy of the operations of human minds, & modest in our decisions about them.

132/6–9   As we have two eyes, we have undoubtedly two perceptions of every object we see. Each eye hath its own sphere of vision & its own images,
133/9ff.   independent of & unrelated to the other. Yet in fact, when the optic axes are both directed to the same object, or when they have the same position with regard to it, so that the two images are formed upon corresponding parts of the retinæ, we see objects simple, & cannot by the strictest
[21]   attention per | ceive any kind of duplicity in them. But when the two images fall upon dissimilar parts of the retinæ, that is one upon the center, another at a distance from it &c in such cases we always see the object double, the two objects always appearing at a certain angular or visible distance, greater or less according as the position of the images upon the retinæ is more or less dissimilar. The Anatomists of the body have failed in their attempts after a solution. The Anatomists of mind have not thought that it concerns them; & yet I can see no other resource but to resolve it into some unaccountable quality of the mind.

152/20–3   Either the mind unites the two perceptions into one from the beginning, or seeing objects at first double, it comes by use & experience to perceive
154/15–25   them single. The last is the opinion of Dr Smith in his Optics. If it is true it discovers to us a strange process of the mind, by which a duplicity of visible objects being found by experience a sign of unity [by] to the touch, we lose the sense of the visible duplicity by passing immediately from this to the tangible unity; in like manner as we think we see the tangible figure of a globe, when in reality we only see a circle variously shaded. But I think the common opinion were probable, to wit, that from

the beginning we see objects single when our eyes are properly directed, & that by our original make, objects whose rays fall on corresponding parts of the retinæ are seen in the same place. For 1st if there was a double appearance to the eye, however habit might bring us to give no attention to it but immediately to pass to the tangible unity signified by it, yet it is probable that by repeated endeavours we might be able to attend to this double appearance & overcome the habit, as we see like habits in other cases may be overcome tho' not without difficulty. It might particularly be expected of Painters, who are accustomed to separate the visible appearance of objects from the tangible idea it suggests, that by looking at an object first with one eye & then with both, they might be able to perceive a duplicity in the latter case. 2dly in all the instances of double vision the two images are seen as it were in different points of the same sphere & at a certain angular distance. I cannot indeed form a conception of two objects seen at the same time without having a certain distance or proximity, & I apprehend every other person will find it impossible for him to have I such a conception. Now it is as difficult to account for this as for single vision. For it is impossible to assign a reason why the mind in seeing an object double with two eyes, should naturally place the images at one distance rather than another. It may as well place them at no distance as at any particular one, & then vision will be single. And indeed when in double vision the two images are seen at a certain distance (as I think they always are) it seems necessarily to follow, that by moving the axis of one of the eyes in a certain direction while the other is fixed, the distance between the images would be diminished, & at last vanishing would give single vision.

I shall mention a fact from Cheselden that seems to determine the point. A young Gentleman whom he couched in the 13 Year of his age; after he had seen for some time upon one eye, the other being couched, he thought he saw the object twice as large when he looked upon it with both eyes, as when with the first couched eye only, but not double (says Mr Cheselden) that we can any way discover – There are indeed some facts that seem to make for Dr Smiths opinion. A Clergyman who had been blind for some years of a gutta serena, being cured by a salivation by Dr Hepburn of Lynn did at first see objects double, but by degrees the images approached & at last he saw single & as distinctly as before. One or two other instances of this kind are mentioned by Dr Briggs in his nova visionis theoria. In these cases it is probable the double vision was owing to the persons having lost the habit of directing their eyes properly, & when they recovered that faculty they had no more double vision.

155/9f.   We have another instance from Cheselden of a person who had one eye distorted by a blow on the head, who at first saw objects double, but by use came to see single, first the more familiar objects, & afterwards any object whatsomever, tho the distortion continued. It were to be wished the circumstances of this case had been more particularly narrated. Perhaps for some time he directed his eyes, so as to deviate equally from the object; & then he had two indistinct images. But he might learn at last to direct one eye to the object & so have one distinct image, the other eye being too oblique to give any image, or giving one so faint that he got the habit

[23]   of not attending to it. |

153/17–154/6   Dr Smith thinks there is the same difficulty in accounting for our hearing sound single with two ears as our seeing objects single with two eyes. But I apprehend the cases are very different. Sounds have not properly any place, & there is nothing by which two sounds perfectly similar & synchronous can be distinguished. But every visible object hath a place, which distinguisheth it from objects seen at a different place at the same time, be they ever so like. Now the difficulty lies in this, why every point in one retina has a certain point in the other so corresponding to it, as that images falling upon these corresponding parts, are always the same.

163/23f.   Newton thought that the fibres of the optic nerves from corresponding parts of the retinæ united; Yet the accurate Vesalius hath given us several facts that absolutely overturn this theory.

158/15–19   Dr Porterfield has another method of accounting for single vision Med. Essays Vol. 4 but it must fall to the ground if Bp Berkely's theory of vision be true, to wit, that we do not naturally see the distance of objects from the eye, & therefore can give no satisfaction to those who believe that distance from the eye is not properly an idea of sight but of touch: which I think very probable after all that Dr Porterfield hath said to the contrary.

166/11–15   From what hath been said, it seems we must resolve single & double vision at last into an unaccountable consent or harmony established in our constitution betwixt the corresponding parts of the bottom of our eyes, by which the objects painted on those corresponding points are seen always in the same place, & so give one perception.

101/24f.   The perception of visible figure & visible extension are nearly related, the first being a mode of the latter, & therefore shall be considered together. Figure is reckoned by Mr Locke to be an idea got both by sight

& touch. But it seems more proper with Berkley to distinguish that figure of objects which we see from that which we feel; & to call the one <u>visible</u>, the other tangible figure, & after examining them separately, to consider how they come to be so closely united by the mind as to have one name in all languages, & to be mistaken by such accurate Anatomists of the human mind I as Mr Locke was, for one & the same thing perceived by two different senses.

If we could find a being endowed with sight, without the sense of feeling or any other external sense, but capable of reflecting & reasoning upon what he sees; the notions & philosophy of such a being might enable us to distinguish the pure perceptions of sight from those which have an admixture from other senses, which is otherwise a matter of no small difficulty.

Let us suppose such a being as well as we can, & that several white circles of different diameters & at various distances are presented to him. He might, as these objects grew familiar, compare them together & discern the relations of greater, less, & equal. If one of these circles was divided in the middle by a black line, he might compare the parts, & perceive their similarity & equality. If the circle should in like manner be divided by more right lines, he might perceive the sectors into which it was divided to be bounded by two right lines & a curve line, & that the sectors were to one another in the ratio of their angles. And thus by comparing the objects of sight & reasoning upon them, he might by degrees acquire the idea of points, angles, right obtuse & acute, of lines streight & curved, & of spaces bounded by lines; he might discover the relations of these & form Geometrical conclusions built upon self evident principles. He might likewise form ideas of numbers & erect a system of Arithmetic. It is not material to say in what order he might proceed in such discoveries, or how much time & pains might be employed in them: But <u>what</u> such a Philosopher, by reason & ingenuity, without any materials of sensation but those of sight, might discover.

A supposed extract from Joannes Rudolphus Apodemus a Rosecrucian Philosopher concerning the Idomenians, who have only the sense of seeing.

The Idomenians, sayeth he, are many of them very ingenious & much given to contemplation. In Arithmetic & Geometry there hath always been an unanimity among them, but in Physics & Metaphysics they have had many disputes carried on with great subtilty, & are divided into various

105/3–30

[25]

sects. Their principles relating to Arithmetic & numbers, making allowance for their notation, differ in nothing from ours; but their Geometry
differs considerably from that of the human species. Their definitions of
points, lines streight & curved, of angles right acute & obtuse & of |
parallel lines do correspond exactly with ours. They have no conception of
solids, nor even of the distinction of surfaces into plain & curve: but they
have distinct notions of trilateral, quadrilateral, circular & other figures
bounded by lines.

As a specimen of their geometry, which we may call the Geometry of
visibles, I shall mention a few elementary propositions of many which
they demonstrate with Geometrical accuracy from self evident principles.
1   Every right line being produced will at last return into itself. 2 Any two
right lines produced will meet in two points & include space. 3 If two lines
be parallel they cannot both be streight. 4 Every right lined triangle hath
its three angles greater than two right angles. 5. Triangles that are [equal]
{similar} are also equal. 6. The circumferences of small circles are to one
another nearly as their diameters, but those of larger circles in a less ratio.
7 A right lined triangle may be assigned equal to a given circle. 8 A right
line being given, a point may be assigned which is equally distance from
all parts of it. pp. 19–25

(*The following is a record of substantive variants between* HM, *pp. 109–11,
and* MS, *pp. 25–7.*)

109/8–10   As our . . . thus:] As to their Metaphysicks it is generally agreed,
               that p. 25
109/11   essential] common p. 25
109/15   space.] . . . Therefore colour is the only thing by which body is
               distinguished from space. p. 25
109/20–2   incapable . . . whole.] They conceive it to be infinite, that is without any
               limit, & in its nature one interminable whole, yet they do not at all imagine
               it immense, but on the contrary, it is universally agreed that every the least
               part of space, bears a finite ratio to the whole. p. 25
109/23   common and natural] universal p. 25
109/24–5   and the . . . universe.] a measure not settled by custom, but pointed | out
               by nature. pp. 25–6
109/26   common and natural] universal p. 26
109/27–8   returns . . . line.] makes one unlimited whole; & every other length is
               expressed by the ratio it bears to a whole right line. p. 26

39/33 essential attributes] primary qualities. p. 26

10/23 upon] . . . by his followers p. 27

10/39 they can no more doubt of it, than they can] to doubt it would be to p. 27

11/3 penetration.] . . . Therefore body is allowed to be penetrable by body. p. 27

11/12 many volumes] the Vatican p. 27

(The record below is a full transcription of MS, pp. 27–30, which corresponds to portions of HM, pp. 100–188. The abbreviation 'cf.' indicates that the MS text bears some comparison to the HM portion specified, but cannot strictly be said to correspond.)

11/15–25 But the founder of the inductive sect, laying aside Hypotheses, began to investigate the laws of this phænomenon. He proved by a very particular induction, that this quality is common to all bodies, but in very different degrees; & that it not only differs in degree in different bodies, but in the same body at different times. That as the same body varies in its magnitude, it varies also in its over-coming quality, which diminishes or |

8] increases in the subduplicate ratio of the magnitude of the body. The ratio of the overcoming quality in different bodies is a matter of very difficult investigation. There are cases in which it can be discerned from the colour & distinctness of [the] parts of the body. And there are other cases in which even the vulgar learn by experience to judge of it in a manner which the Philosophers are at a loss to account for; as their indications are not taken from any thing in the object, but in the manner of perceiving it. Some of them attribute this to instinct, others to external sense – Thus far Apodemus – Now for some remarks. .

1/32–112/6 The ingenious Bishop of Cloyne hath proved, that we could never by the eye alone have any conception of distance of objects from the eye or proximity to it. I think we may add, that an Idomenian, tho' he assigns a place to every object of sight, yet would never assign a place to himself; or if he did, he would be as much puzzled to find his own place in the whole extent of space, as we are to find the seat of the soul. Now if it is allowed that an Idomenian can have no notion of distance or proximity betwixt himself & what he sees, I think after careful examination, their Geometry must be such as Apodemus hath described it. Nor does his account of their Philosophy appear to contain any evident marks of imposture.

101/25–102/4 Taking it for granted then, that this is in the main a just account of the philosophy of things purely visible, I observe, that visible extension & figure, tho of all our perceptions the most frequent & familiar, yet the human species have got a habit of not giving the least attention to them. The mind perceives some things by sight others by touch which it ascribes to the same body; the perceptions are equally real, yet we conceive the tangible qualities only to be really in the object, & its visible qualities as phantoms which have no real existence in the body but are signs of {its} tangible qualities. Perhaps the reason of this may be, that the visible qualities are so fleeting & inconstant, varying in every different position & distance, & evanishing quite in darkness, that they make no lasting impression upon the mind. But the tangible qualties are of a more durable & stable nature. The visible appearance being too changeable & inconstant for the mind to rest on, it only uses that as a step to lead us

[29]

to the tan l gible. Besides that most things we are acquainted with in our early days, can do us little good or hurt but by touching us; & necessity obliges us to observe carefully the tangible figure magnitude & distance of objects we have any concern with.

cf.102/29f.

Whether this be a just account of the matter or not, it is pretty remarkable, that the perceptions of visible figure & visible magnitude should have no name in any language. That tho they admit of mathematical reasoning, & have their peculiar properties, yet no Mathematician ever considered them. Dr Saunderson found himself at no loss to comprehend every part of Mathematicks, which shews plainly, that that kind of quantity which is perceived by the eye only hath never been admitted into that science. By this habit of giving so little attention to things every moment before our eyes, we become at last quite unacquainted with them; it is with great difficulty we can make them an object of thought & reflexion. Their most obvious properties surprize us & can hardly gain belief.

cf.188/2–14

If a globe & a circle {of the same colour} are set upon the table before a plain man, he thinks he sees the globe of one uniform colour with the circle. Yet it is certain, the globe is in every part variously shaded according to the position of the light. But he is so accustomed to make allowance for shades, & to take no further notice of them than as indications of figure, that he instantly draws the conclusion & loses sight of the premises. He thinks he sees the circle plain & the globe convex, but both of one colour, wheras in truth there is no convexity in the one more than the other to the eye, but a real difference of colour.

cf.102/14–20

The great difficulty which the ablest painters find in giving just shading & relief to their figures, arises solely from this, that it is very difficult to conceive & retain in the imagination even what we see before our eyes, when we have been long accustomed to use that perception only as a sign of something else. Could the Painter disjoin the perceptions he has by sight from all others, & fix them steadily in his mind, shading, giving relief & just perspective proportions would be as easie as plain colouring. |

[30]

cf.100/32–5

I think both Berkly & Hume affirm that there can be no idea of visible space without colour. I am of a contrary opinion & think I have a distinct conception of visible extension without colour. This idea seems indeed to be very refractory, & not easily made to ply with their systems. But as the same difficulties may occur with regard to tangible space, I shall refer them till that comes under consideration. (*MS ends*) pp. 28–30

Discourse 2.

'Analysis of the Sensations of smell and Taste', delivered 14 March 1759 (MS 3107/1/3, 58–72, in Gordon's hand).

(The following is a record of substantive variants between portions of HM, pp. 25–9, and MS, pp. 58–72.)

25/9–15

IT . . . give the] (*MS begins*) The order in which the sensations are to be considered, is by giving p. 58

25/21–3

Natural . . . forth] All animal & vegetable bodies continually emit p. 58

25/27–31

All . . . subtile] (*omitted*) p. 58

25/32–5

Whether . . . inquire.] That which the Chemists call the spiritus rector in plants, is such a volatile substance, which has indeed a greater affinity with the oyl of the plant, than with its other known principles, & therefore adheres to the oyl in a chemical analysis of the plant, but in time | flies of⟨f⟩ even from that & leaves it common oyl. All the distinguishing smell of the plant is caused by this spiritus rector, & is smelled wherever that is scattered in the air. And we are beholden to the sense of smelling as the only mean, by which we could have discovered this principle, the only principle in the composition of plants, which is peculiar to each species, the others that are known being the same in all the vegetable kind. p. 58–9

25/35–26/8

This . . . smelled.] (*omitted*) p. 59

27/35

thought of.] . . . It is the immediate object of the mind in all these cases. p. 60

27/38

accompanied] necessarily accompanied p. 60

28/5

mind.] . . . ¶ I said that smell is the immediate object of the mind, whether it is smell'd, or remembered or imagined, & so every man believes till he is taught otherwise by Philosophy. I know indeed that Philosophers have a Theory directly contrary to what I have now advanced; a theory of great antiquity & authority; & which is either taught or supposed in all the

systems of the understanding I have heard of from Plato ⟨to⟩ the present
time. Yet as it is a theory, if there appears no sufficient reason to support
it; the authority of great names or even their common consent ought not
to bear down the dictates of nature & common sense. p. 61

28/6   once, and only once,] for the first & onely time p. 61

28/18   or in my sensorium] (*omitted*) p. 61

28/20–32   This is . . . men.] Before we proceed farther it will be necessary to examine
            this theory. p. 61

(See § 2.2 for a full transcription of MS, *pp. 61–72.)*

28/33   In the mean time] Therefore till this hypothesis be better explained or
            more conclusively proved p. 72

29/3   imagination.] (*MS ends*) p. 72

Discourse 3.

'Analysis of our sensations continued', delivered 15 March 1760
(MS 3107/1/5, 12r–15r, in Gordon's hand).

(The following is a record of substantive variants between portions
of HM, *pp. 38–53, and* MS, *fos 12r–15r.)*

38/34   We have . . .] (*MS begins*) fo. 12r

38/39–39/1 the air . . . odours] odoriferous plants diffusing their fragrance fo. 12r

39/7   plants is] . . . , & how it is perceived fo. 12r

39/9   but in a mind] where it is not smelt fo. 12r

40/13   cold] . . . , colour & figure fo. 12r

40/20–1   In order . . . is,] We are next to consider in what sense we ascribe smell
            to the rose, as a quality perceived by the act of smelling & whether this
            quality be the same with the sensation or what relation it bears unto it. |
            In order to this fo. 12r–v

40/23   powers.] . . . It seeks such connexions among things as that one may shew
            when & where to expect the other. fo. 12v

40/29   but in a popular sense] (*omitted*) fo. 12v

40/34   human] men in common fo. 12v

41/3–4   and knowing . . . calendar] eager to find a cause of his misfortune, but
            uncertain where to fix it, he concludes perhaps at last that that day of the
            year is fatal to him, or that he met an evil eye. fo. 12v

41/28–30	give . . . both] distinguish this power from the effect: So that both have the same name, which by this ambiguity is capable of being applied either to the effect or the cause fo. 12v
41/32–5	This . . . said.] (omitted) fo. 12v
42/15	centre.] . . . ¶ The <u>spring</u> signifies a certain season of the year, it signifies some genial power in the Sun & Air, & it signifies a disposition in vegetables to put forth their leaves & blossoms. These three things are very different one from another, yet as they are all constantly connected in the course of nature, they are so united in the imagination, that we give them one name without being sensible of any ambiguity; but if anyone should infer from this, that the vulgar imagine some quality to be in the air or in the month of march like the putting forth of blossoms, he would certainly do them great injustice. fo. 12v
42/22	time] . . . but believes that the water has the same uniform degree of heat. fo. 13r
42/30–2	or virtue . . . matter.] (omitted) fo. 13r
42/32	act of the mind] act, operation, feeling, impression; fo. 13r
42/36–8	Therefore . . . name.] (omitted) fo. 13r
43/2	when . . . percieved] in being smelt fo. 13r
43/3	virtue] modification fo. 13r
43/4–6	hath . . . us.] is the cause or occasion of that sensation. fo. 13r
43/9	cold] . . . & in a word in all those qualities of bodies which Mr Locke calls secondary qualities fo. 13r
43/30	like] & therefore we use them as we do fo. 13r
44/2	altogether unprofitable] unworthy of a Philosopher fo. 13r
44/15	peaceful retirement] (omitted) fo. 13r
44/20	impulse] impression fo. 13r
44/23–5	the Peripatetics . . . intellect] I see no reason I to suppose, with the Peripatetics an <u>intellectus agens</u> fo. 13r–v
44/28–35	Sensation . . . characters] (omitted) fo. 13v
44/36	bears to] . . . the consciousness, fo. 13v
46/3	Of TASTING] Of Taste fo. 13v
46/6–8	applied . . . repetition] applicable to those of taste & hearing that it is unnecessary to repeat it. fo. 13v
46/12	had . . . to] was attracted by & in some measure dissolved in fo. 13v
46/39–47/1	as well . . . shops] (omitted) fo. 13v
47/5–10	Sir . . . examined?] (omitted) fo. 13v
49/26	hautboy] . . . an Organ fo. 14r
50/10–13	Nature . . . nature.] (omitted) fo. 14v

50/19	It is the effect] The belief, after a little experience, instantaneously follows the sound, by fo. 14v
51/3	offer . . . subject] beg leave to submit to the judgment of this society what occurs to me on this subject fo. 14v
51/22–38	Had . . . language.] (*omitted*) fo. 14v
52/17–22	A man . . . nations.] (*omitted*) fo. 14v
52/34	learned.] . . . & understood fo. 15r
53/15	every . . . orator] this would carry all the fine arts to a higher pitch of perfection than ever they attained fo. 15r
53/17	loss] . . . nor even that skill in artificial languages is absolutely incompatible with ability in the natural fo. 15r
53/22	arts.] (*MS ends*) fo. 15r

Discourses 2 and 3.

'Analysis of the Sensations of Smell and Taste', delivered 14 March 1759 and 15 March 1760 (MS 1/I/3, 16–33, in Reid's hand).

(The following is a record of substantive variants between HM, pp. 28–29, and MS, pp. 16–17.)

28/33	In the mean time] Therefore till this Theory be better explained or more conclusively proved p. 16 (*See § 2.2 for full transcription of MS, pp. 7–16*)
28/35–36	immediate . . . memory] the thing remembred p. 16
28/37–29/3	But . . . imagination] The Sen{s}ation must go before either the Memory or Imagination. These various Acts of the Mind of which the Smell is the common Object are as distinct and different as things can be and besides that I {am} certain that Memory is not Sensation and that Imagination is different from both p. 16
29/5	a smell] one Yesterday p. 16
29/10–12	Sensation . . . principles of belief.] This may be otherwise expressed by saying that Consciousness and Memory are Simple & Original Principles of Belief, altogether distinct & independent and we can no more resolve memory into consciousness than [Memor] consciousness into Memory. p. 16
29/13–16	Sensation . . . *apprehension.*] (*omitted*) p. 16
29/22	ideal . . . teaches] we meet with the Theories of Philosophers. They teach p. 16
29/26–7	of . . . ideas] (*omitted*) p. 17

29/28   or knowledge] (*omitted*) p. 17

29/28–32   Now . . . of.] Now as far as I can perceive Sensation is one of the first Operations of the Mind and we see it is necessarily accompanied with belief. Imagination or Simple apprehension of the Objects of Sensation is posterior. p. 17

29/36   judgement] . . . & by separating the Sensation from {the belief of its} Existence with which it was originally joyned. p. 17

29/36–30/2   And . . . separated.] (*in MS margin*) p. 17

(The record below is a full transcription of MS, pp. 17–18, which corresponds to portions of HM, pp. 30–31.)

30/9–15   But what is {this} Belief? Every Man knows, but no Man can define it. Does any man pretend to define Sensation or to define Consciousness. It is happy indeed that no Man does and it had been happy if no Man

31/9–30   had pretended to define belief. It is, say Philosophers, a Perception of the agreement or disagreement of Ideas. Let me apply this to the instances of belief now under consideration. I believe that the Sensation I have exists, and that the Sensation I remember does not exist but did exist yesterday. Here I must compare the idea of Smell with the Ideas of past and present Existence. The perception of certain agreements and disagreements is the belief. Is it not apparent that this ⟨is⟩ mere Theory without the least foundation in Nature. Belief therefore at least in Sensation and Memory is not a perception of the agreement or disagreement

[18]   of Ideas. |

30/15–18   Mr David Hume has been at pains to shew that belief is onely a Modification of simple Apprehension, and since many of our Apprehensions are capable of no other Modifications but different degrees of Strength or Vivacity he concludes that belief is onely a lively conception. Lord Kames agrees with him that belief is onely a Modification of the Idea but

30/25–33   makes it a Modification that cannot be explained. By the same Arguments that these Gentlemen use I could prove that Anger is a Modification of Love or Will of Understanding. These three are all the Theories I have seen of belief ⟨and⟩ they are all founded on the Doctrine of Ideas. The first contradicts Experience in the Instances I have mentioned and the two last shock common Sense. If any One asks me to define Judgment I desire him first to define Apprehension. They are both Original Operations of the Mind and perfectly understood but incapable equally of being explained or defined. Why should Judgment be a Modification of Apprehension any more than Will is of Understanding or hearing of Sight. pp. 17–18

(The following is a record of substantive variants between various portions of HM, *pp. 32–47, and* MS, *pp. 18–30.)*

32/22	or believe] *(omitted)* p. 18
32/24–37/8	Yet . . . self.] *(omitted)* p. 18
37/9–19	But . . . then?] [And tho we can infer nothing from Smelling but some unknown being that has this Power or Faculty nor can give a Reason why we should draw this Inference yet the inference is unavoidable, and is not the Effect of Philosophy or of Education but of Nature.]	When we come to be conscious of other Powers & faculties of this same Being which we call our Selves, we distinguish them by Names as the Sense of Smelling tasting & the like and however different these Powers are we are naturally determined to ascribe them all to one Mind. So that here are several Notions that can in no tollerable Sense be said to be impressions upon the Mind even in their first appearance, but suggested or presented to the Mind by means of an Impression. Smell may be called an Impression but the Sense or Power of Smelling is no Impression. It may remain when there is no smell nor any Impression whatsoever. The Mind or Sentient being is something different both from both *(sic)* the Sensation and faculty for it may continue the same when that faculty is lost. pp. 18–19
37/20–1	our . . . it,] the Sensation to the faculty from the faculty to a Mind p. 19
37/24–5	immediately inspired by] [the immediate Effect of] {a belief inspired immediately by} p. 19
37/33–4	cannot . . . being] or thought cannot be without a Mind p. 19
38/2	sensation] . . . which we are conscious of p.20
38/6	are . . . ideas] cannot be accounted for by the System of Ideas p. 20
38/9–10	passing . . . produces] and instantaneously produces not onely p. 20
38/16–21	sensation . . . thoughts.] But the Suggestion of a Mind from its Sensations is previous to all Experience and is the Work of Nature. The effect of it is that we get at once the Notion of a Mind which we had never before and at the same time the belief of its Existence and of its Relation to our Sensations. p. 20
38/21	principle] Suggestion p. 20
38/23	cause] . . . which we could not have otherwise p. 20
38/35–6	or sentient being] as its Subject p. 21
38/39–39/1	the air . . . odours] odoriferous plants spreading their Fragrance p. 21

39/7	plants is] . . . and how it is perceived p. 21
39/9	but in a mind] that is not Smelt p. 21
39/18–19	without . . . truth] (*omitted*) p. 22
39/27	am apt to think] shall suppose p. 23
40/13	cold] . . . colour and figure p. 23
40/20–1	IN order . . . is,] We are next to consider in what Sense we ascribe Smell to the Rose as a Quality perceived by the {mind} [act of Smelling] & whether this Quality be the Same with the Sensation or what Relation it bears to it. In order to this p. 23
40/23	powers.] . . . It seeks such Connexions among things as that one may shew us when and where to expect the other. p. 23
40/29	but in a popular sense] (*omitted*) p. 23
41/4	conceive . . . calendar] ascribe it to the day of the Month or to some person he last met with. p. 24
41/15–17	and a . . . come.] (*in MS margin*) p. 24
41/28–30	give . . . both] distinguish this power from the Effect, so that both have the same Name which is by this Ambiguity capable of being applyed either to the Effect or the Cause p.24
41/32–5	This . . . said.] (*omitted*) p. 24
42/15	centre.] . . . Thus the Spring signifies [both] {a certain Season of the Year} some genial Power in the Sun and Air, and a Disposition in Vegetables to put forth their leaves and blossoms. These three things are extreamly different from one another, yet as they are all constantly connected in the course of Nature they go all under one Name and are united in the Imagination. But if any one would infer from this that the vulgar imagine a Quality really in the Air or in the Month of March like the putting forth of blossoms he would certainly do them great Injustice. p. 25
42/16	one] . . . which like light and darkness are irreconcileable p. 25
42/26–8	The . . . they] That Smell in the Rose is not imagined even by the vulgar to be a Sensation seems to me evident from this that [we] {they} p. 26
42/30–2	or virtue . . . matter.] (*omitted*) p. 26
42/32	act of the mind] Act Operation feeling Impression p. 26
42/33–4	the sensation . . . being] Sensation from its very Nature inferrs a Mind as its Subject p. 26
42/35	thing] . . . therefore they are not the Same p. 26
42/36–8	Therefore . . . name.] (*omitted*) p. 26
43/2	when . . . percieved] in being felt p. 26
43/3	virtue] Modification p. 26

43/4–8	hath . . . it;] is the Cause or occasion of that Sensation. We are determined by our constitution to seek an external Cause of it p. 26
43/18	we] . . . immediately and p. 26
43/20	sensations] . . . accompanying hunger p. 27
43/27	most properly and] more p. 27
44/2	altogether unprofitable] unworthy of a Philosopher p. 27
44/15	peaceful retirement] (*omitted*) p. 28
44/23–5	the Peripatetics . . . intellect] I see no Reason to suppose with the Peripateticks an Intellectus agens p. 28
44/28–35	Sensation . . . characters] (*omitted*) p. 28
44/36	bears to] . . . the consciousness p. 28
45/1	or virtue] {or Modification} p. 28
45/2–4	colour . . . senses] & perhaps Colour. So that if we form clear and Distinct Notions of these Relations in the case of Smelling it will be easy to apply them to other Sensations p. 28
46/3	Of TASTING] Of Taste p.29
46/6–8	applied . . . repetition] applicable to taste that it is unnecessary to repeat it. p. 29
46/12	unless . . . to] [which are always full of] {unless it was attracted by & in some measure dissolved in} p. 29
46/26–7	savage state] State of Nature p. 29
46/35–6	cannot . . . by] may appear to be the same to p. 30
47/5–10	Sir . . . examined?] {See Nehemiah Grew's Discourse on Taste read before the Royal S. 1675} p. 30

(MS, pp. 30–31 corresponds, without substantive variation, up to HM, p. 47/29. The following is a full transcription of MS, pp. 31–33, which bears some comparison to material in HM, Chap. 7.)

cf.203ff.   I beg leave to conclude with an observation which seems to me to give some Light to the various Philosophers that have prevailed in the World concerning Sensation and Sensible things. The words Smell Taste Colour Extension Solidity and the like are beyond all doubt understood by mankind to signify things which are External and which do not exist in the Mind but are perceived by it. It was therefore natural for Philosophers first to seek them in external things and to examine or conjecture about their Nature, without looking inward to our feelings which are of all others the Objects we are least disposed to attend to. This method of Philosophizing about Sensible things and the Senses I beg leave to call the Exoteric

Method. It seems to me to have obtained with little Interruption from the beginning of Philosophy to De Cartes.

It were easy to shew how this method of Philosophizing naturally produced the Peripatetic System. The Universalia a parte Rei, the Materia Prima, and Substantial Forms however Ridiculous they may appear to Moderns seem to me a Natural Consequence of this Method of Philosophizing. Had Aristotles doctrine been onely hard Words without a meaning {as we are apt to imagine} or had it had no foundation in human Nature it could not have been the birth of so extraordinary a Genius nor could it have obtained for so many Ages Among sensible & thinking Men. I believe it is the best System his method could Produce. But the Method was Defective. The Powers & faculties of the Human Mind are the Engines we work with in the Mine | of Truth. These Engines are liable to disorder themselves and till we understand the Nature and Use the natural State the disorders and Remedies of them; we shall never be able to do any great Execution with them.

[32]

De Cartes seems to have been the first happy mortal who duly thought of this; and began a Scrutiny into the Mind it self and the first principles of human Knowledg⟨e⟩ by looking inward. This I shall call the Esoteric Method. Des Cartes had great Talents for it but being in too great hurry to erect a System; he satisfied himself with some of the most Obvious principles of Evidence particularly those of Consciousness & Mathematical Evidence & endeavoured to reduce all others to these. He likewise adopted into his System the Machinery of Ideas which has no Natural Connexion with [it] {his Method} tho it has with the Exoteric.

The Writers since Cartes not onely have given us no new principles but taken it for granted that there can be no more ways of coming at truth than those he has Mentioned. They have indeed pursued with Ingenuity the principles he laid down and so have landed us in a forlorn Scepticism. Nor can we ever get out of this dismal State but by throwing off the Hypothesis of Ideas and [making farther progress] by discovering the other original and Natural Principles of belief which by the Constitution of the human Mind, operate upon our Consent as well as Consciousness and a Perception of the agreements or Disagreements of Ideas.

There is a considerable Analogy between De Cartes System of the Mind and his System of the Material World. He thought no More necessary to solve all the Phænomena of the Material World but Matter & {Vortical} Motion, later Philosophers have not onely shewn these Principles to be insufficient {& the last of them Chimerical} but have found out others.

[33]   As Gravity & Cohesion. And there are no doubt many | more yet undiscovered. In like Manner Cartes thought to Solve all the Phænomena of Minds by Consciousness and Ideas. The Machinery of Ideas appears to be built on no firmer foundation than that of Vortices. However this was not contrived by Des Cartes he borrowed it from his predecessors & his Successors seem neither to have carefully examined his Principles in this Part of Philosophy nor made any considerable add{ition to} the foundation he has laid down but have built upon it very curious [Fabricks] Structures which however at last {hath both dissolved by the breath of Scepticism and} like the <u>baseless Fabric of a [Dream] {Vision} left not a tract behind.</u>

It needs not appear Strange that the Men of Genius who have [supported] built upon the Ideal Scheme have not all been Sceptics tho the Scheme naturally leads to Scepticism. Des Cartes & Malbranche had a Roman Catholic Faith to ballance it & Berkley a good Protestant Faith. Locke besides his Religious Faith seems to have too great a regard both to common Sense & the good of Mankind to yield to Scepticism himself or introduce it into the World. But a late Enquirer into human Nature who was less fettered by these restraints has espoused this Scheme for better and for worse and like a true inamorato seems to [like it] be in love even with its blemishes. pp. 31–33 .

Discourse 4.

'Of the sense of touch', delivered 23 Sept 1760, (MS 3107/1/6, 29r–37r, in Gordon's hand).

(The following is a record of substantive variants between portions of HM, pp. 54–76, and MS, fos 29r–37r.)

54/9   THE Senses . . .] (*MS begins*) fo. 29r
54/10–11   each . . . bodies] there being to each of them only one species of object, that is, one quality of bodies, which we perceive by their means. fo. 29r
54/26   though . . . sensation] (*omitted*) fo. 29r
54/28   there is no sensation at all] it is not perceived fo. 29r
56/5   use] to consider it only fo. 30r
56/29–30   distinct . . . signifies] (*omitted*) fo. 30r
56/31–57/21 But . . . mind.] However, a Philosopher by some practice may be able to attend to it; & to compare it with that hardness in the table which it indicates. fo. 30r

7/31–58/27	Nor . . . explain.] I perceive indeed, that the feeling has various degrees, as the hardness likewise has; but this is common to almost all sensations. This feeling, beyond a certain degree, is a species of pain; but a body may have the greatest degree of hardness without being capable of pain or any thing like it. From what hath been said we may draw these conclusions. – 1st that there is a certain sensation of touch which we receive as often as the hand or any other part of our body is pressed against a hard body; & although this sensation is so frequent & familiar, it is not in the least attended to, when it is so moderate as not to give a considerable degree of pain. It serves no other purpose but to introduce the notion of hardness in the body pressed upon. It has no name in any language as far as I know, nor have Philosophers ever attended to it; for if they had, it is impossible that they should have always confounded it with that quality in body which we call hardness, to which it has not the least similtude. fo. 30r
8/33	As] 2dly I conclude that hardness is not a sensation but an external quality whereof a certain sensation is the natural sign. As fo. 30v
8/34–5	nor . . . things] (omitted) fo. 30v
8/36–7	nor . . . substance] (omitted) fo. 30v
9/5	It . . . language] I shewed in a former discourse fo. 30v
9/24–7	What . . . them?] (omitted) fo. 31r
9/28	chemistry] . . . & every art, by which we can produce any change on natural bodies for the conveniency of life fo. 31r
9/28–32	And . . . them.] (omitted) fo. 31r
9/33–4	and . . . signified.] (omitted) fo. 31r
0/13–15	Nay . . . place.] (omitted) fo. 31r
0/19	formerly] in a former discourse fo. 31r
0/23–31	varied . . . how.] constantly changing. Here it is true that comparing sensation with mind, we perceive that the former cannot be without the latter. This I say is [the truth] true, but it is not the whole truth. The truth is that the former brings into view the latter as well as the relation it has to it, & gives the first conception of a mind to which all our sensations and thoughts belong. fo. 31v
0/36–7	most . . . nature] vulgar & by Philosophers fo. 31v
1/1–4	It . . . explained.] (omitted) fo. 31v
1/29–30	though its cause is not] (omitted) fo. 31v
2/1	know] . . . without the aid of Philosophy, (omitted) fo. 32r
2/9–16	The distinction . . . nature] (omitted) fo. 32r
2/24–7	Their . . . suggest.] (omitted) fo. 32r
3/1	implied] included fo. 32r

63/25–6   how . . . for] (*omitted*) fo. 32v

63/34   the notion and belief of] (*omitted*) fo. 32v

63/38–64/6   Hence . . . unlike.] This is always the case where these feelings are not
so interesting as to give considerable pleasure or pain. fo. 32v

64/13   to . . . subject] even to understand what we have advanced upon it. fo. 33r

64/17   ideas] . . . by a kind of intuition or instinct fo. 33r

64/28   nor . . . felt] (*omitted*) fo. 33r

64/29–30   and . . . over.] (*omitted*) fo. 33r

65/15   we . . . any] & reason we can give any tolerable account of the origine
of our fo. 33r

65/34   sciatica.] . . . A grain of sand or concreted matter in the ureters may give
a very smart sensation without giving us the least notion of the figure of
the body that causes it. fo. 33v

66/2   or train of sensations] (*omitted*) fo. 33v

66/6–7   but . . . extension.] of its hardness, figure & position. fo. 33v

66/24   succession] *suite* fo. 34r

67/1–11   our . . . so.] the first origine of our notions of space, motion, extension,
& all the primary qu⟨a⟩lities we ascribe to body, has not yet been
explained. fo. 34r

67/25–68/32   philosophy . . . at] reason, & cast as notorious usurpers & imposters?
This might do very well; but alas! they decline this tribunal; they despise
reasoning, & look down with a sovereign contempt upon fo. 34v

68/37   better] prudent fo. 34v

69/3–70/36   In order . . . explained.] (*omitted*) fo. 34v

71/2–32   But . . . things.] (*omitted*) fo. 34v

72/2–3   We . . . sensations.] (*omitted*) fo. 34v

72/4–6   the . . . uniform.] his own memory & senses & the memory & senses
of others may be trusted. We cannot prove that fire will burn tomorrow
unless we take it for granted that the course of nature will continue the
same till that time. fo. 35r

72/7–8   upon . . . reasoning] (*omitted*) fo. 35r

72/8   remember:] . . . I shall not call them innate, fo. 35r

72/19–20   Perhaps . . . operations] (*omitted*) fo. 35r

72/25–6   short . . . existence] time after fo. 35r

72/26–8   by which it perceives . . . faculties] (*omitted*) fo. 35r

74/14–15   which . . . nature] that fo. 36r

75/6   and . . . ground] nor a shaddow of reason fo. 36v

75/7–9   If . . . of.] (*omitted*) fo. 36v

75/13–18   This . . . proof.] The minor proposition of this argument, the ingenious author has made evident to all that understand his reasoning; but the major proposition is left without any proof, as being universally allowed by Philosophers. fo. 36r

/24–8   and . . . metaphysics.] (*omitted*) fo. 37r

/32–7   On . . . done.] But the conclusions themselves are so contrary to fact & to the common sense of mankind, that they need a stronger support than a general opinion of Philosophers who were not aware of the consequences of this opinion. fo. 37r

/6   sensations.] . . . And it requires no more but attending properly to our own thoughts, to be convinced of it. fo. 37r

/7   a belief . . . education] (*omitted*) fo. 37r

/13   philosophy.] . . . ¶ We may see upon the whole, that the impressions of sense, & the qualities of bodies suggested by them, tho' no ways like, are so associated by our constitution before we come to the use of reason, that the ablest Philosophers & most acute Metaphysicians have still confounded them. And in consequence of that confusion & of the doctrine of ideas all our systems of the mind have either maintained that the qualities of inanimate matter are like our sensations, or that we can have no conception of any such qualities, & that their names signify nothing but sensations. (*MS ends*) fo. 37r

2.2 Reid's Examination of the Ideal System, 1758–1759.

In July 1758, Reid proposed a question to the Aberdeen Philosophical Society, and, in accordance with the Society's rules for discussion, read out his own reply. This question appears to mark the first stage of Reid's direct criticism of the ideal system. His initial objections were then refined and expanded in both a large section of the discourse, 'The Analysis of the Sensations of smell & Taste' (14 March 1759), and his Orations III and IV (April 1759, 1762). Reid did not publish this material until 1785 in the *Intellectual Powers*, where it appears having undergone further revision. The importance of this development in Reid's intellectual biography cannot be over-emphasised. His own claim is that the chief merit of his work lay in his "having called in question the common theory of ideas."[3] Presented below, therefore, is a transcription of Reid's unpublished criticisms of the ideal system.

---

[3] Letter to Dr. Gregory (1790) in *The Works of Thomas Reid, . . .* ed. W. Hamilton, 8th ed. (Edinburgh, J. Thin, 1895, reprint with introduction by H. M. Bracken, Hildesheim, Georg Olms Verlag, 1985): p. 22a.

There are three extant manuscript versions of Reid's question to the Society regarding the ideal system. The first version, transcribed below as Version 1, is untitled and appears to be an early version (6/III/5, 1r–2r). The final paragraph of this version occurs on the same page as, and immediately above a different work bearing the date 'Dec 1 1758' (see § 3.2); hence we at least know that it was written prior to that date. The second version, reproduced below as Version 2, is in Reid's own hand (6/I/11, 1r–2v). Its conformity to Thomas Gordon's transcription (3107/2/1, 9–11), suggests that it was this version which Reid delivered to the Society. Substantive divergences between Gordon's transcription and the second version are noted immediately following the latter.

Version 1.

2131/6/III/5, 1r It seems to be agreed among our Philosophers that the mind can onely perceive where it is consequently that nothing with out the mind or that has a separate existence from it can be perceived but by means of some impression made upon the mind itself. This impression being present to the mind is perceived by it and is the proper object of perception. These

20 impressions when revived by memory or imagination are Ideas. And these two are all the Objects of human thought.

This system has very extensive consequences which D Hume has deduced at large in his treatise of Human Nature, which is almost entirely built upon it. The foundation therefore deserves carefully to be

25 examined if we would form a judgment of the solidity of the fabric built upon it.

I suspect this way of explaining perception however common is unphilosophical not to say puerile. A body we commonly think can not affect another without touching it and making some impression upon it,

30 hence I apprehend we are led to imagine that things perceived by the mind must be united to it by a kind of contact. but as the properties of Mind and Body have not the least similitude we cannot reason from the one to the other.

Besides this reasoning supposes the Mind to have a place & objects

35 to have a certain distance from it. Whereas our Nature leads us to assign visible place onely to visible Objects & tangible place to tangible Objects. Volition ⟨and⟩ Remembrance are said to be in the Mind not locally but as the Subject of which they are qualities. the Sun Moon a tree &c are in my mind onely as perceived by it but it does not appear that what I perceive is

either in my mind locally or near or at a distance from it. All which would suppose that the mind had a place, which I think has not been made out and Supposing the Mind had a place so as that it could be properly said to be in such a place and in no other yet it cannot be shewn that the mind

5 cannot perceive things at a distance from it. |

Further there are many of our Ideas that do not seem to have had any preceeding impressions of which they are copies. Space void of Body is a thing of which we can have no impression since it can neither be seen nor felt nor be the Object of any Sense.

10 Duration, Past & future &c

Our own Existence the Operation of our minds.

Ideas are not like to impressions or copies of them, but differ from them as much as Spirit does from body the table I write upon is hard Smooth round combustible &c but none of these qualities belong

15 to the Idea of the table, for that Idea is neither hard nor soft rough nor smooth it hath no colour nor quality of body, being a mode of thinking

I would ask whether Impressions made upon the Mind are any thing different from the faculty of perceiving them, if they are, it is as difficult

20 to concieve how the mind perceives its own impressions as how it should perceive other things and these impressions are a meer fiction of Philosophers. If they are not different, to say we perceive things by the impressions they make on the mind is a tautology and makes not the manner of perceiving any clearer but more obscure. Nature teaches us to

25 distinguish between the act of perceiving and the thing perceived to which of these do we give the name of impression.

If the Name of Impression is given to the object or thing perceived then If I see a black ox I have upon my Mind a black horned hairy fourfooted impression. And since Ideas are copys of Impressions when I think of

30 this Ox I have a black hairy fourfooted Idea. This language is too gross for common Sense but it is strictly philosophical, if impression is what we perceive & Ideas are onely fainter Impressions. And if the Mind is like a painters Canvass it may no doubt receive such Impressions but if we cannot properly ascribe to it colour Shape & extension to ascribe such

35 impressions to it is absurd & puerile.

If by impression be meant the Act of perceiving not the thing perceived. I am apt to think that the Act of perception conveys a very different Notion to me from any thing I use to call impression and that if it is at all applyed to the Mind with any analogy to its common Acceptation it

[2r] ought to be applyed to the Passions rather I than to the perceptions of the human Mind.

Version 2.

2131/6/I/11, 1r Question 12 Are the objects of the human Mind properly divided into impressions and Ideas? and must every Idea be [an Image] a Copy of a preceeding Impression?

It seems to be agreed among our Philosophers that the Mind can onely
10 perceive where it is, consequently that nothing without the Mind or which has a separate Existence from it, can be perceived but by means of some Impression made upon the Mind itself. This impression being present to the Mind is perceived by it & is the onely proper Object of our Perception. And that those Impressions when revived or copyed by Memory or
15 Imagination are Ideas. And that these two make all the Objects of human Thought.

This System of Perception has very large & extensive Consequences which B Berkley and D Hume have deduced at large and their Philosophy of the human Mind seems to be almost entirely built upon it. The
20 foundation therefore deserves to be well examined if we would form a Judgment of the Solidity of the Superstructure.

1 There seems to be reason to suspect that this way of accounting for Perception is unphilosophical & founded on vulgar prejudices. A Body we think cannot affect another without touching it & making some
25 Impression upon it, hence we are led to imagine that things perceived by the Mind must be united to it by a kind of Contact. But as the properties of Body and Mind have not the least Similitude we cannot Reason from the one to the Other.

Besides this way of explaining Perception supposes the Mind to have
30 a Place and Objects to have a certain Distance from it, or proximity to it. Now tho we must necessarly assign a visible Place to visible Objects and a tangible place to tangibles, yet it is doubtfull whether we ought at all to assign a Place to the Mind, and consequently whether any thing can be with propriety said to be in the Mind or out of it locally. Volition &
[1v] Remembrance may be said to be in the I Mind as it is the Subject of those Operations. So likewise Perception being an Act of the Mind may be said to be in the mind as its Subject but when I say that a tree or a house which I perceive is in my Mind and not at a Distance from it, this evidently supposes the Mind to have a place which I think has not yet been made out.

And Supposing the Mind to have a place so that it could be said to be in such a place and in no other yet it cannot be proved that the mind may not immediately perceive {a} thing at a distance from it without the intervention of Impressions made upon it.

5   Nature undoubtedly teaches us to distinguish betwe⟨e⟩n the Act of perceiving and the Object perceived. When I see a horse, seeing a horse is an act of My Mind, but the horse which I see is not an Act of my Mind there is therefore a real Distinction between the act of Perception & the Object.

10   Now I would ask whether by impressions upon our Minds Philosophers mean the Objects we perceive or the act of perceiving them?

Suppose First it should be said that Impressions mean that act of the Mind by which we perceive an Object. To pass over the impropriety of the word Impression to signify an Act of the Mind: we may observe two

15   things that would follow from this Supposition. first. That to say we perceive things by impressions made on the Mind would be a meer Tautology and signify no more but that we perceive them by perceiving them. And Secondly if Impression be the Act of the Mind in perceiving there must be an Object distinct from the Impression as has been shown above.

20   But let us Suppose in the next place that by impressions they mean not the Act of perceiving but the Object perceived. It must necessarily follow that whatever can be affirmed of the Object may be affirmed of the Impression thus when I see a black Ox I have upon my Mind a black hairy horned fourfooted Impression and since Ideas are onely copys of

25   Impressions, When I think of this Ox I have a black hairy fourfooted Idea. This language however repugnant to common Sense is strictly philosophical, if impressions are the Objects we perceive & Ideas are

[2r]   onely fainter impressions. And if the Mind is like a | painters Canvass it may no Doubt receive such Impressions, but if we cannot properly ascribe

30   to it colour Shape and Extension to ascribe such Impressions to it seems absurd & puerile.

But supposing the Mind capable of such Impressions and that these impressions are the Objects we perceive. Is it not as difficult to conceive how the Mind perceives its own Impressions as how it {should} per-

35   ceive[s] other Things. So that upon the Whole these Impressions upon the Mind seem to be either an ill chosen Word for the Objects of Perception which leaves us where we set out or if they signify any thing more they seem to be a Mere fiction of Philosophers.

2   Whereas these Philosophers reduce all our Impressions to those of

Sensation and Reflexion, & make all our Ideas copys of our Impressions. There seems ground to apprehend that we have many Ideas which are not copys of Impressions got either by Sensation or Reflexion.

5   We have undoubtedly Ideas of Number Space Duration past & future Resemblance Identity Existence & many others which cannot be with any propriety called copys of any Impressions either of Sensation or Reflexion.

3   It is not worth while to dispute Whether Ideas are properly called Images or Copys of Impressions whether they resemble or are like them.
10   It must certainly be allowed that if an Idea be a copy of the object and has a Resemblance, it is a Resemblance sui generis, nor can we reason from the Consequences of other Similitudes to the consequence of this without shocking common Sense or abusing Language.

The Idea of a horse is a Thought and can resemble a Horse onely as
15   a thought can resemble a horse. The Idea of heat is not hot the Idea of Extension is not extended nor the Idea of colour coloured. The Idea of a Century has no more Duration than that of a Minute. Nor does the Idea of Anger imply the least degree of that Passion. Or the Idea of Pain any the least degree of Pain. Colour Extension Sound Taste & other sensible
20   qualities cannot be predicate of the Mind or said to be in it in any consistency with common Sense. Yet the Ideas of these Sensible Qualitys can as little be in any other Subject but a Mind, nor can they have any other existence but in being perceived. Pain & pleasure are real things.
[2v]   Yet can onely exist | in a Mind capable of pleasure and pain. The Ideas of
25   Pleasure and Pain are as different from the things as the Idea of Extension is from Extension.

(The following is a record of substantive variations between Version 2 and MS 3107/2/1, fos 9–11.)

292/9	our] . . . modern p. 9
292/12	This] That this p. 9
292/14	And that] That p. 9
292/14	revived] received p. 9
292/14	by] . . . the p. 9
292/15	that] *(omitted)* p. 9
292/17	very] *(omitted)* p. 9
292/18	deduced . . . and] made great use of in their systems; & indeed p. 9
292/19	almost] *(omitted)* p. 9

2/29	Besides] (*no new paragraph*) p. 9
2/30	a certain] (*omitted*) p. 9
2/32	tangibles] tangible objects p. 9
2/34	with propriety] (*omitted*) p. 9
2/37	a tree or a] the tree or p. 10
2/39	the Mind . . . out.] that the mind has a place as bodies have; which is a principle that ought not to be taken for granted. p. 10
3/1–4	And . . . it.] (*omitted*) p. 10
3/5	Nature] 2 Nature p. 10
3/6	seeing a] seeing this p. 10
3/7	which I see] (*omitted*) p. 10
3/9	Object] . . . perceived p. 10
3/10	Now] (*no new paragraph*) p. 10
3/12	Suppose] (*no new paragraph*) p. 10
3/12	the] that p. 10
3/17	signify no more but that] would signify no more than p. 10
3/18	if] . . . the p. 10
3/19	shown above] observed p. 10
3/20	But] (*no new paragraph*) p. 10
3/20	next] <u>second</u> p. 10
3/28	And] (*omitted*) p. 10
3/29–30	Impressions . . . Extension] {as colour, shape & extension}, but if we cannot p. 10
3/32	But] . . . farther, p. 11
3/34	{should}] might p. 11
3/35	Things] . . . If we know not how it perceives its own impressions, we cannot possibly know, whether it may not perceive things at a distance from it, without the intervention of any impression. p. 11
3/35–6	upon the Mind] so much talked of, p. 11
3/36	for] to signify p. 11
3/37	out] . . . without giving the least light to the nature of perception, p. 11
3/39–294/1	2 Whereas . . . Reflexion.] 3. There are many things perceived by us, which are neither impressions upon the mind, nor ideas of such impressions. Such as <u>number</u>, <u>space</u>, <u>duration</u>, <u>past & future</u>, <u>resemblance</u>, <u>identity</u>, <u>existence</u>, & many others. p. 11
4/8	3] 4 p. 11
4/8	are properly] may be p. 11
4/9	Copys] . . . or images p. 11
4/9	or are like them. It] them or not. But it p. 11

294/10–11	if . . . it] this resemblance p. 11
294/14	The] (*no new paragraph*) p. 11
294/18–19	Or . . . Pain.] (*omitted*) p. 11
294/20	or said] nor be said p. 11
294/22	as little be] be as little p.11
294/23–4	things. Yet] things, & p. 11

There are three versions of the section against the ideal system that Reid removed from the *Inquiry*. The first is located within Thomas Gordon's transcription of Reid's discourse 'The Analysis of the Sensations of smell & Taste' 14 March 1759 (3107/1/3, 61–72). A second version is found in Reid's third *Oration*, a translation of which may be found in *The Philosophical Orations of Thomas Reid delivered at Graduation Ceremonies in King's College Aberdeen*, 1753, 1756, 1759, 1762. ed. D. D. Todd, trans. S. M. L. Darcus, *Philosophical Research Archives* 3 (1977): pp. 916–90. Finally, there is an early draft of this section in Reid's hand (1/I/3, 7–15). This latter version appears to be at least one stage prior to that which Reid delivered to the Society. Various portions are deleted and Reid indicates that others are to be relocated. The result of these editorial changes would have been a text very similar to that recorded by Gordon. Reid's draft is reproduced below in full, as Version 1. Immediately following this transcription is a record of Reid's instructions to delete or relocate portions of the text, along with his marginal additions. Gordon's transcription is also reproduced in full, as Version 2.

Version 1.

131/1/1/3, 7

[Thirdly] the [System] {Hypothesis} of Ideas seems to me not to answer the Purpose for which it is intended, namely to solve the
5 Phænomena of Remembrance, and Perception of things external. It leaves those Operations as Mysterious and unaccountable as it found them. The difficulty to be resolved is, how a thing that is external or a thing that is past and has now no Existence can be represented to the Mind. Says the Idealist it is represented by a present Idea or Picture of it. I have
10 been at pains to conceive this Solution but must confess I cannot find that it makes the thing plainer. Sometimes I conceive the Idea appearing as Proxy for an unknown Constituent but I cannot find its commission. Sometimes I conceive it as a Picture the Object being the Original. But here the Difficulties increase upon me. For there are a great many things
15 which [I know not how they can] {cannot} be pictured. What is a picture of a Smell a Sound or Taste? How can Time be pictured and the preterit distinguished from the present and future? {What can Picture Existence & Nonexistence}. And as to the things that may be pictured which have figure Colour and Dimensions I can conceive them pictured on a Canvass
20 or table but how they {can be} pictured upon the Mind I am quite at a loss to conceive.

And if I could get over all these Difficulties and suppose a passive part of the Mind that had dimensions of length and breadth fit for receiving these pictures, the difficulty still remains. It is as {if} every man were
25 born and lived all his time singly in a little Camera Obscura where he had no intelligence but from the pictures in his Chamber. I say that in this Case he [would] never {would} he [could] never {could} dream of any Originals or conceive any object but his pictures themselves. If he should be informed by [revelation] {his good Genius} that I these were
30 intended to represent something else, what else could he possibly Imagine but another Camera obscura like his own, [stored] {tho} perhaps {stored} with more & better furniture. Certainly if he could go a Step beyond this in his conclusions it must be by means of some other Principles than Philosophers have discovered.
35 But perhaps the Idea represents the Object as a Sign does {the} thing signified. So we see Words and writing can be made to express every thing. And so the little World of Ideas is a kind of book or language that acquaints us of every thing without. Here again unsurmountable difficulties arise. How do we learn to understand this language, or to read

this Ideal Book. Shew a book to a Savage who never heard of letters
and he does not know that these Characters are Signs far less what they
Signifie. Speak to a man in an unknown tongue. Your words may be signs
to you but they are none to him. All signs must be interpreted. If Ideas are
5   Signs the Art of Interpreting Ideas behoved to be the most essential part of
human knowledge and the Ground of all. Yet this is an Art never thought
of. Civilians [know] {have considered} how Laws and Contracts are to
be interpreted. Grammarians and Critics how {to} interpret Language.
Nay we have arts of Interpreting Cryptographical Writing of Interpreting
10   Dreams and Riddles. But where are the Rules of Interpreting Ideas or from
what principles are they to be deduced.

Having thus considered the Nature of Ideas, & their Use either as
Mediums of Thought or as Representatives of Objects; Let us next
consider the Reasons that have led Philosophers to suppose such Beings.
15   They will I conceive Appear to be mere{ly a} fiction and Hypothesis
contrived to solve certain Phænomena of the Mind which appear other
wise Unaccountable.

It must be allowed by all (say the Philosophers) that whatever the Mind
immediately perceives must be present to it. It cannot act where it is not.
[9]   It may be conscious | of what passes within itself its own joys and fears
and Desires and thoughts–but how can what is at a Distance affect it or
be known to it, but by some Image or Representation of it in the Mind
itself? When we {see or} think of the Sun and Planets and fixed Stars does
the Mind traverse those immense Regions? No surely, it has a little world
25   within it self in which as in a Mirrour it perceives the great One. Far less
can what is past & perhaps has now no Existence be an immediate Object
of the Mind, it must be represented by something present and existing.

Upon this Reasoning, which is expressed by some of our Philosophers
and supposed by the rest, stands the whole Fabric of Ideas or Rep-
30   resentative Beings in the Mind, and all our Systems about the human
Understanding. And therefore it deserves to be carefully examined.

First then I would observe that this reasoning takes it for granted that
we may be conscious of {what is in the Mind} and upon that Principle
explains how we come to perceive to remember to imagine, by resolving
35   all these Operations into Consciousness. But why is not consciousness
accounted for as well as the others? if it is inexplicable and to be taken for
a first principle possibly the rest may be so likewise: And then it will be in
vain to ask how the mind should immediately perceive what is past. It is
[10]   no more necessary that we should know this, than it is necessary that | we

should know how we are conscious of what is present. Suppose then I am quite unable to show how the Mind can immediately perceive that such a smell existed yesterday does it follow that it cannot happen because I cannot tell how it can happen. Malebranch thought that we see all things in God, other Philosophers that we see them by images of them printed on our own Minds. Suppose the former Hypothesis effectually confuted will it follow that the second must be true.

But says the Philosopher we not onely do not see how perception & Rem{em}brance can happen otherwise we plainly see they cannot. This indeed is directly to the point and now the whole Strength of the Argument [stepes] {comes} forth, & It is this. {Neither} The Mind [cannnot act but where it is] nor [can] any other being {can} act but where and when it is. Whether therefore you suppose Perception to be an Action of the Object upon the Mind, or an Action of the Mind upon the Object, in either case they must necessarily meet together otherwise neither can any wise affect the Other.

In the Name of common Sense I would ask the Philosopher. Do you know how the Mind and Object do act upon one another when they do meet? We are told indeed that there is an Impression or Stamp made upon the Mind; that the Mind comprehends or grasps the Object. But I suppose these expressions are {not} to be understood strictly but metaphorically. Let us therefore strip them of the Metaphor & speak literally & philosophically, & then they mean no more but this that the mind thinks of remembers perceives | the Object. These are not metaphorical [or pictoral] words, but simple and perfectly understood. and when we substitute them for the words <u>Acting upon</u> <u>Impressing</u> Comprehending and the like we shall find that the Argument is onely a [Petitio Principii] {begging of the thing in Question} and takes for granted what it should prove, to wit, that we can not think of any thing but what is present {& existing}.

We say indeed in common Speech that such a thing was not in my Mind, meaning I did not think of it, but whether this way of Speaking is figurative or not, is the point in Question.

And the proper way to determine this Question is not to consider Thought as an Act as an Impression as a Comprehension; These are vague and obscure terms when applyed to thought. It is it self clear and Distinct {and perfectly understood when called by its proper Name} and when I take it in this Light & consider whether thought of an Object supposes contiguity both in time and Place between the Mind and that Object, I cannot see that it does.

I find indeed that I have been so accustomed to think of Bodies and
their Operations that I am apt to measure every thing by their Standard.
We commonly think that a Body to act upon another must be in contact
with it, that it can onely act by impulse and that there can be no impulse
5   without contiguity. These Notions are not perhaps very Philosophical
even when applyed to Body, but suppose they were, they are evidently
got by Experience [& what Right have we to apply them to Mind, where I
we have had no Experience of their Truth.] {of the Operations of Bodies
and however prone mankind have been to apply them to mind, there does
[12]   not appear to be the least ground I either from Reason or Experience to
justify our doing so.}

I might farther observe that this Maxim of the Mind being onely able
to act where it is, supposes it to have a place. Which must at least be
acknowledged to be very dubious.

15   So that in reality this Notion so universal {among Philosophers} That
the Mind cannot [immediately] remember or think of past or distant
Objects, {immediately}, but onely by the Mediation of certain Ideas
Images or Representative Beings presently existent in the Mind. seems
to me a fiction of Philosophers grounded in vulgar Prejudices not unlike
20   those by which we are apt to ascribe human figure to the Deity or cloven
feet to the Devil. Yet this fiction has been the chief Cause of that Darkness and Perplexity which every one is sensible of in our Systems about
the Understanding and of those Paradoxes and that Scepticism which
very ingenious Men have been led into by endeavouring to make them
25   consistent. [That the Mind and Object should act upon each other by the
Medium of an Idea which is in the mind onely appears as absurd as it
would be to keep a Ship at Anchor by the Medium of a Cable which lyes
coyled up in the hold & is not tyed to the Anchor.]

How{ever} I shall suppose it to be true that Ideas presently existing
30   in the Mind can alone be the Immediate Objects of thought, and shall
beg leave to consider a little the consequences of this Theorie. It appears
to me that we must necessarily on this Supposition either go back to the
Exploded and ridiculed Peripatetick System, or into absolute Scepticism
and disbelief of every thing, but the Ideas or feelings of the present
35   Moment. And that there is no Scheme betwixt these that is tenible upon
the Supposition we are presently grulling. I

[13]   [For first] we agree with Aristotle that a medium is necessary betwixt
the Mind and the Object that they may act upon each other, this Medium
is an Idea or Phantasm. We likewise agree in joyning this Medium to one

of the Extreams to wit the Mind so that all is safe on that side but then
the Moderns {by rejecting intelligible Species} have untied this Medium
from the other Extream to wit the Object, which undoes all operation of
the Extreams on one another. For it is evident that if a medium is at all
5   necessary it must lay hold of both the Mind and Object and go all the
way between them without any gap or interruption otherways it remains
as impossible for the mind and Object to affect each other as if there was
no Medium at all. And I may as well take hold of the Moon with my
hand, as apprehend an Object by means of an Idea which does not reach
10   it. That the Mind and Object should act upon each other by the medium
of an Idea which is in the Mind onely, appears as absurd as it would be
to hold a Ship at Anchor by the Medium of a Cable which is not tyed to
the Anchor but lyes coyled up in the hold.

Aristotle was sensible of this Absurdity and has avoided it. [For he
15   makes the{se} Ideas or Intelligible Species to be continually sent forth
from the Object in all directions, to be received by the Passive Intellect
& that the active Intellect which may be supposed at no great Distance
observes them. These impressions on the passive Intellect may remain
when they are not perceived from whence it is easy to see how Memory
20   & Reminescence may be accounted for. [Here] {Therefore} I cannot
help thinking that we do great Injustice to [Aristotle] {the Stagarite}
in ridiculing this Scheme while we hold the principles on which it is
founded {in retaining one half of his Hypothesis & rejecting the other} |
14]   for to say that a Medium is necessary and yet that it is not necessary that
25   this Medium should reach from one extream to the other is a palpable
Absurdity.

To avoid the Peripatetick Scheme we have no resource left consistent
with the Doctrine of Ideas but to say that there is no Action or
Operation of the Mind and Object on one another but these Ideas are
30   produced in our Minds by God or we dont know how. This Scheme I
say leads to Absolute Scepticism; for by it our present feelings or Ideas
are not onely the Immediate but the Sole Objects of the Understanding.
Nothing past or to come nothing external can possibly enter into our
thoughts.

35   For such things upon the principles we are now Supposing can neither
operate upon us nor we upon them. they can not be immediate objects
of thought because they are not present Ideas nor ⟨can⟩ they be mediate
objects of thought because our Ideas {and Minds} are no ways connected
with them.

This is the pure genuine unmixed Ideal Scheme and indeed if Prejudices and Authority of great Names were not very powerfull, one might with less Labour and at first View see that the Principles we are now supposing lead to this: for if we will resolve perception & memory into {present} Consciousness we must necessarily [cut off] exclude every thing from the Intellectual World which we are not presently conscious off. This Ideal Scheme tho' admirable for its simplicite and shortness, yet leaves so little play to the human Mind that it is no wonder that those who hold the principles from which it flows should boggle a little at the Conclusion. Berkley took onely a part of it. He shook of⟨f⟩ the External World indeed which he thought might be easily spared, but could not find in his heart to part with {his own & other} Minds {a Supreme Mind} and every thing past I but his principles justly pursued would have led him [farther] {to this} and left him nothing but [the Berkley of this Minute] {Ideas and feelings of the present}.

Berkley owns that he has no Idea of a Mind, that is, a Subject or Substratum of his Ideas; yet he is certain there is one, he is certain too that there is a Supreme Mind who is the Cause or Author of his Ideas and he believes there are other {finite} Minds {like his own}, now if he can think of these things and believe them & prove their Existence without having Ideas of them, why should he conceive it impossible to [. . .] {think of} or believe other Existences without having Ideas of them. Therefore I cannot help thinking Berkleys Scheme untenible as he takes a part of the consequences of the Ideal Theory and rejects the rest without giving a just Reason for it.

To sum up what I have said about Ideas and what I think about them. If by the Idea of an Object is meant the thought of an Object, I shall contend with no man about a Word. Onely I would desire any Person that has leisure, to put Thought in place of Idea in the Writings either of ancient or modern Philosophers about them; And he will find the most celebrated Systems of the Understanding, to be such Jargon as no thinking Man could have wrote nor would any Man have patience to read. But if the Idea of an Object does not mean the thought of the Object, but some more immediate Object of thought which must come between what the vulgar call the Object and the Mind. I say if this is the meaning of Ideas, I can find none of them in my Mind. I can neither conceive their Nature, nor in what way they serve as a Medium. The Reasons which have lead Philosophers to invent such Beings appear to me inconclusive and founded upon gross prejudices. And the same Reasons if they were conclusive would lead me

[16] either back to the Peripatetick System, or I plunge me into the Abyss of Absolute Scepticism.

(The following is a record of Reid's instructions to relocate or insert additional portions of text. For example, take the record for 297/11 : Reid indicates in the MS that a portion of text located in the margin of p. 7 is to be inserted after 'plainer'.)

297/11 plainer.] . . . ⟨⟨ I consider all the different ways in which one thing may represent another, but cannot find any of them applicable to Ideas. ⟩⟩ p. 7

298/11 deduced.] *(Reid indicates that two portions of text, labelled 'E' and 'F', are to be inserted after 'deduced.'. Unfortunately, these cannot be firmly identified, as Reid does not provide the necessary labels. However, if Gordon's transcription is accurate, then we may surmise that Reid is referring to the following portions: The first, presumably 'E', is located on the final page of MS 1/I/3, and is recorded below. The second, presumably 'F', is that portion of the transcription above running from 300/29 to 302/25, 'How{ever} . . . for it.')* ⟨⟨ All Ideas are supposed to be things present and really existing [in the Mind] and internal and to be perceived by the faculty of Consciousness. Yet of these Ideas {one} represents a thing present, another a thing past; one a thing existent, another a Non entity; one a thing external another a thing internal or in the Mind. One idea affirms, another denies, another presents an Object without affirmation or Denial. Every Attempt {made} to explain how Ideas should express such various and contrary things has onely increased the difficulty. What do we gain then by this Hypothesis? Instead of explaining *(MS ends here)* ⟩⟩ p. 33.

298/20–39 I of . . . that I] *(Reid places the following text in the margin of MS, p. 9; however, there is no clear indication of where he wished it to be inserted.)* ⟨⟨ Suppose the Mind Stored with Images, it must more over have a faculty of perceiving them otherwise it will have no Consciousness no perception. A Seal has an Image upon it perhaps severals but it does not perceive these Images. Why? Because it has no perceiving faculty. There must therefore be a faculty of perceiving in the Mind as well as Images. But this faculty can onely extend to things present to the Mind. How do we know that? Why we cannot conceive how it should perceive things past or at a Distance. But do we conceive how things present are perceived? By no means. Then our not being able to conceive how is no argument against the one more than the other. ⟩⟩ p. 9

299/4 happen.] . . . ⟨⟨ The same Argument would prove that I cannot be conscious of what is present to the mind for I can as little conceive the Manner of my Consciousness as of my Remembrance. 〉〉 p. 10

299/7   true.] *(Reid indicates that a portion of text, labelled 'D' is to be inserted after 'true.'. Unfortunately, this cannot be identified, as (i) Reid does not provide the necessary label, and (ii) there is no portion of his MS that corresponds to the text that occurs at this point in Gordon's transcription.)*

299/31   it,] . . . 〈〈 And this way of Speaking is perhaps common to all Languages, and founded on a natural Prejudice by which we are apt to conceive the Operations of Mind like those of Body. For the same Reason the Words comprehend conceive imagine or equivalent ones are common to all languages. 〉〉 p.11

300/28   Anchor.] *(Reid gives an instruction here that the portion of the transcription above from 297/3 to 298/11, '[Thirdly] . . . deduced.' is to be inserted following either the word (i) 'Anchor.' – if the text 'That . . . Anchor', 300/25–28, was not deleted prior to the instruction, or (ii) 'consistent', 300/25 – if it was.)*

300/36   grulling.] . . . 〈〈 Aristotle thought, as the Modern Philosophers also do, that in thought the Mind and Object must act on each other, by means of some Medium, and he contrived a Medium that seems to answer the Intention, namely certain intelligible Species which are constantly sent forth from the Object in all Directions, and make an Impression on the passive Intellect. He conceived the active Intellect to observe these Impressions, and by that Means the external Objects. It is easy to see how by this Hypothesis he accounted for Perception Memory Reminiscence and all the other Operations of the Understanding. The Modern Hypothesis is built upon the same Principle and intended for the same End but it does not at all answer the End. 〉〉 p. 13

302/6   off.] . . . 〈〈 There being no Principle of Reasoning allowed by Philosophers by which we can infer from the Existence of our Ideas, the Existence of any other thing whatsoever. 〉〉 p. 14

302/25   it.] . . . 〈〈 Mr Humes Scheme seems conʒistent with itself and justly deduced from the received Doctrine of Ideas. But as it is wholly built upon that Hypothesis of which he never offers the least Proof If that Hypothesis is shewn to be without foundation this grand Bulwark of modern Scepticism must fall to the ground. 〉〉 p. 15

302/25   *(Reid indicates that a portion of text, labelled 'H' is to be inserted after the marginal note above. Unfortunately, this text cannot be firmly identified, as Reid does not provide the necessary label. However, if Gordon's transcription is accurate, then the following text, located on the final page of MS 1/I/3, may be that to which Reid refers.*) ⟨⟨ To conclude this long digression concerning Ideas. The Word Idea I have observed to be used in four different Senses by Philosophers, tho' they commonly use it as if it had always the same Meaning. 1 By the Idea of an Object they sometimes mean no more but the thought, the Memory, the Imagination of that Object. To deny the Existence of Ideas in this Sense would be to deny these faculties of the Mind which we are all conscious off. But I observe that the (*sic*) we are conscious of these acts and if any man chuse to call them Ideas it is not worth while to dispute about a Name. Yet Idea seems an improper Word to express these Acts of the Mind because it has nothing Active in its Signification. And we may as well call love hatred and all the Affections and Appetites Ideas, as thinking remembrance & Imagination. I observe farther that in this Sense, the Idea {is indeed in the mind but it} is not the Object of thought but the act of thinking. [Far less] {as little} can the Idea be said ⟨to be⟩ a picture or Image of the Object. Thought of the Moon has not the least Similtude to the Moon, nor the thought of Anger to Anger. Secondly The word Idea is often used to signify [the real] {every} Object of Thought perception [and] {or any} other Operation of Understanding. In this Sense ⟨it⟩ is onely a vague general Word like thing or Object and serves onely to confound plain understandings; nor is it true or agreable to common Sense to say that all Ideas are in the Mind, or that they have no Existence but when thought of. Thirdly Idea is sometimes put for what we conceive or Comprehend of an object as distinguished from the whole Nature of that Object. ⟩⟩ p. 33

Version 2.
Excerpt from 'Analysis of the Sensations of smell and Taste',
delivered 14 March 1759 (MS 3107/1/3, 61–72, in Gordon's hand).

07/1/3, 61   1st If this phantasm of a smell do presently exist in my mind, I ought to be acquainted with it, no less than I am with the smell itself when I have the sensation of it; yet upon the most diligent examination I can neither find it in my mind, nor form a conception, what kind of thing it is. The philosopher tells me it is a picture, an image, a representation

35 of a smell: this give me no further light, for I can conceive nothing like smell but smell. Mr Hume tells me that this idea of smell differs from smell in no other respect but this, that it has a lesser degree of strength

2] | & vivacity. If I understand this aright, it means that the idea is a very weak smell. But I am sure there is no such thing in my mind, & that I

can think of the smell of the tuberose when I have not the least degree of
the sensation. If any one should say that the philosophers mean no more
by the idea of smell, but the thought of it, that is, that act of the mind by
which we remember or imagine it; this I understand perfectly; but why so
5   many hard words of ideas, species, representations & images, to express
improperly what every man understands & can express properly in plain
english. But in reality this is not what philosophers mean by ideas. For
they always define them to be, not the act of the mind when it imagines
or remembers any thing, but the immediate object of the mind. If the idea
10 of extension were conceived to be only the remembrance or imagination
of it; it could never have entered into any mans imagination that this
idea is an image or picture of the object; for what similitude can there be
between remembrance & extension. The idea of extension in the mind is
conceived to be the same whether we remember or imagine it; but these
15 acts of the mind are very different. From hence it is evident that the word
idea is not at all intended by Philosophers to express the thought or act of
the mind, but an object of thought which is always in the mind even when
that which the vulgar call the object is without. Such ideas I can neither
find in my mind, nor can I conceive what kind of beings they are.
20   2dly I am as much at a loss to conceive the use of ideas as the nature
of them. They are said to be the immediate object of the mind when it
remembers or imagines any thing. So then what the vulgar calls the object
is something more remote & mediate, & its idea the more proximate &
immediate object. Now this distinction of an immediate & more remote
25 object of thought, does not appear to me to have any foundation in nature
nor indeed can I at all comprehend it. – All thought must be about some
one thing or another; What we think about we call the object of thought or
object of the mind. Now all objects of thought seem to me to be immediate
objects of thought; nor can I conceive what it is to think of any thing by a
30 medium. – You cannot think of Hannibal, says the Idealist, but by having
an idea of him. But what is this idea? Is it the thought of him? It is very
[63]   true I cannot think of him without having a thought of him; | but this is
not philosophy, it is trifleing. If you say, the idea is not the thought, but
the object of the thought; then it is the idea I think of, & not Hannibal; so
35 that there is no thought of Hannibal at all, but of his idea. But this idea
perhaps leads me to think of Hannibal. Be it so. Whenever it leads you
to think of Hannibal, he is then as immediate an object of thought, as the
idea was before. One object of thought may introduce another by the laws
of our constitution, but when the second object is actually thought of, it

is as immediate an object as the first was. The sound of a coach may lead me to think of a coach, & to believe that one is passing by; here the sound is the immediate & only object of sense, but the passing of a coach is as immediate an object of thought & belief.

5   3dly Having considered the nature of ideas & their use, let us next consider the reasons that have induced philosophers to suppose such beings. It will appear, as I apprehend, that no solid proof has been advanced of the existence of ideas. That they are a meer fiction & hypothesis contrived to solve the phænomena of perception, memory & imagination. That they do

10   not at all answer this end, & that the same reasons which have led men to conceive the existence of ideas, will if justly pursued, either lead us back into the exploded Peripatetic system, or plunge us into the most forlorn scepticism.

The existence of ideas in the mind which are images or representations

15   of all external & past objects of thought has been taken for granted, without any solemn proof by all the Philosophers I am acquainted with. The reasons that have induced them to do so, as far as I can collect them from their writings, are as follows.

"It must be allowed by all (say they) that whatever the mind immedi-

20   ately perceives must be present to it. It cannot act where it is not. It may be conscious of what passes within itself; of its own joys & fears & desires & hopes; but how can what is at a distance affect it or be known to it, but by means of some image or representation of it in the mind it self? When we see or think of the Sun, planets & fixed stars, does the mind traverse

25   those immense regions? No surely, it has a little world within itself, in which as in a mirror it perceives the great one. Far less can what is past, & perhaps has now no existence, be an immediate object of the mind; it must be represented by something present & existing."

Upon this reasoning which is expressed by some of our philosophers

30   & supposed by the rest, stand both the fabric of ideas & all our systems of the understanding & therefore it deserves to be carefully examined. |

4]   1st then I would observe, that this reasoning takes it for granted that we may be conscious of what is in the mind, & upon that principle explains how we come to perceive, to remember to imagine, by resolving all these

35   operations into consciousness. But why is not consciousness accounted for as well as the others? if it is inexplicable & to be taken for a first principle, a simple & original faculty that cannot be resolved into others; possibly the others may be so likewise. In analyzing & accounting for the faculties of the human mind we may possibly proceed till we find

those that are simple & original; but it is impossible to proceed one step further, or to give any other account of them than that it is the will of our maker to bestow them upon us. If therefore remembrance, perception & imagination be really original faculties & perfectly simple; it will be in vain to attempt any solution or account of them. They must be considered as laws of nature, which may serve for the solution of other phænomena, but cannot be solved themselves. But if these faculties be not simple & original the solution of them ought not to be taken from hypotheses or con- jecture, but from such laws of nature or such facts as are certainly known to exist. Des Cartes thought that the heavenly bodies could not be carried round in the manner we see, but by a vortex of subtile matter, therefore he concluded there must be such vortices. In like manner philosophers have imagined that perception, memory & imagination cannot be produced without images & representations of things in the mind, therefore they have concluded that there must be such images. But this way of reasoning is now acknowledged by all who have any true taste in philosophy to be fallacious & vain; for this plain reason that the wisdom of God is far beyond that of men; & if we were to conjecture to the end of the world how the phænomena of nature are brought about, we should hardly have a chance to hit upon the truth. I conc⟨lud⟩e therefore that the doctrine of ideas ought to be rejected for the very same reason as the vortices of Des Cartes or the intelligible species of Aristotle, namely that they are only a hypothesis: nor is it any proof of their existence that we cannot account for certain phænomena by other means.

But, says the Philosopher, we not only do not see how perception & memory can happen without ideas. We plainly see they can not.

This indeed is directly to the point, & now the whole | strength of the argument comes forth & it is this. "Neither the mind nor any other being can act but when & where it is: Whether therefore you suppose perception to be an action of the mind upon the object, or of the object upon the mind; in either case, they must necessarly meet together, otherwise neither can any way wise (*sic*) affect the other." – In the name of common sense I would ask the philosopher "Do you know how the mind & object act on each other when they do meet"? We are told indeed that there is an impression or stamp made upon the mind. That the mind comprehends or grasps the object. But these expressions surely must not be understood strictly & literally, but metaphorically. Let us therefore strip them of the metaphor & speak literally & properly; & then they mean no more but this that the mind thinks of, remembers, perceives the object. These are simple

& literal expressions & perfectly understood, and when we substitute for them the words <u>acting upon</u>, <u>impressing</u>, <u>comprehending</u> & the like, we shall find that the argument is onely a begging of the question, & takes for granted what it ought to prove, to wit, that we cannot think of any thing
5 but what is present & existing.

We say indeed in common speech, that such a thing was not in my mind, meaning, that I did not think of it, & this way of speaking is perhaps common to all or most languages & founded on a natural prejudice by which we are apt to conceive the operations of the mind like those of
10 body. For the same reason the words comprehend, conceive, imagine, or equivalent ones, are common to all languages. But the question is, whether these expressions are not figurative when applyed to the mind. And the proper way to determine this question is not, to consider thought as an act, as an impression, as a comprehension; for these are vague &
15 obscure terms when applyed to thought; thought itself is a thing distinctly & perfectly understood when called by its proper name: and when I take the question in this light & consider whether thought of an object supposes the existence of the object, & contiguity in time & place between the mind & object, I confess I cannot see that it does.

20 I find indeed that I have been so accustomed to think of bodies &
•6] their operations, that I am apt to measure every thing | by their standard. We commonly think that a body can only act by impulse, & that there can be no impulse without contiguity. Whether these notions are strictly true & philosophical, I do not presently enquire, but suppose they were,
25 they are evidently got from our experience of the operations of bodies, & however prone mankind have been to apply them to mind, there does not appear to be the least ground either from reason or experience to justify our doing so.

So that in reality this notion so universal among philosophers that the
30 mind cannot think of past or distant objects, immediately, but only by the mediation of certain ideas images or representative beings presently existent in the mind, seems to me a fiction. A fiction grounded upon prejudices, which do indeed cleave very fast to human nature, & which have produced many other opinions very general & of long continuance,
35 which thinking men have at last laid aside. Even to the time of Des Cartes, it seems to have been the general opinion that the soul was either of an aerial or igneous nature. It is owing to a prejudice not unlike to this that we are so apt to ascribe human figure to the Deity & to Angels, & cloven feet to the Devil. There is no doubt an analogy betwixt some faculties of the

mind, & certain actions of the body, as between imagination & painting, between memory & laying up things for future use, hence things are said to be laid upon the memory, to be painted in the imagination. Philosophers have been laid away by such metaphorical expressions, which are so natural & so common to all languages, that they are taken to be literal. Therefore we find that as far down as Des Cartes & Hobbes, Memory & Imagination were explained by traces & images in the brain, & perhaps this opinion is still as common as that of ideas in the mind. Aristotle conceived as was most natural that these images were sent forth from the object, when it was found that this was a hypothesis, Philosophers placed them in the brain without enquiring strictly how they came there, but the notion seems now generally to be laid aside by the more thinking & they are placed in the mind; I conceive this is no less an Hypothesis than the rest, & that there does not appear the least proof of any such images at all. I acknowledge that memory & imagination | cannot be explained, that is reduced to consciousness without them. But why is such an explication necessary? or how does it appear that perception memory & imagination are only different modes of consciousness? But

2dly The Hypothesis of ideas seems to me not to answer the purpose for which it was intended, namely to solve the phænomena of remembrance, perception & imagination. It leaves these operations as mysterious & unaccountable as it found them. The difficulty to be resolved is how a thing that is external, or a thing that is past, & has now no existence, or a thing which never had or never will have existence, can be represented to the mind. I have been at pains to conceive this solution, but must confess I cannot find that it makes the thing plainer.

I consider all the different ways in which one thing may represent another, but cannot find any of them applicable to ideas. Sometimes I conceive the idea appearing as proxy for an unknown constituent, but I cannot find its commission. Sometimes I conceive it as a picture, the object being the original. But here the difficulties increase upon me. For there are a great many things which cannot be pictured. What is a picture of smell, of sound or of taste? How can time be pictured & the [present] preterite distinguished from the present & future? What can picture existence & non–existence. All these things may undoubtedly be the objects of imagination, yet it is impossible to conceive things presently existing in the mind which represent them. And as to the things which may be pictured, which have colour, figure & dimensions, I can conceive them pictured on a canvas or table, but how they can be pictured on the mind, I [find it impossible] {am quite at a loss} to conceive. And if I could get over all these difficulties & suppose a passive part of the mind that had dimensions of length & breadth fit for receiving these pictures, the greatest difficulties still remain. For this hypothesis makes every man to be confined all his life to a little <u>camera obscura</u> where he has no intelligence of things without, but from pictures in his chamber. I say that in this case he never would, he never could dream of any originals, or conceive any objects but his pictures themselves. If he should be informed by his good genius, that these were intended to represent something else, what else could he possibly imagine but another <u>camera obscura</u>, like his own, tho' perhaps stored with more & better furniture. I Certainly if he could go one step beyond this in his conclusions, it must be by means of some other principles than Philosophers have hitherto admitted.

But perhaps the idea represents the object as a sign does the thing signified. So we see words & writing can be made to express every thing. We shall conceive the ideal world then, not as pictures in a <u>camera obscura</u>, but as a book or language that acquaints us with every thing from without. Here again unsurmountable difficulties arise. For how do we learn to understand this language, or to read this ideal book. Shew a book to a savage who never heard of letters; he does not know that these characters are signs, far less what they signify. Speak to a man in an unknown tongue; your words may be signs to you but they are none to him. All signs require interpretation. If ideas are signs, the art of interpreting ideas behoved to be the most essential part of human knowledge & the ground of all: Yet this is an art never thought of. Civilians have considered how laws & contracts may be interpreted &c Grammarians – Cryptology – dreams & riddles – but where are the rules for interpreting ideas or from what principles are they to be deduced?

All ideas are supposed to be things present & really existing in the mind as pain or anger exists in the mind; yet one idea is a type or image of a thing past, another of a thing present, one of a thing existent, another of a non-entity; One of a thing external, another of a thing in the mind. One idea affirms, another denies, another represents an object without affirmation or denial. Every attempt made to explain how ideas made to express such various & contrary things, has only increased the difficulty. What do we gain then by this [difficult] Hypothesis? Instead of explaining any one faculty of the mind we make them more mysterious, & inexplicable.

3dly The same reasons which have led Philosophers to conceive the

existence of ideas, will if justly pursued either lead us back into the
exploded Peripatetic system, or plunge us into the most forlorn scepticism
& disbelief of every thing, but ideas & feelings of the present moment. –
Aristotle thought, as the [present] modern philosophers do, that in thought
the mind & object must act upon each other by means of some medium.
And he contrived a medium that seems to answer the intention, namely,
certain intelligible species, which are constantly set forth from the object
in all directions, & make an impression on the passive intellect. He
conceived the active intellect to observe these impressions, & by that
means the | external objects. It is easie to see how by this hypothesis he
accounted for perception, memory, reminiscence & the other operations
of the understanding. The modern hypothesis of ideas is built upon the
same principle & intended for the same end, but it does not at all answer
the end. We agree with Aristotle that a medium is necessary, that the mind
& object may act upon each other. This medium is an idea or phantasm.
We agree likewise in joining the idea to one of the extremes, to wit the
mind, so that all is safe on that side; but then Des Cartes & the moderns
by rejecting intelligible species, have [. . .] {untied} this medium from
the other extreme, to wit the object; which undoes all operation of the
extremes upon one another. For it is evident, that if a medium is at all
necessary, it must lay hold on both the mind & object & pass all the way
between them without any chasm or interruption, otherwise it remains as
impossible for the mind & object to affect each other, as if there was no
medium at all. And I may as well take hold of the moon with my hand
as apprehend an object by means of an idea which never reached it. That
the mind & object should act upon each other by means of an idea which
is in the mind only, is as absurd as it would be to pretend to hold a ship
at anchor by the medium of a cable which is not tyed to the anchor, but
lyes coyled up in the hold.   Therefore I cannot help thinking that we do
great injustice to the Stagarite in ridiculing his scheme while we hold the
principles upon which it is founded, in rejecting one half of his hypothesis
& retaining the other. For to say that a medium is necessary & {yet} that
it is not necessary that this medium should reach from one extreme to the
other, seems to me a palpable absurdity.

    To avoid the Peripatetic system we have no resource left consistent
with the doctrine of ideas, but to say, that there is no action of the mind &
object on one another, that these ideas are formed in our minds by God, or
we do not know how. This scheme I say leads to absolute scepticism; for
by it our present feelings or ideas are not only the immediate but the sole

objects of the understanding. Nothing past or to come, nothing external can possibly enter into our thoughts. For such things on the principles we are now supposing, can neither operate upon us, nor we upon them. They cannot be immediate objects of thought because they are not present ideas; nor can they be mediate objects of thought because our ideas & minds are no ways connected with them. This is the pure, genuine, unmixed modern ideal scheme; & indeed if ⟨the⟩ authority of great names did not [. . .] {work} very strongly upon the understand I ing, one might at first view see that it must land in this Universal scepticism. For if we will resolve perception & memory into consciousness of present ideas, we must necessarily exclude from the intellectual world every thing which we are not presently conscious off. There being no principle of reasoning allowed by philosophers by which we can infer, from the existence of our ideas, the existence of any other thing whatsoever.

Des Cartes may justly be said to have laid the foundation of this scheme of scepticism by rejecting intelligible species & retaining ideas. Nor needs it appear strange that neither he nor Malebranch, Lock, or Berkley who adopted his principles were sceptics, though their principles lead to scepticism. A regard to religion, to the good of mankind & to the principles of common sense, did not suffer them to plunge themselves or draw others into so desperate a system. But a late enquirer into human nature, less followed by those restraints, who had both the genius to discern the just consequences of the doctrine of ideas, & the courage to adopt & recommend them to mankind, hath brought this scheme to perfection. One may se⟨e⟩ Malbranch & Mr Lock, in several places of their writings, when ready to be thrown into the abyss of scepticism by their philosophical principles, catching hold, the one of religious faith the other of common sense as a rope to keep them above water. Berkley indeed clearly perceived, & has unanswerably demonstrated that the received doctrine of ideas leaves no ground to believe the existence of an external material world. And therefore conceiving that the material world may be thrown off without detriment to religion or the interests of mankind, he in so far adopts the consequences of the ideal scheme. But he could not find in his heart to part with his own & other minds, a supreme mind, & every thing past & to come; tho' his principles justly pursued would have led him to reject every thing but the ideas & feeling of the present moment. – In other things Berkley takes to the dictates of common sense in opposition to the doctrine of ideas. He owns he has no idea of a mind, that is of a subject or substratum of his ideas & feelings, yet he is certain

that there is one, he is certain too that there is a supreme mind of whom
he has no idea, & that this supreme mind is the cause or author of his
ideas, and he believes that there are other finite minds like his own, that
there is a past present & future. Now if he can think of these things &
5   believe them & prove their existence without having ideas of them, why
should it be thought impossible to think of or believe other existences
[71] without having ideas of them. I Therefore I cannot help thinking Berkley's
scheme untenible as he takes a part of the consequences of the ideal
theory & rejects the rest without giving a just reason for it. Mr Hume's
10   scheme seems consistent with itself & justly deduced from the received
doctrine of ideas. But as it is wholly built upon that Hypothesis, of which
the author never offers the least proof: If that Hypothesis is shewn to be
without foundation, this grand bulwark of modern scepticism must fall to
the ground.
15   To conclude this long digression, we may observe that the word <u>idea</u>
is ambiguous, & we shall often find the same author in the same page or
paragraph using it in several various senses without giving any notice of
the ambiguity to his readers or observing it himself. It cannot be doubted
that this ambiguity hath contributed much to hide the weakness of that
20   hypothesis about ideas, which I have been endeavouring to confute, as
well as to darken the writings of Philosophers about the operations of the
understanding, in which this word occurs so frequently, & therefore it may
be of some use to take notice of the various ways in which it is used.
1st To have the idea of any thing sometimes signifies no more than
25   to think of it. And thus <u>having an idea</u> is meerly that figure of speech
which Critics call a <u>pleonasm</u>, as if I should say, <u>I have a remembrance</u>,
for <u>I remember</u>, I have a love for such a person, i,e, I love him. In this
sense of the word, ideas are not either the mediate of immediate objects
of the mind. They are indeed nothing at all but an useless implement
30   of speech.
2dly Ideas are sometimes used as a general word to express every object
of thought. Thus I understand that common saying of philosophers, That
words are the signs of ideas, For words are surely the signs of every thing
we think about. Thus <u>mind</u> is the sign of a thinking being; <u>Sun</u>, the sign
35   of that vast globe which enlightens our planetary system. In this sense
then idea is only a general name & has the same use & signification as
the words thing or object, which may always be used or substituted in its
place without danger of mistake. But let it not be taken for granted, that
all ideas in this sense of the word, are in the mind.

3dly My idea of an object often signifies what I conceive or comprehend of it as distinguished from the whole nature of the object. Thus my idea of Peekin is perhaps only <u>a vast & populous city in China</u>. One who has seen it may have a much more | perfect notion or idea of it, tho ⟨the object of their⟩ thought & mine be the same individual city, yet our ideas of it differ. If it be asked where my idea of Pekin is when I take the word in this sense. I answer it is in China, or wherever the object is & it cannot be otherwise, for it is a part of the object or something belonging to it. The multitude of houses, streets & inhabitants, I conceive, is in China; the thought of them or indeed in my mind; but to call <u>that</u> the idea, is to change the meaning of the word, & to take it in the first sense [above] I before mentioned.

4thly The word idea is often applied to objects of thought, which have no real existence but are called creatures of the mind. Thus the commonwealth of Utopia or that of Oceana may be called <u>ideal</u> commonwealths. If it should be asked where those commonwealths are? I answer, no where, as far as I know. But are they not in the mind then? To this I answer that if <u>being in the mind</u>, is only a pleonasm of expression & signifies no more but that they are thought of, I admit that in this sense they are in the mind. But if being in the mind signifies a real existence either of these commonwealths, or of any image of them in the mind; I see no reason to think that they are or can be in the mind.

5thly Ideas in the writings of philosophers about the understanding most commonly signify certain images or types formed in the mind, which are immediate objects of thought or consciousness, & without which we cannot think of their originals or archetypes. In this last sense I take ideas to be a meer hypothesis & fiction. I can find none of them in my own mind. I can neither conceive of their nature, nor in what way they serve as a medium. Instead of explaining, they darken the operations of understanding. The reasons that have induced Philosophers to invent such beings appear to me inconclusive & founded on vulgar prejudices; and the same reasons if they were conclusive, would lead us back to the Peripatetic system, or plunge us into the abyss of absolute scepticism.

3 MISCELLANEOUS

3.1 On the self (22 Oct 1748)

2131/6/I/18, 1 ⟪ 1748 Oct 22 ⟫

Among the various objects of thought & Reflexion there is none that is
more familiar or seems at first view to be better understood by us than
Self. It seems very hard to doubt whether the most ignorant understands
what he means by himself. Yet ask the Philosopher what this Self is and
I am afraid he will be to seek for an answer.

I mean not now to Enquire whether I am body or Spirit whether Substance or Accident but what is the (I) concerning which these enquiries
may be made. As he that would enquire into the Nature of Fire or water
must previously have Some Idea or Notion to which he Affixes these
Names, So it would seem some Notion or Idea of our selves is supposed
in all talk or Reasoning or Enquiry about our Nature. Now I want to know
what this Idea this Notion is, to which I give the Name of my Self.

Suppose I call my Self a Thing that perceives Reasons remembers
Resolves &c Be it So. Here I think I understand what is meant by perception Remembrance Reasoning &c. But that is not enough. For I am
not perception Remembrance and the rest but a perceiving Remembring
thing. Perception, it may be said, cannot be without a Percipient. I am apt
to think so, but I know so little of the Matter that I cannot give a Reason
for it. It Seems as clear to most men that Colour Gravity Solidity cannot
be but in a Coloured Solid Heavy thing which they call Body Yet others
think Body is onely a Name that includes these Ideas and others that are
connected together by certain Laws of Nature So as that Use or Necessity
makes us Include them under one Name and Account them one thing.
According to the Opinion of the First we may call Body a Real Substance
according to the opinion of the latter we call it a nominal one. Let me
First Suppose that I am a Nominal Substance & consider how this opinion
hangs together and consists with what I know of my Self.

According to this Supposition I am nothing but a train of Thoughts
Ideas Resolutions Volitions Sensations Passions &c. But what ties these
into one and gives them Unity? Besides these are all Transient things
wheras I continue the same when these are changed. Perhaps they are con-

nected by Consciousness that I had these feelings passions & Volitions.
But what is this same Consciousness. I know nothing that is meant by
Consciousness of past Perceptions but the Remembrance of them nor by
Consciousness of Present Perceptions but the perceiving that we perceive
5   them. I cannot imagine there is any thing more in perceiving that I
perceive a Star than in perceiving a Star Simply otherwise there might
2]   be perceptions of perceptions in Infinitum I our Present Perceptions then
Joyned with the Remembrance of what are past Make up that Consciousness which knots us into a Person or Self.
10   What is Remembrance {of past perceptions}? Something more Sure
than the Idea [of Perceptions that are past] {of them}. It [implys a Co] is
the Remembrance of my having had Such perceptions Memory this Seems
to Suppose An Idea of Self. & not to Constitute it
         The Nature of Memory ought to be more carefully enquired into. This
15   Self seems to be Strictly connected with Memory. I can make no more of
it presently but this I see, I hear, I think; I Remember to have seen felt &
thought before now; It appears quite natural and unavoidable for me to
attribute these perceptions to my self. I am not Sight but I see I am not
thinking but I think The Distinction betwixt the Substance and Accident
20   seems here unavoidable But 'tis Memory alone that gives me Assurance of
My past Existence and all my past perceptions. What I presently perceive
and what I remember makes a train of things which is still flowing, my
present feelings changing to Remembrances & being Succeeded by other
feelings. Tis memory that connects all this train together. Upon this all
25   these Successive Ideas are Strung as it were in order. But this train of
Ideas thus knit together by Memory is not my Self but my Ideas. These
I can class & divide & Separate. But I cannot so much as Suppose my
Self divided or Separated. Yet when this train of Ideas is taken away what
remains? I confess I know not. When my thoughts and Ideas and passions
30   change what it is that continues and is called the Mind I know not. I seem
to have no Idea of it and yet am under an invincible Necessity of believing
there is some {such} thing. It seems one of the most natural & original
principles that we continue the same individual unchanged{Self} in all the
changes vicissitudes and varietys of thought & perception. That we are
35   not thought or Remembrance but think & Remember. The Notion of our
Selves may lead us to imagine other thinking things like ourselves. The
Relation of thought to us may give us the Notions of Subject & Accident
Substance and Quality
         If it should be said that we have at least a relative Idea of our Selves.

viz that we are that which has Such Ideas passions & Volitions. Self is the Subject of these Qualities the Principle of these Operations. I ask how we know that these Qualities are in a Subject or that these which we call operations have a principle. Besides this Supposes that all the different
5 Qualities powers & operations we are conscious of have a Relation to one Common Subject or principle and how come we to know this?

Perhaps besides the Consciousness of past & present Perceptions there is also a Consciousness or Perception of my being, which is simple & original to my Nature & cannot be explained tho it be felt by every one. If
10 this be so it ought at least to have a Name I shall call it Self-Consciousness. It would methinks be improper to call it an Idea or an Impression at least it seems not to have been considered under either of these heads by those who have treated of them. And I apprehend it will be hard to say whether it is an Impression of Sensation or Reflexion?

3.2 On perception and principles of belief (1 Dec 1758)

2131/6/III/8, 1r   Decr 1   Of the Perception we have of Distance by Sight   1758

1. We do not perceive Distance from us [immediately] [{naturally &
20 originally}] by Sight 1 Because it is a line drawn from the Object to the Retina. which if seen at all must have the Same appearance to the Eye whether it is long or Short. 2 Children at first cannot Judge of Distance

3 Neither have we any Perceptions by Sight from which we can infer Distance by any logical Deduction.
25   4   It remains that Distance must in Experience ⟨be⟩ associated with certain perceptions or feelings which accompany our perceptions of Sight. So that those perceptions or feeling⟨s⟩ come by Habit to suggest the various Distances of Objects with which they have been found by constant Exerience connected.
30   5   We see Distance in no other sense than we hear Distance {or as we see Anger or Shame in a Mans face}, & the Reason why Use does not so well admit the Expression of hearing as of seeing Distance is that we are more apt to confound Ideas of Sight & Touch than those of hearing & Touch. The latter being either more frequently & constantly associated
35 in Experience Or our Condition making us more early attentive to this Association & Strengthning it before we come to the Use of Reason, so as to make the associated Ideas seem one Simple Perception. Or perhaps the Ideas of Sight and touch have in their own Nature some kind of Analogy and aptness to mix & unite in one compound which has the

appearance of perfect Simplicity, which the Ideas of hearing & Touch have not.

Of the Perception of Extension by Sight

Even what we may call visible Extension seems not to be an Object of Sight. Shall we say it is not seen but discerned. Nothing is properly visible but Colour extension is not Colour & therefore is not visible. It seems to be a Law of Our Nature that objects [seen] whose Images have certain Distance on the Retina should be perceived at a certain Distance from each other. yet this distance is not Seen for tho it be perfect Darkness between two visible objects that does not bring them nearer the Distance between them is perceived to be the same as if filled up with coloured Objects. So that Visible Extension is an Original Perception.

If we should suppose that one uniform Colour had always filled the Eye at one time, we should probably [always] {never} have had any Idea of visible Extension nor thought of it as an Inseparable attendant of Colour. |

Again Suppose that the Impressions made in the various parts of the Retina affected the mind the same way so as that there was distinction of an Impression upon one part from that of another then Various colours impressed on the Retina at the Same time would onely have made one mixed Impression without figure or Extension as various Sounds affecting the Ear at the same Time or Various Smells affecting the Nose at the same Time but we could in this Case have no more had the Idea of Extension by the Eye than we can presently have it by the Nose or the Ear As we can I think conceive the meer Sense of hearing to be separated from the Musical Faculty by which we perceive two or more tones at once discern their Intervals their Harmony or Discord & their Measure as to time. So I conceive the meer Seeing facultie by which we perceive Colour is distinct from that faculty by which we perceive in every Coloured object figure & Extension & betwixt one and another a Certain Quantity of Distance

《《I apprehend that most people who have Cataracts in their Eyes from their Infancy have Ideas of Colour without visible Extension. This seems particularly to have been the Case of the Young Man Couched by Cheselden whose Observations he hath recorded. I do not mean that the Colours which such persons see are in their Nature unextended & incapable of figure (for this seems a Contradiction) but that having never seen those Colours Modified by Figure or to have any limits, their figurability and the various modifications of Extension they are capable

of can never enter into their Imagination nor be an Object of thought. As
every Sound must in the Nature of things have a certain tone and a certain
interval from any other Sound yet their may possibly be persons who
never had an Idea of the Tone of a Sound or of any Interval of tones.⟩⟩

5

Of the Perception of Tangible Extension

Must it not in like manner be by an original & inexplicable law of Our
Nature that we perceive tangible Distance in the parts of our Own bodies
10   & bet⟨w⟩ixt other bodies by means of our own. Certainly All that we
properly feel is hard or Soft rough or Smooth hot or cold. yet all these are
distinct from Extension it ⟨can⟩ never be made out of any combination or
Association of them it appears to be as simple an Idea as any of them.

15

Of External Existences

I do not see that External Existences can be inferred logically & demonstratively from any of our Perceptions. Our Perceptions are all as it would
seem transacted in our Own Minds. Nor is there perhaps any one of them

[2r]   respecting external Existences I which we cannot conceive fallacious, & it
seems possible that there may be no such External Existences as we seem
to perceive: Yet on the other hand the belief of such External Existences
both Spirits and Bodies seems to be so universal so natural & unavoidable, that we can not ascribe it reasonably to prejudice of Education or
25   principles of false Philosophy. We seem therefore to be led to this belief
by principles of our Nature & frame. It is therefore undoubtedly a very
curious Enquiry What {are the} principles of our Nature which Lead us
to this belief of External Existences and whether they produce this belief
immediately or if not by what Means?
30   1 When we consider the Operations of our own Minds it is onely
thoughts Volitions passions and affections we are conscious of. We
cannot by reasoning {from these} conclude {the Existence of} a Being
of which these are Opperations or Attributes we cannot demonstrate that
these things cannot be with a Subject of which they are Powers or prop-
35   erties. Indeed it seems utterly inexplicable how we come by the very Idea
of a Subject or to imagin that these thoughts have a necessary Relation
to some thing else which we call their Subject. We are onely conscious
of the thoughts, yet when we reflect upon them there arises necessarly
and unavoidably a Notion of a thinking thing, & that this thought we are

conscious of is its Operation or Act. Here seems to be a Relation arising
not from the comparison of the things but both the Relation and one of the
Relatives is begot by the Other. I can make no other Account of this but
that we are so made as that thought necessarly appears to us as the Act
5   or Operation of a Being we call Mind & yet we can give no reason why
it should be so. If any Man will affirm that thought may exist without a
Subject & that the conceiving it as an Act or Operation of some Being is
a vulgar or a Philosophical Prejudice, I do not see how he can be confuted
but by appealing to his own Sense or the Common Sense of Mankind.
10   2   Again when a Man has several Successive Thoughts which he
recollects, suppose it granted that each of them must belong to a Mind
{& that each of them did exist in Succession}, yet how does it appear that
they belong to one & the same Mind, I believe no man can give a Reason
but his immediate perception or rather discernment that it is so. Here
15   then are two natural Principles that force our assent tho we cannot give a
Reason for them, nor do they seem either to have that kind of Evidence
which Mathematical Axioms have. Viz that thought Supposes a thinking
thing, or is the Act or Operation of a Being which we call Mind And that
Successive thoughts attended with that consciousness we commonly feel
20   must belong to the same Mind or thinking thing.
          3   Remembrance is a kind of thought that does not appear to have
any necessary Connexion with what is past. I remember I saw a Comet
in 1744. this Act of the Mind is present & whatever it is it might be I for
aught I know tho I had never seen a Comet how do I know then that this
25   perswasion which the kind of thought I call Remembrance gives me is
not entirely fallacious. No man can give a Reason why it should not. yet
every man is constrained to believe his memory when it gives a distinct
Report. This ⟨is⟩ the more remarkable when we consider that our memory
does sometimes deceive us. Nay in dreaming in fevers & frenzies it is
30   altogether fallacious. Here then seems to be a third natural Principle like
to the two preceeding Namely that what we distinctly remember to have
happened when we are neither dreaming nor distempered must really have
happened.
          4   If these I have mentioned be natural Principles of the Mind of which
35   no Account can be given but the will of our Maker I think it follows that
the Ideas of Mind or Spirit or thinking Substance of Powers & Operation
and Consequently of Cause & Effect. Of past Existence & the Relation
between Remembrance and past Existence Of Duration {Identity}. These
I say are all of them Original Ideas without any Preceding Impressions.

5   We have undoubtedly a perswasion of {the Existence of} other thinking Beings like our selves before we are capable of Reasoning And I think those who deny the Existence of Matter yet acknowledge the Existence of Men like themselves endowed with like powers and faculties. Yet I apprehend it will be impossible to account for the Universality firmness and Earliness of this Belief unless we allow that by an Original Property of our Nature the Human Form & Features suggests a Human Mind without Reasoning or Reflexion. Nay we see that the passions and affections of the Mind are suggested even to infants by the features voice and other Natural Indications by a kind of Instinctive Discernment. So that the Existence of other Beings like our selves is as much a Dictate of Nature and not a Deduction of our Reasoning facultie as the Affections we feel towards them, which do necessarly suppose their Existence.

6   Are we not led by Natural Principles to consider our Body as belonging to us. And that [there are] like bodies stand in a like Relation to other Minds. Nay I conceive that from a natural inclination to conceive other beings {to be} like our Selves we are apt at first to attribute life thought & affections to every thing we see and that it is by Experience onely we find out that there are bodies unanimated & meerly passive. The distinction betwixt Soul and Body as different Substances one thinking but not Extended the other Extend⟨ed⟩ but meerly passive and incapable of thought, this Distinction seems meerly a Deduction of Reason & Philosophy & what untaught Men never think off |

2131/6/III/5, 2r   7   Is it not from a Natural Principle that Children believe every thing that is told them? They surely do not ponder whether the person that tells them a Story had access to know the truth of it whether he may have any interest or pleasure in deceiving them. Whether he be a person of Veracity & which are the logical grounds of our Belief in Testimony. But they swallow down with a greedy Belief whatever is told till they are by Experience convinced that they do by this means expose themselves to deceit. Indeed if we should suppose them to have the caution & diffidence of a Man of the World in believing what is told there would [not] be {no} sufficient hold in their Minds for their receiving instruction from their Elders. Here then is a natural principle of belief which is peculiar to infancy at least is strongest in that Age. A principle which often misleads which Years & Experience ought to check and restrain.

8   Is it not from a Natural Principle that we are led to expect a steadyness and uniformity in the Course of Nature that like Causes will produce like Effects, & like Appearances happen in like Circumstances this is a

principle we are obliged to rest upon through our whole lives even in the most important Transactions.

9   That every new Existence & every Change that happens in Nature must have a Cause seems to be another Natural Principle which we always rest upon tho we can hardly give a reason for it. And that the Cause must be adæquate to the Effect. |

10   We certainly do very early begin to conceive that Sensible Objects exist when they are not perceived. All Mankind imagine that the same Individual Sun which they saw lately continues his existence unchanged when they shut their Eyes or when he is under a Cloud. It is in vain to say he may then exist in the mind of another. for this certainly is not what we mean by his continued existence besides no Man is so absurd as to imagine that the same individual impression that was lately in my Mind is now in the Mind of another.

Now the belief of the real & separate Existence of [External] Sensible Objects must be {at least} as early and as universal as that of their continued Existence for the last supposes the first. And if their real Existence is believed {the belief of} their continued Existence may be accounted for from the 2, 6, 8, & 9 principles above mentioned. It is to be considered therefore whence this Opinion of the Real Existence of Matter takes its Rise.

It seems to be imagined by Berkley that the rise of it is this that we feel Certain Impressions of Hot Cold rough Smooth &c which we call impressions of Sensation we are Sensible that we are not the Cause of these Impressions hence we judge that they are made by some External thing of which they are the Images. We therefore conceive some External Being whose properties are the Archetypes of those Impressions we feel. But I apprehend upon a narrower Examination it will appear that any thing we feel or any impressions made upon us {are not taken} to be the Attributes of Bodies or even images of them. Nor are these Impressions considered as Effects caused by Bodies.

I conceive their are many Impressions of Sense {(indeed all of them which can be separated from Extension & Motion)} which would never lead us to imagine any thing external. Heat & Cold for instance, are manifestly feelings which as far as I see could no more lead us to the conception of an external Existence {as their Cause or Archetype}, than good or bad Humor. Roughness or Smoothness Hardness or Softness when we consider the bare feelings are things that can onely exist in a Mind and can no more exist in an Unsentient thing than the pain of the

Gout or the Headach. The same may be said of Sounds smells and Tastes. the me{e}rest Idiot does not Imagine that an Orange has any feeling like what we call the Smell or Taste of An Orange or that a Bell Hears.

5   We do not therefore Ascribe to bodies the feelings excited in us or any like feelings. Is there not then a Roughness and Smoothness {a softness and hardness which we conceive to be} really in Bodies I answer there is but these are no ways like the feelings that go by that Name the roughness that is conceived to be really in a body is not like any feeling it is a certain Unevenness in the Surface of the Body the Hardness that is conceived to 10 be in a body is a certain Cohesion of the Parts which makes it difficult to remove them from one another. There are things not onely entirely unlike the feelings which we call roughness & hardness but such things as we cannot conceive to exist in a Mind. And therefore if we have any conception of them at all we must conceive them to be in some other 15 Subject. |

[3r]   In like Manner the Motion we conceive to be in a Body is a Successive Change of Place. Now there is no impression upon the Mind that has the least Resemblance to this. A Succession of feelings of touch is as unlike {the} Motion of a Body as a Song or Air in Music is unlike the Motion 20 of a Body. In a Word all the Qualities of Body which Suppose Extension Motion or a tendency to Motion are thing⟨s⟩ quite unlike any Impression upon the Mind.

    Colour seems to be another Impression upon the Mind which I conceive can have no Archetype but in a seeing thing. The Impression 25 that Light makes upon the Sense cannot be like to any {Quality of an} external inanimate Existence But Colour by our Constant Experience is so associated with Visible Figure & even with tangible Figure that we are apt to think they cannot exist Separate. That Visible figure can be without colour I think evident by supposing the whole field of Vision of one 30 uniform Colour excepting one Triangle perfectly black or without Colour. We should have as distinct an Idea of this Triangular Space as if it was coloured. A Body being perfectly black is not less capable of figure on that Account. And as Figure may be without Colour so I conceive Colour may be impressed upon the Mind with⟨out⟩ being accompanied with any 35 Notion of Figure as in the Instance of Persons born with Cataracts in their Eyes. Perhaps in such a Case Colour alone would never Suggest to us any External Existence more than heat or Cold.

    Other feelings or Impressions on the Mind might in certain circumstances be associated with figure as Colour is, in which Circumstances I apprehend it would be as difficult to separate those feelings from tangible figure as it is in our present circumstances to separate Colour from visible figure. Thus the Surface of a body may be hot through a certain square Space & could (*sic*) through another Space of another figure & temperate through a third Space, and if all our Sensations of heat and Cold were thus limited and circumscribed by figure I apprehend it would be very difficult to seperate heat & cold from figure. In like manner a part of a Surface of a Certain figure applyed to the organ of Taste may be Sweet another bitter another Sour. And if taste was always thus associated with figure we should be apt to imagine that Taste behoved to be figured as well as Colour.

If this is true that Colour is imagined to be necessarly extended & Figured onely because the Perceptions of Extension & figure do constantly accompany it then Colour may be an Impression upon the Mind but Extension & figure I think can not be So. |

From what hath been said it seems probable that there are certain feelings or Sensations we have & to which we give the Names of Taste Smell Sound Colour Hardness softness Roughness Smoothness Heat Cold. bodily pain and Pleasure. To which the name of Sensation or Impression may very properly be given, because they require nothing to their Existence but a Mind capable of feeling them. And tho our [Nature] {Reason} may lead us to think that there is some external Cause that produces them in us because we are conscious we do not produce them in our Selves, yet neither Reason nor any other natural principle leads us to ascribe them to a cause that is like them or to imagine that they are images of any thing that really exists in an inanimate being as far as we can perceive nothing can resemble them but like Sensations in the mind of another sentient being. And I think the name of Sensation feeling Impression ought to be limited to things that have the properties above Described.

But there are other notions conveyed to us some how by the Sight & touch viz bulk figure extension number Motion {Situation} Cohesion of parts & the like. That all men have such Notions and that very early even before the use of Reason seems undeniable. From which I think it probable that those Notions must be suggested by some Natural Principle. In like manner as the consciousness of thought Suggests a thinking being, tho we are not conscious of a being nor have any Impression of it. Those are Notions or Ideas of real Existences. Distinct from Mind from its Impressions or Ideas. Nay I cannot conceive any Impression

upon a Mind that has the least resemblance of real figure real Motion real Solidity. Now I ask how do we come by these notions. If they are not natural it seems impossible to account for their ever entring into the human Mind, much more is it unaccountable that all Mankind should not
5   onely have such Ideas but believe that there are really such things. I allow that their Existence cannot be logically inferred either demonstratively or probably from our feelings. But as little can past existences be inferred from Memory Is it not probable that there is some Original Principle in our Nature that both suggests those Ideas to us and forces our belief. Just
10   as any new Appearance in the Course of Nature both Suggests to us the Notion of a Cause and forces us to acknowledge that it must have a Cause tho we can neither give a probable nor necessary Reason why a thing that begins to exist must have a Cause.

11 It seems farther Evident that Mankind from the beginning believe
15   [hardness] extension figure not to be things that can exist of themselves but the properties or Qualities of Some extended & figured thing just as thought appears to us as a thing that cannot Exist of itself but in some
[4r] Mind. If it was not from some Natural Principle that we consider I Body as a Substance, I see no other Account that can be made of it but this
20   that these and Necessity makes us joyn the several Sensible Qualities of a body under one Name & hence we come at last to consider as one Real thing. But if this were the Case I do not see how it never happens that other mixed Modes are taken for Substances but this always is. I cannot conceive a Reason a Song or a Word is never taken for a Substance these
25   are early associations yet we never seem to be in the least disposition to take them for Substances. the same may be said of dancing ploughing and twenty other things

That all Mankind should agree that thought Memory love & hatred need a Substratum which they call Mind & that Solidity fluidity Motion & Rest
30   need a Substratum which they call Body will be difficult to account for if we do not resolve it into some Natural Principle.

If these Opinions which I have represented as the Effect of natural Principles can be shewn to be false; or if true, if they can be shown to be deducible from selfevident truths by demonstrative or probable reasoning
35   in such Manner as to account for the earliness & universality of these Opinions I shall then be ready to throw aside these natural Principles as useless or Imaginary.

This Suggestion of external Objects to the Mind by the Senses ought not to be called Sensation but Perception. It is like the Suggestion of the

place of a Coach by hearing the Noise: In this case it is not proper to say
I hear the place of it but I perceive it to be in such a place by the Sound.
Here the association betwixt the Sound & place is formed by Habit. In
perceiving external Objects by the Eye or touch the Association between
5   the Impression upon the Mind & the consequent belief of an Object is
natural not acquired.

In this perception of external Objects there must no doubt be an Act of
the Mind as well as an Object. That act of the Mind does not necessarly
infer the Existence of the Object we may possibly be dec{e}ived as
10   memory is an act of the Mind which may be without any past Existence
yet both gives us the Idea of past Existence and makes us believe it
at once so this perception of Seeing or touch both gives us the Idea of
external Existence and compells our belief of it. The Act of perception
can onely be in a Mind but the Object which it presents to the Mind is as
15   necessarly something which cannot be in a mind either locally or as an
Act or Operation of the Mind.

There may likewise be means of perceiving Such as a proper disposition
of the Organ and some Impression made upon it. Where such Impression
is felt it may be always and is naturally distinguished from the Object Thus
20   the Hardness I feel is an Impression but the Cohesion of parts which this
suggests is quite a different thing. |

Of the Perception of Harmony {Number Order} Beauty
& others of that ⟨kind⟩

25

It is universally acknowledged that we have a Perception of Harmony
in certain Sounds and Discord in Others. And the faculty by which we
perceive this is called an Internal Sense. the Perception itself is called a
feeling To call this in Dispute may be thought to dispute about Words. All
30   that I plead therefore is that the Perception of Harmony is not a Sensation
feeling or Impression in the Sense I have given of that Word. If it was a
meer feeling no reason can be given why all Mankind should consider it
as a certain relation of Sounds and not as an Impression upon the Mind.
In like manner I can find no Reason why the Perceptions of Beauty Order
35   Number Grandeur should be called feelings because Nature leads us to
consider them as belonging to things and not to the Mind.

It is easy to apply what has been said to Moral Perceptions which our
Nature leads us to merit and Demerit duty and Obligation to persons in
whom they are said to be. Our Modern Philosophy which affirms these

to be onely feelings in us is vain and contrary to Nature as it is to the common Sense & Apprehension of Mankind. We may as well Attribute Extension figure & motion to the Mind or consider them as nothing really in things but certain impressions upon us, and we have equal Reason to look upon these past Existences which are presented to us by Memory to be onely present Impressions upon our Minds without any reality, or truth. In a word the same Reasons would lead us to deny any Real Existences in Nature but the Impressions which we are conscious to present to the mind and so would land us in the most ridiculous Scepticism.

Our Immediate Natural and Original Perceptions are the onely Evidence we can have of things of the last consequence to us if we trust not these we cannot have a Shaddow of Evidence that there ever was any thing past or that there is any thing present but what is felt in Our Minds this Instant.

The Wisdom of Nature hath thought fit to give us such original Perceptions for the Direction of our Conduct to supply the Defect of Reason which could never give us an Idea of an External Existence far less give us Evidence of any such. So that as in Infancy we are guided by instinct without know⟨ing⟩ what we are about so in Riper Years we are Guided by principles indeed but such principles as are inlaid in our Nature and wrought into our frame. Reason in the Generality of Mankind is so little improved that it would never be sufficient to direct our Conduct in the most common affairs. Natural Principles may be considered as a kind of Natural Inspiration or Revelation.

3.3 On seeing objects single (undated)

2131/6/I/23, 1r

That we see objects at first single when our eyes
are properly directed

1   If there was a duplicity to the eye, however custom and habit might bring us to pass immediately from this perception to the tangible unity signified by it; yet it is probable that by accurate attention we might be able to check that custom and attend to the pure objects of Sight since we find this in other like instances tho' difficult is not impossible. When a common man sees the inside of a Church he thinks the pillars appear to his eye of equal height and thickness. But a person accustomed to attend to his perceptions can easily be convinced that tho they have really the same tangible dimension yet their visible dimensions diminishes as they are more distant from him and that in perspective they must be so represented.

Now as we can by strict attention perceive the visible dimension of an object tho accustomed constantly to consider it onely as a sign of the tangible it is probable that by care and pains we might be able to attend to the visible Number of Objects tho commonly onely used as a Sign of the
5   tangible Number. [Yet I never found] This might be particularly expected of painters who are accustomed to separate the visible appearance from the tangible that by looking first with one eye and then with both they might be able to perceive some duplicity in the latter case yet I think there is no evidence that any person ever saw an object double when his eyes
10   were properly directed to it.

    2   In all the Instances of double Vision we know the two Images are seen [at a certain] as it were in different points of the same Sphere and at a certain angular Distance, [now this is as difficult] nor can I form a conception of two objects seen at the same time which have no distance
15   nor proximity. And I apprehend every other person will find it impossible for him to conceive this. Now it is as difficult to account for this as for single vision. For it is impossible to give a reason why the mind in seeing an Object double with the two eyes should {naturally} place the two
1v]   images I at one certain distance rather than another. It may as well place
20   them at no distance as at any particular Distance & then the Vision will be single. And indeed when in double Vision the two Images are seen at a certain Distance (as I think they always are) it seems necessarily to follow that by moving the axis of one of the eyes {in a certain manner} while the other remains fixed the distance between the images would be
25   diminished and at last evanishing would give single vision.

    Dr Jurin mentions a case of a Clergyman who having been blind for some years with a Gutta serena was cured by a Salivation and for some time after saw objects double but by degrees the Images approached [and at last saw] and at last he saw as distinctly as before, he tells us of an
30   Instance or two {one or two others} of this kind mentioned by Dr Briggs in his Nova Visionis Theoria. It seems very probable that in these cases the double vision was owing to the persons having lost the habit of directing their eyes properly to an object and when they recovered that faculty they had no more double vision

35   [Dr Smith mentions] we have another Instance from Cheselden of a person who had one eye distorted by a blow on the head who at first saw objects double but by use came first to see the most familiar objects and at last all objects {tho the distortion continued} It were to be wished we had been more particularly informed of the circumstances of this case.

Perhaps {he learned to turn} when one eye was [turned] directly to the
Object which might take some time the other was too oblique to give any
image or gave so faint an Image that he soon acquired the habit of not
attending to it.

5   These are all the Instances I have met with that may be brought in
support of Dr Smiths opinion that we naturally see things double but
by use come to judge them single. And I think it appears from what is
observed above that they do not conclude the point. He [gives a Reason]
observes farther that there is the same difficulty in accounting for our
10   hearing [objects] {sounds} single with our two ears as in seeing objects
single with two eyes: But here I apprehend the cases differ Sounds have
not properly any place and there is noting by which two perfectly similar
& synchronous sounds can be distinguished. But every visible Object hath
a visible place, which distinguisheth it from objects that have a different
15   place tho ever so like to it and seen at the same time. Now the Difficulty
lys in this why [when the eyes have a certain Direction with regard to
an Object] every point in one retina [has a point] corresponds in such a
manner to the point similarly situated in the other that images falling upon
these corresponding points are seen the Same Place |

20

[2r]   A Phænomenon in Optics

Let A, B be the two Eyes, a, b two objects seen by them, in the three
following ways successively; first by interposing the Obstacle (g) so as
25   that the Eye {A} sees b, but not a & the Eye B sees a but not b Secondly
by removing all obstacles so as each eye may see both objects at once;
Thirdly by interposing the two Obstacles e & f so that the Eye A may see
a & not b & the Eye B may see b & not a. I find from Experience that [in
the first Case] keeping the Eyes & Objects in the unmoved all along, in
30   the first Case the Objects will appear nearest to each other in the second
case they will appear more distant and in the third case most distant of all.
        Explained. 1 When both Objects are seen by both Eyes their apparent
Distance will be measured by the Angle bAa or bBa. 2 When the obstacle
g is interposed the apparent distance of the Objects will be measured by
35   the Angle bDa and when the obstacles e & f are interposed the apparent
distance of the Objects will be measured by the angle bCa.
        Cor⟨1⟩   When Ba & Ab are parallel the Objects a & b tho they are as
far asunder as the Eyes are may be seen coinciding. This I find holds in
Experience.

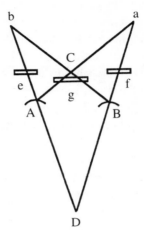

Cor 2   This phænomenon {in Cor 1} Confirms what I have advanced of the Cause of Single Vision viz. that by an Original law of our Nature pictures on the corresponding parts of the Retina are Seen in the same place. It seems also to Confute Porterfields Theory. For when Ab & Ba are parallel the Objects ought to be seen at an Infinite distance by his Theory The laws of our Nature may be supposed more constant and invariable than those that are founded upon habit & Custom. What Porterfield has laid down as a law of Nature is transgressed in innumerable instances. Indeed in every instance where it does not fall in with what I have laid down as a law of Nature. What I have laid down as a law of Nature does not appear to be transgressed in any one Instance.

Is it not probable that in hares & other Animals whose eyes are averse the two eyes have opposite hemispheres so that two objects in the Axes of the two eyes appear diametrically opposite, but if we suppose the hare to have human eyes these two opposite objects would seem to coincide. |

3   If Custom could bring us to see Objects single which in the same circumstances were seen [Single] {double}, it might be expected that we might by practice acquire the Habit of seeing Objects single when their Images do not fall upon correspondent parts of the Retina. We are every day of our lives receiving images in this way, when we know they belong to one Object those that have made innumerable Experiments to examine the Circumstances of double Vision, find that this double Appearance never vanishes by Custom.

Prop   If the Rays coming from a Point of the Object do not meet in

a point of the Retina but {on a point} either before or behind it they
will be dissipated upon the Retina through a Space similar to the Pupil
& therefore in the human Eye Circular, which we may call the Circle
of Dissipation. And the Di⟨a⟩meter of the Circle of Dissipation is to the
Diameter of the Pupil as the distance of the Focus from the Circle of
Dissipation to its Distance from the Pupil

Cor 1.   The Circle of Dissipation is least cæteris paribus when the
pupil is least & by admitting Rays onely through a small hole in an opaque
plain before the pupil the Radius of Dissipation may be diminished at
pleasure

Cor 2   The Confusion of an object will be greater or less as the Ratio of
the Diameter of Dissipation to the Diameter of the Image is greater or less

Cor 3   Hence a larger object will appear less confused (cæteris
paribus) than a small one in the Ratio of the Diameters inversely this is
the Reason why a large print may be read distinctly at a great Variety
of Distances. But the limits of Distinct Vision in a small print are much
more confined. Take a Book that has three different Sizes of Print; hold
it so near the Eye that the Smallest begins to be confused; & the middle
& largest print will still appear distinct; bring it nearer till the Middle
Size begin to appear confused & the largest will still appear distinct &
the smallest very confused. We ought therefore to distinguish between
perfect Vision and distinct Vision calling that perfect Vision where the
Rays from one point of the Object do meet in one point of the Retina &
calling that Distinct Vision where the Radius of Dissipation bears but a
small proportion to the Diameter of the Image

Prop. Let r be the Radius of the true Image of a Circular Object in the
Eye, p the Radius of [the circle of] Dissipation. And suppose the Object to
be bright white upon a black ground. And first let r > p I say the Image
upon the Retina will consist of a Circle as bright as the Object whose
Radius is r – p & annular Penumbra surrounding the Circle whose breadth
is 2p & whose brightness gradually diminishes from the inner side till it
evanishes qu⟨i⟩te at the outter side of the Annulus. (*MS ends*)

REGISTER OF EDITIONS

1. *An Inquiry into the Human Mind on the Principles of Common Sense*, Edinburgh, Printed for A. Millar, London, and A. Kincaid & J. Bell, Edinburgh, 1764.

2. *An Inquiry* [etc.], Dublin, Printed for A. Ewing, 1764.

3. *An Inquiry* [etc.], The second edition corrected. Edinburgh, Printed for A. Millar, London, and A. Kincaid & J. Bell, Edinburgh, 1765.

4. *Recherches sur l'entendement humain d'après les Principes du sens commun,* 2 vols, Amsterdam: chez Jean Meyer, 1768.

5. *An Inquiry* [etc.], The third edition corrected. Edinburgh, Printed for T. Cadell (Successor to A. Millar) in the Strand, and T. Longman, in Pater-Noster Row, London; and A. Kincaid & J. Bell, Edinburgh, 1769.

6. *An Inquiry* [etc.], The third edition. Dublin, Printed by R. Marchbank for the Company of Booksellers, 1779.

7. *Untersuchung über den menschlichen Geist, nach den Grundsätzen des gemeinen Menschenverstandes.* Aus dem englischen nach der 3 Aufl. übers. Leipzig, 1782.

8. *An Inquiry* [etc.], The fourth edition corrected. London, Printed for T. Cadell in the Strand, London; and J. Bell and W. Creech, Edinburgh, 1785.

9. *An Inquiry* [etc.], The fifth edition. Edinburgh, Bell and Bradfute, 1801.

10. *An Inquiry* [etc.], The sixth edition. Glasgow, Printed for Gray, Maver & Co. And Vernor and Hood, Lackington, Allan and Co and T. Ostell, London, By W. Falconer, 1804.

11. *An Inquiry* [etc.], The sixth edition. Edinburgh, Bell and Bradfute [etc.] 1810.

12. *An Inquiry* [etc.], The seventh edition. Printed for Bell and Bradfute, and William Creech, Edinburgh; and T. Cadell and W. Davies, London, 1814.

13. *An Inquiry* [etc.], Glasgow, Printed by W. Falconer, 1817.

14. *An Inquiry* [etc.], Edinburgh, Printed for Anderson and Macdowall, and James Robertson, Parliament Square, 1818.

15. *An Inquiry* [etc.], London, The Proprieters, 1818.

16. *An Inquiry* [etc.], Edinburgh, Stirling and Slade [etc.], 1819.

17. *An Inquiry* [etc.], Edinburgh, Printed for Thomas Nelson, Westbow, 1821.

18. *An Inquiry* [etc.], London, Printed by W. Wilson, 4, Greville Street. For J. Bumpus, Holbrn Bars; Sharpe, King-Street, Covent-Garden; Samms, Pall-Mall; Warren, New Bond-Street; and Reilly, Lord Street, Liverpool, 1821.

19. *An Inquiry* [etc.], Edinburgh, Published by William Aitchison, 1823.

20. *An Inquiry* [etc.], London, Printed for Thomas Tegg, 1823.

21. *An Inquiry* [etc.], *with an account of the life and writings of the author.* Cupar, R. Tullis, 1823.

22. *An Inquiry* [etc.], New York, Johnstone and Van Norden, 1824.

23. *The Philosophy of Reid as contained in the 'Inquiry into the human mind on the principles of common sense'*, ed. E. H. Sneath, New York, H. Holt and company, 1892.

24. *An Inquiry into the Human Mind*, ed. T. Duggan, Chicago, University of Chicago Press, 1970.

25. *An Inquiry* [etc.], Photographic reprint of the 1785 Edition. With a new Introduction by Paul B. Wood, Bristol, Thoemmes Antiquarian Books, 1990.

---

26. *The Works of Thomas Reid* . . . With an account of his life and writings by Dugald Stewart, F.R.S., with notes, by the American editors. Charlestown, Printed and published by Samuel Etheridge, jun'r, 1813-15 (4 vols).

27. *The Works of Thomas Reid.* With an account of his life and writings, by Dugald Stewart. New York, E. Duyckinck, Collins and Hannay, and R. and W. A. Bartow, 1822 (3 vols).

28. *Œuvres complétes de Thomas Reid, chef de l'école écossaise*, publiées par M. Th. Jouffroy, avec des fragments de M. Royer-Collard et une introduction de l'éditeur . . . Paris, V. Masson, 1828-36 (*Inquiry*, 1828).

29. *The Works of Thomas Reid* With notes, sectional heads and synoptical table of contents, by G. N. Wright; and 'An account of the life and writings of Thomas Reid', by D. Stewart, London, Printed for T. Tegg, 1843 (2 vols).

30. *The Works of Thomas Reid, D.D. with Notes and Supplementary Dissertations*, ed. W. Hamilton: 1st ed., Edinburgh, Maclachlan and Stewart, 1846; 2nd ed., Edinburgh, Maclachlan and Stewart; and London, Longman, Brown, Green, and Longmans, 1849; 3rd ed., Edinburgh, Maclachlan and Stewart; and London, Longman, Brown, Green, and Longmans, 1852; 4th ed., Edinburgh, Maclachlan and Stewart, 1854; 5th ed., Edinburgh, Maclachlan and Stewart, 1858; 6th ed., Edinburgh, Maclachlan and Stewart, 1863, reprint Thoemmes press, 1994; 7th ed., Edinburgh, Maclachlan and Stewart, 1872; 8th ed., Edinburgh, Maclachlan and Stewart, 1880; 8th ed., Edinburgh, J. Thin, 1895, reprint with introduction by H. M. Bracken, Hildesheim, Georg Olms Verlag, 1967, 1983, 1985.

31. *Thomas Reid's Inquiry and Essays* (Abridged resetting of Hamilton 6th edition), eds. K. Lehrer and R. Beanblossom, Indianapolis, The Bobbs-Merrill Company, Inc., 1975; Hackett Publishing Company, Inc., 1983.

32. *An Inquiry* [etc.], Photo-reproduction of Hamilton. Charlottesville, Virginia, Ibis Publishing (undated).

PAGE CONCORDANCE

The following list provides a concordance between the pagination of the present edition (EUP), and the most commonly used previous editions, namely, the 1785, Hamilton (6th ed), T. Duggan, and Lehrer and Beanblossom editions. See the *Register of Editions* for bibliographical details.

INDEX